Translators through History

Benjamins Translation Library (BTL)

The Benjamins Translation Library (BTL) aims to stimulate research and training in Translation & Interpreting Studies – taken very broadly to encompass the many different forms and manifestations of translational phenomena, among them cultural translation, localization, adaptation, literary translation, specialized translation, audiovisual translation, audio-description, transcreation, transediting, conference interpreting, and interpreting in community settings in the spoken and signed modalities.

For an overview of all books published in this series, please see
http://benjamins.com/catalog/btl

EST Subseries

The European Society for Translation Studies (EST) Subseries is a publication channel within the Library to optimize EST's function as a forum for the translation and interpreting research community. It promotes new trends in research, gives more visibility to young scholars' work, publicizes new research methods, makes available documents from EST, and reissues classical works in translation studies which do not exist in English or which are now out of print.

Volume 101

Translators through History. Revised edition
Edited and directed by Jean Delisle and Judith Woodsworth

Translators through History

Revised edition

Edited and directed by

Jean Delisle
University of Ottawa

Judith Woodsworth
Concordia University

Revised and expanded by Judith Woodsworth

John Benjamins Publishing Company

Amsterdam / Philadelphia

The paper used in this publication meets the minimum requirements of
the American National Standard for Information Sciences – Permanence
of Paper for Printed Library Materials, ANSI z39.48-1984.

Published under the auspices of
the International Federation of Translators (FIT)
and UNESCO

Library of Congress Cataloging-in-Publication Data

Translators through history / edited and directed by Jean Delisle, Judith Woodsworth.
    -- Rev. ed. / revised and expanded by Judith Woodsworth.
   p. cm. (Benjamins Translation Library, ISSN 0929-7316 ; v. 101)
Includes bibliographical references and index.
1. Translating and interpreting. 2. Translators. I. Delisle, Jean. II. Woodsworth, Judith.
PN241.T745   2012
418'.02--dc23   2012010744
ISBN 978 90 272 2450 7 (Hb ; alk. paper)
ISBN 978 90 272 2451 4 (Pb ; alk. paper)
ISBN 978 90 272 7381 9 (Eb)

John Benjamins Publishing Co. · P.O. Box 36224 · 1020 ME Amsterdam · The Netherlands
John Benjamins North America · P.O. Box 27519 · Philadelphia PA 19118-0519 · USA

*No higher service can be rendered to literature
than to transport the masterpieces of the human mind
from one language to another.*

Germaine de Staël (1766–1817)
French-speaking Swiss author and thinker

*The history of the different civilizations is the history
of their translations. Each civilization, as each soul,
is different, unique. Translation is our way to face
this otherness of the universe and history.*

Octavio Paz (1914–98)
Mexican writer, poet, and diplomat,
winner of the 1990 Nobel Prize for Literature

*Translation is not a matter of words only:
it is a matter of making intelligible a whole culture.*

Anthony Burgess (1917–93)
English author, poet, playwright,
linguist, critic and translator

Cover photo (paperback edition)

Émilie du Châtelet (1706–49)

The marquise du Châtelet, née Émilie de Breteuil, was fluent in English, Italian and Latin. She translated the *Aeneid* and other classical works into French, though no examples have survived. She showed great interest in the abstract sciences, devoting herself to the study of mathematics as shown in this portrait. She was the first to translate and comment on Isaac Newton's *The Mathematical Principles of Natural Philosophy* (written in Latin). Completed shortly before her death, the translation was published posthumously by Voltaire, her lover of fifteen years.

Source: Portrait by Maurice Quentin de La Tour (1704–88), photographed by Philippe Sébert. The painting now hangs in the Château de Breteuil, near Paris, owned and managed by Madame du Châtelet's descendant, Henri-François le Tonnelier, Marquis de Breteuil. Used with permission.

Table of contents

Table of illustrations

Foreword to the second edition

Great strides have been made in the field of translation studies in the past quarter century. The history of translation, in particular, has burgeoned, providing fertile ground for students and scholars around the world to tackle topics with breadth and depth through time and across geographical areas. The history of translation, and of translators, has a robust past, a vibrant present, and a promising future. In this context, *Translators through History* remains a useful tool for a variety of readers – students, scholars and professionals working within the discipline of translation – and continues to be of interest to scholars from other disciplines and the wider public. With the exception of a reprinted version in 1997 that contained a few straightforward adjustments, however, there has not been a thorough revision. In 2007, Jean Delisle issued a new French version of the book, *Les Traducteurs dans l'histoire* (University of Ottawa Press), in which he corrected errors that had been identified by readers and critics, made improvements in both form and substance, and provided updated bibliographical information. It was clearly time for a new English edition with current information, corrections and new theoretical perspectives, not the least of which recognizes new thinking in the discipline of history.

In the first edition, we referenced the nineteenth-century historian Leopold von Ranke who sought to "determine what actually happened" (Delisle and Woodsworth 1995: 245). Academic historians have long since moved beyond the Rankean paradigm, and approaches to history continue to evolve. In our time, the very notion of objectivity has been set aside in favour of multiple points of view. To begin with, the range of possible objects of inquiry is limitless; the rules and regulations of the discipline, as well as the methods and nature of historical interpretation, are all open to debate. A work of history can be compared to a musical composition, as in Paul Cohen's account of the Boxer Rebellion, which he has called a history "in three keys", building his narrative on history as event, experience and myth (Cohen 1997). A weaving together of different strands, drawing on diverse stores of evidence, history is a creative, interpretive act, to some extent an act of imagination. Not unlike translation, in other words.

This all has implications for the history of translation, and the various methods of constructing history all have relevance for what *Translators through History* seeks to accomplish. Whereas traditional history tended to look at momentous events and the "great deeds of great men", recent decades have seen an increasing number of scholars focus on ordinary people and attempt to tell "history from below". Historians of translators are adopting this vantage point to good effect. For millennia, translators have accompanied the "great men" in their "great deeds", but they have been defined by their subordinate status (as captives, slaves or ethnic hybrids, for example). Yet, their social, cultural and geographic identities have allowed them to cross borders, negotiate across cultures and contribute to intellectual and cultural exchange. Just as decolonization, feminism and identity politics have transformed historical writing, so, too, have they made their mark on the narratives of translation. The examination of the agents in translation history, along with the cultural, social and political structures that define them, can yield compelling and textured historical explanations. Once reliant on archives and historical records in a culture dominated by the written word, furthermore, newer historians now take oral accounts into consideration: for example, Evan Haefeli "reads" Hudson's voyage up the river that flows through present-day New York State through the eyes of native peoples using both written and oral accounts (2007). This can be a productive technique for us as historians of translation in delving into non-textual cultures and in examining interpreting, in particular.

The new directions in researching and writing history, set in motion some time ago, are in fact becoming mainstreamed. For instance, since Ranajit Guha penned the classic text of subaltern studies, *Elementary Aspects of Peasant Insurgency in Colonial India* (1983), we have moved to a point at which subalternity has become an accepted framework through which to view all kinds of history and "reading against the grain" has become widespread.

The field of translation studies, too, has evolved considerably, particularly since the "cultural turn" heralded by Susan Bassnett and André Lefevere (1990), who went on to link the "translation turn" to the field of cultural studies in general (1998). Translation scholars have become familiar with new theoretical perspectives through contact with other disciplines, and translation has become an area of interest, even a fruitful metaphor, in other realms of inquiry. This confluence is very rich in consequences for the history of translation. To name only a few of the titles that will be referred to in the following pages, the nineties saw the publication of feminist studies by such scholars as Sherry Simon (1996) and Luise Von Flotow (1997). In *Translation and Power* (2002), Maria Tymoczko and Edwin Gentzler extend the boundaries of the "cultural turn" and advance the notion of a "power turn". Michael Cronin's *Translation and Identity* (2006) draws on various forms of translation to show its role in shaping identity and promoting difference.

Postcolonialism, in particular, provides a corrective lens for the field of translation and has opened new avenues of reflection – in edited volumes by Susan Bassnett and Harish Trivedi (*Post-colonial Translation: Theory and Practice*,

1999) and Sherry Simon and Paul St-Pierre (*Changing the Terms: Translating in the Postcolonial Era*, 2000), for example. The postcolonial perspective is applied in monographs examining translation in a non-European context: Paul Bandia's *Translation as Reparation: Writing and Translation in Postcolonial Africa* (2008); and Wang Hui's *Translating Chinese Classics in a Colonial Context: James Legge and his Two Versions of the 'Zhongyong'* (2008), which offers a fresh look at the work of missionary translators. There may be a danger of this becoming the "new orthodoxy", as Peter Burke warned of the earlier "history from below" movement (1992: 38), with translation scholars attempting to explain or critique all past forms of translation in postcolonial terms. Yet, the approach remains useful in taking into account the transnational dimensions at play and in providing a framework for understanding "power relations and relations of alterity" (Simon and St-Pierre 2000: 13).

This new edition preserves a good part of the original publication. The preface and introduction to the 1995 edition of *Translators through History* have been left virtually intact since they tell the story of our history, documenting its genesis from an idea launched at a translators' congress over twenty years ago through the rather daunting task of drawing on the talents of a team of historians from around the world to compile a collective work – much like putting together the pieces of a puzzle.

In writing *Translators through History* in the first place, we focused on the translator – the agent rather than the product or the process. This was not an obvious choice in a discipline that had hitherto been so focused on the text: for example, on the extent to which the translation replicated the source text or, on the other hand, was made to fit the norms of the target culture. We identified certain themes, or spheres of activity in which translators have played an important role, and in telling the selected stories, dealt to different degrees with the social, political, economic or religious context in which the particular translators worked. The structure has not changed: readers will recognize the original chapters and many of the subheadings. This history of translators continues to be organized around the same nine key themes, and the narratives and voices of the original contributors have been preserved to a large degree. At the same time, an effort has been made to achieve a greater degree of scholarly rigour, cohesion and seamlessness while keeping the text clear and readable.

The content has been updated and expanded, and some completely new elements were introduced. Chapter 8 was completely rewritten for the 2007 French edition and appears here in English for the first time. Additional material has been added to the other chapters: for example, a brief history of machine translation in Chapter 4; an overview of the way recent theory has framed issues of power in Chapter 5; and a look at English versions of sacred texts of the East made by such translators as James Legge. Revisions have extended beyond stylistic changes to the correction or updating of factual information – the number of translator associations in the world, the number of languages now spoken, and so on – made possible by increasingly available sources. More importantly, the revised edition alerts readers to new directions in translation scholarship, which provide a more nuanced view of past events. One "error" that has attracted particular attention in the field of translation history is the notion of a so-called school of Toledo: it has been clarified and perhaps put to rest, although the "myth" may well continue to circulate.

As much as possible, newer references were used and information from them incorporated into the text. A wide range of sources are quoted and referenced in cases where the authors have provided a particular point of view or interpretation of facts, or have shed light on particular events that are less widely known. References are sometimes not provided when information originates from publicly available sources such as online encyclopedias or where it forms part of common knowledge. To annotate all sources would have yielded a cluttered and less readable text. All works mentioned in parenthetical references in the text are listed in the "Works Cited" section, which now reflects the 100 additional titles consulted during the editing process. The "Further Reading" sections that were included in the original edition, now somewhat outdated, have been removed. Translation history has flourished to such a degree in recent years that an exhaustive bibliography would be out of the question in a single volume such as this. However, there are enough references to point interested readers in the right direction should they wish to pursue a particular topic, especially given the relative ease of accessing bibliographic information using today's electronic resources.

Dates of birth and death have been eliminated for historical figures, and are now reserved primarily for translators and interpreters. In the case of variations – and there are many – several sources have been consulted, including catalogues of major libraries; the generally accepted dates are accompanied by the notations "c." (*circa*, around) or "fl." (*floruit*, flourished), and in some cases only a date of birth or death is given. Inevitably, there continues to be some repetition from one chapter to another. Some important figures, such as St. Jerome, Chaucer, Luther and Tyndale, appear in more than one place, but the endnotes and index will guide the reader to the multiple references.

The illustrations, finally, have been refreshed in keeping with the importance attached to the iconography of translation we set out to establish in the first edition. Descriptions of all illustrations, with revised versions of the ones that remain from the previous edition, can be found in Appendix I.

There are, and will continue to be, gaps. "If we think of the history of translation as a *mosaic*, there can be little doubt that there are still many small pieces or
tesserae missing, as well as large empty spaces yet to be filled" (Santoyo 2006: 13).
This is where the "future" of translation history lies. This is a project that sets out
a framework for further research, whether it be by filling in the blanks geographically or temporally, whether by focusing on the agency of the translator or on the
nature and impact of the texts or discourse translated.

Once again, I would like to express my gratitude, in my own name and on behalf of
Jean Delisle, to all the contributors to the original edition of this book, published
simultaneously in English and French in 1995, and to those who have participated
in various ways in the production of this new edition. The names of writers, translators and proofreaders are all listed in Appendix II. We are also indebted to translators of this work, and their respective teams, for disseminating it to Portuguese,
Spanish, Arabic and Romanian readers, as well as others, potentially, as new translations are completed. Readers and reviewers, whom we have met personally, or
whose comments we have read through individual correspondence or published
texts, have been both generous and helpful. In drawing our attention to errors and
omissions, large and small, they have enabled us to make necessary changes and
improvements, first to the 2007 French edition and now to this one.

A few individuals deserve special mention. I am grateful, first of all, to Isja
Conen, Acquisition Editor at John Benjamins, who commissioned this updated
English edition. She has been both encouraging and patient. Jean Delisle contributed immensely with unfailing support, encouraging words, and immediate
attention to my every request for information. He led the way by undertaking his
revision of the French edition, and kindly provided me with his edits to set the
stage. Long-time friend and colleague Sherry Simon has been a motivating influence and source of affection throughout the years. Philippe Caignon, my department chair and colleague at Concordia University, brought Ray Kurzweil to my
attention in the course of a conversation during which he so warmly welcomed
me back to my department. Philip Noss expertly and promptly revised the section on Gbaya in Chapter 2, offering positive, supportive comments. Jean-Claude
Boulanger, author of Chapter 8, offered a thorough commentary on the English
translation of his chapter. I extend my appreciation to Hilary Parker for her meticulous work constructing a new index for this edition, and to Douglas Parker
for drawing on his acute sense of language, along with his vast knowledge of literature and culture, to proofread the manuscript.

I owe so much to a devoted family: to Michael, by now a historian in his own
right, who has provided guidance in new thinking on history, and who, along

with Amy, has been my beacon; to Vince, the history buff, Patrice, the linguist and world traveller, and their partners; to my grandchildren Julien, Mia, Mathieu, Will and Eleanor, who each in his or her own way has provided inspiration. To Lindsay, who has lived and breathed this project since the beginning, I offer my thanks; once again, he has read every word – many of them several times – with immeasurable patience, while sharing my adventures through this vast history. This piece of work, finally, is offered in memory of my parents, Zsuzsanna and Zoltán Weisz. Displaced and dislocated, they inhabited the fertile spaces between cultures, instilling in me a passion for languages and cultural exchange. My journey began with theirs.

Judith Woodsworth
Montreal, 2012

Preface

"Turning translations into instruments of humanism, peace and progress – such is our noble task". These are the words of Pierre-François Caillé (1907–79), founding President of the International Federation of Translators / Fédération internationale des traducteurs (FIT). They reflect his personal philosophy, which he passed along to the Federation when it was established in 1953 (Lilova 1979). In Article 6 of its bylaws, FIT invites translators to "assist in the spreading of culture throughout the world". The tens of thousands who belong to the seventy-three [now 100] member organizations of our Federation spare no effort to fulfil this mission. The work they perform on a day-to-day basis attests to the fact that translation permeates all facets of human activity and is an inexhaustible source of progress.

People have translated since time immemorial. Long before FIT, translators served as vital links in the vast chain through which knowledge was transmitted among groups of people separated by language barriers. Ever since humans first devised writing systems, translators have been building bridges between nations, races, cultures and continents. Bridges between past and present, too. Translators have the ability to span time and space. They have enabled certain central texts – works of science, philosophy or literature – to acquire universal stature. Translators breach the walls created by language differences, thereby opening up new horizons and broadening our vision of reality to encompass the entire world. "Translators live off the differences between languages, all the while working toward eliminating them" (Edmond Cary 1956: 181).

Yet translators have been widely scorned at times and their work severely criticized. These educated men and women of letters have been distrusted, even called turncoats and traitors. But if we think about it, what people actually fear is not the translators themselves, but rather the new, foreign and sometimes strange values that they introduce into their own cultures. We are always somewhat unsettled by novelty, difference and otherness, which challenge our own values and hold up a mirror that forces us to examine ourselves. Translation, in the final analysis, is about discovery – a journey of exploration through the fabulous realm of knowledge.

If we stand back and assess the work of translators over the centuries, as the authors of this volume have done, we can see that receiving cultures have generally considered themselves enriched by their work. Just think of Livius Andronicus, a Greek slave in the third century BCE, who introduced the stern Romans to the treasures of Greek literature; Ibn al-Muqaffaᶜ, the eighth-century Persian translator who enriched the Arab culture with the famous Indian *Fables of Bidpai*, which later inspired the fables of Jean de La Fontaine; Geoffrey Chaucer, a translator before becoming an author, who brought the ballad, the romance, the fabliau and animal fables into his culture; Jagannatha, the eighteenth-century Indian astronomer who translated Ptolemy's *Almagest* and Euclid's *Elements* from Arabic into Sanskrit; Voltaire, who acquainted his eighteenth-century compatriots with Shakespeare and shook their aesthetic values; Émilie du Châtelet (pictured on the cover), who was the first to translate the seminal work of Newton into French; Yan Fu (Figure 15), who introduced the work of the prominent British thinkers Thomas Huxley, Adam Smith, Herbert Spencer and John Stuart Mill to China; and finally, closer to home, Constance Garnett (Figure 23), the eminent English translator, who made the Anglo-Saxon world familiar with great Russian writers such as Tolstoy, Dostoyevsky, Chekhov and Turgenev. There are thousands upon thousands of examples. "Please, never despise the translator", Alexander Pushkin advised. "He's the post-horse of human civilization". These words will be all the more compelling as readers become better acquainted with the function of translators as unassuming artisans of communication.

The purpose of *Translators through History*, published by the FIT Committee for the History of Translation with the assistance of UNESCO, is twofold: first, to bring translators from the ancient and recent past out of oblivion and, second, to illustrate the roles they have played in the evolution of human thought.

"Historians of translation are needed more than ever before", said José Lambert (1993:22). There are two main reasons for this. The history of translation helps translators, those discreet labourers, to emerge from the shadows and enables us to better appreciate their contribution to intellectual life. The pages that follow are teeming with figures who have left their mark on the profession in various ways. Inventing alphabets, enriching languages, encouraging the emergence of national literatures, disseminating technical and scientific knowledge, propagating religions, writing dictionaries – their contributions have been prodigious. Translation cannot be dissociated from the notion of progress; some even maintain that a society can be measured by the translations it accepts. This points to the importance of the work done by translators.

"The construction of a history of translation is the first task of a *modern* theory of translation" (Berman 1992:1). The study of our profession's antecedents will help to legitimize translation as an independent discipline, capable of defining itself, of sustaining a discourse *sui generis*. It has already been given a name: "translation studies" or "*traductologie*" in French. This young discipline cannot claim a future if it is unable to build upon earlier experience and seek fresh ideas based on models from the past. Constructing a history of translation means bringing to light the complex network of cultural exchanges between people, cultures and civilizations through the ages. It means drawing a portrait of these import-export workers and attempting to unravel their deep-rooted reasons for translating one particular work instead of another. It means finding out why their sponsors (kings, aristocrats, patrons, high-ranking clergy, etc.) asked them to translate a given work. It means taking into account what the translators themselves have written about their work, its difficulties and constraints. In short, as Lieven D'hulst has observed, history "is virtually the only means by which the discipline of translation studies can achieve some measure of coherence – by showing how divergent traditions of thought and activity are in fact similar or interconnected, by linking the past to the present" (1994: 13).

I hope that today's translators will recognize themselves in this book devoted to their predecessors. And I include the many administrative and technical translators of the latter half of the twentieth century who, while they may not participate in cultural advances to the same extent as the individuals from the past presented here, nonetheless fulfil an essential function in modern society.

Readers will appreciate the immense task involved in mapping the vast but uncharted territory of the universal history of translation. This work, itself only a beginning, could never have been carried out without an international team reflecting the make-up of FIT itself. We would like to express our heartfelt gratitude to all those who had a hand in the project, as contributing authors, editors, translators or proofreaders, helping to produce this original work from a wealth of documents. Some fifty individuals from twenty different countries helped to mount this impressive portrait gallery of translators. All the authors are to be thanked for their rigorous and highly professional efforts. Above all, our appreciation is due to the initiators and driving forces behind the project, Jean Delisle and Judith Woodsworth, Chair and Vice-Chair of the Committee for the History of Translation, respectively. Through their determination, enthusiasm and talent, they were able to achieve the objectives set out by Jean Delisle at the Twelfth World Congress of FIT, held in Belgrade in 1990. We would like to offer them our deepest appreciation.

Monuments have been erected to various translators: Mesrop Mashtots (Figure 2) in Yerevan, Jacques Amyot (Figure 4) in Melun, Joost van den Vondel (Figure 6) in Amsterdam, William Tyndale (Figure 13) in London, and St. Jerome (Figure 20) in Washington, to name but a few. This volume, which celebrates the achievements of many other translators, should also be seen as a monument to their memory.

History would be a fascinating curiosity, but merely a sterile exercise, if we did not draw lessons from it for the present and future. I am convinced that *Translators through History* will be interesting, even inspirational, to a broad range of readers, who will learn a great deal from this work. Translators themselves will undoubtedly be the first to gain from it. Embarking on this fascinating voyage through the annals of their profession, they will encounter many pioneers who crossed borders and influenced the course of the history of ideas. These portraits will remind them that theirs is one of the most useful and noble professions, one in which they have every reason to take great pride.

Jean-François Joly
President
International Federation of Translators
Montreal, June 1995

Introduction

This book comes at the end of a long gestation period; it is the culmination of an idea that took root in the early 1960s when the International Federation of Translators (FIT) was only ten years old. At the Fourth World Congress of FIT held in Dubrovnik in 1963, it was unanimously agreed that a comprehensive history of translation should be written. One of the principal initiators of this project, Dr. György Radó (1912–94) (Hungary), called upon historians of translation to carry out preliminary studies and write monographs on this subject, which had previously received little attention. "We have to show the way and lay the foundations; in other words, we must create a framework and a method that will enable us to carry out the research and ultimately write the proposed history of translation" (Radó 1964: 15).

At the FIT Congress held three years later in Lahti, Finland, Dr. Radó raised the matter once more and outlined to the delegates his concept of how a comprehensive history of translation should be written. The reaction was enthusiastic, and the FIT Council decided to establish a Committee for the History of Translation. The scope of the project was enormous: the proposed study was to cover no less than twenty-five centuries, encompass every continent and deal with hundreds of languages. Studying the history of translation in this way would be tantamount to rewriting the history of the world, the history of civilization – but from the perspective of translation (Van Hoof 1991: 7).

Given the amount of work involved, the state of research in history of translation and the limited financial and human resources of FIT, some people were sceptical about whether so ambitious a project would ever be completed. In an article that appeared in *Babel*, Radó nevertheless presented a detailed outline of the book as he saw it (Radó 1967: 4–8).

Years went by. Despite a steady increase in the number of publications on the subject, the vast compendium of translation history envisioned by the early members of FIT had not yet been written. Would it be possible to produce this "worldwide encyclopedia of translation", full of dates and facts, containing all the milestones along the "glorious road which the art of translation has travelled" (Radó 1964: 15)? Even the most enthusiastic and daring of historians would feel daunted by such an undertaking, and justifiably so.

A new Committee for the History of Translation was struck at the Twelfth World Congress of FIT in Belgrade in 1990. Moved by the same spirit as those who initiated the original history project, the Committee developed plans for a publication that would be more limited in scope. The goal remained the same: to enhance the translation profession throughout the world by revealing the immeasurable contribution of translators to the intellectual and cultural history of humanity. To borrow the words of Pierre-François Caillé, founding president of FIT, translators are those "lonely soldiers" who plunge into the fray of ideas and cultures to bear messages from one to the other, often becoming agents of profound ideological and social change (Caillé 1955: 3). It was felt that their work, their dignity and their place in the "Republic of Letters" had yet to be highlighted (Larbaud 1946: 9).

Interest in the history of translation has grown in recent years. Since the 1980s, in particular, translation scholars have been aware of the importance of historical research and have begun to define appropriate methods and theoretical models for the new subdiscipline. In their conference papers, scholarly articles and books, they have addressed the subject of the history of translation from a variety of perspectives, each drawing the boundaries of history in a different way and looking at the past through different lenses.

The Committee for the History of Translation set out to make a contribution to this area. One of its first tasks was to compile as complete a list as possible of historians of translation around the world and to gather information about their research. This groundwork led to the publication of the *International Directory of Historians of Translation* in 1991, with further editions released subsequently (Delisle 2011). This valuable tool enabled us to set up research teams, create an international network of historians and get the preparation of *Translators through History* under way.

While broad-ranging and ambitious, *Translators through History* does not claim to be an exhaustive study of the history of translation. Instead, it is a *selective* and *thematic* overview of the principal roles played by translators through the ages. Nine broad themes were chosen to reflect the various areas in which the work of translators has been most apparent. Translators have been viewed not so much from a psychological point of view, but rather in terms of their position in a cultural and temporal space. The result is rather like a canvas drawn with a broad brush, and readers will undoubtedly discover significant omissions in the pages that follow. We are well aware of the lacunae, which inevitably derive from the approach we decided to adopt.

Each of the nine themes was assigned to an international team of historians, headed by a principal author. The participating scholars had the freedom to illustrate their remarks by means of examples drawn from any period of time and any cultural or linguistic community. Through teamwork, we have drawn on the expertise of scholars living in various parts of the world and have sought to move beyond a Eurocentric view of translation, thereby respecting the vocation of FIT. It is undeniable that the West in general, and Europe in particular, have been given preferential treatment, as it were, owing to the sheer number of historians in that part of the world, and to the important strides they have made in historical research in the past twenty years. And yet we have been fortunate enough to include history specialists from the major regions of the world: from Europe, the Americas, the Middle East and – to a lesser extent – from Africa and Asia.

Underlying our task as editors were two concerns: one was for our readership, which was intended to be an international one, and the other was for stylistic and methodological consistency. Without compromising our standards of scholarship, we have sought to make the book readable and accessible to as wide an audience as possible. For this reason, we have been careful to avoid using some of the highly specialized terminology particular to the field of translation studies or related disciplines. In addition, explanations have been added, either in the text or in endnotes, to clarify allusions to specific historical events or cultural features that might not be familiar to every reader.

Translators through History can be regarded as a guide to the field of translation history. References are intended to help readers find more information on specific topics of interest to them. All the works mentioned in parenthetical references in the body of the text are listed in the "Works Cited" section. An index of proper names is also provided to make the book easier to use.

Illustrations have been inserted between the chapters. These illustrations, in our opinion, are not simply decorative.They are another means of portraying the role and status of translators through history. The iconography of a field is an essential element in any meaningful history of it. A description of all illustrations is included in Appendix I.

It is our sincere hope that you, the reader, will take pleasure in reading this collective work, and that the wide range of material presented will arouse your curiosity about the history of translation.

Jean Delisle
Judith Woodsworth
Ottawa and Montreal, 1995

Figure 1. Double Egyptian interpreter

Figure 2. Mesrop Mashtots

CHAPTER 1

Translators and the invention of alphabets

Human beings have been living and dying for some four million years, but they have been writing for fewer than six thousand. The earliest form of writing, Sumerian cuneiform script, was born humbly in Mesopotamia to facilitate agricultural and commercial bookkeeping. Other systems soon appeared in Egypt and China. Wherever writing existed, it was regarded as a divine gift and became the exclusive privilege of an elite or a powerful aristocratic class. In Egyptian mythology, for example, the invention of writing is attributed to Thoth, the god of knowledge, language and magic, who served as adviser and scribe to the other gods. The word "hieroglyphics", in fact, means "sacred inscriptions". With writing, history was born. Translation, too. Archaeologists have uncovered Sumerian-Eblaite vocabularies inscribed in clay tablets that are 4,500 years old.[1] These bilingual lists attest to the existence of translation even in remotest history. Writing quickly became the preferred medium for commercial contracts, religious teachings, law and literature. In ancient civilizations, scribes were the masters of writing, teaching and translation. They performed most administrative functions and controlled both the sacred and secular sciences. There is no doubt that they played a role in the invention of writing, but their names have been erased with the passage of time.

The invention of an alphabet by the Phoenicians around 1000 BCE, most probably in Byblos (north of present-day Beirut), was truly revolutionary. Using alphabetic abstraction (i.e. assigning a character or symbol to represent each sound), one had to know only about thirty letters in order to write, instead of memorizing hundreds, or even thousands, of signs or complicated drawings such as pictograms, hieroglyphics or ideograms. Because the Phoenicians were merchants and navigators, their alphabet spread to other peoples living on the shores of the Mediterranean. The Aramaic, Hebrew, Greek, Coptic and Arabic alphabets were all derived from the Phoenician one. The Greeks were the first to introduce vowels to accurately reproduce the sounds of their language graphically, using signs that represented consonants in the Aramaic alphabet. This gave rise to the letters A, E, O and Y. The letter I was a Greek innovation, as was the use of wax tablets. In the seventh century BCE, Greek writing in turn gave rise to the Latin alphabet with Etruscan acting as an intermediary step. The alphabet is regarded as the key to the history of humanity and its advent considered to have initiated the democratization of knowledge (Diringer 1952; Jean 1987: 52).

Today, linguists have identified nearly seven thousand languages spoken the world over, although only a few hundred of these have a literary tradition (Lewis 2009).[2] Some traditional writing systems are gradually being displaced by the Latin alphabet, preferred by linguists, who add diacritical marks to indicate the distinctive features of indigenous languages. In the long and complex history of the invention of writing, it is not always easy to determine the precise contribution of translators. Nevertheless, some of them are known to us. This chapter will highlight the efforts of four translators who have helped to give nations a memory: Ulfila, the inventor of the Gothic alphabet (fourth century, Bulgaria); Mesrop Mashtots, the inventor of the Armenian, Albanian and Georgian alphabets (fifth century, Armenia); Cyril, the inventor of the Glagolitic alphabet (ninth century, Moravia); and James Evans, the inventor of the syllabic writing system for Cree (nineteenth century, Canada).

Ulfila, evangelist to the Goths

Ulfila ("little wolf") was born around the year 311, probably somewhere in Romania.[3] On his mother's side, he was descended from Roman Christian prisoners who had been carried off from Cappadocia by Goths in the latter half of the third century.[4] The Goths formed the eastern band of Germanic peoples who inhabited the basin of the Vistula River and the northern shores of the Black Sea from the second century onward. They conducted periodic raids against the Roman Empire until the year 410 when the Visigoths, or West Goths, sacked Rome under their chief Alaric I.

These historical circumstances explain how Ulfila came to receive a Christian education while living among pagans. At the age of thirty, he was a lector, or reader, during religious services. As part of his duties, he studied the Bible. This was direct preparation for his later work as a translator. Around 340, he was consecrated bishop by Eusebius, one of the most influential churchmen of the time and a proponent of Arianism.[5]

Ulfila was responsible for the Christian community, comprised primarily of descendants of poor Christian prisoners, now living among the Visigoths. For seven years he served as bishop there and worked to spread Arianism. As a result of the persecution of Christians in 348, Ulfila and his followers crossed the Danube and took refuge to the south, in Roman territory. With this exodus he earned the title "the Moses of our time" (Thompson 1966: 97). He settled near Nicopolis in what is now the city of Trnovo, Bulgaria, where he remained for thirty-three years.

A translation of the Scriptures proved essential to Ulfila's evangelical work, and he soon realized that an alphabet would have to be invented for this purpose. Up to this point, Gothic had been strictly a spoken language. Ulfila used characters taken from Greek and Latin to transcribe Gothic sounds. He also added some runic[6] letters, borrowed from ancient Germanic and Scandinavian alphabets. Ulfila's alphabet, which consisted of twenty-seven characters, is not to be confused with the German script also known as "Gothic", which is simply a graphic transcription of the Latin alphabet (Van Hoof 1990: 42).

With the assistance of a team of collaborators, Ulfila undertook to translate the Bible. This monumental task occupied him for the forty years he was bishop. Mindful of the aggressive nature of the Goths, he refrained from translating the Book of Kings for fear that its numerous descriptions of battles might arouse their passion for war. Ulfila felt that his compatriots were far too fond of combat and inclined to indulge in pillaging and plundering.

To carry out the translation, Ulfila worked from the Greek text, scrupulously following its word order and syntax. He was often forced to coin new words or phrases. "With this translation [...], Ulfila stands out as the founder of Gothic literature, which enables us to understand the evolution of Germanic languages over fifteen centuries. Elements of the language forged by Ulfila have been passed on to all the Germanic idioms. One example is the verb *fastan*, which in Gothic meant 'to hold out' and to which Ulfila added the religious sense of 'to fast'. The term is still used in this way in contemporary English, as well as in Dutch (*vasten*) and German (*fasten*)" (Van Hoof 1990: 39).

In 380, the Roman Emperor Theodosius I, who had proclaimed Christianity to be the State religion, took measures to suppress Arianism. Although Arianism had been declared a heresy at the Council of Nicaea in 325, the Empire had continued to tolerate it. The Emperor now excommunicated its followers. Ulfila was summoned to Constantinople to defend his beliefs, but was never permitted to speak before the Council. When he fell ill and died in 382 or 383, he was over seventy years old.

Bishop Ulfila wrote a great deal, particularly on the subject of Arianism. Unfortunately, few documents from that period have survived. Among the rare samples of the Gothic language are fragments of Ulfila's translation of the Bible, the famous *Codex Argenteus*, written in gold and silver ink on red parchment and dating back to the sixth century. This precious document is now kept in the library of the University of Uppsala in Sweden. Ulfila's Bible is the oldest record of a Germanic language to have endured in so substantial a form – a work that helped reinforce the religious zeal of new converts, spread Arianism among the Goths and preserve their ethnic identity (Wolfram 1988: 85).

Mesrop Mashtots and the flowering of Armenian culture

According to tradition, the Armenian Church has apostolic origins, as Armenia is said to have been evangelized by two of Christ's twelve apostles: St. Bartholomew and St. Jude (also known as St. Thaddaeus). Early in the fourth century, Armenia embraced Christianity under the influence of St. Gregory the Illuminator.[7] Armenia's official conversion was marked by the baptism of some four million Christians in only a few months. This occurred just after Roman Emperors Constantine and Licinius issued the Edict of Milan, tolerating the practice of Christianity, but not yet granting official recognition to the religion. Soon after, St. Gregory built an edifice over a pagan sanctuary: Echmiadzin Cathedral, the first cathedral in Christendom.

Toward the end of the fourth century, Armenia lost its independence: the Western part was governed by the Byzantines and the rest, the greater part, dominated by the Persians. In Armenia, the Scriptures were initially taught in Greek and in Syriac. Interpretation was often required during religious services. Furthermore, Greek and Syriac, and occasionally Pahlavi (a Persian language), were used for public administration since they were written languages and Armenian was not. Foreign languages were thus used in the realms of religion, culture and public administration, with serious disadvantages to the Armenian people. It became increasingly urgent to create an Armenian alphabet.

It was during the reign of Vramshapuh that St. Mesrop Mashtots (c.361–440) made his invaluable contribution to Armenian culture: the Armenian alphabet, which he invented between 392 and 406 (Figure 2). A native of Hatsekats in the canton of Taron, Mesrop (or Mesrob) held a variety of administrative and military posts at the Arsacid Royal Chancery. He had a gift for languages, speaking Greek, Persian, Syriac and Armenian. He chose to become a monk, and spent time in a monastery preparing for a missionary life spreading Christianity. However, the Scriptures and liturgy, which were written in Syriac, were largely unintelligible to the faithful, and Mesrop found it difficult to preach in Armenian. He sought the advice of Sahak Partev (Isaac of Armenia or Isaac the Great), a descendant of St. Gregory and the Patriarch of the Armenian Church. With Sahak's blessing, and assistance, he undertook to create an alphabet for his people.

The idea of creating a script for the Armenian language was not totally new. A Syriac bishop by the name of Daniel owned a large collection of documents about various alphabets. In one of these, the elements of Aramaic were dominant. Mesrop and Sahak began teaching this alphabet to young children, but after two years, the experiment was deemed a failure: this system of writing did not adequately convey the sounds of their own language. Mesrop continued his research in Syria, Edessa and Amida. It was there, or perhaps in Antioch, that he determined the phonetic content of each letter. Later, in Samosata (today Samsat, Turkey), he improved on the design of the characters, enlisting the help of a specialist in Greek calligraphy named Rufanos (also known as Rufinus).

By the time he returned to Armenia, he had all the elements required to put together an alphabet of thirty-six letters; two further letters were added to this alphabet around the end of the twelfth century, completing what is considered to be the classical Armenian alphabet (Grousset 1973: 173). Mesrop followed the Greek rules for forming syllables, introducing vowels and writing from left to right, unlike Syriac and other Semitic languages. The details of his linguistic borrowings are still hotly debated, but "the basis for the Armenian system is essentially alphabetic and Greek. It is supplemented Greek, like the Gothic system or the Slavic system. Just as the Gothic system is Greek supplemented by Latin and runic characters, the Armenian system is Greek supplemented by non-Greek, or Semitic, characters" (Peeters 1929: 219). Mesrop's alphabet is phonetically accurate: it consists of twenty-two signs which correspond to Greek letters, and fourteen others which indicate sounds unique to Armenian.

Once they had an alphabet at their disposal, Mesrop Mashtots, Sahak and their disciples began to translate the Bible into Armenian. To obtain complete copies of the original Greek text, Sahak sent Mesrop and Bishop Dinth to the court of Emperor Theodosius II in Constantinople. Between 431 and 435, Sahak and Mesrop sent two of their disciples, Eznik and Joseph, to Edessa, where they were to translate the Scriptures from the Syriac text into Armenian. Eznik and Joseph then travelled into Byzantium, where they learned Greek, so that they could translate that language as well. Other translators, Leontius Vanandotsi and Koriun Skancheli, joined Eznik and became part of his team. Once they had completed their work, they left the Byzantine Empire and headed home. They brought with them copies of the Scriptures, patristic texts and the canons of the Councils of Nicaea and Ephesus.

Sahak and Mesrop Mashtots had translated most of the ecclesiastical texts from Greek copies that were either incomplete or inaccurate. The copies brought from Constantinople gave them the opportunity to revise their earlier drafts. The translation of the Bible was instrumental in promoting widespread literacy and evangelization in Armenia. Once the Bible was completed, the country's leaders devised a plan that was astonishingly modern in nature: they proposed to make the entire population literate by creating a network of public schools. In so doing, they hoped to build a powerful political and cultural identity that would strengthen the nation's resistance to assimilation by the Byzantines and Persians.

The invention of the alphabet marked the beginning of the golden age of Armenian literature. In addition to sacred texts, many of the world's masterpieces were translated: works of history, philosophy and mathematics by authors such as Aristotle, Plato, Xenon and Eusebius. This also led to the production of original works, various genres written in a broad range of disciplines: history, geography, mathematics, astronomy, cosmography and medicine. Thanks to the efforts of Mesrop and Isaac, Armenia was in a position not only to build up its own intellectual capital but also to make a unique contribution to civilization at the crossroads of East and West.

Mesrop Mashtots is said to have created an alphabet for the Albanians[8] after completing the Armenian alphabet (Grousset 1973). This long-lost alphabet was discovered in a manuscript kept at Echmiadzin. He is also believed to have invented the Georgian alphabet, although historians are not unanimous on this point. "It is possible that Mesrop's work encouraged the Georgians and the Albanians to create their own national alphabet. But it is not possible to give him full credit for these inventions, as his biographer and disciple Koriun has done, acting out of naive admiration for his master rather than national pride" (Dédéyan 1982: 157).

Shortly after Mesrop's death, Koriun, one of his pupils and translators, wrote his biography, one of the first major original works to be written in Armenian. Koriun writes with the enthusiasm of a hagiographer, particularly when describing Mesrop's triumphant arrival at the cathedral of Echmiadzin, carrying his translation of the Book of Proverbs like Moses descending Mount Sinai with the Ten Commandments.

Mesrop's popularity, combined with a widespread interest in cultural matters, has nourished the collective imagination of the Armenian people. His accomplishments are celebrated annually with a "translators' day" called Tarkmanchatz. It marks the beginning of the school year and honours translators, writers and teachers – those whose mission it is to replenish the nation's intellectual resources and mould new generations. Pictures of Mesrop, a true national icon, and of his alphabet grace the covers of many school books.

In the Echmiadzin Cathedral, a Gobelin tapestry made in 1981 by the painter Grigor Khandjian depicts in epic fashion the presentation of the Armenian alphabet to the court of King Vramshapuh. In Yerevan, the capital of Armenia, an imposing statue of Mesrop stands before the Matenadaran national library, which bears his name and which houses some ten thousand rare manuscripts, an invaluable national treasure.

Cyril and Methodius among the Slavs

The powerful and formidable Constantinople, capital of the Byzantine Empire (or Byzantium), saw itself as the successor to Rome, heir to its glory and henceforth the heart of Christianity and civilization. Nations seeking to change their "barbaric" ways now turned to Constantinople.

Up until the ninth century, the Slavs had had little contact with the major centres of ancient civilization. In 862, an unexpected event with important historical repercussions occurred: Prince Rastislav, the Christian ruler of the Slavic state of Great Moravia, asked Byzantine Emperor Michael III to send missionaries to educate his people and preach the Christian faith in the Slavic language.[9] Frankish clerics in Moravia refused to speak anything but Latin, which the people did not understand. The prince expressed the wish that, like the Greeks, Romans and Goths, his people have the sacred texts translated into their language. Behind his religious intentions lay political motives: the Moravian prince aimed to bring about the political emancipation of the Slavs from the Frankish empire through religious emancipation (Dvornik 1970: 156; Tachiaos 2001). In concrete terms, Rastislav wanted to be free of the tutelage of the Germanic clergy, who were more concerned with domination and interference in Moravian affairs than with education.

To Emperor Michael and the Patriarch of Constantinople Photius,[10] no one seemed more suited to carrying out this diplomatic, cultural and religious mission than the brothers Cyril (c.827–69) and Methodius (c.825–85) (Figure 3).[11] Natives of Thessaloniki in Macedonia, they spoke Greek and also had an excellent knowledge of the Slavic dialect spoken in that region. Methodius had been the commander-in-chief of a Slavic province in Macedonia and, in 860, he and his brother had taken part in a diplomatic mission among the Khazars, inhabitants of the Lower Volga region. Cyril (originally named Constantine) was one of the most eminent scholars of Constantinople. Well respected at the court, he had a brilliant mind and had received a rigorous education under renowned masters, including Photius himself, considered the greatest humanist of his time (Obolensky 1967: 588). A philosopher well versed in the art of dialectic, Cyril was exceptionally gifted in languages and took a particular interest in philology and archaeology. During his stay among the Khazars, he is said to have learned Hebrew, Arabic, and Khazar – a Turkic language – very quickly. It was there that he discovered the Gothic Psalter and Gospels translated by Ulfila, which he managed to understand with the help of a local inhabitant.

According to the biography of Cyril and Methodius attributed to their companion and disciple Clement of Ohrid, about whom more will be said later, Cyril inquired whether the Moravians had a system of writing. If not, he said, it would be like trying to "write on water", and he would surely be considered a heretic. He was told that if he invented a writing system, the Almighty would come to his aid, since "God gives to those who ask in good faith and opens the door to those who knock" (Dvornik 1970: 158–159).

Why did Cyril ask such a question? Why did his biographer, or hagiographer, suggest that the invention of an alphabet for the Slavs was the work of God? At that time, the first task of any nation aspiring to become "civilized" was to develop its own writing system. The Goths and the Armenians are classic examples. The Roman clerics, however, believed that only Hebrew, Greek and Latin could be used in prayer. Cyril did not want to be called a heretic for translating the holy texts into the vernacular of the time, Old Slavonic, so he sought the protection of the Emperor and the Patriarch, and obtained their approval for his undertaking.[12] His biographer even provides him with divine approbation: since God himself revealed the Slavic letters to Cyril, he could not be suspected of heresy. This was not the first time in the history of writing and translation that a new writing system was given a divine origin. The Sumerians, Egyptians and Chinese all regarded writing as a gift of the gods. But in asking Cyril to come up with an alphabet for the Slavic language, the Emperor was motivated by political considerations as well: "Before Byzantium and the Byzantine church could make any significant inroads into the Slavic world, they had to provide Slavs with a writing system that was perfectly adapted to their language" (Dvornik 1970: 161). Such was the political and religious climate in 862, the year when Cyril began to develop a new alphabet in order to carry out his work as a translator, missionary and diplomat.

Cyril is said to have invented the so-called "Glagolitic" alphabet, named for *glagol*, meaning "utterance" or "word" in Old Slavonic. The true origins of the Glagolitic alphabet remain obscure, but it is believed that the writing system was fitted to the Macedo-Bulgarian dialect of Slavonic, and that it was formed on the model of the Greek minuscules, or lower-case Greek cursives of the ninth century with recourse also to some Latin and Hebrew (or Samaritan) signs, or signs that Cyril may have used to represent non-Greek sounds. The precise number of letters in the original alphabet is not known, but is assumed to be around forty. It is not clear why the script was based on a South Slavonic dialect, while its use was intended for a totally different area and tongue in North Slavonia, but it has been argued that Slavonic tongues in the ninth century were more nearly related to one another and that the notation system could thus more readily be adopted by all members of the linguistic group (Jagic 1936: 225).

With a writing system at his disposal and with the help of Methodius and some disciples, Cyril was now in a position to undertake the translation of the Holy Scriptures, the Psalms and several books of liturgy into Old Slavonic. The first words translated using the new Glagolitic alphabet were: "In the beginning was the Word, and the Word was with God, and the Word was God". There could not have been a more appropriate text for the inception of a new writing system and the birth of Slavonic literature than the opening verse of the Gospel according to St. John. The dialect of the Macedonian Slavs thus acquired the status and prestige of other written languages. Assessing the quality of Cyril's translations, Roger Bernard wrote: "He recorded the ancient language of the Slavs with astonishing precision; his translations, based on a sound methodology, were clearly superior to all other medieval translations" (Bernard 1990: 1031).

In 863, alphabet and translations in hand, Cyril and Methodius finally set off for distant Moravia. On their arrival, Rastislav bestowed honours upon them. In a letter to him, Emperor Michael III said: "Please accept this gift, which is greater and more precious than gold or silver, jewels or treasures" (Obolensky 1967: 590). The Emperor was of course referring to the alphabet, the instrument required to carry out the mission and also the cornerstone of medieval Slavic civilization. The liturgical translation begun in Constantinople continued. Cyril introduced more Slavonic into religious services until soon the entire mass was celebrated in that language. He dared to sing the praises of God in a "barbaric" language, and that was a bold move at the time. He was not foolhardy, however, and wisely adhered to the rite prescribed by the church of Rome.

Yet despite this precaution, the new liturgical practice drew a sharp response from the Roman clergy and provoked a dispute with the Archibishop of Salzburg, who were anxious to maintain tradition as well as control over liturgical matters. After being taken to task over the Slavonic liturgy in Venice in 867, the two missionary-translators set out for Rome, likely at the behest of Pope Nicolas I. By the time they reached Rome, in 868, Pope Adrian II had succeeded Nicolas. Far from condemning them, the Pope welcomed them as veritable heroes. The warm reception was due, in part, to the fact that the brothers were bringing with them the relics of Saint Clement, but the brothers were also cultivated for their influence over the Slavs, at a time when Rome vied with Constantinople for jurisdiction over that territory. The Pope officially recognized the Slavonic liturgy and, by some accounts, even promoted them to the rank of bishop.

Two years later, on February 14, 869, Cyril died in Rome. His brother Methodius returned to continue his work of Christianization and translation among the Slavs, although not at first in Great Moravia, where Rastislav had been taken captive. Methodius himself was taken prisoner. While the Pope remained on his side and Methodius was later freed, the use of Slavonic liturgy was restricted. When he died, some years after his brother, the funeral service was held in Latin, Greek and Slavonic. Soon after their deaths, the two missionary-translators were regarded as saints. They are known as the "Apostles of the Slavs". They are still venerated in both Roman Catholic and Orthodox churches and commemorated in various ways in many eastern European countries.

The "Cyrillic" alphabet itself was not invented by Cyril, but adapted from Glagolitic. After the death of Methodius, the disciples of the brothers were exiled from Great Moravia and fled to the First Bulgarian Empire. There they created the Cyrillic alphabet. The development of the forty-three character alphabet called "Cyrillic", a simpler form of Glagolitic, is attributed to St. Clement of Ohrid (c.840–916).[13] After taking part in the mission of Cyril and Methodius to Moravia, Clement became the first Slavic bishop in Bulgaria, where he founded three monasteries and a church, and translated the Byzantine liturgy into Old Bulgarian (Février 1948: 431).

The Catholic Slavs continued to use Glagolitic longer than the Orthodox Slavs, who replaced it with Cyrillic in the thirteenth century. The Russian, Byelorussian, Macedonian, Ukrainian, Bulgarian and Serbian alphabets derive from Old Cyrillic. Glagolitic has apparently survived and is said to be in use today in some Catholic parishes of Dalmatia. The invention of this alphabet has played a significant role in the history of the Slavic world and has immortalized Cyril. Thanks to this apostle-translator and his brother, Old Slavonic achieved the status of a literary language. The members of this linguistic group were gradually able to attain religious autonomy and pursue their cultural aspirations, thereby ensuring the link between East and West.

James Evans and the Cree of Canada

Closer to our time, another missionary-translator invented an alphabet to facilitate his work as an evangelist and educator among the First Nations of Canada. Born into a Methodist family in England, James Evans (1801–46) emigrated to Canada in 1822 and began his life on the new continent as a teacher in an eastern Ontario village. It was while attending a revivalist meeting with his wife, Mary, that James Evans felt the call to become a missionary. This was an "era of frenzied missionary work by all the Christian churches in Canada", who were eager to "save the souls of the Indians" (Burford Mason 1996: 4) and Evans was no exception.

James Evans went to set up a mission at Rice Lake, north-east of modern-day Toronto, on behalf of the Canadian Methodist Conference. This was Ojibway (Ojibwa, Ojibwe) territory and James and Mary showed a particular interest in the native culture and language they encountered there. In fact, Evans was one of the few missionaries who made an effort to understand the belief system of the native people, which is what made him so successful in his work with the Ojibway and later the Cree (Burford Mason 1996:12). After being ordained a minister in the Wesleyan Methodist Church of British North America, Evans was sent to the St. Clair mission, near the present-day Ontario town of Sarnia, and then travelled to other parts of Ontario, or what was known as Upper Canada.

It is said that Evans had a talent for languages: "He had a rare ear for languages, for their vocal music and their phonetic elements, and he had made this a special study" (Burwash 1911:5). He learned Ojibway, which he transcribed into Latin characters, and he began translating although some translations existed already. He systematized the Indian languages along the lines of contemporary European philological thought. He began to develop a writing system for the Ojibway language, using symbols that were different from Latin characters based on the shorthand he had learned in England while apprenticing in the grocery business.

At the time, however, the British and Foreign Bible Society was printing religious material for the Indians using the Latin alphabet and tried to put a halt to the development of Evans's syllabics. Consequently, Evans at first directed his attention to improving the approved alphabet-based version of Ojibway. In 1837, he went to New York to arrange for the publication of the hymns and excerpts of the Bible that he had translated, as well as a pamphlet entitled:

> The SPELLER and INTERPRETER in INDIAN AND ENGLISH for the use of
> THE MISSION SCHOOLS and such as may desire to obtain a knowledge of the
> OJIBWAY TONGUE.

Evans was not yet fully satisfied. He found that the Indians were confused when learning both English and their own language using the Latin alphabet (Burford Mason 1996:10). At the St. Clair Mission, therefore, he persisted in developing a syllabic alphabet specifically adapted to the sounds of their language. This would stand him in good stead for the work he was to undertake among the Cree of Northern Manitoba.

Evans's missionary work took a decisive turn in 1840 when he was appointed superintendent of the North-West Indian Missions at Norway House, a strategic post at the north end of Lake Winnipeg, in Manitoba. He moved there with his wife, his daughter and three other missionaries. His appointment to this post had been encouraged by the Hudson's Bay Company, but it was grounded in political and economic motives as much as religious ones.[14] The Company was not in favour of educating the Indians, but they were aware that the work of the missionaries was attracting Indians to southern settlements and enticing them to leave their trapping and hunting areas unattended. Missions to the northern Indians, under the control and scrutiny of the Company, might alleviate the problem (Burford Mason 1996: 28).

Evans quickly realized that in order to communicate effectively with no-madic Indian bands spread out over a vast territory, he would need to know their language. "How can a man reach these people", he wrote, "if he doesn't speak their language? To work through an interpreter is like hacking one's way through a forest with a feather" (Shipley 1966: 16–17). He also needed material written in their language and would have to institute a program of translation and publication. He would then have to teach them to read and write, which requires extensive instruction and a sustained effort. Very few of the hunters and fishermen, who made up the population, had time for this. Evans thought about this constantly: "Why cannot a simpler, easier method of learning to read be invented than our old, slow, cumbersome one with the alphabet?" he asked himself (Young 1899: 185).

He undertook this task with determination, energy and perseverance. With-in two months, he had developed the Cree syllabic alphabet using his Ojibway syllabary as a model, since the two languages, part of the Algonquian family, resembled one another. What makes James Evans's syllabary so valuable is its sur-prising simplicity. It is essentially composed of nine symbols (triangles, angles, arcs, pothooks, etc.) representing the consonants, each of which can be written in four different positions for the vowels which accompanied them, facing right, left, up or down. These nine symbols can thus represent the thirty-six sounds of the Cree's musical language. The mnemonic quality of this orthographic system, which is free from spelling and grammar rules, accounted for its instantaneous success. A bright student could learn it in a single day. "[…] a clever Indian, on being shown the characters in the morning, was able to read the Bible […] be-fore the sun went down the same day, and […] one week was all that was neces-sary for the average Indian to master thoroughly all the characters, and to use them accurately" (McLean 1890: 170). The natives, never having been to school, were astounded to find they could learn to read in so little time, without long and tedious study. The minister-translator became known as "the man who made birchbark talk" because, as he had no paper, he inscribed the characters of his syllabary on the bark of the birch tree. He made ink out of soot scraped from the inside walls of chimneys. The Rossville Mission, in the community that grew up around Norway House, became a primary centre of translating and publishing in the Cree language (Burford Mason 1996: 59; Peel 1974). It is surmised that James Evans himself spoke only a little Cree and could not have done all the translations with which he is credited. For this work, he relied on his assistants, who lived in both cultures, Henry B. Steinhauer, Thomas Hassall, John Sinclair, and Reverend William Mason and his wife Sophia Thomas.[15]

Evans requested that a printing press be shipped out to him. In 1841, he received word that the Missionary Society had agreed to send him one, with the proviso that anything printed on it would require the approval of the Hudson's Bay Company. In the meantime, casting movable type became Evans's new obsession. Several attempts ended in failure, but the tenacious and inventive missionary succeeded in printing seven pamphlets, using crude type fashioned out of lead from the lining of tea chests and ink made from a mixture of soot and sturgeon oil. A jackpress used by traders to pack furs served as a press (Burwash 1911: 10). Despite his primitive tools, this Canadian Gutenberg managed to print several hundred copies of his translations. The first book was printed on birchbark, bound with buckskin and sewn with animal tendons. The two largest publications to emerge from the valiant beginnings of Cree printing were two hymn booklets of sixteen and twenty pages.

It was not until five years later, in 1845, that a proper printing press made out of wood was sent from England. But it would arrive too late: by this time James Evans was in the final year of his life and did not live to see his syllabic alphabet put to use among native people from Hudson Bay to the Rockies. Others would reap what he had sown.

The death of his best teacher and interpreter, Thomas Hassall, whom he accidentally shot with his rifle, seems to have been a turning point and to have contributed to his premature ill health. He was also increasingly distressed by the open hostility of the governor of the Hudson's Bay Company. The more educated the Indians became, the less inclined they were to trap and hunt for the Company; Evans was also fiercely opposed to work on the Sabbath and advocated that the Company's men take Sundays to rest and worship.

Rumours about Evans's conduct also affected him deeply: he was accused of impropriety with native girls who lived in his house. Upon investigation, these allegations were found to be unsubstantiated, but a "deliberately ambiguous report of the proceedings" was sent to Evans's superiors in London, which resulted in his recall to appear before the annual Methodist conference (Burford Mason 1996: 69). Despite his ultimate exoneration, his health continued to deteriorate. He suffered a heart attack and died on November 23, 1846. He did not live long enough to witness the complete Bible translated and printed in syllabic characters. It was published by the British and Foreign Bible Society fifteen years after his death.

The syllabic writing system, so well suited to transcribing the Cree language, was adopted by many native communities and even by rival denominations such as the Anglicans (Church Missionary Society) and the Catholics (Oblats de Marie-Immaculée). The Cree syllabary was adapted for the language of the Inuit of the far North by John Horden and E.A. Walkins. This enabled Edmund Perk to translate several books of the Bible into Inuktitut in 1876.

The assimilationist attitudes and actions of the different churches and indeed the government of Canada have been decried in recent years. Attention has been paid, in particular, to the profound and lasting ill effects of residential schools, at which the use of indigenous languages was prohibited and that of English imposed, and at which First Nations children were subjected to abuse. However critical one may be of James Evans and other missionaries from today's perspective, his contribution to the survival and vitality of indigenous languages must nevertheless be recognized. Having a written language has been indispensable. And whereas there is a tendency nowadays for some indigenous languages to be written in Latin script, the syllabic alphabet pioneered by James Evans is still in use.

This chapter has profiled four translators who invented alphabets. The translators who developed writing systems extended the boundaries within which knowledge could be disseminated (Bulgaria, Moravia and Armenia); they helped awaken the collective consciousness of ethno-linguistic groups (Goths and Slavs); they participated in the emergence of national pride (Armenia, Georgia and Moravia); and they promoted the communication of new ideas (Ojibway and Cree). They gave an impetus to literacy and the democratization of education and contributed to the birth of literature and the preservation of cultural heritage.

For many missionary-translators of the past, the invention of an alphabet was required to spread the faith. Yet, in every case, the use and transmission of alphabets went beyond evangelical purposes. Writing was not simply bestowed upon human beings by heavenly powers, as was once believed. Translators played a part in the development of writing, often providing an entire community with a means to develop and grow through intellectual pursuits. In the words of Lord Dufferin, Governor General of Canada from 1872 to 1878, "What a blessing to humanity is the man who invented that alphabet! [...] The nation has given many a man a title, and a pension, and then a resting-place and a monument [...], who never did half so much for his fellow creatures" (McLean 1890: 175–177). Although directed at Evans, the "Apostle of the North", the Governor General's words could just as easily apply to Ulfila, Mesrop Mashtots, Cyril and other translators who have given a written form to language.

Notes

1. See the "Ebla tablets" (http://en.wikipedia.org/wiki/Ebla_tablets), accessed January 2012.

2. The online edition of M. Paul Lewis's 2009 edition of *Ethnologue: Languages of the World*, considered the most comprehensive available reference source of world languages, catalogues 6,909 languages (http://www.ethnologue.com/ethno_docs/introduction.asp, accessed April 2011).

3. Ulfila is also spelled Ulfilas, Ulphilas and Wulfila.

4. Cappadocia is the ancient name of a region in Asia Minor, in what is now part of Turkey.

5. This doctrine was formulated by Arius (Alexandria, c.256–c.336), who claimed that the Son of God was not consubstantial with the Father. The Son of God was "like" the Father, but not "of one and the same substance". This heresy, which denied the deity of Christ, was condemned by the Council of Nicaea in 325 and the Council of Constantinople in 381.

6. The runic alphabet was an ancient Germanic alphabet used from the second or third to the sixteenth centuries, mainly for charms and inscriptions on stone, wood, metal or bone. The number of letters ranged from sixteen runes in Scandinavia to over thirty in Anglo-Saxon England.

7. St. Gregory the Illuminator, or Enlightener, (c.257–c.331) is the patron saint and first official head of the Armenian Apostolic Church. He is credited with converting Armenia, making it the first nation to adopt Christianity as its official religion.

8. The Albanians discussed here are not to be confused with modern-day Albanians. The Albanians of the Caucasus were a people living on the southwest shore of the Caspian Sea. This territory is now part of Azerbaijan and borders on Armenia.

9. In the ninth century, the Great Moravian Empire stretched from Dalmatia to Poland. Today, Moravia is a region located in the east of the Czech Republic.

10. The work of Patriarch Photius is highlighted in Chapter 8.

11. The principal sources for the biographies of Cyril and Methodius are various Slav, Latin, and Greek legends. None of these legends is without difficulties and none, so far at least, has obtained general acceptance. Most scholars agree that the two Slav (the so-called Pannonian) Legends, *Vita Cyrilli* and *Vita Methodii*, are highly credible. There is also a shorter Latin legend, the so-called *Translatio S. Clementis*, which sometimes confirms these legends, along with statements of the Popes and other Vatican documents (Jagic 1936:215).

12. Old Church Slavonic or Old Church Slavic was the first literary Slavic language, based on the old Slavic dialect of the Thessaloniki region. It served as the basis for later Church Slavonic traditions, used to this day in some Eastern Orthodox and Eastern Catholic churches as a liturgical language.

13. Cyrillic is closer to Greek in the shape of its letters. It was simplified in 1708, under Peter the Great (1672–1725), and became the official Russian alphabet. The Cyrillic alphabet was modified again in 1917, by decree, and lost several letters.

14. Founded in 1670 by charter of British King Charles II, the Hudson's Bay Company had driven the French out and amalgamated with the competing North-West Fur Trading Company to increase its influence as far as the Rocky Mountains to the West and the border with Upper Canada to the East. "To counteract the mission as an agent of unwelcome change, by 1825 the Hudson's Bay Company had drawn up a policy for coping with the unsettling influence of the missionaries at its trading posts. These missionaries were not to impose their moral scruples on Company officials and their way of doing business", writes Burford Mason (1996: 44). Governor Sir George Simpson upheld this policy: he wielded considerable power and would eventually undermine the work of James Evans and his followers.

15. Sophia Thomas Mason, whose mother was Cree, translated the Bible. Her translation was "considered so competent that her name appears on the fly-leaf, the only female missionary to be thus honoured" (Burford Mason 1996: 59).

Figure 3. St. Cyril and St. Methodius

Figure 4. Jacques Amyot

CHAPTER 2

Translators and the development of national languages

Translators have helped to develop systems of writing. In their efforts to transpose certain fundamental texts from one culture to another, they have also had an impact on the evolution of language itself. As French philosopher Jean le Rond d'Alembert (1717–83) wrote in his "Observations sur l'art de traduire" (Remarks on the Art of Translating), "well-made translations [are] the fastest and surest way to enrich languages" (quoted in Lefevere 1992: 112). This chapter will examine the various ways in which translators have contributed to the development, enrichment and promotion of national languages, with particular emphasis on six of them: English, French, Swedish, German, Gbaya and Hebrew.

In the case studies presented in these pages, translation is not an isolated phenomenon. Rather, it is associated with certain major projects – nationalist, ideological and religious in nature – which often had the support of monarchs, aristocrats and institutions. The power of the sponsors, or the critical context in which translation took place, helped provide impetus and, in some cases, ammunition to translators, and gave legitimacy to their work. This in turn made it possible for them to make their mark on their language and culture.

We begin with the example of England, where foreign influences enriched the language and at the same time stimulated a need for a truly native tongue. In France, the combined factors of nationalism and strong monarchies encouraged translation and the domestication of great foreign works, often with the express purpose of strengthening and emancipating the national language. In Germany, it was the translation of Christian texts that sparked the development of a standard German language. The case of Martin Luther will receive particular attention; quite apart from his ecclesiastical role, Luther stands out as the driving force behind the establishment of a literary language in his country. In Sweden, too, the emergence of a written vernacular coincided with Christianization. In the late Middle Ages, the Monastery of Vadstena, referred to as the "cradle of Swedish translation", was the site of a vast translation enterprise which helped develop modern written Swedish. In Africa, as in many of the countries on the European continent, language and religion were closely linked: the missionaries who arrived during the colonial period to spread the Christian gospel also did much to promote the local languages. An institution such as the Gbaya Translation Centre in Meiganga, Cameroon, reinforced the ideological necessity of promoting a native tongue. As a final example, Hebrew has been chosen for its particular status: an ancient language which for centuries was the holy language of the Jewish people was revived in the twentieth century for use by a new nation. Translators helped to foster new linguistic resources and transform Hebrew into a truly modern language.

A language for England

"The English language is the sea which receives tributaries from every region under heaven", said American poet and essayist Ralph Waldo Emerson (quoted in McCrum et al. 1986: 11). The English language is a hybrid, an intermingling of several branches of the Indo-European family. Its development is linked to successive invasions and raids, its history one of conquest and conversion. As cultures and languages clashed and converged in Britain, translation played its usual role of mediation and cross-fertilization, especially when translators were in a position to alter the course of events, either through the position of authority they occupied, or through the influential nature of the work they accomplished. This section will focus on the contributions of four men: King Alfred the Great, Geoffrey Chaucer, William Caxton and William Tyndale.[1]

The British Isles were first settled by Celts, an Indo-European people who retreated westward before advancing Italic and Teutonic peoples. Julius Caesar invaded Britain in 55 BCE, although the Roman conquest did not begin in earnest until 43 CE. Despite a certain degree of Romanization, Latin did not replace the Celtic language as it had in Gaul, and it declined with the withdrawal of the Romans after 410 (Baugh 1957).

In 449, another series of invasions began, this time by the Angles, Saxons and Jutes, Teutonic tribes who introduced the Germanic language that was to become the foundation of English. But there were soon new influences: in 596, Latin returned to Britain – through conversion rather than conquest – when Augustine, the first Archbishop of Canterbury, Christianized England and began to organize the English church.[2]

Learning flourished mainly in the monasteries of the time. While scholarship was based on Latin, some early, largely religious, translation work occurred. Aldhelm, Bishop of Sherborne (c.640–709), a classical scholar, is credited with having translated the Psalter, although there is no evidence to substantiate the claim. In addition to Latin verse, Aldhelm apparently also wrote poetry that he set to music, but none of these compositions have been found either. He is said to have drawn a crowd by singing songs in the vernacular, so that he could then preach to the assembled listeners on sacred subjects (Aldhelm 1925:69).

The Venerable Bede (c.673–735), writing a generation later, produced the *Historia ecclesiastica gentis Anglorum* (*Ecclesiastical History of the English People*) and numerous works of scholarship in Latin (Figure 21). He is remembered as a translator as well, thanks to his disciple's account, "Cuthbert's Letter on the Death of Bede" ("Epistola de obitu Bedae") in which Bede is reported to have dictated a translation to a scribe, a young boy named Wilberht, on his death bed:

> During those days there were two pieces of work worthy of record […] which he desired to finish: the gospel of St. John, which he was turning into our mother tongue to the great profit of the Church, from the beginning as far as the words 'But what are they among so many?' [Joh. 1:1 to 6:9] and a selection from Bishop Isidore's book on the Wonders of Nature [*Liber Rotarum*, or *De natura rerum*].
> (Bede 1969:582–583)

This scene was depicted in a painting exhibited in 1902 by James Doyle Penrose. Although nothing that Bede may have written in English has survived, he is nevertheless considered a great and "distinctively English" writer. He made his mark as a "champion of the vernacular", having urged the use of English in the translation of sacred texts. He later influenced the Lollards, who believed he had in fact translated the Bible into the vernacular, making a reference to this in the *General Prologue* to the Wycliffite Bible (Frantzen 2010).

Viking invasions began in 793 as plunder raids; they lasted some three hundred years and ended with the settlement of Norsemen in England. The Norsemen, referred to as "Danes" by the Anglo-Saxons, had a decisive influence on the development of Old English. They brought with them place names such as those ending in "by" (Derby, for example) and approximately nine hundred words such as "sky", "skein", and so on. Equally important, however, was the reaction to the Norse incursion.

The only English king to have been called "the Great", Alfred (849–99) stood out equally for his skills as a political leader and his love of learning. When he became King of Wessex in 871, about half the country was in the hands of the Danes. He waged his battle against them on two fronts, one political and the other cultural. Military victory led to the signing of a treaty, the subsequent withdrawal of the enemy to the north of the country and the solidification of what would become an Anglo-Saxon kingdom.

Alfred recognized that learning had declined with the destruction of monasteries by the Vikings. On the other hand, the earlier domination of Latin as the language of learning had inhibited the development of a standard form of English

(Blake 1996: 83). Alfred's response and great achievement was to seize upon this opportunity, using the English language as a vehicle for not only reviving learning but also fostering the English language. Just as his military exploits saved the English nation from destruction, so did his intellectual activities save the English language and further literacy among his subjects. The first monarch to become a symbol of national unity, he set out to gain political control over the English-speaking peoples in the South by appealing to "a shared sense of Englishness, conveyed by the language" (McCrum et al. 1986: 69).

Relatively late in life – he was nearly forty – Alfred learned Latin so that he could translate, or commission the translation of, key texts. The King began with Pope Gregory's *Cura Pastoralis*, or *Regula Pastoralis* (*Pastoral Care*). Gregory was of particular interest in Britain as the initiator of the Augustinian mission; his *Pastoral Care* (which Alfred called the "Shepherd's Book") was considered a standard manual for clerics. It was in the preface to this work that Alfred highlighted his motive for translating the book into English.

> Then I remembered how the law was first found in the Hebrew language, and afterwards, when the Greeks learned it, they translated it all into their own language and all the other books as well. And afterwards in the same way the Romans, when they had learned them, they translated them, all into their own language through learned interpreters. [...] we also should translate certain books which are most necessary for all men to know, into the language that we can all understand, and also arrange it [...] so that all the youth of free men now among the English people [...] are able to read English writing well.
>
> (Quoted in Swanton 1975: 30–32)

King Alfred commissioned the translation of Bede's *Historia ecclesiastica* and Boethius's *De Consolatione Philosophae* (*The Consolation of Philosophy*), among other works, and also sponsored two texts, considered as important as his translations, a Book of Law, or Dooms, and the *Anglo-Saxon Chronicle*.

Translation, legitimized in this way by Alfred, served to enhance the status of English, which came to be viewed as a suitable, if still inferior, alternative to Latin. This marked the "beginning of the continuing influence of translation on the development of English" (Blake 1996: 83–84). Alfred also initiated the practice of distributing copies of the translations, showing his support for the use of a single variety of English throughout the country, a political support that was critical to the rise of a standard form of the language (Blake 1996: 86).

Translation continued to flourish after King Alfred, in monasteries and other religious establishments, in particular. The Benedictine monk Ælfric (955–1020), for example, translated *Lives of the Saints* and *Homilies* into Old English, accompanied by prefaces that set out his intention to make his language simple and clear for common people with very little education. Surnamed "the Grammarian", he was the author of a Latin grammar and a Latin-English dictionary which was the first of its kind.

Geoffrey Chaucer (c.1340–1400), one of England's greatest poets, was also a translator. He translated such important works as Boethius's *Consolation of Philosophy*, which was printed by William Caxton around 1478. In his epilogue to the Boethius, Caxton praises Chaucer and, in words that echo those of other writers of his day, calls him a father of the English language: "the worshipful fader & first foundeur & enbelissher of ornate eloquence in our englissh" (quoted in Blake 1991: 157).

After the Norman Conquest of 1066, which had triggered another "major linguistic collision" (McCrum et al. 1986: 73), French was widely used in official circles and Latin was the chief language of scholarship and learning. By the fourteenth century, however, English began to take its place as an official language. It was introduced into schools in 1350, into the courts in 1362 and into Parliament in 1399. Making a conscious choice to write in English, Chaucer embodied the re-establishment of English as a national language.

Chaucer was educated as a squire in a noble household and enjoyed a successful career in the service of the royal court. He worked as a courtier in various capacities, including diplomatic missions to France and Italy. Chaucer was familiar with classical and vernacular literature in at least three languages: Latin, French and Italian. He adapted many works from French, notably the *Romaunt of the Rose* (one section of which he translated – two others are attributed to him) from *Le Roman de la Rose* by Guillaume de Lorris and Jean de Meung. This translation, albeit partial, is considered to represent Chaucer's "first significant literary endeavour" (Sánchez-Martí 2001: 217).

Since the Norman Conquest in 1066, English-French contact had resulted in a primarily one-way movement, in that English writers imitated both the form and content of French and other Continental writers. Chaucer, therefore, found himself in a "mediocre literary tradition, and with a language [...] lacking the prestige of French and Latin" (Sánchez-Martí 2001: 218). It is of some significance that the intended audience for the *Romaunt*, members of the court who would have been familiar with the French language, did not actually need this translation. As in some of the other cases of literature translated into the vernacular that will be examined in Chapter 3, Chaucer was using this as an exercise to stretch the resources of his own language. Thus the *Romaunt* confers prestige both on Chaucer and on the English language, and the language itself is given a workout of sorts (Machan 1989, quoted by Sánchez-Martí 2001: 222). Chaucer also translated works of Ovid and Virgil from Latin, and Boccaccio from Italian. He translated freely, for the most part, making additions where he deemed necessary. Chaucer influenced the lyric, laid the ground for narrative poetry and imported many genres into England: the ballade, the romance and the fabliau, for example (J. M. Cohen 1962: 10–12).

Even in his *Treatise on the Astrolabe*, a work of science, Chaucer made a deliberate choice to use English rather than Latin. In his prologue, Chaucer makes the point that English has allowed him to draw "nahwt only as trewe but as many and as subtil conclusiouns as ben shewed in Latyn". To this he adds: "God save the King, that is lord of this language". This is the earliest reference to the "King's English", an indication of Chaucer's awareness of the influence of the royal Chancery in establishing the official form of written English (Chaucer 1977: 909).

Chaucer's style embodied the "richness of Middle English, Latinized and Frenchified by Christianity and Conquest" (McCrum et al. 1986: 81). But as a court poet, above all, his usage reflected the speech of the court and a literary tradition influenced by French. It was not the English used in administrative documents of the time, nor was it the ordinary speech of London. Chaucer did not determine the form that standard English was to take during the following century (Baugh 1957: 233).

While English was widely spoken, official records in the fourteenth century remained in French or Latin. In 1362, for example, when Parliament was addressed for the first time in English by King Edward III, the records of that meeting were in French. English gradually became the written language of the official administration and parliament under the impetus of the Lancastrian monarchy. King Henry V, who reigned from 1413 to 1422, was the first English king since the Conquest to use English in his official documents. The war he waged with France contributed to English nationalism and the rise of the English language. Through his authority, King Henry, like Alfred earlier, helped establish a certain standard form of the language. Inspired by the King, the brewers of London, an influential guild, adopted English writing in 1422, although the decision itself was recorded in Latin (Blake 1996: 174–175).

This decision marked the beginning of the end of the supremacy of Latin and French over written English. The establishment of printing in England was another decisive factor and William Caxton, England's first printer, was "as important for the language, in his own way, as Geoffrey Chaucer, whose work he printed" (McCrum et al. 1986: 85).

William Caxton (c.1422–91) began his working life as a merchant adventurer, engaging in the lucrative and flourishing trade between England and the Low Countries (Figure 5). Wool was the most important commodity at the time, but Caxton traded also in illuminated manuscripts, written mainly in French and destined for courtly circles in England. Caxton rose to become Governor of the English Nation of Merchant Adventurers in Bruges, and as such was involved in negotiations between England and the Dukes of Burgundy, then in control of the Low Countries. He held this post from about 1462 until 1471.[3]

Relatively late in life, Caxton embarked upon a career as a translator and printer. He began translating French texts into English around 1469. In 1471, he started work on his translation of Raoul Lefèvre's history of Troy, and went to Cologne to learn the art of printing. He printed his translation, *The Recuyell of the Historyes of Troye*, in Bruges in 1473–74. This was the first book printed in English. In 1476, by this time retired as a merchant and diplomat, Caxton returned to England and set up a press within the precincts of Westminster Abbey, conveniently situated for the British court, whose members were his best clients (Blake 1973). The first book that he printed there was a translation by Anthony Woodville, *Dictes and Sayenges of the Phylosophers*.

From that time until his death in 1491, Caxton printed extensively for his aristocratic clientele. His publications consisted of two types of works: writings of the courtly poets such as Chaucer, Gower and Lydgate, and English prose versions of French books translated by himself or his patrons. Caxton printed a number of significant translations: Ovid's *Metamorphoses*; the *Golden Legend* (from a French version of Jacobus de Voragine's thirteenth-century collection of saints' lives called *Legenda Aurea*); *Mirrour of the World* (from the popular medieval compendium of knowledge entitled *Image du Monde*); and *Aesop's Fables* (from a French version printed in Lyon in 1480) (Blake 1973).

While considerable diversity existed in spoken dialects, the London variety of English was gaining acceptance in writing in most parts of the country by the time Caxton established his press. One of the difficulties, however, was that most of the compositors working for his press were foreigners without training in the English writing system. This resulted in variations in spelling, although over time the press became the "guardian of the standard" (Blake 1996: 205). Caxton's decision to reproduce the English, and in particular the spelling, of London and the Southeast in his numerous translations and other works he printed was crucial: "the books that issued from his press and from the presses of his successors gave a currency to London English that assured more than anything its rapid adoption" (Baugh 1957: 235).

Whereas linguistic changes on the Continent had taken place prior to the appearance of the printing press, the English language was still evolving when Caxton set up shop. Printing, under Caxton, had the "unfortunate" consequence of crystallizing the "orthography of a language still in flux" which is why, today, there is such a difference between how English is written and how it is pronounced (Bühler 1960: 4).

Caxton describes his translation method in the Prologue to *Eneydos*, published in 1490 as an "englisht" version of the French *Eneydes*, which in itself was a free paraphrase of Virgil's *Aeneid* that likely borrowed from earlier French versions, with influences of Boccaccio and other authors (Caxton 1490: v–xxviii). In his own version, Caxton made an effort to use a language that would be comprehensible to his audience: "I haue reduced and translated this sayd booke in to our englysshe, not ouer rude ne curyous, but in suche termes as shall be vnderstanden" (Caxton 1490: 3). This kind of self-promotion was common in the prologues and epilogues that Caxton attached to his printed works. Perhaps out of a need to sell books, or simply to affirm how the English language would benefit from his translations, he makes frequent references to the still unsophisticated – or "rude" – quality of the language and to his own efforts to "embellish" it, in the tradition of Chaucer and others (Blake 1996: 184).

At the same time, Caxton's particular approach to translation, governed by the origin of his source texts as well as the tastes of his readers, led him to maintain a French "flavour" in his translations, adhering to French word order and often borrowing French terms, a practice that contributed to the enrichment of the English style and vocabulary.

Caxton and the printers after him recognized "the toil of translators" as a normal part of their work; they stimulated the habit of vernacular composition, and thereby enhanced "the literary prospects of the domestic language" (Lee 1968: 94). More generally speaking, printing facilitated the spread of learning and knowledge. Before 1500, the total number of books printed in Europe was about 35,000, most of them in Latin. In England alone, some 20,000 items were printed in English over the next 150 years. By 1600, nearly half of the population had achieved a certain degree of literacy. Thus the vernacular was not merely a medium of expression increasingly used by writers; it was actually being read by a significant number of people (McCrum et al. 1986: 93).

As scholars debated the merits of Latin and English, the "issue was being decided by the translators" (Baugh 1957: 247). The Renaissance brought about a revival of learning, renewed interest in classical models and new discoveries. The wisdom of ancient times and other lands did not remain the property of the learned. Translations poured forth to meet the demand for this knowledge among diplomats, courtiers and merchants. Thomas North translated Plutarch; Thomas Elyot translated Plato, Cicero, Seneca and other classical authors; and Erasmus, Calvin and Luther were rendered into English. The impact on the English language was the introduction of myriad scholarly borrowings and coinings: an addition of approximately 10,000 new words to the English tongue (McCrum et al. 1986: 95). A battle between "inkhorn terms" – pedantic or scholarly language – and "plainness" was waged throughout the sixteenth century.

Bible translators played a role in the development of the vernacular in England as in other European nations. John Wycliffe (Wyclif or Wiclif, d. 1384) and his followers, the Lollards, produced the first complete version of the Bible in English based on the Latin *Vulgate* produced by St. Jerome in the fourth century.[4] Wycliffe and his associates are credited with having introduced over a thousand words of Latin origin into the English language. Many of these words had technical meanings, with endings like *-able, -ible, -ent, -al, -ive*, which are now common elements in English derivatives (Baugh 1957: 222–223). The Lollard translation paved the way for further English Bible translating and left its mark on the English language in general. But the determining influence was Tyndale (Figure 13), whose Bible sprang from the original Greek and Hebrew.

William Tyndale (c.1494–1536) was born in Gloucestershire, attended Magdalen College, Oxford, and was ordained in 1519. Accused of heresy early on, he was acquitted but censured as a rabble-rouser. After failing to enlist the support of the Bishop of London in his plan to translate the Bible into English, Tyndale left for the Continent, where he lived a fugitive's life. In Germany he met Luther, then translated and published the New Testament. In Antwerp he published his version of the first five books of the Old Testament, the Pentateuch. Betrayed by a fellow Englishman to agents of Charles V, he was strangled and burned at the stake on October 6, 1536 at Vilvorde, near Brussels.

Tyndale has only recently been rescued from "unfair neglect" and hailed as the patriarch of English language and literature. David Daniell, a Shakespeare specialist with a lifelong interest in theology, has led the rehabilitation movement. He first restored Tyndale's Old and New Testaments in modern spelling (1989 and 1992), and then produced the first full-scale biography of Tyndale in nearly sixty years (1994). In a thorough and impassioned study of Tyndale's rhetorical skills as a translator, Daniell shows how Tyndale achieved for the English language what Newton did for physics.

Tyndale was undoubtedly familiar with the books printed in English by Caxton and other London printers, yet Latin was still the language for anything serious or official. As late as 1600, only thirty of the 6,000 volumes in the Oxford University Library were in English. The impetus for Tyndale to write in English has its origins, of course, in the Lollard movement and the example of Luther. It also derived from a "rhetorical nationalism" just beginning to take shape in the Oxford of his time (Daniell 1994: 46). Tyndale believed that both Greek and Hebrew translated much more easily into English than into Latin, and that English reflected the wide spectrum of styles contained in the Old Testament a "thousand times" more effectively than did Latin (Daniell 1994: 290).

Tyndale's language was shaped by the sounds, syntax and vocabulary of his native Gloucestershire, but he managed nevertheless to write in a style that had much wider appeal. He was influenced, too, by the speech forms specific to the cloth-making industry of his district, where the wisdom of the people was conveyed through sayings that were crafted in rhythm and near rhyme. These sayings, used in preaching and the art of rhetoric which had recently been re-established in schools under the influence of Erasmus, are echoed in Tyndale's near-proverbial creations such as "seek and ye shall find" (Daniell 1994: 16–18).

Tyndale was a remarkable scholar and linguist whose principal attribute was clarity. His skills derived from his Oxford logical and rhetorical training, his knowledge of eight languages including Greek and Hebrew (exceptional for a man of his time), his experience as a preacher and his awareness of a native English tradition of writing. Tyndale translated into the language people spoke, not the way the scholars wrote. At a time when English was struggling to find a form that was neither Latin nor French, Tyndale gave the nation a Bible language that was English in words, word order and lilt. He made a language for England, Daniell says, just as Luther did for Germany (1994: 3).

He made use of plain, monosyllabic English vocabulary and coined many new words which have now become part of the language: "Passover", "scapegoat" and even the word "Jehovah" itself. More importantly, perhaps, he crafted phrases which have gone deep into English-speaking consciousness. Some of them are so familiar to us that they sound like proverbs, or seem like clichés: "eat, drink and be merry"; "the powers that be"; "the salt of the earth"; "the spirit is willing…". But Tyndale went beyond words and phrases; his skills extended to structures, rhythm, and cadence. Using simple, straightforward English syntax, he forged memorable lines such as this passage from the parable of the prodigal son: "this thy brother was dead, and is alive again; and was lost, and is found".

By contrast with the enormous Bibles produced on the Continent, Tyndale's Bibles were pocket sized. The only complete surviving copy of his 1526 New Testament was on display at the British Library in 1994, on the occasion of the quincentenary of Tyndale's birth. It was a little book, as was Tyndale's 1534 New Testament, "a small thick book of four hundred pages which sits comfortably in the hand" (Daniell 1989: xiv). This had important implications: the Bible could easily be smuggled (the English Church was still opposed to reading the Bible in the vernacular) and carried around and perused by ordinary readers.

As Tyndale once said to a learned man, one of his opponents in the religious controversies of the time: "If God spare my life, ere many years I will cause a boy that driveth the plough shall know more of the Scripture than thou dost" (Daniell 1989: viii). That he accomplished what he set out to achieve is evident in the following observations of a London newspaper columnist:

All writers stand upon the shoulders of their predecessors, using and developing
their language as it has been handed down. William Tyndale is the ghost at the
bottom of the pyramid of English language and literature. He introduced the revolutionary notion that the common English spoken by the man in the street is as
good as Latin or French or any other "learned" language for expressing profound
or poetic thought. [...] He was a fiery English scholar who kept the common
touch, and died at the stake. We shall celebrate the quincentenary properly this
year. But the true monument of the invisible man rests not in the British Library
or the celebrations, but in the language itself in all its glory.   (Howard 1994: 16)

Tyndale's influence on the English language, unlike that of Alfred, Chaucer or
Caxton, is linked not to his personal stature – since he was on the wrong side of
those in power – but rather to the status of the source text, the Bible, and its overriding importance for the theological, ideological and political battles waged at
the time of the Reformation and beyond. The Authorized Version of 1611, eighty
per cent of which derived from the work of Tyndale, was the culmination of efforts to shape the English language: "[it] became one of the great totems of the
power and elegance of the English language. Since the word of God could find
such complete expression in English, it was no longer possible to believe that English was not a fit language for literary composition" (Blake 1996: 186).[5]

The emancipation of French

The languages first spoken in Gaul (Iberian, Ligurian, and Gaulish) left few traces
in the language that was to become French. The Frankish and Visigoth invaders
who arrived from the third to the fifth centuries were rapidly Romanized. As far
as the links between language and translation are concerned, the determining
influence was the Roman conquest, which took place between 58 and 51 BCE. It
was through translation that Rome had inherited the cultural wealth of Greece.
Written Latin became the *lingua franca* of medieval Europe (the language of the
Church, the law and scholarship).[6] It was the *lingua romana rustica* (the Latin
spoken by occupying soldiers, administrators and merchants), on the other hand,
that gave birth to the various Romance languages, including French. As early as
the ninth century, the gap between the two branches – classical Latin and the
Latin of the people, or so-called "vulgar" Latin – was such that both the Church
and royalty had to recognize it. It was then that translation came into play. The
Council of Tours (813) authorized the clergy to translate ("*transferre*") homilies
into the vernacular. The Oaths of Strasbourg (842), if not actually translated from
one language to another, were transcribed in the form of a bilingual text (Romance and Teutonic).[7] This is the first known document to have been written in

langue d'oïl. A dialect spoken north of the Loire River, as opposed to *langue d'oc*, which was spoken in the south, *langue d'oïl* split off further into a variety of dialects, of which the two best known were Norman – destined to a brilliant but brief future, thanks to William the Conqueror – and Francien, a central dialect, which was to become fourteenth-century French.[8] Later on, the Renaissance also played its part in the development of the French language, which was then codified and standardized in the seventeenth century. As we are about to see, translators were instrumental in this long process of maturation.

Medieval translators found themselves in the same situation as their Roman predecessors: they were translating from a rich culture and an advanced language into an idiom that was still emerging, as well as for a readership that was discovering antiquity through their work. They looked to the Romans, therefore, for models – for translation methods, of course, but also for ways to overcome the inadequacies of their language. These pioneers were soon to encounter cultural and linguistic problems inherent to the art of translation, problems that were all the more arduous because they were breaking new ground (Chavy 1974: 565 and 1988).

Originally carried out in monasteries, primarily for religious purposes, translation spread to other fields as early as the tenth century. Secular works such as *fabliaux*, a specifically medieval genre of short narrative verse, and comedies or romances based on ancient models soon appeared in Romance languages. The first great poets, like Chrétien de Troyes, Marie de France, Rutebeuf and Jean de Meung, were essentially translators, writing at a time when translation, imitation and creation were inextricably bound. It was not until the fourteenth century, once the first universities were established, that translation left the monasteries and briefly flourished under the protection of the Crown. King John II, or John the Good, commissioned his secretary, a Benedictine monk named Pierre Bersuire (c.1290–1362), to translate Livy's *Ab urbe condita*, or *History of Rome* (1355–56). Bersuire noted that classical Latin was understood by very few people at the time, and therefore decided to preface his translation with a lexicon of approximately seventy new words he had had to create: *augure, auspices, cirque, expier, sénat, triomphe* and so on. Around the same period, the preface to the Metz Psalter, a collection of psalms translated from Latin into a Lorraine dialect, set out two ways to compensate for the lack of French terminology: borrowing (*iniquitas* becomes *iniquiteit* and *redemptio* becomes *redemption*, for example) and paraphrase, made necessary by the fact that equivalents for certain Latin words could only be attained through "circumlocution and explanation" (Horguelin 1981: 162). It is interesting to note that Cicero had already used and recommended both of these techniques.[9]

Charles V, or Charles the Wise, succeeded his father John the Good in 1364. He established translation as the underpinning of a "royal cultural policy" (Lusignan 1986:162). He built a library in the Louvre and filled it with about a thousand manuscripts; then he engaged the services of some ten translators, who were generously rewarded for their work. The most illustrious of these, Nicolas (Nicole or Nicholas) Oresme (c.1320–82), had been the king's private tutor and then his adviser.[10] A man of vast knowledge, Oresme (Figure 16) translated works of Aristotle and Ptolemy, and wrote various treatises in Latin and French, most notably on numismatics and astronomy. He pointed out the role played by Roman translators in the transmission of Greek knowledge, and emphasized the benefits of making this knowledge accessible in French. But French would have to be turned into a scientific language, and for this purpose technical terminology would have to be used in translations, even if it could not be easily understood by most people (Oresme, quoted in Horguelin 1981:34). Oresme often coined these technical terms himself. He has been credited with approximately 450 neologisms still present in modern French: *aristocratie, démagogue, législation, politique, sédition*, and even *langue maternelle*, to give just a few examples (Taylor 1965).

The neologisms the translators created were accompanied by glosses, or explanations. Translators would also make use of word pairs in order to convey the full meaning of some Latin or Greek terms. Examples of this are: "*le pris et la somme de rachat*" (the purchase *price and cost*) and "*selon la manière et coustume du pays*" (according to the *ways and customs* of the land). This technique was widely used by translators, and even writers, up to the end of the sixteenth century. There are still some traces of it in the French language, and in English too, for that matter, in expressions such as *sain et sauf* (safe and sound). Translators were not merely inventors of words; they also helped popularize knowledge and make it accessible to French readers.

But a language is not limited to its lexicon. In their effort to endow the great authors of Greek and Latin antiquity with a French voice, medieval translators were comparative linguists before their time. When they compared the stylistic resources of the source and target languages, they discovered deficiencies in the vernacular. They set out to remedy these, not without bemoaning the difficulties of their task in the prefaces that accompanied their translations. The main obstacle to producing a clear and understandable vernacular translation from a Latin original was lexical and rhetorical in nature, rather than syntactical. As Serge Lusignan points out in his study of fourteenth-century translators, those working from Latin models did more than just translate: they created a standard for French scholarly writing. Operating not only on the textual level, but on the level of language itself, they helped forge new structures (Lusignan 1986:149).

This is how the vernacular gradually became a medium in fields previously reserved for Latin.

During the fifteenth century, translation once again went into decline. The few translated works were from classical and medieval Latin. The end of the Middle Ages was marked by the invention of the printing press, which would benefit translation in the following century. Whereas medieval translators had translated for the "glory of God" and the "common good", the mission of the translators who succeeded them during the Renaissance was, as du Bellay claimed, to raise French to the level of other famous languages.

The sixteenth century was a period of effervescence distinguished by two great movements: humanism, whose reaction against the scholastic tradition led to renewed interest in ancient languages and literature, and the Reformation, which also advocated a return to sources, in this case to the Bible in its original Greek and Hebrew languages. During this period of emerging ideas and religious conflicts, of discoveries and inventions, translation was to enter a new golden age. But the pivotal role of translation derived primarily from the rise of a national language and literature. Translation was once again supported by royalty. In 1530, François I created the *Collège royal*, also called *Collège des Trois Langues* (for Latin, Greek and Hebrew). In 1539, he promulgated the famous Edict of Villers-Cotterêts which made it compulsory to replace Latin with French ("*le langaige maternel françois*") in official documents.

As early as 1509, a translator named Claude de Seyssel had appealed to King Louis XII to create a body of French literature, and had advocated translation as a means to enrich and extend the French language. Throughout the century, however, there were two opposing schools of thought about the way in which this was to be achieved. Following Clément Marot, a group of court poets and translators considered translation a good stylistic exercise that would contribute to the enrichment of their language. The Hellenist scholar Thomas Sebillet took this position in his 1548 book *L'Art poétique*. Like Horace in his *Ars poetica*, he considered *version* (or translation) a literary genre and a branch of rhetoric. This opinion was not shared by the *Pléiade*, a group of humanist poets led by Ronsard, who held that translation was dangerous to both literature and language. The group requested that Joachim du Bellay (1522–60) reply to Sebillet; the result was the 1549 *La Deffence et Illustration de la Langue Francoyse*, an "anthology of all the arguments against translation" (Mounin 1994: 13). Du Bellay recommended that language be enriched through "imitation", and not translation, of the best Greek and Latin authors. He suggested that neologisms of Greco-Latin origin be created, and also that terms be drawn from regional dialects and the vocabulary of craftsmen. He did not believe that style and eloquence could be learned from translators. Excessive borrowing from foreign languages under the guise of scholarship was already being discredited. Rabelais, for example, had made fun of "peddlers of used and mouldy Latin words". In the fourth rule of his translation treatise, Étienne Dolet (1508–46) warns translators not to make use of words that resemble Latin too closely or that have seldom been used in the past. Toward the end of the sixteenth century, Henri Estienne (1531–98) published an indictment of the "new, Italianized French language".

Jacques Amyot (1513–93), known as the "prince of translators", also set out to enrich the French language (Figure 4). His translations themselves, as well as his *Projet d'éloquence royale* (1574), reflected an overriding concern for absolute clarity: "être le plus clair possible". To achieve this, he proposed avoiding awkward neologisms, indicating the logical connections between sentences and paragraphs, using a simple, natural style and trusting one's ear to ensure harmonious phrasing. Amyot has been acclaimed for his contributions to the French language. Montaigne considered him the best French writer; literary critic Gustave Lanson wrote that Amyot's translation of Plutarch represented the supreme effort of the French language to equal the languages of antiquity. The Larousse dictionary categorizes him as "one of the creators of classical prose".

Renaissance translators were extremely versatile. Writers as well as translators, many of them were also lexicographers, proofreaders, printers and booksellers. As such, they contributed to the proliferation of works on every aspect of language: poetics, rhetoric, grammar, spelling, pronunciation and so on. These translators were also responsible for the first dictionaries, which will be the subject of Chapter 8.

A survey of sixteenth-century translation would not be complete without mentioning the Reformation, which led to increased translation activity with obvious implications for language. The Catholic Church had always opposed the translation of sacred texts, fearing heresy and maintaining that Latin alone was the language of the Christian faith. The first vernacular Bibles to appear in the Middle Ages were reserved for the use of the clergy. Until the end of the seventeenth century, most Bible translators were forced into exile, like Marot after he published a translation of the Psalms. For the Reformers, however, it was essential that the Bible be made available in the "language of the country" (Lefèvre d'Étaples). This opinion was shared by Erasmus, who believed that the translation of the Scriptures was the task of translators and not theologians. Jean Calvin (1509–64) also held this view. After studying Greek, Hebrew and theology at the *Collège royal*, Calvin took refuge in Switzerland, where he published, first in Latin and then in French, his central work, *l'Institution de la religion chrestienne* (1541). Calvin translated his own work into French as a service to his country: "*à notre nation françoise*". As the first work of theology to be published in French, it opened up the possibility of writing in the vernacular about a subject which until that time had been dealt with exclusively in Latin.

Many historians of the French language have recognized the role of Reformation writers and translators in the emancipation of the language. Compared with the Bibles of Olivétan and Robert Estienne, the Psalm translations of Marot and Théodore de Bèze, and the numerous pamphlets produced in Geneva and distributed throughout the French countryside by peddlers, Calvin's work stands out. He is considered one of the initiators of French eloquence, and his *Institution* is one of the founding texts of modern French, along with Rabelais's *Pantagruel* and Amyot's *Plutarch* (another translation). Calvin's *Institution* is viewed as the "first masterpiece of pure religious and moral philosophy to have been adequately expressed by vernacular French" (Lanson 1964:266–274).

The prefaces of seventeenth-century translators reveal a marked change of attitude toward the influence of translation on the evolution of the language. The objective remained the same – to make French a literary language by imitating the authors of antiquity. However, the process of imitation had become selective: the aim was now to endow the language with the most pleasing elements of antiquity. Translators even became openly critical. One corrected obscure elements in Livy; another condemned Tacitus for his lack of logic; still another admitted he was troubled by Cicero's faulty transitions and repetitions. These corrections were thought to be justified on the grounds that every nation had different tastes in matters of style, and that French was "much more strict and scrupulous than Latin". This was a far cry from the humble complaints of translators of the Middle Ages and Renaissance.

The century of Louis XIV had begun with a vast enterprise of purification and codification of the language. Writers and grammarian-translators such as Malherbe, Vaugelas and Chapelain, along with literary salons and the newly founded *Académie française*,[11] played a significant role. As was the case in previous centuries, translators also took part in this process. They were prominent members of the *Académie*, whose first secretary, Conrart, considered translation an excellent means of providing prose models for French writers. Their translations became part of the corpora used to compile the first dictionaries (Richelet's *Dictionnaire français* in 1680; the *Dictionnaire de l'Académie* in 1694). They participated in every debate relating to the language. Their prefaces discussed matters of vocabulary, spelling and pronunciation. Most importantly, they published numerous translations, in some cases as many as fifty or sixty titles, most of which reflected their concern for style.

Nicolas Perrot d'Ablancourt (1606–64) advocated three basic qualities: clarity, concision and elegance. He added explanations in order to clarify certain points, as he repeatedly says in the various observations that accompany his translations: *"pour l'éclaircissement"*, *"pour éviter l'obscurité"*, or *"pour la clarté du raisonnement"*. To strengthen the impact of his style, on the other hand, he sought to write concisely; this he achieved by using expressive terms, arranging words and sentences carefully and deleting anything cumbersome or unnecessary. He crafted his sentences with great concern for elegance (called *embellissement* at the time), created proverbial phrases through symmetry and opposition, and paid close attention to rhythm and harmony. He admitted to adding words for ornamental purposes: *"pour mieux lier le discours"*, *"pour la commodité de l'expression"*. Perrot d'Ablancourt is considered the father of the *"belles infidèles"*.[12] The way in which he practised translation has been criticized over the centuries, but from Boileau to Valery Larbaud, he has been praised by many a celebrated writer for his "magnificent French" (Paul Claudel, quoted in Zuber 1968: 283).

Although the first half of the seventeenth century was dominated by translators of the *Académie*, the Port-Royal translators took over, discreetly, by 1660.[13] Probably better known for their *Grammaire générale* and their *Logique*, the "*Messieurs de Port-Royal*" were also the authors of works and translations intended for doctrinal and pedagogical purposes. (As a young man, Racine attended their *Petites écoles*, where translation was part of the curriculum.) The *Bible de Port-Royal*, translated primarily by Le Maître de Sacy and published by Elsevier in 1667, had a lasting success and was reprinted as recently as 1990. All this translation work gave rise to much discussion of language-related questions. As a result, the precise meaning and use of many words and expressions were determined, and this was of great benefit to the language (Brunot 1966: 31). Around 1650, Antoine Le Maistre formulated ten "Rules for French translation"; four of these dealt with translation as such, while the remaining six had to do with rhyme, symmetry, repetition, harmony, rhythm and the length of sentences.

For these translators and their contemporaries, translation and writing went hand in hand. Their influence on the French language was undeniable, although it has been generally underestimated or even overlooked. In his book *Les "Belles Infidèles" et la formation du goût classique*, Roger Zuber makes the point that seventeenth-century translators were also literary critics who applied principles of creative writing they had learned from Guez de Balzac and Boileau. Now that their contributions have been recognized, they can take their place alongside Balzac and Descartes, Chapelain and Vaugelas (also translators) – writers who have traditionally been considered the "builders of classical literature" (Zuber 1968: 10–12).

At the dawn of the Enlightenment, French translators could legitimately claim to have honourably accomplished one of their missions: they had contributed to the development of the language by endowing it with every known register of expression and by allowing it to convey every area of human knowledge.

Martin Luther: artisan of the German language

Translation is a fundamental element in the history of the German language. The tradition of translating biblical and literary texts from other languages dates back to the eighth century, when the first biblical glossaries were compiled. It continues with interlinear versions and translations of a more liberal and poetic nature. The high points of the history of translation into German include the translation of the New Testament from Tatian's second-century Latin version, carried out at the Monastery of Fulda around 820; Otfried von Weissenburg's *Book of Gospels*, completed in Old High German around 870; and the translation of the psalms by Notker the German (c.950–1022) made around 1000.[14] The particular qualities of Notker's translations were his precision, stylistic rigour and an orality that reflected the spoken language. The point of departure in his translation work was exegesis, the understanding of the original text by means of explanations and commentaries (Sonderegger 1984: 144; Copeland 1991).

Medieval translations of the Bible were not based on Greek and Hebrew originals, but rather on the Latin *Vulgate*. Old High German as a written language arose and developed from the translation of the Bible into the vernacular (Sonderegger 1984: 136). Under the influence of Latin, German developed into a language of literature and was soon used not only in Bible translations, but in other types of writing. By the late Middle Ages, German was able to express sophisticated theological and philosophical ideas, thus superseding and finally replacing Latin as the language of literature and science. Nonetheless, German remained a regional language with a wide variety of dialects, serving mainly functional and social purposes.

As the High German language developed and began to establish itself as a legitimate form of communication, with the potential to express a broad range of ideas, translation played a less critical role in its history. Yet, it never ceased to be a factor in the continued development of language (Koller 1984: 122). Of special note are the translations produced during the Enlightenment: of Homer by Heinrich Voss (1751–1826), Shakespeare by Christoph Martin Wieland (1733–1813),[15] Milton by Johann Jacob Bodmer (1698–1783) and French literature by Johann Christoph Gottsched (1700–66). Equally important during that period were the frequent discussions of linguistics and the principles of translation. It was a long time, however, before a unified, national German language emerged, and the process was not concluded until the end of the eighteenth century. In this thousand-year evolution, the translation of the Bible by Martin Luther (1483–1546) was a decisive factor. His work and particular contribution will be the primary focus of this section.

The effect of Luther's work as a translator can be understood only against the backdrop of the Reformation and its linguistic and communicative requirements, as well as the tradition of translation prevalent at the time (Schildt 1983). It is also important to bear in mind not only Luther's theological views, but also his personality, linguistic abilities and unique creativity.

By the beginning of the sixteenth century, social conflicts had reached such a point in Germany that a broad movement arose which for a time united all social classes against the Roman Church. At that time, social reforms could take place only in conjunction with a reform of the church. Luther's systematic rendering of the Scriptures into the language of the common people provided this movement with an ideological framework, that is, with a program (Arndt and Brandt 1987), although it was not Luther's intention to do so, for his actions were a consequence of his theology. The Bible already existed in early High German.[16] It had been completed before Luther, and had already demonstrated the extent to which common people needed a Bible they could read in their own language (Gelhaus 1989–1990: 1).

Luther was born and raised in the linguistic area of East Middle Germany where a normative language, a literary language of some sophistication, had already developed. His use of this East Middle German variant of literary German for translating the Bible encouraged the further establishment and standardization of this form. The technical precondition for the mass distribution of the Bible was, naturally, movable printing type, developed by Gutenberg eighty years earlier.

The desire for a unified national language was expressed to varying degrees among the different classes of society of the time, but was especially strong among the rising middle classes. Luther took the new communicative needs into account by using forms of speech that enjoyed widespread regional usage and also had a broad social basis. He was open to all influences, but to those of the Upper German linguistic area in particular.

Luther studied Latin, Greek and Hebrew intensively, but also paid particular attention to the language spoken by the people. In order to achieve the most appropriate and effective renderings, he enlisted the support of different specialists,

such as Philipp Melanchthon for Greek, Matthäus Aurogallus (or Goldhahn) for
Hebrew, and Caspar Cruciger for Latin. He also consulted professional people
such as foresters and game wardens, for example, to address specific terminological problems. In addition, Luther's own creativity and poetic sensitivity were
unsurpassed. All these factors contributed to the broad influence that his translations have enjoyed to this day.

Luther's linguistic achievements were grounded in a certain number of translation principles. First of all, he advocated the return to the original languages
of the Bible: Hebrew for the Old Testament and Greek for the New Testament
(without, however, completely neglecting the Latin *Vulgate*). This was an innovative philological approach, which had grown out of the increasing influence of
humanist philosophers. Although the *Vulgate* had been proclaimed the official
version of the Bible by the Catholic Church, Luther rejected it as a truly authentic
text. A further principle was Luther's target-culture approach. He transformed the
text of the Bible into a German text by reworking it to fit the mentality and spirit
of his time. He recognized that semantic equivalents alone were insufficient. He
sought to make the historical, cultural and social realities expressed in the Bible
comprehensible to his readers, so distant in space and time from the original audience (Bondzio 1984).

Luther tried to formulate his translation in accordance with the rules of
the target-language (Arndt and Brandt 1987: 45), but the German language had
not yet reached a stage of development which made this fully possible. Another
principle to which Luther adhered was that the word should follow the meaning
of the text, and not the other way round (Stolt 1983: 244). This was not a new
idea: the notion of the subservience of words to things is found in a number of
sources during the same period (Rener 1989: 21). It nonetheless required courage on Luther's part since he was dealing with a sacred text. He believed that
translation was always interpretation, to some extent as least. Philological accuracy, therefore, was not his main concern. Translators, he felt, should strive for
moral and situational appropriateness, and to this end he advocated that they
be educated in philosophy and theology and have pastoral experience (Bondzio
1984: 268).

Luther's translation principles and strategies can be further demonstrated by
comparing different editions of the translations that appeared during his lifetime,
specifically between 1522 and 1546, since these were the versions which he edited
personally. The various versions reflect a tendency toward straightforward, but
vivid, expression – through the substitution of verbal expressions for noun phrases, for example. This is particularly evident in his translations of the Psalms.[17]
Luther always took the sound of the spoken language into account. As a preacher,

he was in a position to observe the direct reaction of his audience and judge their ability to digest his words, and he drew on this experience when translating.

Luther defended his translations in two texts: *Sendbrief vom Dolmetschen* (1530) (Circular, or Open, Letter on Translation) and *Summarien über die Psalmen und Ursachen des Dolmetschens* (1531–33) (Defence of the Translation of the Psalms). These texts were written to counter accusations made by Catholic officials that Luther had changed or falsified the Holy Scriptures. The Archbishop of Mainz had forbidden the translation of clerical documents from Greek and Latin on the grounds that the German language did not have an adequate vocabulary and was unsuited to the presentation of theological concepts (Gelhaus 1989). The *Sendbrief* and *Summarien* were defensive texts, perhaps not intended to set out a treatise on translation or propose a novel method of translating (Rener 1989: 129–131). Nevertheless, Luther does take the opportunity to reflect on certain theoretical problems that remain the subject of debate even to this day. Among the issues he discusses are free versus literal translation, naturalization versus foreignization of translated texts, questions of style, and the importance of taking the contextual framework into account (Stolt 1983).

In these texts, Luther presents some examples from the *Vulgate*, contrasting literal translation with his own translations, in which emphasis is placed on the meaning of the whole phrase rather than the meaning of individual words. One often quoted example deals with Luther's addition of the word *allein* (alone / only), in the sense of *nur* (only), in the Epistle of St. Paul to the Romans (3 : 28), a place where the Latin word *sola* is not found in the original. The sentence "*Arbitramur hominem iustificari ex fide absque operibus legis*" is formulated by Luther as: "*Wir halten / das der mensch gerecht werde on des gesetzs wreck / **allein durch den glauben**" (Arndt 1968: 25).[18] This sentence, translated in English as "We hold that a man is justified without the works of the law, by faith alone", conveys a central theme in Luther's teachings. He justifies the addition of the word "alone" on both theological and linguistic grounds. When talking about two things, one of which is affirmed and the other negated, he explains, the word "alone" must be added to make the contrast clearer. The use of *allein*, therefore, takes on special significance in Luther's theology (Brendler 1983: 264).

Another example is taken from Matthew 12 : 34, which in the Latin text says: "*Ex abundantia cordis os loquitur*". To replace the obscure literal translation ("The mouth speaks out of an excess of heart"), Luther proposes a free translation using a widespread German proverb: "*Wes das hertz voll ist / des gehet der mund uber*" (Arndt 1968: 33). The literal meaning of the German proverb is "When the heart is full the mouth overflows"; its equivalent in biblical English is "Out of the abundance of the heart the mouth speaketh". Using these examples, he tried to show how a faithful rendering can betray the meaning of the entire sentence. Translators, he believed, must sometimes look for a phrase in the target language that renders the thought clearly with different words. This is what earned Luther a "special place in the history of the language and also in that of translation" (Rener 1989: 131).

Luther claims to have made his translation more colloquial and more understandable, too. His objective in this case was to strike the right balance between high and low registers, liturgical and everyday language, as no one before him had been able to do. In the *Sendbrief*, he states that German should be spoken like "the common man in the marketplace". The language of the people was an inspiration to him and an infinite source, but it cannot be said on the basis of Luther's translation of the Bible that he actually spoke or wrote like the common people. In fact, his celebrated statement about the "common man" is not to be taken too literally, but rather as a figurative description of usage, the authority behind idioms (Rener 1989: 131).

The example just quoted shows how important the heart was for Luther. In the world of biblical representation, the heart was the seat of reason and the intellect, as Birgit Stolt (1990) has shown. For Luther, thoughts, feelings and words were inseparable and all located in the heart, which was also the seat of faith. This is how Luther defines the qualities required of a good translator: "Translation is not an art for anybody, as the misled holy ones think. What is necessary is a fair, devout, faithful, diligent, pious, Christian, learned, well-versed, experienced heart" (quoted in Arndt 1968: 37).

The influence of Luther on language and translation was apparent soon after his death. The first German grammars, published in the sixteenth century by Valentin Ickelsamer and Fabian Franck, were directly based on Luther's translation of the Bible. Also worthy of mention is Johannes Clajus (1535–92), whose text bore the title "Grammatica Germanicae linguae ex bibliis Lutheri Germanicis et aliis eius libris collecta" (Grammar of the German language based on Luther's Bible and his other collected works). It was only in the eighteenth century that a more differentiated evaluation of Luther's language appeared. Johann Christoph Adelung (1732–1806), author of a *Grammatisch-Kritisches Wörterbuch der hochdeutschen Mundart* (Grammatical and Critical Dictionary of the High German dialect), regarded Luther's Bible more as a useful source than a model for correct language (Sonderegger 1984: 141). However, the normative influence of Luther's language can be observed right up to the nineteenth century, in Grimm's dictionary, for example, where it serves as the most important source.[19]

Through his translation of the Bible, Luther helped bring about the enrichment and standardization of the German lexicon, as well as the development of a balanced syntax using formal means such as verb position and conjunctions. His main contribution, however, is in the field of stylistics. Clarity, simplicity, vividness and general comprehensibility were the most important features of his translation of the Bible, which even today serves as a model for good writing. All revisions of the Bible and modern translations are consistently measured against Luther's text.

Luther may not have actually created the new High German written and spoken forms, but his translations were a driving force, catalyst and benchmark in the development of the German national language (Koller 1984: 122). His collection and selection of the means available to him within the language system of his day, combined with his own creations and innovations, influenced the entire German language itself (Arndt and Brandt 1987: 140). But the influence of Luther extended well beyond his own country, setting an example for Bible translators elsewhere.

The flowering of the Swedish language

The Nordic countries occupy the northwestern corner of Europe. In this region, often but erroneously referred to as Scandinavia, there are six "national languages" in use today, spoken in five states: Swedish in Sweden; Danish and Faroese in Denmark; Norwegian in Norway; Icelandic in Iceland; and Finnish (along with Swedish) in Finland.[20] Together, the six languages are spoken by some 23 million people. Background information will be provided on the entire group of languages, with particular attention to Scandinavia proper, and more specifically, to Swedish.

Traditional concepts like Nordic and Scandinavian are geographical, historical and cultural entities. They refer to the fact that these five countries – though politically separated during most of their history – share a cultural heritage that is specifically Nordic.

The most important aspect of the Nordic/Scandinavian unity (though far from the only one) is that of language. Nevertheless, this unity is limited and complex. Historically, the three Scandinavian languages, together with Icelandic and Faroese, derive from the North-Germanic or Nordic branch of the Germanic languages, their closest living relatives being the West-Germanic languages (German, Dutch and English). Finnish, on the other hand, is totally unrelated. Like

Lappish and Estonian, which are spoken in the same or adjacent areas, Finnish does not even belong to the Indo-European group of languages, but is classified as a Finno-Ugric language. The three Scandinavian languages are in principle mutually intelligible, as are Icelandic and Faroese.

The five Nordic languages (all those mentioned above except Finnish) trace their common origin back to a "Proto-Nordic" stage of development. During the first eight centuries CE, this was the language of southern and central Scandinavia (the northern Scandinavian areas and the North Atlantic islands not yet having been colonized). This language is attested by primitive runic inscriptions, dozens of which have survived.[21] What appears obvious from these traces is that Proto-Nordic was a strikingly stable and geographically uniform language.

During the Migration Period and the Viking Age, the Nordic population came into contact with foreign languages that left their mark on Scandinavian vocabulary.[22] This pre-literary level of loan words testifies to early contacts with the culturally more advanced peoples of Western and Southern Europe primarily. Some thousands of runic inscriptions from the Viking Age, preserved on stone monuments in central parts of Sweden and Denmark, do not reflect this picture; their linguistic form is entirely domestic. It was not until the final integration of Scandinavia into medieval European civilization that foreign influence began to have an identifiable effect on vernacular language. The decisive step in the integration process was the emergence of written vernaculars, using a script based on the Latin alphabet and employed in text production on a substantial scale.

This change in the state of linguistic culture in Scandinavia came as a result of the Christian mission and the subsequent introduction of Latin texts. This took place mainly in the tenth and eleventh centuries. By the twelfth and thirteenth centuries, a rich literature in West Norse appeared in Norway and Iceland, of which the most well known works are the classical sagas and Eddic poetry. In Sweden, the first "books" written in vernacular East Norse languages (but in a Latin script) were not produced until the early thirteenth century. The oldest complete copies extant today date from the end of that century.

The documents of this pioneering epoch of Swedish literature were written records of provincial law (Andersson 1987). Their appearance marked the very genesis of civilized written Swedish. This signalled not only a language written in the Latin alphabet, unlike previous Swedish, which was written in runes, if at all. It also reflected a language carrying the fundamental notions of Christian culture and western civilization: in a word, a Swedish language basically integrated into a living West-European community, at a medieval phase of its historical development. Somewhat paradoxically, the establishment of a "national language" required integration into an international linguistic community. This was principally achieved by different kinds of linguistic transfer; translation was one notable example.

The Monastery of Vadstena, the cradle of Swedish translation, was posthumously established in accordance with the very exact instructions of St. Bridget (1303–73).[23] An Augustinian Monastery for both men and women, it was the institution that most effectively promoted the Swedish language through translation. Since translation of religious texts was done anonymously, no specific translators were normally credited with the works published. Consequently, even though they contributed a great deal to the development of the Swedish language, their names are not recorded as they are in some other countries.

One of the great initial challenges of the new institution was to translate the foundress's entire collection of *Revelations* from the Latin in which they had been rendered by her confessors back into her own Swedish mother tongue. This task was indeed herculean. It seems to have been performed in connection with the inauguration of the monastery in 1384. The result, in today's printed editions, fills up more than 1,200 pages – in good, stylistically adequate Old Swedish. This work was of the utmost significance for the further development of written Swedish (Wollin 1991 and 2000).

In a subsequent phase of development, the Swedish language benefited from the translation efforts of the Swedish reformers. Their first achievement was the New Testament (1526). The source text was probably the Latin version of the Renaissance edition of Erasmus. King Gustav I (c.1495–1560) of the Vasa dynasty, who established a Lutheran state church in his country, was responsible for the oldest complete Swedish Bible, the so-called Vasa Bible. Translated by Olav and Laurent Petri, the Vasa Bible was printed at Uppsala in 1541, and is considered to be based principally on Martin Luther's contemporary High German translation. This sixteenth-century version was to become the canonized Holy Bible of the Swedish state church. It remained in active use until 1917, when it was replaced by a new official translation.

The Vasa Bible holds a unique position in Sweden's literary and linguistic culture. For almost four centuries, this fundamental confessional document of the established church was listened to from the pulpit, read by the literate, quoted and referred to in literature and in everyday life. It also functioned naturally as the ruling example in the standardization of the written language. From the perspective of the history of language, this translation is by far the most important text ever written in Swedish.

In the 1541 text, the Swedish Reformers skilfully balanced different patterns of stylistic inspiration. The Old Swedish Vadstena tradition is obvious at several levels of language, particularly in orthography and morphology. In syntax, partly even in the lexicon, some constructions may be traced back to the German original. As regards the relationship to contemporary usage, the Bible translators reduced variation significantly. Thus, more distinctly than their medieval monastic forerunners, they anticipated the normalizing efforts of later centuries. In particular, the relative uniformity of biblical orthography was a pioneering achievement, laying the historical basis of modern Swedish spelling. On the whole, the Swedish Reformation Bible is a very tangible example of a translating achievement that directly and decisively influenced language development.

Translation, then, is not exceptional writing, but rather an integral part of the normal process of text production. Written texts are naturally and frequently produced through translation. The role it has played in the history of the Swedish language has been critical. For a language such as Swedish, which has a relatively small number of speakers and is used in a country that has always been situated on the margins of European civilization, translation is perhaps even more central than elsewhere. In the Middle Ages and in early modern times, most Swedish-language writers were translators, not "authors". Even to this day, in fact, the production of literary texts is not necessarily dominated by original writers (Hansson 1982; Torgerson 1982).

The evolution of the Gbaya language in Cameroon

For many centuries, translation has been an important means of communication in Africa. Translation of religious texts, in particular, has been a long-standing and widespread practice across the continent. The Septuagint, a translation of the scriptures from Hebrew into Greek made from c.250–130 BCE in Egypt, is one example. Translations of the scriptures into Coptic languages occurred as early as the third century, and into Ge'ez, an Ethiopic language, in the fourth and fifth centuries. By the eighteenth century, the complete Bible was available in two African languages, namely Ge'ez and Arabic, while a New Testament was available in Coptic. During the nineteenth century, growing Christian missionary activity generated a "steady stream of versions of the Bible" (Metzger and Coogan 1993: 772). Some of the earliest translated Bibles were in Malagasy in 1835 and Amharic in 1840 in Ethiopia. The complete Bible is now available in over 170 African languages.[24]

The development of national languages and the evolution of translation in Africa are interrelated. Owing to the contributions of early missionary translators in Cameroon, for example, national languages such as Isubu, Douala, Ewondo, Bulu, Fulfulde, Mungaka and Bamoun were developed and used for the purpose of spreading the gospel (Nama 1990a: 356–369). This phenomenon occurred in many other African countries.

This section will articulate the historical origins and evolution of the Gbaya language as nurtured and promoted by translators. The Gbaya Translation Centre (currently called the Gbaya Literature Centre), in particular, has made significant contributions to the evolution of translation theory and practice, the development of national languages and the dissemination and preservation of Gbaya culture and philosophy. It has its roots in the so-called Sudan Mission, founded by American Evangelical Lutheran missionaries in Mboula, Cameroon, in 1923. The Centre itself was established in Ngaoundere in 1971, and was later transferred to Meiganga.

The Gbaya inhabit parts of the East and Adamawa provinces of Cameroon, the Central African Republic and the Democratic Republic of Congo. At least two million people in three African countries speak some dialect of the Gbaya language. The Gbaya, especially those in Cameroon, are hunters and nomads as well as farmers. They migrated principally from what is now the Central African Republic into the Adamawa plateau and the eastern regions of Cameroon. That is why the Gbaya were culturally and linguistically influenced by the Fulbe (also called Fula or Fulani, whose language is called Fulfulde) for several generations.[25]

The Gbaya language has been classified as a subgroup of the Niger-Congo family (Koenig et al. 1983). Gbaya consists of a great many dialects including the following: Yaayuwee, Lay, Mbodomo, Ganginda, Dooka, Gaymona, Mbusuku, Yaangele, and Bangando. "Gbaya Mbere", the language variety spoken around the Mbere Valley, as far as the Central African Republic, is distinct from "Gbaya Bertoua", which is spoken around Bertoua, capital of the East Province of Cameroon, and its environs. The Gbaya Translation Centre in Meiganga works mainly in one dialect, Yaayuwee, since the Yaayuwees, who inhabit the northern part of the territory, are the most prominent group among the Gbaya. Even though Yaayuwee is the principal language of translation and interpretation, especially in the Gbaya Translation Centre at Meiganga, it is not the only vehicle of dissemination of Gbaya culture and philosophy. To varying degrees, the other dialects have also been vehicles of translation and interpretation among the Gbaya since the late nineteenth century, when the earliest attempts were made to write the language.

Two groups of Europeans can be credited with having shown the way in the development of the Gbaya language and translation and interpretation activity: first, European ethnographers, linguists and translators, who came to study indigenous language and culture; and second, those who came to spread the Christian faith among the Gbaya of Cameroon, the Central African Republic and the Democratic Republic of Congo. Ecclesiastics of the Sudan Mission, for example, came from the United States to Mboula and Meiganga in 1924 and played a pioneering role in promoting the Gbaya language.

Evangelization, education, the promotion of national languages, and translation and interpretation were so closely interwoven among the Gbaya from 1924 to 1940 that it is difficult to discuss any one of them in isolation. As these early missionaries converted and educated the locals, they were assisted by a team of indigenous people who were highly educated and knew at least two European languages. Joseph Garga, a prominent convert, was baptized in 1928, along with others who subsequently assisted the missionaries in their translation activities. Garga, known among the Gbaya as the *Kaigama* (a notable and assistant chief), requested that the missionaries translate the life of Christ and the Ten Commandments into Gbaya. By 1932, the Gbaya were converting so fast that even the chief of Mboula was baptized. By 1942, local evangelists such as Paul Baoro and Daniel Mbarkao had started preaching and interpreting the gospel in the Gbaya language. These indigenous people played a dominant role in translation and interpretation activities similar to that of Akwa Mpondo, Timba and André Mbangué, among others, who pioneered the profession among Douala Catholics in 1908. However, the comparison ends there, because unlike André Mbangué and his colleagues, who were sent to Germany for further training so that they could later assist in translation, the Gbaya pioneers participated in translations of the Bible without having been sent to America to perfect their linguistic abilities.

Rev. Adolphus Gunderson (c.1890–1951), a linguist and translator, contributed enormously to the development of the Gbaya language. He was at home in English, French, Hausa, Fulfulde and later the Yaayuwee dialect of Gbaya. Some German ethnographers and linguists had already attempted to write in Gbaya. After learning Gbaya and setting it down in writing, Gunderson opened a school to teach Gbaya and French to the indigenous peoples. Translation activity took on new life in 1933 when Gunderson began writing the Gbaya language with Rev. Arthur Anderson at Abba, a small town in the Central African Republic, in order to spread the gospel among the Gbaya in both countries. The first scripture published in Gbaya was the Gospel of Matthew in 1939. The collection, transcription and translation of oral literature seem to have been another preoccupation of the early missionary translators (Noss 1981b and 1993), and Gunderson was among those who collected and translated Gbaya folklore.

Working in areas related to the physical and social well-being of the local people, women translators also contributed to the development of the language. As far back as the 1920s, missionary translators like Anna Gunderson, Olette Bertson, Anne Olsen and Olga Kristen translated documents on such subjects as health care, social welfare and home economics into Gbaya.

Right from the beginning, teamwork seems to have been the dominant method of translation. Translation workshops and revisions by native speakers and linguists who had an excellent mastery of the culture played an important part. Eugene Nida has frequently underscored the vital role that the local informant, or native speaker, plays in this kind of translation activity (Nida and Taber 1969). Rev. Adolphus Gunderson and his team, most of whom were missionary translators, laid a solid foundation for the promotion of Gbaya language through the numerous translation and interpretation activities which had become an integral part of Gbaya life and culture.

Between 1942 and 1972, the year in which the Gbaya Translation Centre was transferred from Ngaoundere to Meiganga, there seems to have been a lull in translation and interpretation activities among the Gbaya, with some notable exceptions. During this period, Rev. Lloyd Sand translated the *"commentaire biblique"*, comprised of sections of the New Testament, and his wife Beryl translated the Song of Songs. During the same period, the École de Théologie (at present, Institut de Théologie Luthérienne) was founded in Meiganga. In 1961, it graduated six Gbaya pastors charged with disseminating and interpreting the gospel in the Gbaya language (Christensen 1990). Through the leadership of the Canadian missionary translator, Madel Nostbakken, the New Testament in Gbaya was completed and published in 1968.

A second phase of translation and interpretation activities among the Gbaya of the Mbere Valley began in 1971 when the American linguist Philip Noss (b. 1939) opened the Gbaya Translation Centre in Meiganga, a centre that enjoys full collaboration with the Catholic Church.

An eminent scholar of Gbaya life and culture, Noss grew up in Cameroon and learned Gbaya as a child. In 1979, he became literature coordinator for the Evangelical Lutheran Church of Cameroon and in 1984 a translation consultant with the United Bible Societies. He works in five languages: English, French, Gbaya, Fulfulde and Sango. He is the author of an authoritative book on Gbaya grammar (1981a), co-author with Father Y. Blanchard, OMI (Missionary Oblates of Mary Immaculate) of a Gbaya-French dictionary (1982), and translator of books in many fields from French and English into Gbaya. In addition, Noss has published several significant theoretical essays which view translation from the perspective and context of African culture, and of Gbaya language and culture specifically (Noss 1982b and 1987, for example).[26] In his works, Noss discusses the translation or adaptation of biblical names or titles in an African context. He has also made valuable observations on the "ideophone": a sound pattern or effect, similar to assonance, consonance or alliteration, which functions as an adjective, adverb or modifier and may replace a verb or even a complete sentence to express human sensations (Noss 2001 and 2003). Because of the complicated nature of the ideophone, it has often been ignored, but translators at the Gbaya Centre have used it in translating sections of the Bible to convey both meaning and dramatic effect (Noss 1985).

As in other parts of Africa, national languages in Cameroon began to develop in the late nineteenth century. In a relatively short time, languages such as Ewondo, Douala, Bulu and Gbaya – our particular focus in this section – have evolved quickly, thanks to the crucial role played by missionary translators.

Hebrew: a modern language for Israel

Hebrew is an ancient language belonging to the Canaanite branch of the Northwest Semitic family of languages. The earliest traces of ancient Hebrew are inscriptions from the eighth century BCE, but the language was preserved mainly in the text of the Hebrew Bible, whose compilation was completed by the fourth century BCE. After the diaspora – the dispersion of Jewish communities outside Palestine following the Babylonian exile in the sixth century BCE – Hebrew ceased to be a working language, but survived as a holy language, used mainly for religious purposes. However, in certain periods it was also used by Jewish authors in composing secular literature (e.g. Hebrew literature of the Golden Age in medieval Spain, and the literature of the Jewish enlightenment movement in nineteenth-century Europe). The Hebrew language was not used in everyday life; for that purpose, Jews spoke the languages of the various countries where they lived, as well as some special dialects used exclusively by them, such as Yiddish and Ladino.[27]

Zionism, the nationalist revival movement of the Jewish people, first emerged in Europe in the nineteenth century.[28] Its goal was to renew life in Eretz-Israel (the land of Israel, or pre-state Israel). In the early stages of Zionism, the movement did not necessarily envisage the revival of Hebrew for everyday use. Such a change did not seem realistic. Even Theodor Herzl, the first leader of the Zionist movement and the first to envision a Jewish state, thought that German would be the language of that state. But a desire to revive Hebrew emerged within the Zionist movement, and it gained strength with the immigration of Jews to Eretz-Israel.

Of the people who struggled for this ideal, the most important was Eliezer Ben-Yehuda (1858–1922), known as "the reviver of Hebrew". He was a linguist and journalist who immigrated to Eretz-Israel in 1881. In the magazines he published (*Ha-zvi*, *Hashkafa*), he tried to persuade people to use Hebrew in their everyday lives. He set a personal example by speaking only Hebrew to his own family and by educating his son using Hebrew, which was quite unusual at that time. Ben-Yehuda wrote a Hebrew dictionary and began to adapt old Hebrew to modern life by coining a vast number of new words. Many of them became part of modern Hebrew.

Yet in Ben-Yehuda's time and afterwards, the inhabitants of Eretz-Israel came from many lands, and many of them did not speak, read or write Hebrew. Hence life was multilingual. Various organizations strove to change this state of affairs. One of the most fervent was The Language Defenders' Corps, established in 1923. This youth organization fought zealously for the exclusive use of Hebrew in public life. Its members, encouraged by Zionist leaders, used to demonstrate and interfere with public events held in languages other than Hebrew. The campaign for the primacy of Hebrew was also directed against imported books and local newspapers in foreign languages which were read by the immigrants. Ultimately, Hebrew won the battle: today it is the first official language of the State of Israel, which was established in 1948. Hebrew is the language used in literature and journalism, in scientific and technological writing, and in everyday speech.[29]

Translations contributed to the revival of Hebrew in two ways. First, translation helped disseminate the language. During the years when original texts written in Hebrew in all fields (popular literature, teaching materials, etc.) were still scarce, translations filled the void. Second, translation enriched the language itself through contact with other languages.

It is very difficult, however, to isolate the influence of translations on the development of modern Hebrew. Texts originally written in Hebrew (for example, literature and newspapers) also played an important role in disseminating the language. And the development of Hebrew through its contact with other languages – a process not always welcomed by purists – was not associated with translations alone. Hebrew absorbed, and continues to absorb, elements of foreign languages, because Israel even today remains a country of immigrants, a country whose inhabitants speak and read several languages. Israeli culture has always been affected by other cultures: Russian, Anglo-American, Middle Eastern, Mediterranean and others. The languages spoken by different ethnic and linguistic groups have penetrated Hebrew not only through translations but also through other channels such as original-version foreign television programs and films.

The following discussion will nevertheless try to determine the specific influence of translations on the development of modern Hebrew, and will focus on some important work carried out in the field of literary translation.

One of the leading figures in Jewish literary life in the diaspora during the late nineteenth and early twentieth centuries was Mendele Mokher Sforim (1835–1917) – a pseudonym meaning "Mendele the bookseller" used by Shalom Ya'akov Abramovitz. Mendele, who lived in Odessa in Tsarist Russia, wrote fiction in Yiddish and translated it into Hebrew himself. One of his most important works is *The Travels of Benjamin the Third*, a sharp satire on Jewish life in the diaspora. The Hebrew version appeared in 1896. Translations usually serve readers who are not acquainted with the language of an original work, but this translation was intended for readers who already knew the book in Yiddish, and was meant to contribute to the revival of Hebrew, playing both a linguistic and a cultural role (Perry 1981).

The main difficulty faced by Mendele in this self-translation was that he had written the source text in a rich and lively Yiddish, a living language spoken by Jews in the diaspora, while the language of his translation was old and petrified. Stylistically erudite, it echoed the Bible instead of real life. But Mendele succeeded in turning this limitation into an advantage: the gap between the high-flown style and the ridiculous character of the protagonists produced a strongly ironic effect. This gap itself helped to create a social satire. Mendele's effective use of old Biblical Hebrew was adopted by other authors and is popular even to this day in Hebrew satire.

Chaim Nachman Bialik (1873–1934), the Hebrew national poet, also used translation to help Hebrew become a living language. Bialik began his career as a poet in Russia, but in 1924 he emigrated to Eretz-Israel, where he continued his work. In the poetry and fiction which he composed in Hebrew, Bialik portrayed Jewish life in the diaspora both critically and compassionately. Besides his own creative writing, he translated classical works from world literature into Hebrew: Cervantes's *Don Quixote*, for example, probably from the Russian and German versions. He also wrote folk poems and rhymes for children, which naturally did not exist in Hebrew before it became a living language. These texts were in part adaptations of existing Yiddish songs (Sadan 1965; Shamir 1986a and 1986b). As in the case of Mendele's translation, the language he used was sophisticated and evocative of the Bible. Reflecting on how children would cope with such a language, Bialik suggested that they would manage as they did with nuts, which strengthened their teeth (Ofek 1985: 79). Despite the language problem, Bialik's folk poems and rhymes for children became very popular. Many of them have been set to music and are still sung today. Through them Bialik proved that Hebrew could function like any normal language.

Translations also contributed to the development of modern Hebrew by enriching the language. In the process of revival, Hebrew users had to cope with two sorts of voids (Dagut 1981; Ivir 1987). Since it had become a holy language alone, Hebrew had stagnated. It therefore lacked the means to express many of the concepts of everyday life. Whole areas of contemporary reality, such as science and technology, were absent. Moreover, Hebrew had long existed only in written form and completely lacked the spoken variant which other languages possess.

Translators had to resolve these difficulties, since the source texts included both spoken language and references to modern phenomena. This need was met by renewing Hebrew and extending its own range of resources. This included reviving old words by changing or enlarging their original meaning, giving new meaning to words whose old meaning had been forgotten and, in addition, coining new words or creating neologisms, on the basis of existing grammatical forms. When translators wanted to create "a spoken variant", they sometimes disrupted the old language on purpose by using idioms incorrectly. Hebrew also benefited from its contact with various source languages, enriching the stock of Hebrew resources by imitating grammatical and syntactical forms, borrowing words, and translating expressions literally in the form of *calques*.

What began as an objective necessity turned, with time, into a voluntary aesthetic norm. From the early twentieth century on, Hebrew gradually developed into a living language capable of meeting all verbal needs. Even after it had become as stratified as any "normal" language and included an actual spoken variant, each translation created the language anew in the ways described above (Even-Zohar 1976; Toury 1977 and 1980; Ben-Shahar 1998; Weissbrod 1989). In coping with the spoken language that was used in certain source texts, the adoption of a "fictitious spoken language" was encouraged, since it was felt that "authentic spoken Hebrew" suited the street, but not literature. Over time, there was less hostility to the use of spoken Hebrew in literature, but there was another reason for using fictitious spoken language in literary translations. A spoken language belongs to a specific social and historical context, it is said, and one cannot be substituted for another. It is considered preferable to use an invented spoken language in translation, one which belongs to "the third territory", the place where source and target language meet (Mirsky 1978).

Linguistic creativity in Hebrew translation is identified with the work of Abraham Shlonsky (1900–73), one of the most distinguished Hebrew poets and translators of the twentieth century. In his poetry and translations, linguistic inventions were not only a means of filling the gaps, but an aesthetic end in themselves.

Shlonsky renewed Hebrew through his own range of creative resources. He used the various historical strata of Hebrew skilfully and also invented a vast number of neologisms on the basis of existing grammatical forms. The tendency to coin new words was probably accentuated by the fact that Shlonsky was a modernist poet, and modernism allowed all sorts of liberties, including the licence to play with language. Many of his neologisms, which were collected by Ya'akov Kna'ani (1989), became rooted in Hebrew literature and everyday language.[30] Shlonsky's work was written in an era when Hebrew culture – politics, theatre, popular songs, clothing, and so on – was heavily influenced by Russian culture. In translating Russian poetry and prose, Shlonsky created a sort of spoken language which was unique to literature. It was characterized by sentence structure, words of address, connecting words and diminutives which derived from Russian. The strong influence of Shlonsky on Hebrew letters is revealed by the fact that even Hebrew authors who were born in Eretz-Israel, and did not speak or read Russian, adopted his Russian-Hebrew style (Even-Zohar 1990).

Shlonsky's work strengthened the conception of literary translation in Hebrew culture. Translation was regarded not just as an intermediary between Hebrew readers and world literature, but also as a means of developing modern Hebrew. To quote the critic Israel Cohen (1957):

> The translation of the finest of world literature not only enriches our national literature and broadens the horizons of its authors and readers, but it also forges the national language, hammers it, forces it to scour its treasures, to plumb its depths to find equivalent expressions; it accustoms the language to give voice to feelings and thoughts and sights that until then had not set foot in its realms, to create new modes of expression.

Through the efforts of translators working on literary as well as sacred texts, national languages have been born, developed, enriched and given new direction and new life. Although such efforts often met with opposition, and even led in some cases to the outlawing, persecution and execution of translators, they also enjoyed the support of powerful individuals and institutions. Through their association with great projects of religious reform or nationalism – or both of these causes – translators played a significant role in the development of receiving cultures, and in the genesis of language itself.

Notes

1. Owing to the significance and complexity of their work, some of these individuals will reappear further on in the book: Chaucer in Chapter 3, Caxton in Chapters 5 and 8, and Tyndale in Chapter 6.

2. Augustine of Canterbury (d. 604) is not to be confused with St. Jerome's contemporary, Aurelius Augustinus or St. Augustine (354–430), Bishop of Hippo Regius in North Africa, and a father and doctor of the Church. Not totally unfamiliar in Britain, Christianity had made some progress by the third century. In the fifth century, St. Ninian did missionary work in Scotland and St. Patrick in Ireland. When Augustine and his monks arrived, in fact, their task was made easier by the fact that there were already a small number of Christians in the kingdom of Kent, where they landed, and that King Æthelbert had married a Christian.

3. Because of its predominance as a market, Bruges served as a gathering place for merchants from all over Europe who established themselves in national communities, each one ruled by a governor. A merchant adventurer was essentially any English merchant who engaged in overseas trade (Blake 1969: 31).

4. For more on the *Vulgate*, see Chapter 6.

5. See also Chapter 6.

6. The term "*lingua franca*", borrowed from Italian, originally meant Frankish tongue, the language of the European traders who ventured into the Eastern Mediterranean, rather than the Franks who colonized Gaul in the fifth century. It was a mixture of mainly Romance languages, used in the Mediterranean region from the time of the Crusades up to the end of the nineteenth century. Today the term refers to any common language, either an actual national language or a hybrid one (Calvet 1981). In India, the Mogul conquerors developed Urdu (from the Turkish *ordu* meaning "army") as an idiom of communication in the army and administration of their empire. Swahili (from the Arabic *Sahel* meaning "coast") was originally used by Arab traders along the east coast of Africa.

7. The so-called "Oaths of Strasbourg" was a treaty of alliance sworn by two of Charlemagne's grandsons, Charles the Bald and Louis the German, at the time they were dividing up the empire. In proclamations that took place in Strasbourg in 842, Charles and Louis pledged to defend each other against their brother Lothair. The Oaths are transcribed in the Romance language of Charles and the Teutonic (Old High German) language of Louis, and are reproduced in Nithard's *Histories* (ninth century), otherwise written entirely in Latin.

8. The term "Francien" was coined by the philologist Gaston Paris (1889) to replace "*dialecte de l'Île de France*". As the language of the court, *Francien* spread with the expansion of royal influence and became the national language, winning out over competing written languages used by educated people in the *langue d'oïl* provinces. The question of Francien is controversial: some are of the view that its existence was put forward in the nineteenth century to support the idea of the French language enjoying a direct and pure lineage from Latin, thus minimizing the importance of other regional languages of France.

9. Marcus Tullius Cicero (106–43 BCE) was a Roman statesman, philosopher, orator and translator. He introduced the Romans to Greek philosophy and created the Latin philosophical vocabulary required to make it intelligible. These ideas on translation were expressed in *De oratore* ("On the Orator"), dated 55 BCE, and in *De finibus bonorum et malorum* ("On the Limits of Good and Evil"), dated 44 BCE (Lefevere 1992:46–47).

10. Nicolas Oresme's contribution to terminology and lexicography is the subject of further examination in Chapter 8.

11. The Académie française was established in 1634 by Cardinal Richelieu and received its charter from King Louis XIII in 1635. Richelieu gave it the mission of developing and purifying the French language, a task begun by Malherbe. To this day, the body continues to act as the official authority on the French language, and to revise and issue its official dictionary. See also Chapter 5.

12. The expression "*belle infidèle*" has been attributed to Gilles Ménage (1613–92). Ménage is said to have commented on a translation by Nicolas Perrot d'Ablancourt in these terms: "I called it *la belle infidèle* (beautiful and unfaithful), which is how I used to refer to one of my mistresses when I was young" (Ménage 1715, 2:186). The term "*belles infidèles*" has been used since the seventeenth century to designate a particular attitude or approach in which a free translation is preferred to a literal one. For the origins of the expression, see Zuber (1968:195 and 196, note 35).

13. Port-Royal was an abbey built in Paris in 1626. It became a stronghold of Jansenism, and a gathering place for prominent writers and philosophers such as Blaise Pascal, who carried out their studies of logic, grammar and theology there, and also translated religious texts.

14. Notker the German (*Notker der Deutsche*), also known as Notker III or Notker Labeo, was a monk of St. Gall, which was one of the thriving centres of classical culture in Germany in his day. St. Gall is now located in Switzerland.

15. Other German translators of Shakespeare, particularly Schlegel and Tieck, will be discussed in Chapter 3.

16. There are records of at least fourteen complete Bibles having existed in High German before Luther. Johann Mentel (1410–78), one of the first printers to have used movable type, printed a complete Bible in Strasbourg in 1466. Four Low German editions were also published after 1478.

17. Striking examples from Psalm 63 ("My Heart Thirsts for God") and Psalm 23 ("The Lord is my Shepherd") are set out in Arndt (1968). Luther's 1524 translations are compared with the less literal, more colloquial formulations of later versions.

18. German quotations are given in original spelling, including lower case for nouns, as reprinted in Arndt's 1968 edition (quoted in Marlowe 2003).

19. The *Deutsches Wörterbuch* (Dictionary of the German Language), the first instalment of which was published in 1852. See Chapter 8.

20. The term "Scandinavia" more appropriately refers to the central and main part of this region, and comprises Sweden, Denmark and Norway, but not Finland and Iceland, as is sometimes assumed. Today, Scandinavian languages are spoken by some 18 million people.

21. See Chapter 1, note 6.

22. The Migration Period, also called the Barbarian Invasions, was a time of human migration in Europe, precipitated by upheaval within the Roman Empire and beyond its borders. Following this period (300–700 CE) were other movements of peoples, including the Vikings or Norsemen (eight to eleventh centuries), who set out across Europe for purposes of trade and warfare.

23. Born of a noble family near Norrtälje, Birgitta (Bridget or Brïte) Persson was the wife of Ulfo, governor of the province of Närike. She had eight children, including St. Catherine of Sweden. After the death of her husband she became a religious mystic and founded the Vadstena Monastery and then the Brigittine order of St. Saviour. She spent the last twenty-three years of her life in Rome, where she served as an adviser to the Pope. The Brigittine Revelations, which combine stories of the life of Christ and the Virgin with calls for the reformation of the Church, include the seven books of the *Liber Celestis,* the *Revelationes extravagantes* and the *Opera Minora.*

24. The complete Bible, according to the United Bible Societies, is available in 469 languages, of which 173 were African languages as of December 31, 2009 (http://www.biblesocietyinisrael. com/index.php?option=com_content&view=article&id=31&Itemid=27&lang=en, accessed June 2011).

25. The Fulbe penetrated northern Cameroon in the 19th century as jihad warriors of Usman dan Fodio. Originally from the most western regions of West Africa, they spoke Fulfulde, a West Atlantic language. They are comprised of two broad divisions, urban dwellers and cattle people. As herdsmen, they are seminomadic, moving often to find pasture land and water required for their herds. Over twelve million Fulbe live in western Africa. For the complexities of inter-ethnic relations in Cameroon, see Burnham 1996.

26. Extensive research on language and culture has been carried out on other dialects since the 1970s: for example "Bodoe, a neighboring Gbaya dialect in the Central African Republic", by the French scholar Paulette Roulon-Doko who has also written a Gbaya-French dictionary (Paris: Karthala, 2008).

27. Yiddish (literally "Jewish") is a Middle High German language. It originated in the Rhineland in about the tenth century as a variant of *tiutsch* (which the Jews referred to as *taytsh*). Written in the Hebrew script, it has been enriched with borrowings from Hebrew and Slavic languages. It was the primary spoken language of the Ashkenazi Jews, who occupied the Rhineland and then spread over Central and Eastern Europe. Once spoken in Jewish communities throughout the world, Yiddish is now in decline. The number of Yiddish speakers on the eve of World War II was around 11,000,000; the number of speakers is now estimated at several hundred thousand (Shandler 2005: 1; 203). Cultural production – books, newspapers, theatrical performances – is merely a fraction of what it once was, although in some parts of North America, Europe and Israel, there has been a revival of interest in Yiddish culture, particularly in what Shandler describes as "postvernacular" Yiddish. Ladino, also known as Judeo-Spanish, is a blend of medieval Castilian, Hebrew, Arabic and other elements. Originally spoken by Sephardic Jews, when they lived in Spain and Portugal in the Middle Ages, it has since been spoken by Sephardic exiles around the world.

28. From the time of the Jewish diaspora, the exiled Jews longed for their homeland, symbolized by Zion (or Jerusalem). While Zionism reflects this tradition, it refers, more strictly speaking, to the more recent nationalist movement responsible for establishing the modern state of Israel. Zionism is generally attributed to Theodor (Binyamin Ze'ev) Herzl (1860–1904) and other nineteenth-century figures and groups.

29. Arabic is the other official language of Israel; since Supreme Court rulings from the 1990s on, it has been used more extensively than it once was.

30. Ya'akov Kna'ani devoted two decades to the production of a *Comprehensive Hebrew Dictionary* (1998).

Figure 5. William Caxton

Figure 6. Joost van den Vondel

CHAPTER 3

Translators and the emergence of national literatures

For Geoffrey Chaucer (c.1340–1400), who is generally recognized as England's greatest medieval poet, translation was a fundamental activity. Writing in the vernacular at a time when Latin still enjoyed considerable cultural prestige, Chaucer obtained status and authority through his work as a translator and *compilator* (Machan 1989). He translated, or claimed to have translated, classical and vernacular work from Latin, French and Italian; building on *Le Roman de la Rose*, Boethius, Boccaccio, Petrarch and Dante, he wove the primary philosophical and artistic concerns of his age into his own work. For Chaucer, as for other early vernacular writers, there was an overlap between translation, compilation, rewriting and original authorship. The conception of translation as re-creation was a means to resolve these tensions. While eclipsed during certain periods of history by the supremacy of original authorship, this view of translation has remained a common thread throughout history. Chaucer's metaphor of ploughing old fields to produce new corn, opposed though it is to Dryden's seventeenth-century notion of the translator as a slave labouring in another man's vineyard (Lefevere 1992: 24), has transcended time and place.

> For out of olde felds, as men seyth,
> Cometh al this newe corn fro yer to yere,
> And out of olde bokes, in good feyth,
> Cometh al this newe science that men lere.
>
> Geoffrey Chaucer, *Parliament of Fowls* (1977: 566)

Literary translation is distinct from both sacred and scientific translation. Historically, scripture translation was akin to that of science: in both cases, writes the early Jewish translator and philosopher Philo Judaeus (c.20 BCE–c.50 CE), there is "a wording which corresponds with the matter" (Kelly 1979: 69). Literal translation was espoused by the early Christian translators, advocated by St. Jerome for his Scriptural work, then reaffirmed by Boethius (480–524) and the medieval translators after him who were concerned primarily with the transmission of intellectual information. The translation of literature into vernacular languages evolved within a different tradition. Although it has been the subject of the same debates on faithfulness as other forms of translation, literary translation has been more concerned with the creation of new forms through translation. In Roman times, translation was theorized as a "rhetorical project of achieving difference with the original text". In the same way, medieval translation of the classical *auctores* into the vernacular grew out of exegesis, commentary and textual appropriation (Copeland 1991:65). Throughout history, admiration for the original work has been coupled with a sense of making something new: hence, as in the case of Chaucer, the concepts of translation and creation, of imitation and displacement, of import and conquest have been inextricably linked.

This chapter illustrates the ways in which translators contribute to the development of national literatures. Translation has often preceded creative writing, and has been described as "giving birth" to literature (Cary 1962). This has been a *leitmotiv* in writing on translation, as illustrated by Octavio Paz:

> [...] there is constant interaction between the two [translation and creation], a continuous, mutual enrichment. The greatest creative periods of Western poetry [...] have been preceded or accompanied by intercrossings between poetic traditions. At times these intercrossings have taken the form of imitation, and at others they have taken the form of translation.
>
> (Paz, quoted in Schulte and Biguenet 1992: 160)

A series of examples of this phenomenon will be presented in the pages that follow. In each of the cases, the end result is fundamentally the same: translation has provided models and inspiration to individual writers, and at a broader level has given new direction to literature within the target culture. The process is interesting to examine: the motivation for translating in the first place, the perception or theorization of the process by translators, and the nature of the impact on the receiving culture. Translation takes place within a context and its great moments are grounded in history. Emergence of one literature always occurs in relation to another; it is a matter of differentiation, hence of relations between centre and margin, between dominant and minor cultures. Translation as a practice and discourse will be examined in relation to other events and discourses (social, political, ideological and so on). What emerges from this view is not only the importance of these external factors to translation, but also the centrality of translation itself to intellectual history across cultures.

The term "emergence" is to be taken in its broadest sense. This study will show how translators have contributed to their own literature at various stages of its development, either by forging a nascent literature or by helping to redirect it at a crucial moment of history.

Although nations with sharply defined geographical boundaries are generally regarded as a "universal form of sociopolitical organization", the concepts of nationhood and nationalism as they are understood today are actually relatively recent (Bjornson 1991). National states as such began to emerge in Renaissance Europe. The discovery of printing and the subsequent spread of print culture, the passion for Greek and Latin erudition, the conquest of new worlds, and the importance of making the Bible accessible in vernacular languages: these were some of the factors that led to increased translation activity during the Renaissance, and to the parallel emergence of national languages, national literatures and a sense of nation itself. It is appropriate, therefore, that this chapter begin with Renaissance translation: a case study of a writer/translator of the Dutch Golden Age.

By the late seventeenth and early eighteenth centuries, many of the European literatures had already achieved the status of "national" literatures and were no longer in a state of emergence *per se*. However, they did undergo significant shifts through a convergence of political and literary events. One such literary event, the translation of Shakespeare on the Continent, is the subject of the next case study. This situation more properly has to do with the re-emergence or redirection of national literatures. National languages already existed, as did the literatures they expressed. New national identities were proclaimed or strengthened in reaction to French hegemony following the Napoleonic subordination of much of Europe. Cultural communities were also finding ways to assert their own identity – through literature, notably.

Much of the focus of this chapter is on more recent literatures, linked to efforts to achieve self-determination. Two separate instances of differentiation from a dominant English culture will be presented: the first case involves Ireland, a nation that achieved political independence from Britain, and the second Scotland, where cultural differentiation from England seems to have occurred but where independence remains on the agenda. The two remaining sections will examine postcolonial cultures for which translation has been a fundamental means of promoting national literature: the case of Argentina, and the more problematic case of Africa, which raises the question of the relevance of the concept of "national literature" itself.

Joost van den Vondel and the Dutch Golden Age

The translations of Joost van den Vondel (1587–1679) (Figure 6) offer a unique insight into the nature and function of translated literature in the seventeenth-century Dutch Republic (Hermans 1985a and 1991). His translations are important historical documents in themselves in that they reflect the willingness of at least some sections of a given cultural configuration to invest considerable intellectual and material resources in the importation, by means of translation, of foreign texts of high cultural prestige. This happened, moreover, at a moment when the leading classes in the Dutch Republic – a newly formed political entity born out of rebellion – were intent on legitimizing their position through the creation of a consciously national culture. Vondel is generally regarded as the greatest poet and playwright of the Dutch Golden Age. Translations formed an integral part of Vondel's entire literary production, just as they did for Chaucer. In typical Renaissance fashion, this resulted in a seamless web of *translatio, imitatio* and *aemulatio* informing the writer's own *inventio* and supplying him with a series of textual models.

Vondel's literary output was prodigious and continued well into old age. As a translator, he was no less versatile and prolific. His translations span more than half a century. He began to translate not long after 1610 with Du Bartas's *Les Sepmaines*[1] and ended in 1671, at the age of eighty-four, with Ovid's *Metamorphoses*. His work includes several substantial prose renderings from the Italian and Latin done purely as exercises and not intended for publication. He published the first integral translations of Latin plays by Seneca and the first renderings into Dutch of five Greek plays by Sophocles and Euripides (only one other play by Sophocles was available in Dutch until then). He also produced two complete versions of Virgil, one in prose, the other in verse.

In more ways than one, Vondel may be regarded as a typical vernacular writer of the later Renaissance. He exemplifies not only the dependence of vernacular literature on classical sources through the mediation of humanist learning, but also the way in which these sources were absorbed and integrated into the increasingly self-conscious culture of a newly independent, economically powerful state. As an individual, Vondel showed a high regard for foreign, mostly classical, examples and prototypes, and a constant willingness to model his own writing on them. Having only limited schooling, he learned Latin and then Greek at a mature age, and thus relied on friends better versed than he was in classical philology to help him with translations from Latin and especially Greek. In a sense, his own development parallels the growth of Renaissance writing in Western Europe generally and in the Low Countries in particular. Europe initially discovered the classics through the work of the Italian humanists, and always remained more familiar with Latin than with Greek Antiquity. In turn, most of the new Renaissance forms and ideas first reached the Low Countries via France. The parallel with Vondel's development as a translator is striking: starting with translations from the French and Italian, he moved on to Seneca, Horace, Ovid and Virgil, before bringing out four of his five translations from the Greek when he was in his seventies.

There is much in Vondel's social and intellectual complexion that marks him as an exponent of the society that produced the culture of the Dutch Golden Age, even though in religious terms he occupied a marginal position. The son of an immigrant family from the southern Netherlands, Vondel grew up in an Anabaptist community in Amsterdam, but he eventually became a fervent Catholic in a Calvinist-dominated country. His economic position was at once comfortable and vulnerable. As a silk merchant running his own business, he could devote only limited leisure time to his literary pursuits and wrote his huge *œuvre* at tremendous speed.

In the 1650s, the market for luxury goods collapsed as a result of an economic crisis. Vondel, then seventy years of age, was forced to accept a salaried post as an accountant to cover the debts of his son who had gone bankrupt during the crisis. Although barred from direct access to the corridors of power due to his religious affiliation, Vondel found patrons for his literary work among his immediate social superiors, the rich merchant class of Holland and particularly the powerful Amsterdam "regents" who controlled the country's commercial wealth and whose political interests Vondel served in his public discourse.

In intellectual terms, too, Vondel remained dependent on those who could supply him with models of high cultural prestige – classical models, that is. His social background and education had only partly prepared him for this. Having been trained for a commercial career, he had learned French but no classical languages. The references to Latin and neo-Latin sources in his first major poem, a hymn on navigation from 1613, are all based on existing Dutch translations. His first play, *Passover* (1612), contains reminiscences of *Les Sepmaines*, two books of which Vondel translated around this time or shortly afterwards (*The Patriarchs* in 1616 and *The Magnificence of Solomon* in 1620). In the preface to *The Magnificence of Solomon*, Vondel made his first significant statement about translation, pointing out the difference between translation and *inventio* and advocating a literalist approach to translating.

As his contacts with leading cultural circles in Amsterdam increased, Vondel took private lessons to learn Latin (1613–20); he also acquired Italian and made a prose version of Torquato Tasso's *Gerusalemme liberata*, which was never finished, however, and which remains in manuscript form to this day. His second play, *Jerusalem Destroyed* (1620), derived its story line from Flavius Josephus, but its language and structure bore the imprint of Seneca's *Troades*, labelled "the queen of tragedies" by the internationally renowned neo-Latin writer Hugo Grotius,[2] whom Vondel greatly admired and eventually befriended. But when Vondel set out to translate two of Seneca's plays into Dutch (*Troades* becoming *The Amsterdam Hecuba*, 1626, and *Phaedra* recast as *Hippolytus*, 1628), he still needed to collaborate with others on a prose crib which he subsequently put to rhyme. In the early 1630s, he translated all of Horace into prose as an exercise for his own benefit. It was published twenty years later, in 1654, only to prevent an unauthorized version from coming into print.

The classical forms he absorbed underpinned a great deal of his original writing, including Horatian satires on public events, tragedies in the Senecan vein and triumphal poems in the grand heroic manner celebrating national victories in the ongoing war with Spain. There is an unbroken continuum from one end of the spectrum to the other: from his translation of a neo-Latin poem by his humanist friend Caspar Barlaeus, written in imitation of Catullus's famous "sparrow" poem, for example, to his attempt to write a Christian epic in Virgilian style about the Roman Emperor Constantine. Another example, thematically closer to home, is the tragedy *Gysbreght van Aemstel* (1637), Vondel's greatest box-office success on the Amsterdam stage. He again combines Virgilian motifs with Christian ones, but this time applies them to national and even local situations, projecting the Second Book of the *Aeneid* onto an episode in the medieval history of Amsterdam and casting the protagonist Gysbreght as a Dutch Aeneas fleeing the burning city on Christmas day.

As Vondel was establishing himself as the leading tragic playwright of his age, two drama translations in the 1630s provided the basis for a slow but momentous reorientation in his conception of tragedy, away from the Senecan mode and toward Greek models. His *Joseph or Sophompaneas* (1635), which later became known as *Joseph at Court*, was a translation of a contemporary play by the exiled Hugo Grotius. This play about Joseph as the wise viceroy at Pharaoh's court remained Vondel's only substantial translation of a neo-Latin work. Through his contacts with humanists like Grotius, Gerardus Vossius and others, Vondel discovered the superior value of the Greek tragedians. He decided to learn Greek even though he was by now in his forties. Soon afterward, he translated Sophocles's *Electra* (1639), although he still required help since his command of Greek was not, and would never be, sufficient to translate Sophocles or Euripides. In translating these two plays, Vondel took a noticeably freer approach than in his earlier work as a translator. The prefaces to both texts recognize that the literary and linguistic requirements of the receiving culture militate against a literalist rendering. In verse translation, he adds, "pouring something from one language into another through a narrow bottleneck cannot be done without spilling". Both plays proved popular on the stage. *Joseph at Court* became one of the most successful translated plays in the Amsterdam theatre.[3] In 1640, Vondel brought out two original plays concerning the biblical Joseph, and the three were often performed together. His play *Brothers*, also from 1640, which depicts King David's anguished wavering between mercy and duty as the high priest instructs him to execute the innocent sons of Saul, is generally recognized as Vondel's first "Greek" tragedy. It was dedicated to his learned mentor Vossius.[4]

In the early 1640s, Vondel translated, again as a private exercise, Ovid's *Heroides*, which did not appear in print until the eighteenth century. It led, however, to another Christianizing *imitatio*, this time with strong Catholic overtones, in the form of the *Epistles of the Holy Virgins, Martyrs* (1642). But his major and most remarkable work as a translator in this period was the consciously source-oriented prose version of the complete works of Virgil (1646). Whereas Vondel's mature verse translations, beginning with *Sophompaneas* and *Electra*, paid heed to the formal demands of the receiving pole, this prose version of Virgil represented at once his most reverent homage to a supreme literary model and a determined attempt to penetrate and lay bare for the Dutch reader what Vondel referred to as Virgil's "spirit" and "soul", "the mystery of meaning or sound concealed beneath every word, syllable and letter". The echo from St. Jerome is not entirely fortuitous. Nor was this Vondel's last word on Virgil. In 1655, he published a verse rendering of the *Aeneid*, Book II, and the complete verse translation followed in 1660. Vondel dedicated these works to members of Amsterdam's regent class, for whom Virgilian heroes, he believed, could serve as models of moral and civic virtue. Interestingly, however, it was his prose translation of Virgil that was later reprinted most frequently, suggesting a reading public with sufficient curiosity about the intricacies of the source text to appreciate Vondel's painstaking but nonetheless elegant crib. At the same time, his translations helped trigger a vogue of Dutch renderings of Virgil: between 1650 and 1670, half a dozen other writers came up with partial or complete versions of the *Aeneid*, in prose or verse. Vondel himself went on to produce his own *imitatio* in the biblical epic *John the Baptist* (1662). A few years earlier, he had brought out a translation of the Psalms, employing a variety of metres (1657).

Apart from the preoccupation with Virgil's poetry, the 1640s and 1650s also witnessed a series of ambitious plays, increasingly following Aristotelian principles as Vondel's discussions with scholars like Vossius and others continued. In 1648, when the Treaty of Münster brought an end to decades of war between the Dutch Republic and Spain, Vondel responded to an official invitation with a patriotic pastoral modelled on Guarini's *Pastor Fido* but incorporating Vossius's views on the genre as articulated in the latter's brand-new *Institutiones Poeticae* (1647), in which Vondel saw a correction of Guarini's example. While his grandest play of all, *Lucifer* (1654), was an original work set among the angels in heaven, his biblical *Jeptha* of 1659 was intended as the definitive Aristotelian-model tragedy in Dutch.[5]

By the time *Jeptha* appeared, Vondel was over seventy years of age and secure in his reputation as the greatest writer of the Dutch Golden Age. The loftiness of his style and themes commanded respect and attracted a loyal readership, but not necessarily a theatre audience. His *Lucifer* had enjoyed a *succès de scandale* as the target of fierce Calvinist attacks alleging blasphemy. As a result, the play was taken off the stage after just two performances but went through seven reprints in its first year. His *Jeptha*, for all its Aristotelian merit, held only limited appeal for theatre audiences. Vondel continued on his chosen path, but on the Amsterdam stage at least, his brand of classicism had had its day. The nine or so original plays and the four translations from the Greek of Sophocles and Euripides that he produced after 1660 barely reached the stage, or failed to do so altogether.[6] The reason lay in the increasing popularity and profitability of the more spectacular tragedies and tragicomedies in the English and especially the Spanish vein, a genre borne of translations of Thomas Kyd, Cyril Tourneur and, above all, Lope de Vega. Just as humanist culture generally ceased to be a primary shaping force after approximately the middle of the seventeenth century, so was Vondel's stage classicism finally left without an audience. When, around 1670, a bourgeois reaction against the swashbuckling spectacle and amorous intrigue of the nonclassical line set in, the new norm bore a French neoclassicist stamp and derived directly from the newly dominant cultural centre of Europe. A different cultural era had begun.

Translating Shakespeare to/on the European Continent

European Romanticism was marked by a series of translations that permeated and enriched literary systems across the continent. The translation of Shakespeare, a truly European phenomenon, is a striking example. New light has been shed on the impact of translations on the reception of Shakespeare, and their role in the replacement of neoclassical values throughout Europe (Delabastita and D'hulst 1993; Larson and Schelle 1989; Monaco 1974). An investigation of these translations and their authors reveals the complex process of translation/mediation, which brought together linguistic, literary and cultural realities as far removed as the Elizabethan Renaissance and continental Romanticism.

Toward the second half of the eighteenth century, drama was rediscovered both as a literary and theatrical art form. Beginning in France, the new interest in theatre gradually spread from one culture to another. Despite strong resistance at first, French translators assumed the role of initiators within their own society. They also became pioneers outside their country. In fact, the history of the translation of Shakespeare can be written as a history of the international dissemination of French versions of Shakespeare, which was later followed by resistance to French models, when the same fate befell translations as original compositions.

The early translators, of course, did not foresee the tremendous repercussions their work would have, although they were well aware of the literary mission which they had taken on. As a critic and translator, Voltaire was at the centre of conflicting literary trends, both opposed and favourable to Shakespearean aesthetics. Not that Voltaire could or wished to reconcile these forces. He was himself fascinated by several texts, *Hamlet* in particular, which he vilified yet attempted to translate, taking contradictory stands on how to go about it. Voltaire's ambivalent attitude and intellectual authority were at the root of a controversy surrounding the Bard's personality and work, which was to influence the way in which the translations of Shakespeare were later received. The controversy was further accentuated by a split in literary ideals: on the one hand, the quest for new and exotic literary forms to replace the outmoded ones that had derived from Greek and Latin models and, on the other, the conviction that French literature alone, strengthened in the glorious seventeenth century, could stand as a true literary model. Supporters of Shakespeare saw features in his work that were lacking in French literature, whereas his detractors, soon to be in the minority, considered him barbaric and contrary to neoclassical ideals of taste and harmony.

The first French translator to enter the debate was Pierre Le Tourneur (1736–88), although Pierre-Antoine de La Place (1717–93) had previously produced eight volumes of free, inoffensive and uncontroversial translations, published between 1746 and 1749 under the title *Le Théâtre anglois*. Le Tourneur went further. The first volume of his twenty-volume *Shakespeare*, published between 1776 and 1783, contained a highly polemical preface in defence of Shakespeare, whose natural greatness, he claimed, had been obscured by previous "travesties". His translation was copiously annotated, and sought to "educate" rather than "please" the reader. Acknowledging the foreignness of the source text, to some extent at least, Le Tourneur also drew attention to the relativity of taste. In holding Shakespeare up as an alternative to French neoclassical literature, he inaugurated a critical tradition of which one of the famous examples is Stendhal's *Racine et Shakespeare* (1823).

Le Tourneur secured the support of the Court by dedicating his work to King Louis XVI, who was more tolerant of new ideas than was his grandfather, Louis XV, at least at the beginning of his reign. The list of patrons included the most influential members of both the French and English courts. This protection was useful in countering attacks from Voltaire and his coterie. Despite some criticism from the press and the Académie française, Le Tourneur's translation was an unqualified success, certainly fuelled by the Anglomania of the time. The genius of Shakespeare challenged values handed down from Antiquity and thereby undermined all that was sacred in French literature. The sense of nation discovered through contact with Shakespeare took on a broader significance, both literary and political. During the Empire and the Restoration, this served to offset the patriotic virtues of Tacitus heroes, who had been glorified during the revolutionary period.

For nearly fifty years, Le Tourneur's translations were used, even pillaged, by other translators, particularly by those adapting plays for the stage. Le Tourneur's versions, however, did not at all overshadow those of his contemporary, Jean-François Ducis (1733–1816), whose stage adaptations enjoyed considerable success until the late 1820s. The French theatrical tradition adjusted to Ducis's cautious translations, which were nevertheless regarded as original because their historical and mythological themes and characters contrasted so sharply with the conventions of ancient tragedy. The versions produced by Ducis occupied a middle ground between tradition and innovation; they were the result of enduring compromises that were fairly widely accepted by the public.

In comparison, the reforms advocated by Victor Hugo, beginning with his *Préface de Cromwell* (1827), were more radical and slower to take effect. Hugo was rather critical and for a long time wary of translations. At the height of the romantic debate, new versions of Shakespeare were published by Alfred de Vigny (1797–1863) and Émile Deschamps (1791–1871), who were directly involved in founding a new theatre. Vigny's *Othello*, staged in 1829 at the prestigious Théâtre-Français, set out to establish a new model for romantic verse tragedy. Shakespeare was the source of a dramatic and poetic theory seeking to renew the "instrument" or style. Translation was presented not as a source but as an example: it was to function as a full-fledged original work in the target language. This was how Vigny's translation was in fact received.

The translations of Le Tourneur, Ducis and Vigny all reflected existing literary practices. But in introducing hybrid forms, these translations were also innovative and progressive compared to other productions in the target language.

At the international level, French translations functioned as intermediaries. Several other literatures became acquainted with the theatre of Shakespeare through French versions, those of Ducis rather than Le Tourneur. The model of French tragedy, rejuvenated and exemplified by Ducis's translations of Shakespeare, was paradoxically a factor in the emergence of national consciousness in countries such as Germany, Poland and Holland. The pre-eminence of French culture in Enlightenment Europe was conducive to the use of French intertexts, which had already been cast in the dominant neoclassical mould, although the influence of these models was more theatrical than literary. The discovery of Shakespeare in the English original was very slow and uneven, and varied from one culture to another. There were often discrepancies between written texts and versions to be staged, as well as inconsistencies between the revolutionary statements made in prefaces or pamphlets and the concessions of actual translation practice. French models were gradually displaced, the process hastened by political resistance to Napoleonic or monarchist rule.

Beyond these general statements, the overall picture is far from clear-cut, from both a literary and a political perspective. A detailed map of Europe would leave numerous grey areas. In West Slavic cultures such as Slovakia, for example, translation also served to standardize the written and literary language.

The example of Germany is as significant as that of France. Plays destined for an international audience, especially those by Christoph Wieland (1733–1813) and Johann Eschenburg (1743–1820), were prose translations which had benefited from the judicious modifications of German stage directors. Some translators rewrote Shakespeare directly for the stage. Gottfried August Bürger (1747–94) and Friedrich Schiller (1759–1805) were the most celebrated interpreters of *Macbeth*: Bürger regarded the Bard as a model for the *Volksdichter* ("poet of the people") which he and Herder had popularized, while Schiller offered verse tragedy as an alternative to bourgeois drama. Other translators also helped reinforce budding literary trends, which flourished upon contact with Shakespearean theatre.

The great project undertaken by Wilhelm Schlegel (1767–1845) and completed by Ludwig Tieck (1773–1853) emanated from Schlegel's theory of Romanticism and concept of organic poetry. In this case, translation was used as a means to defend a theory. That is why these translations were slow to be adapted for the stage. For a long time, directors and audiences preferred modest prose translations, which they considered more suitable than complex formal equivalents for conveying the "total" Shakespeare. However, from the 1870s on, the Schlegel-Tieck version was held to be superior to the original, and the concept of a "German Shakespeare" became a nationalistic theme.

By the end of the eighteenth century, verse and prose adaptations were being derived from Ducis's versions – *Hamlet*, in particular – in northern European countries such as Russia, Denmark and Norway. In reaction to these adaptations, the nineteenth century produced new versions that were regarded as originals rich in new literary concepts. In Russia, for instance, four tragedies translated at the beginning of the century from Ducis's versions, which appeared to reconcile neoclassical ideals with romantic ones, in reality stirred up intense debate. Versions of *Othello* (Ivan Velyaminov 1808), *King Lear* (Nikolaï Gnedich 1808), *Hamlet* (Stepan Viskovatov 1811) and *Macbeth* (Piotr Korsakov 1815) came under fire from the Romantics, who reacted by trying out new techniques they had come up with themselves or else borrowed from German theorists such as Schlegel. Nevertheless, these neoclassical translations were to survive on the stage for a long time, just as they had in France.

Southern Europe saw similar developments toward the end of the eighteenth century. In Italy, for example, stage adaptations of Ducis's French translations were replaced by written and stage versions that took the original text into account. With the retranslations came a re-examination of the function and techniques of translation, the status of foreign literature in Italy and the self-sufficiency of Italian models. As they became aware of the vital role of translators in literary reform, avant-garde authors tackled the translation of Shakespeare. They would not have been able to do so without the neoclassical versions, on the one hand, and critical models, on the other. Voltaire, for example, whose views were either transmitted in French or translated, lent substance to the debate. The role of translations in the creation of new textual forms is even more significant. In trying to reconcile the conventional and the innovative, translators often produced an unclassifiable target-language text. *Verso sciolto* (blank verse) is a case in point: it originated in translations from English and was borrowed by the next generation of poets, the Romantics – in the true sense of the word.

Changing sides: the case of Ireland

In September 1920, at the height of the Irish War of Independence, the magazine *Misneach* (Courage) published a letter calling for writers in Irish to translate great works of world literature into Irish (Mac Nioclais 1991: 108). Aspiration became reality with the establishment of the Irish Free State in 1922. In 1928, a Publication Committee set up by the Department of Education, later to become the *An Gúm*, advertised a translation competition. The two primary reasons advanced for the necessity of translation into Irish were to stimulate literature in modern Irish through the emulation of outstanding foreign works and to provide reading material for children and adults in modern Irish.

The Irish language and its literature were in a beleaguered state at the moment of independence. The first laws against the language, the Statutes of Kilkenny, had been promulgated by Anglo-Norman invaders in 1366, and had stipulated that English people who spoke Irish would have their lands confiscated. This had little real effect, however, and in 1537, Henry VIII brought in a new law forbidding the Irish to speak their own language (Cronin 1993: 80–83). The Tudor and Cromwellian conquest of Ireland was thorough and effective. Under a more explicit policy of cultural colonization, language difference was seen as the unacceptable outward manifestation of political disloyalty. The decisive defeat of the Gaelic aristocracy at the Battle of Kinsale (1601) and the Battle of the Boyne (1690) resulted in the collapse of the sociopolitical structures that had provided a system of patronage for professional writers, the *fili*, in the old Gaelic order. The literature was left without patrons and readers, the language without custodians. By the end of the nineteenth century, only fifteen percent of the population were Irish speaking for a variety of reasons. For one, a great many of those who had died or emigrated during the Great Famine (1845–47) were Irish speakers. The teaching of Irish was excluded from the primary school system in 1834, and the Catholic

Church remained indifferent to the plight of Irish. One of the avowed aims of the revolutionary nationalist movement in the early twentieth century was the restoration and revival of Irish. Translation into Irish was to be the instrument of restitution, an act of reparation.

The translation scheme of *An Gúm* was riven by a contradiction which hampered its effectiveness as a response to centuries of linguistic dispossession. The fundamental conflict, which it never fully resolved, was between translation as re-creation and translation as pedagogy. On the one hand, intellectual commentators such as Liam Ó Rinn and Cearbhall Ó Dálaigh saw translation as a means of creating a new literary idiom in Irish that would reinvigorate the language and revive the high cultural register of classical Irish, used throughout the Gaelic world between 1250 and 1650. As Liam Ó Rinn claimed in *The United Irishman* in 1933, "There is no country in Europe that does not have two kinds of language, the kind used by people in conversation or doing business and the kind found in literature". Underlying Ó Rinn's comments was a more general view of translation which had its origins in German translation theory of the late eighteenth and early nineteenth centuries, according to which translation (of Greek and Latin texts, in particular) would serve to bolster an independent German literature and demonstrate the immense linguistic resources of the German language. The perceived emotional and political radicalism of the *Sturm und Drang* and early romantic movements in Germany was closely identified with the spirit of the 1798 and 1803 rebellions in Ireland (Lloyd 1987: 129–158). German influence extended into the twentieth century as German scholars, such as Kuno Meyers, continued to dominate the field of Celtic Studies (Ó Lúing 1989: 1–33). Hence, the re-creative, generative role of translation in the emergence of a national literature became a familiar theme to Irish intellectuals concerned with cultural independence. Translation was seen as a means of strengthening a weakened target language and making it functional again as a literary medium (Even-Zohar 1978: 121).

This exalted view of translation was not universally shared, least of all by the politicians responsible for the introduction and financing of the translation scheme. In 1931, the Free State Minister for Finance, Earnán De Blaghad, stated that great masses of reading matter to suit all tastes had to be made available in Irish in predominantly English-speaking areas of Ireland. Translation, in his view, was the only way to produce the quantity of texts required (De Blaghad 1931). The pedagogic mission of the translator is reflected in the startling eclecticism of books to be translated. A 1928 list included *Lorna Doone, The Last of the Mohicans, Hajji Baba of Ispahan, Irish Nationality, The Path to Rome, The Wallet of Kai Lung* as well as *Daddy Longlegs, Mrs. Wiggs of the Cabbage Patch* and *The Undying Monster* (Mac Nioclláis 1991: 111).[7] The high incidence of popular fiction and children's literature meant that those with little Irish would have ready access to reading material in that language. This aim, along with the notion of providing reading matter to suit all tastes, was laudable, but did little to further the re-creative project that motivated advocates of high-culture translation.

If translation was to teach language, then its primary function would be to teach the rich vernacular of Ireland's *Gaeltachtaí* (Irish-speaking areas). The translation scheme employed native speakers of Irish almost exclusively: Seán Ó Ruadháin, Séamus Ó Grianna, Nioclás Tóibín and Aindrias Ó Baoighill. These translators adopted a "fluent strategy", to use Lawrence Venuti's term (1992), translating the text so that it would read like a text that had originated in the target language and culture, with no traces of the linguistic and cultural differences of the source text. Translators drawn from different areas (Munster, Ulster and Connacht) retained dialectal differences in their translated work. The effect was conservative rather than iconoclastic, linked with a more general commitment to what was known as *caint na ndaoine* (literally the "speech of the people"). The position was argued most forcefully by Fr. Peadar Ó Laoghaire, author of one of the early classics of modern Irish literature, *Séadna* (1904), and a prominent cultural nationalist. He claimed that the true spirit of Irish people and the essence of the language were to be found in the natural, everyday speech of people living in *Gaeltacht* areas. The implied linguistic relativism was, of course, a common thread of European nationalism in the nineteenth century. The celebration of *caint na ndaoine* had, in fact, a dual purpose: expressing specificity and giving voice to the voiceless, marginalized, rural Irish poor. In the early part of the twentieth century, John Millington Synge embarked on his translation project, which sought to create literature not only in Irish, but also in English, yet drawing on the peculiar rhythms and verbal inventiveness of the Irish spoken in economically impoverished areas (Kiberd 1993). For both Ó Laoghaire and Synge, the aesthetic project was also one of political recovery, of allowing the objects of colonial indifference to become the subjects of new postcolonial literatures in English and Irish.

In the case of Irish, postcolonial empowerment did not lead to a rejection of target-language bias in translation or the sudden emergence of "non-refractory", or non-transparent, translations (Lefevere 1981:68–77). Indeed, the need to express the radical otherness of Irish as a language led translators to scrupulously avoid Anglicisms in their translations from English, the main source language of translation. The Irish experience is a telling example of the recurrent double bind of postcolonial translation. On the one hand, a language claims its right to exist on the basis of its difference from the language of the colonizer. On the other, in translation, this means that the radical unlikeness of the source language of the colonizer is effaced in favour of the cultural and linguistic conventions of the target language of the colonized. Contrary to what Venuti maintains (1992: 5), therefore, "fluent strategies" are not the sole prerogative of imperial cultures.

In fact, one can argue the opposite. Translations with a source-language bias are a luxury that can be afforded by dominant colonial or ex-colonial languages. However, in the high-risk environment of minority languages (Irish in Ireland, French in North America), the powerful presence of the source language in translations can further diminish the specificity of the target language and ultimately stymie its growth.

By 1937, a total of 214 works had been translated into Irish by translators working for *An Gúm*. Twenty-one had been translated from French, eight from German, two from Italian, three from Spanish, eight from Latin and Greek, one from Provençal, one from Russian and 170 from English. Thus, there were four times as many books translated from English as from all the other languages together (Ó Faracháin 1937: 175–176). The high incidence of translation from English raises a number of interesting questions, which can be summed up as dilemmas of influence and competence. English had been the dominant medium of instruction throughout the nineteenth century in Ireland and had been the language of commerce and culture. The literature that most Irish-speaking translators and writers were best acquainted with was English. Hence, they tended to translate Walter Scott, Charles Dickens, Jerome K. Jerome, Mark Twain – the preferred reading matter of the Victorian middle classes. The persistence of cultural influence is hardly surprising among newly enfranchised postcolonial elite (Niranjana 1992). The question of competence is related to socioeconomic conditions. In the 1920s and 1930s, few native Irish speakers had opportunities to study foreign languages. Foreign travel usually took the permanent form of emigration and, even then, the destinations were largely Anglophone. Therefore, the easiest and most popular, albeit most treacherous, option was to translate directly from literature in the English language.

Irish translation occurred in the context of diglossia, or bilingualism. There were few remaining Irish-speaking monoglots in the 1920s: those who could read Irish could also read English. There was little incentive, therefore, for them to read the 1934 translation of *Lorna Doone* in Irish, for example. To some extent, the very cultural influence that dictated the choice of translation deprived those translations of a readership. The repeated criticisms of *An Gúm's* policy with regard to English translations, along with low readership figures and financial cutbacks during the Emergency (as World War II was euphemistically known in neutral Ireland), led to a dramatic curtailment of the scheme by the end of the 1940s and a tendency to concentrate solely on the translation of schoolbooks.

As a result of published remarks by a number of writers involved in the trans-lation scheme – Máirtín Ó Cadhain and Seosamh Mac Grianna, for example – the early translation work of the new State was retrospectively derided as dispirit-ing hackwork that did little to promote new literature in Irish (Cronin 1993a). However, in a major work on the novel in Irish, Alan Titley questions this assess-ment and points to the fact that many of the writers involved in the scheme also produced original work. Furthermore, he argues that "some translations were of a higher quality and more worthwhile than the original works being published around the same time" (Titley 1991:46).

The translators employed by *An Gúm* included many of the important found-ing figures of modern literature in Irish: Máirtín Ó Cadhain, Séamus Ó Grianna, Seosamh Mac Grianna, Seán Ó Ruadháin, Nioclás Tóibín, Seán Mac Maoláin, Tadhg Ó Rabhartaigh, Aindrias Ó Baoighill and Mícheál Ó Gríobhta. Their trans-lation work ultimately led to the emergence of a literary language which had been ardently sought in the immediate post-independence period. The centripetal fea-ture of the translation work was an increasing emphasis on the standardization of spelling and grammar, resulting in the establishment of a simplified and stan-dard spelling of Irish in 1954. The shift was from the orthographic and syntactic diversity of *caint na ndaoine* to an acceptance of norms, which had characterized classical Irish centuries earlier. The centrifugal feature was a resistance to this very standardization, which allowed writers to explore the resources and expressive possibilities of their own variety of Irish. The tension between these two tenden-cies was to endow Irish-language writers of the 1960s and 1970s with a language and literature greatly improved by the earlier pursuit of excellence in translation. The experience of translation in Ireland in the 1920s and 1930s reveals the very specific difficulties of minority languages – centring around questions of influ-ence, competence, linguistic identity, empowerment and reception – which must be taken into account in any chronicle of the emergence of national literatures (Cronin 1996).

Speaking intimately to the Scottish soul – in translation

Writing about *The House Among the Stars*, a Scots translation of *La maison suspen-due* by Quebec playwright Michel Tremblay, one reviewer in the Glasgow *Herald* said, "this is a play which speaks intimately to the Scottish soul". These words sum up the way in which the work of one particular foreign author has been able to penetrate and enrich another culture and literature through translation.

Multilingualism has been a distinct feature of the Scottish literary tradition in its near thousand-year history. While English predominates today, Gaelic and

Scots tenaciously continue to survive in speech, song and literature. Their survival contributes to that cultural differentiation from England which has helped secure a continuing sense of Scottish nationhood within the political fabric of the United Kingdom.[8]

Gaelic is a wholly separate language from English, but historically Scots and English are cognate languages. While Scots developed out of the northern dialect of Old English in the twelfth century, Scots and English grew apart once Scotland regained its political independence in the early fourteenth century. So significant were the differences between them that when a Spanish ambassador visited the Scottish court in 1498, he likened the two languages to Aragonese and Castilian.

By 1450, Scots had become an "all-purpose language" (Murison 1977: 4). The following hundred years have been described as "the heyday of the Scots tongue as a full national language" (Aitken and McArthur 1979: 8–9). The language was mature enough to have been a language of translation: Virgil's *Aeneid*, Livy's *History of Rome*, the entire New Testament and parts of the Old Testament were translated during the sixteenth century. Inspired by the contribution to French literature of the *Pléiade* poets, James VI, King of Scotland, translated himself and encouraged translation by court writers, including versions of Ronsard and poets of *la Pléiade* (Findlay 2004: 2).

Eventually, however, English achieved primacy over Scots. The Protestant Reformation was a contributing factor: in the absence of a Scots translation of the Bible, an English one was introduced to Scotland, giving spiritual prestige to the English language. English subsequently achieved social prestige, too, as a consequence of the Union of the Crowns in 1603: James VI fell heir to the English throne and chose to rule over his two kingdoms, as James I, from the English capital, London. These events not only weakened the status of Scots as an official language, but also led to fatal erosion of the standardized literary register of Scots. Scots was dealt a further blow when the Parliaments of Scotland and England were united in 1707, and English became the official language of Scotland.

Scots lingered in all classes of society as a national spoken language (except in Gaelic-speaking areas), and even achieved a certain international literary prestige in the late eighteenth and early nineteenth centuries through the poetry of Robert Burns and the novels of Sir Walter Scott. In time, however, a social stigma of sorts became attached to the speaking of it. The more it was abandoned by the upper and middle classes, the more it became identified with the speech of the humbler classes. By the twentieth century, Scots was increasingly associated with the speech of the rural and urban working classes. The inevitable encroachment of its sister language, English, has encouraged a perception that Scots is little more than a corrupt dialect of English rather than a distinct language of ancient lineage.

Scots has nevertheless survived as a medium for literature. Indeed, writing in Scots began to achieve new impetus in the twentieth century due to the inspiring example of the nationalist writer Hugh MacDiarmid (1892–1978) and the Scottish Literary Renaissance movement he headed in the 1920s and 1930s. Translation into Scots, MacDiarmid believed, would encourage a reorientation toward Europe and away from the kind of provincialism brought upon Scots by looking to England for approval. He and his disciples translated a substantial body of poetry into Scots. These translations, as well as the original poetry written by MacDiarmid and others, employed a "literary Scots". Subsequently, however, a younger generation of poets, novelists and dramatists began to make greater use of contemporary, urban working-class Scots speech in their writing.

In the late 1970s, Bill Findlay (1947–2005) and Martin Bowman embarked on their first Scots translation: the work they chose was *Les Belles-Soeurs*, a play by Michel Tremblay which they translated and published as *The Guid Sisters*.[9] For Findlay and Bowman, using Scots for translation was a means of "keeping faith" with both family and class roots, as well as an expression of socialist and nationalist sympathies. Bowman, born and reared in Quebec but a son of Scottish immigrants, and Findlay, a Scot with a working-class background, met while they were postgraduate students of Scottish Literature. Following the example of Hugh MacDiarmid, Findlay and Bowman regarded translation of foreign literature as a means to contribute to the continuance of the Scots literary tradition.

In contrast with the long and distinguished tradition of poetry in Scots and the use of Scots in fiction – albeit mostly in dialogue – there had been no sustained body of plays until the twentieth century. In a late-developing dramatic tradition such as this, translations can help establish a national repertoire. Yet, until *The Guid Sisters*, foreign plays translated into Scots were few in number and drawn from a historical repertoire of fairly circumscribed range: three by Molière, two by Aristophanes, and one each by Goldoni, Kleist and Holberg.[10] Extraordinarily, there had been no translation into Scots of a contemporary foreign play.

The Guid Sisters also broke what was then a linguistic mould. The translations of the historical plays mentioned above had invariably drawn on a spoken rural Scots aggrandized with older words and forms, similar to the "literary Scots" used by poets like MacDiarmid. With the flowering of Scottish theatre in the 1970s, playwrights were beginning to make use of the medium of contemporary urban Scots. The translators found it logical to extend that idiom into translation work, thereby giving a new direction to Scots translations.

Michel Tremblay's international stature and the status of *Les Belles-Soeurs* as a modern "classic" played a part in the decision to translate this particular work into Scots. But Tremblay's use of *québécois* (the French idiom spoken in Quebec) was also a crucial factor. Canadian critics having expressed dissatisfaction with existing English translations of Tremblay, the translators decided to experiment with a nonstandard idiom. Since the relationship between *québécois* and "standard" French is not dissimilar to that between contemporary Scots and "standard" English, they felt they would be able to get closer in letter and in spirit to Tremblay's original than English translators had done. An added similarity, which is important to the thematic content of *Les Belles-Soeurs*, was the social stigma attached to both *québécois* (and more particularly *joual*, the variety used by Tremblay) and Scots within their respective cultures. An additional consideration was Tremblay's use of language as a political and cultural arm in the struggle for Quebec independence. The promotion of Scots, likewise, contributed to a mood of cultural nationalism with potential political consequences.

Translating Tremblay's *québécois* into Scots afforded an opportunity to prove the validity and efficacy of contemporary Scots as a translation medium. The long-standing predominance of standard English translations in Scottish (and British) theatre – more often than not delivered in the class-associated accent of Received Pronunciation[11] – had misrepresented both the nonstandard linguistic nature of much Western drama (contemporary and classic) and its rootedness in the texture of a particular national or regional culture. The urban and rural dialects of Scots, together with English where appropriate, were a rich linguistic resource for translators to draw on in the context of Scottish theatre. Findlay and Bowman admired the fact that Tremblay's unapologetic commitment to *québécois* and the specificity of the Quebec experience had proved no barrier to international appreciation of his plays. Thus Tremblay's achievements were both instructive and potentially inspirational for theatre in Scots. The challenge of successfully conveying Tremblay's genius in Scots translation would provide the means to test and stretch the resources of the target language.

Michel Tremblay became the most popular contemporary playwright in Scotland. First staged in 1989, *The Guid Sisters* proved a popular and critical hit. It was revived in 1990 and again in 1992. In the years since 1989, Tremblay's work has also provided a vehicle for Scottish theatre abroad. Glasgow's Tron Theatre took *The Guid Sisters* to the World Stage festival in Toronto in 1990, and another translation of Tremblay, *The Real Wurld?*, to the Stony Brook International Theatre Festival, Long Island, New York, in 1991. Additionally, a production of *The Guid Sisters* by the Tron ran for a month in Montreal in 1992 as part of the official British contribution to the city's 350th anniversary celebrations (this represented the longest foreign run a Scottish production had ever had). *The Guid Sisters* was successful with audiences and critics in Canada and the United States. Not only were audiences not fazed by the language but critics celebrated it as "startlingly fresh" and "a revelation". Canadian critics commented favourably on the appropriateness of rendering Tremblay's *québécois* into Scots. Also, in a welcome reversal of the flow of English-Scottish cultural traffic, English audiences were introduced to *Les Belles-Soeurs* when an English theatre commissioned and staged a Yorkshire dialect adaptation of the Scots translation.

Through his plays, Michel Tremblay became a familiar and respected figure in Scottish theatre. The Quebec playwright was referred to by a Toronto newspaper as "McTremblay".[12] Described by one reviewer as "the best playwright Scotland never had", Tremblay received an honorary doctorate in 1992 from the University of Stirling in recognition of his international stature and unique contribution to Scottish theatre. Tremblay's popularity encouraged translators Bowman and Findlay to continue their work: in addition to translating a total of eight Tremblay plays, they went on to translate other dramatists, from Quebec and other countries.[13]

The reception of the translations in Canada and the U.S.A. has demonstrated the appeal that theatre in Scots can have for English-speaking audiences beyond Scotland. One minority vernacular has assisted another in this regard. The enthusiastic response of Scottish audiences suggests they feel a special affinity for Tremblay's work. While the language of the translations is their own and therefore adds immediacy for them, audiences are responding to a Quebec milieu since the translators on principle have not adapted any of their translations to Scotland. Thus the Scots idiom conveys the specificity of Quebec experience as well as the universality of Tremblay's art. The translations take on the authority of original work; they resonate with audiences rather than distancing them the way some translations are prone to do. The success achieved by the play is reflected in the following assertion, made by a critic by the time of its third run: "[*The Guid Sisters*] has established itself now as a mainstay of the Scottish dramatic repertoire. No wonder, the Québécois situation is so analogous to the Scottish one" (*The Scotsman*, August 21, 1992, quoted in Findlay 2005: 195).

The fortune of the Tremblay translations in Scotland, as this statement suggests, should be seen, not in isolation, but rather in the context of the resurgence of political nationalism in the 1970s, increasing interest in Scotland's history and culture in the 1980s and a growing appeal of works in Scots. Examples of bestselling books of the period include *The New Testament in Scots*, as well as *The Concise Scots Dictionary* and *The Scots Thesaurus*, which reflect a concern for putting the Scots language into use. The repertoire of Scots translations has been expanded with a greater stylistic adventurousness in the Scots employed. Among the most popular productions have been Scots translations of Molière's *Tartuffe*, Rostand's *Cyrano de Bergerac*, plays by Dario Fo and an adaptation of Hašek's novel, *The Guid Sodger Schweik*. Although it is perhaps difficult to measure the precise influence of the Tremblay translations on original drama written in Scots, they have certainly contributed to an acceptance of Scots as an appropriate and effective medium for translating contemporary foreign drama. The transla-tions have served to demonstrate that Scots can convey a range of emotions and moods beyond those with which it is often associated (e.g. humour and pathos) and that, like Tremblay's *québécois*, its ambition and appeal need not be limited to the parochial.

Jorge Luis Borges and the birth of Argentine literature

As they gazed out at the flat and deserted Pampa they had acquired after inde-pendence (1810–16), the intellectuals of Río de La Plata no doubt hoped that the break with Spain would be cultural as well as political. They were concerned about language (should an independent Argentina continue to speak Spanish?) and an association with a school of thought (that of the former metropolis) which they judged to be intolerant and shallow. These intellectuals – Mariano Moreno, Juan María Gutiérrez, Esteban Echeverría, Juan Bautista Alberdi and Domingo Faustino Sarmiento – had been brought up reading or speaking French and Eng-lish. They were familiar with Herder and other Romantics; they had travelled around Europe (excluding Spain) or the United States. Translation was an activ-ity they either promoted or practised themselves. They founded a literary system with some successes – such as gaucho literature – but based primarily on political or autobiographical writings. Many of the elements essential for producing and reproducing a culture were missing. These people were politicians, governors, diplomats, rather than professional writers. There was a dearth of stable publish-ing houses and specialized newspapers. Above all, readers of Argentine literature were scarce. Educated people read hardly anything in Spanish and the general public, as an unfortunate legacy of colonial negligence, was practically illiterate.

By the time Jorge Luis Borges (1899–1986) began to write, this situation had changed. The Common Education Law of 1884 had guaranteed the literacy of the native population. Spanish was being taught to the foreigners who were begin-ning to arrive in Argentina by the millions. Young publishers, mostly first-gen-eration Jewish immigrants, lent their support to what was being written in the country, and there was a proliferation of journals and literary supplements in the newspapers. Official mechanisms were created to promote Argentine literature: a chair of Argentine literature was established at the University of Buenos Aires in 1913, the Argentine Literary Institute was set up in 1922, and generous literary prizes were offered.

However swift and radical the process of change, none of these measures could guarantee the creation of a truly great literature. This was the preoccupa-tion of the young Borges and his contemporaries who, like him, were interested in avant-garde literature and modern culture. In his opinion, quality and originality in literature could be attained only through meticulous work on the language and a liberated reading of traditions.

In the 1920s, Borges wrote a series of articles on the future of Argentine litera-ture.[14] Although over a hundred years old, Argentine literature, as he saw it, had been heavily influenced by French and Spanish literature and lacked a voice of its own. In his program for the future, Borges addressed two fundamental issues: language and cultural tradition. He advocated a policy of enriching his language through translation, drawing on the successful ways in which other languages represented reality. He admired the oral tradition, the "conversational prose of adults", so prevalent in his country. At the same time, he also extolled Latin, the "language of marble", which writers of the Spanish Golden Age such as Quevedo, Cervantes, Torres Villarroel or the anonymous author of *Epístola moral a Fabio* had reproduced in Spanish.

Borges's approach to the problem of tradition was far broader. It was system-atized in a 1953 article entitled "El escritor argentino y la tradición" (The Argen-tine writer and tradition),[15] but it underlies his entire work, particularly articles dealing with translation. Living on the southernmost periphery, unhindered by preconceived notions, Argentines were free to browse through the cultures of East and West and read from the "library" of the universe (Borges, it should be remembered, worked as a librarian in real life). Borges delighted in the literary wonders of the world: Virgil, *The Thousand and One Nights*, Dante, Shakespeare and Cervantes. He also explored works and authors which, like him, lay beyond the margins of canonical Western literature: the heresiarchs,[16] Jewish mystics, medieval Chinese storytellers and Persian poets.

Underlying Borges's attitude was the idea of *Bildung*, one of the concepts cen-tral to the philosophy of the early German Romantics.[17] Hence the importance of the reader. Borges invented an individual capable of generating infinite texts from a single one (Borges 1932, 1936). This hypothesis, "translated" into fiction in "Pierre Menard, autor del Quijote" (Pierre Menard, author of the Quixote, 1939), helped overturn the age-old tyranny of authorship, replacing it with reading, which is regarded as a more civilized and deeply creative operation.[18]

The concept of originality is a theoretical construct of the eighteenth century (Mortier 1982). Prior to that time, great literary traditions were built through reading, then "translating" or imitating foreign sources. In a series of texts, such as "La flor de Coleridge" (The Flower of Coleridge, 1945) and "La esfera de Pascal" (Pascal's Sphere, 1951), Borges showed how certain images, metaphors or ideas had been handed down from one author to another, from one language to an-other. Struck by the idea of the "flexibility of ownership", he wrote about how the nineteenth-century Irish writer Edward FitzGerald found his voice in a Persian poet by publishing an English version of the *Rubáiyát of Omar Khayyám*, parts of which his father, Jorge Guillermo Borges, had translated (Roger 2011). In his theoretical writing on translation, always closely linked to his own practice, Borges also reflected on how Kafka had created his own precursors. For any writer, he believed, the words of the past are contemporary because literature does not recognize differences of nationality or time.

The works of Borges – theoretical writing, fiction and meticulous footnotes – all reflect an obvious identification of translation and creation. Translation is not simply a transfusion of entire texts into another language. Its true function is to transmit stylistic procedures, new poetic forms, narrative methods and models, and even criteria of truth and beauty. In "Las versiones homéricas" (Homeric Translations, 1932), Borges comments on various fragments translated from Greek to English while reproducing them in Spanish. This rather unique procedure is repeated and expanded in "Los traductores de las 1001 noches" (Translators of the Thousand and One Nights, 1936), in which Borges comments on how Arabic texts passed into French, English and German, while transcribing them into his own language as well. Far from conceiving languages as closed symbolic universes, Borges sees them as storehouses of poetic and narrative procedures, which a writer from anywhere in the world is free to appropriate.

Borges praised translation in theoretical texts, as well as in prefaces or essays about various books and authors,[19] but he was also a practising translator. He translated entire books such as Faulkner's *Wild Palms*, Virginia Woolf's *Orlando* and *A Room of One's Own* and Kafka's *Metamorphosis*, but most of his translations were in the form of shorter contributions to periodicals and anthologies.[20] The anthologies demonstrate most clearly that he aspired to produce not just a personal work, but a *canon*, in the etymological sense of the word as "rules". His books of essays, from *Inquisiciones* (1924) to *Otras Inquisiciones* (1952), or the anthologies he compiled alone or with Adolfo Bioy Casares contain translations designed to serve as models.[21] These heterogeneous collections, which bring together disparate fragments of English, Italian, German, Chinese, Latin or other literatures, revealed to writers both young and old that literature is universal and eternal. They encouraged their readers' taste for the fantastic genre and highlighted, in particular, those stories that tell how to tell a story.

Borges was not an isolated case. The writers of his generation – Adolfo Bioy Casares, Silvina Ocampo, Victoria Ocampo, José Bianco, Manuel Mugica Láinez, Julio Cortázar – were all translators who contributed to the cosmopolitan canon that has given shape to Argentine literature. Borges's particular gift was to have theorized, imagined and defended this form for a peripheral literature.

The essays, poems and fiction of Borges resonate with the names of famous translators: St. Jerome, Ulfila, the Venerable Bede, Notker the German, Martin

Luther, Antoine Galland and Edward Lane.[22] There are references to translations by Geoffrey Chaucer, Samuel Johnson, Thomas de Quincey and William Morris; his fiction is inhabited by characters who translate (Pierre Menard, James Alexander Nolan, Marcelo Yarmolinsky, Jaromir Hladik, Emil Schering) and by characters who read and compare translations. This is not a mere web of extravagant quotations; it is not simply erudition. It draws our attention, as twentieth-century readers, to the role that translation has played, to the disparate ways in which writers have interacted with their predecessors, and to the texts of the past that are comingled with those of the present.

Translation and cultural exchange in African literatures

African literature is rooted in an oral tradition. Unlike other parts of the world such as Europe, the Middle East and some regions of Asia, Black Africa does not have an ancient tradition of written literature, and hence does not have a long history of written translation. In precolonial times, pictorial writing was a common form of artistic expression among Cameroonian ethnic groups such as the Bamoums, Bamilekes and Betis, as it was in a number of other African cultures. It is possible, therefore, to speak of a certain kind of writing, as well as a certain kind of translation (the transcription of African narratives into Arabic characters, for example), which predate the arrival of the Europeans. Yet it was not until Christian missionaries arrived in the nineteenth century, bringing with them the Latin alphabet, that translation as it is now known began. The ensuing translation activity had an undeniable impact on the literatures of Africa, the chief result being the emergence of a literate culture.

In the African context, the very concepts of "national language", "national literature", or even "African literature", in general, are problematic. In the wake of Africa's encounter with the West, European languages have taken their place alongside native tongues, and some of them – such as English, French and Portuguese – have been given official-language status. Cameroon is a case in point: it is polyethnic and multilingual; English and French are the official languages, but there is also a *lingua franca* (Cameroon Pidgin English), along with well over 200 indigenous languages.[23]

The definition of African literature itself has been a controversial issue among writers and academics, as has been the choice of language: African writers have felt ambivalent about writing in a European language, which is not a mother tongue but rather the language of the colonizer (Gyasi 1999: 75). In his book *Decolonising the Mind*, Kenyan writer and translator Ngugi wa Thiong'o (1986: 27) says that African literature can be written only in African languages. In an opening statement to his book, he bids farewell to the English language and promises to write in Gikuyu and Swahili thereafter. And yet he does not close the door to continued dialogue through the "age old medium of translation" (1986: xiv). Translation, in fact, brings about "dialogue between the literatures, languages and cultures of the different nationalities within any one country – forming the foundations of a truly national literature and culture, a truly national sensibility!" (Ngugi 1986: 85; quoted in Gyasi 1999: 82).

Another prominent writer, Chinua Achebe, believes that African literature may be written in adapted forms of European languages. In a 1964 essay published in *Morning Yet on Creation Day*, Achebe writes about whether African writers *ought* to write in English: "I feel that the English language will be able to carry the weight of my African experience. But it will have to be a new English, still in full communion with its ancestral home but altered to suit its new African surroundings" (Achebe 1975: 62). Drawing on new resources, the English language is thus re-appropriated to express the imagination of the African writer (Gyasi 1999: 76). Achebe makes a distinction between *national literature*, written in a language such as English, which is *national* in the sense that it can be understood across an entire territory, and *ethnic literature*, written in a native tongue and available to only one ethnic group within the territory. From this perspective, African literature is seen as the sum total of the national literatures and the various ethnic literatures, a "group of associated units" (Achebe 1975: 56).

Another point of view has been expressed by Richard Bjornson in his study of the writing of Cameroon. Whereas eighteenth- and nineteenth-century European states "crystallized around an existing cultural or linguistic community", he points out, nearly all African states inherited a multiplicity of linguistic and ethnic communities. As a result, many Africans continued to identify with their own ethnic groups and did not have a strong sense of attachment to the emergent nation in which they had been born. Yet even in these "ethnically pluralistic societies", further fragmented by religious, political and regional differences, a sense of national identity has begun to evolve, in large part thanks to print culture (Bjornson 1991: 3–6). Despite the language issue, the "proliferation of literary voices" and the "fragmentation of purpose", emergent literatures in African countries reflect "shared reference points". For Bjornson, then, the term *national literature* provides a "legitimate framework for understanding the diversity of literary production in Africa" (Bjornson 1991: 17–18), a framework which he used in his examination of a broad spectrum of literary texts within one particular country, Cameroon.

As the previous chapter has shown, the first missionaries who arrived in Cameroon stimulated the development of African languages. They contributed, similarly, to the evolution of literature in its written form. Rev. Joseph Merrick (1808–49), a Jamaican of African ancestry, joined an expedition to Cameroon led by the Baptist Missionary Society of London. In 1844–45, he founded the Jubilee Mission, the first successful mission on the Cameroon coast. Merrick translated the New Testament into the Isubu and Douala (Duala) languages, which he produced on a printing press he set up. He also began work on instructional materials in Isubu and a Douala-English glossary. Alfred Saker (1814–80), another Baptist missionary, arrived shortly after Merrick and is credited with having founded the Cameroon city of Limbé, formerly Victoria. He also studied the Douala language and published translations of the Bible: the New Testament in 1862 and the Old Testament in 1872. Although criticized subsequently for his literal translations, Saker's publications helped give an impetus to literary work in African languages.

Dr. Adolf Vielhauer (1880–1959), a German missionary, translated the Bible into Mungaka, another Cameroonian language, in collaboration with an indigenous teacher and preacher, Elisa Ndifon (1888–1971). They were assisted by Anna Hummel and Elizabeth Buhler and a team of native Mungaka speakers. It took thirty years to complete the project; the translation of the whole Bible into Mungaka was published in 1961, two years after Vielhauer's death. Reflecting on his work as a translator, Vielhauer made a number of observations that have much in common with those of translation scholars such as Eugene Nida. In order to make biblical truths acceptable to "readers in the grassfields of the Cameroons", for example, he felt it was necessary to make certain environmental adjustments, such as using "leopard" for "wolf" and "bear", and substituting "wine tree" for "vine" (Dah 1986:18–19). Not only did Vielhauer enrich the repertoire of Mungaka literature through his translations of European literature, primarily biblical texts, he also helped enhance and promote the native tradition by collecting and publishing oral literature. In 1910, he published *Tsu Mana* (*Folklore*), a collection of well-known parables and proverbs derived from the Mungaka culture, laying the foundations for one of Cameroon's more vibrant national literatures.

Isaac Moumé Etia (1889–1939) was one of the early indigenous translators in Cameroon. Proficient in four European languages – German, French, English and Spanish – he was a cultured man of letters who worked as an *écrivain-interprète* in the German and French colonial administrations of Cameroon.[24] Both a translator and prolific writer in his own right, Moumé Etia published extensively: folk tales, books on language, and translations from European literatures. He also expressed his views on some aspects of translation theory.

One of Moumé Etia's most popular works was a collection of oral literature entitled *Fables de Douala*, published in a bilingual edition (French-Douala) in

1929. In this pioneering work, he analyses traditional Douala religious literature, ordinary short stories and tall tales. He also translated well-known fiction from Western languages into Douala – for example, *The Thousand and One Nights*, which he translated from Antoine Galland's French version as *Ikol'a Bulu Iwo na Bulu Bo* (1938) and which led to several later adaptations by other Douala writers.

In addition to his own creative work, Moumé Etia produced grammar books and dictionaries aimed at facilitating the work of other writers. These works are still valuable today because they contain some original idiomatic expressions and proverbs in Douala which would have otherwise disappeared by now as a result of language interference. Moumé Etia's unpublished work, completed before his death in October 1939, includes a collection of Douala proverbs and folk tales entitled *Le petit recueil de proverbes douala*, intended to provide a legacy of wisdom for his people. The collection also contains some Douala translations of foreign proverbs which have served to enrich the target culture literature.

As scholars reflect on these events from the vantage point of postcolonialism there has been a tendency to view translation – of missionaries, Orientalists, anthropologists, for example – as an "expression of the cultural power of the colonizer". Translation is seen as "part of the violence […] through which the colonial subject was constructed" (Simon and St-Pierre 2000: 10–11). While he "bridged the gap between people of different cultural backgrounds", Moumé Etia's work collecting, transcribing and translating oral literature from Douala to the languages of the colonial administration was not "well received" by indigenous people of his time, who viewed him as "as a traitor who was not only exposing their culture to the Whites but was co-operating with them" (Nama 2009: 53). It was by virtue of his elevated status as an écrivain-interprète, on the other hand, who "facilitated communication between the two camps" through a range of "administrative, political, cultural and diplomatic functions", that Moumé Etia was subsequently evaluated by one of his own countrymen – Charles Nama – as a monumental figure in the history of Cameroon. He is regarded not only as one of the "pioneers of linguistic nationalism" analogous to the European intellectuals of the Renaissance, but also a writer and translator who helped shape the future of Douala literature (Nama 2009: 48–49).

Literature in East African countries such as Tanzania, Kenya and Uganda was also given new direction by authors who wrote in the national languages and also translated foreign literature (Nama 1990b: 75–86). Translation of works of literature in the post-independence era was pioneered by Mwalimu Julius Kambarage Nyerere (1922–99), former president of Tanzania, who translated Shakespeare's *Julius Caesar* into Swahili. With this translation, Nyerere achieved considerable acclaim in East Africa, where Swahili is widely used.[25] Literature in the Gikuyu (or Kikuyu) and Acholi languages in Kenya and Uganda has also thrived in East Africa as a result of the contributions of major authors such as Ngugi Wa Thiong'o and Okot p'Bitek (Figure 7).

The Ugandan writer and translator Okot p'Bitek (1931–82), like Joaquim Dias Cordeiro da Matta of Angola, Eno Belinga of Cameroon, Wole Soyinka of Nigeria and Ngugi Wa Thiong'o of Kenya, is notable because of his achievements in translating from African into European languages and vice versa. After studying law and social anthropology in Great Britain, he became a lecturer at Makerere University in Uganda. When he later became unpopular with the Ugandan government, he took up posts outside the country and returned to Makerere at the end of the Idi Amin regime.

Okot p'Bitek, like Moumé Etia in Cameroon, was one of the pioneers of literature in his country. His first novel, *Lak Tar* (1953), was recognized as one of the most outstanding works in an African language. He later published several major poems in his native Acholi language, which he then translated into English. *Song of Lawino: A Lament* was published in 1966 and was internationally acclaimed. This work was followed, among others, by *Song of Ocol* (1970) and *Horn of My Love* (1974), translations of traditional oral verse. These works have contributed significantly to the development and enrichment of Acholi literature in particular and African literature in general. Since the publication of p'Bitek's poems, other African writers have emulated him and produced epic poems in national languages. His work has also been translated into French, Spanish and German.

P'Bitek's translation method deserves special mention. In the preface to *Horn of My Love*, he writes: "Here is the poetry of the Acoli[26] people: their lullabies and love songs, their satirical verses, their religious songs and chants, their war songs and funeral dirges" (p'Bitek 1974: ix). He then explains how he has structured the book. In Part One, he discusses the different occasions on which the songs are sung; in Part Two, the texts are set out with the Acholi and English versions side by side. In Part Three, p'Bitek analyses the themes in the songs themselves, examines the role of poets as historians and finally explains "praise names"[27] and provides a glossary of warriors' titles.

P'Bitek stresses that the translations are his own, one version among many possible ones. It is for this reason that he includes the original vernacular, to allow other translators to criticize as well as to attempt their own translations. Translation in *Horn of my Love* takes place on many levels: p'Bitek translates from an oral tradition to a written language (he uses the term "vernacular"); he translates from an African language to a European one; and he reads, explains and in a sense "translates" his own culture for a wider audience. The interesting feature of this "explicative" method is that it paves the way for further translations, or re-translations, and hence for dissemination of the Acholi literature and culture. This potential for continued transmission enhances and promotes the national literature.

This is an example of how an African writer can resolve the difficult choice between writing in the language of the colonizer or writing in his native vernacular. Thus, African literature, as Paul Bandia (2008) has shown, can provide an enlightening case study for postcolonial translation theory. The integration of the oral tradition into written literature is, in fact, a form of translation, which is supplemented in p'Bitek's case with translation into a European – or colonial – language. This "double movement from an oral tradition to a writing culture and from a peripheral colonized language to an imperial or colonial language" goes beyond the "binary oppositions" of traditional translation theory (Bandia 2008: 5), celebrating the hybridity and in-betweenness theorized by Homi Bhabha (1994). This approach, Bandia concludes, is "particularly pertinent in today's world, where constant relocation, displacement and migration have rendered cultural boundaries obsolete, creating hybrid identities and border cultures" (Bandia 2008: 169).

It has become less relevant, therefore, to view translation within the context of nation building. Economic, political and cultural networks of exchange on a global scale have ushered in a new postnational order, in the context of which the concept of "nation" is no longer the primary determinant of identity (Appadurai 1996). Taking place in a new era of cosmopolitanism, translation has become a "process of hybridization", an "activity of critique and intervention" with broad cultural implications (Simon 2002: 139) – one of which is the suggestion that translation studies become the "new disciplinary framework through which literary exchange is studied" (Bassnett, quoted in Simon 2002: 132).

Notes

1. The French poet Guillaume de Salluste du Bartas (1544–90) was the author of a grandiose and influential encyclopedic and biblical epic known as *Les Sepmaines*, referring to *La Sepmaine ou Création du monde* (1578) followed by *La Seconde Sepmaine* (1584) which Du Bartas did not complete.

2. Huig de Groot (1583–1645), known by his Latin name Hugo Grotius, was a Dutch jurist, philosopher, theologian, poet and playwright.

3. Second only to Johan van Heemskerck's 1641 translation of Corneille's *Le Cid.*

4. Gerrit Janszoon Vos (1577–1649), more commonly known by his Latin name Gerardus Vossius, was a Dutch scholar of the classics, Hebrew and theology.

5. The play was presented in the form of an *aemulatio* of the neo-Latin *Jephthes* written around 1545 by George Buchanan (1506–82), and took into account later criticism of Buchanan's play voiced by humanists from Daniel Heinsius to Vossius.

6. Vondel translated Sophocles's *Oedipus Rex* and *The Trachinian Women*, which he called *Hercules in Trachin*. He also translated two plays by Euripides, *Iphigenia in Tauris* and *The Phoenician Women*, the latter largely based on Grotius's Latin version.

7. *Lorna Doone* (1869), a historical romance by English novelist R. D. Blackmore; *The Last of the Mohicans* (1826), a historical novel by the American writer James Fenimore Cooper; *Hajji Baba of Ispahan* (1824), a picaresque romance of Persian life by British diplomat and author James Morier; *Irish Nationality* (1911), by Irish historian and nationalist Alice Stopford Green; *The Path to Rome* (1902), British Catholic Hilaire Belloc's account of his pilgrimage to Rome; *The Wallet of Kai Lung* (1900), a collection of fantasy stories of ancient China by English author Ernest Bramah; *Daddy-Long-Legs* (1912), an epistolary novel by the American female writer Jean Webster (pseudonym for Alice Jane Chandler Webster); *Mrs. Wiggs of the Cabbage Patch* (1901), a novel by the American female novelist Alice Caldwell Hegan Rice; *The Undying Monster* (1922), a werewolf masterpiece that later inspired a popular horror film, by Jessie Douglas Kerruish.

8. With the current secessionist government in Scotland planning a referendum in 2014 on the question of independence, it is not yet clear how the political relationship to the United Kingdom will evolve.

9. *Les Belles-Sœurs* was written by Michel Tremblay (b. 1942) in 1965. It was first produced at the Théâtre du Rideau Vert in Montreal in 1968. It is believed to be the first work of theatre to use *joual*, a form of Quebec French spoken at that time by the working classes. The term "*québécois*" is used here to refer to Tremblay's language, since it is more general than "joual", which strictly speaking applies to the sociolect spoken in Montreal, and which has also had negative connotations in some circles.

10. These are all authors of national and international prestige. Molière (1622–73) was a French classical playwright known for his comedies; Aristophanes (c.446–c. 386 BCE) was an eminent comic playwright of ancient Athens; Goldoni (1707–93) was a Venetian playwright and author of opera *libretti*; Kleist (1777–1811) was a German dramatist and author; Holberg (1684–1754) was a writer, historian and playwright who is considered the founder of modern Norwegian and Danish literature.

11. Received Pronunciation (RP), also referred to as the Queen's (or King's) English, is the accent used in standard spoken English. While not intrinsically superior to regional forms of English, RP has long enjoyed prestige in relation to other varieties.

12. *The Globe and Mail* [Toronto], June 1, 2000. Quoted by Raymond Ross in his obituary of Bill Findlay, *The Scotsman*, May 23, 2005 (http://news.scotsman.com/obituaries/Bill-Findlay.2628820.jp, accessed August 2010).

13. *The Real Wurld?* (*Le vrai monde?*) and *Hosanna* (*Hosanna*) were staged in 1991; *The House Among the Stars* (*La maison suspendue*) received separate productions in 1992 and 1993; *Forever Yours, Marie-Lou* (*À toi, pour toujours, ta Marie-Lou*) was staged in 1994; *Albertine, in Five Times* (*Albertine, en cinq temps*) was produced in 1998; *Solemn Mass for a Full Moon* (*Messe solennelle pour une pleine lune d'été* was staged and published in 2000; and their last Tremblay collaboration, *If Only ... (Encore une fois si vous permettez)*, was performed in 2003. Findlay and Bowman also worked on Scots versions of plays by other Quebec playwrights: Dominic Champagne, Michel-Marc Bouchard and Jeanne-Mance Delisle (Bowman 2000: 25). Findlay introduced Scots audiences to works by other foreign authors: Gerhart Hauptmann's *The Weavers*; Pavel Kohout's *Fire in the Basement*; Teresa Lubkiewicz's *Werewolves*; and Raymond Cousse's *Bairns' Brothers*. Bowman has worked in collaboration with Wajdi Mouawad on adapting Harry Gibson's dramatization of Irvine Welsh's *Trainspotting* for the stage in Montreal (1998).

14. These articles, written in 1925, 1926 and 1928, were later published in *Discusíon* and *Historia de la eternidad*. See Borges 1932 and 1936.

15. The article was originally published in *Discusión* in 1932, but was subsequently reissued.

16. Leaders of heretical doctrines or movements.

17. *Bildung* signifies not only education or "culture", but also the method or process of acquiring or constructing it (Berman 1984: 72).

18. The story originally appeared in the journal *Sur* in May 1939, and was later included in the collection *Ficciones* (1944).

19. Apart from the ones already mentioned: "El Ulises de Joyce" (1925); "Las dos maneras de traducir" (1926); Prologue to Paul Valéry, *El cementerio marino* (translated by Nestor Ibarra, 1931); "Lawrence y la Odisea" (1936); "Walt Whitman; Canto a mí mismo" (1942); "Sobre el doblaje" (1945); "Cansinos-Asséns y Las mil y una noches" (1960); "Las mil y una noches" (1980); "El Traductor" (1985).

20. Borges translated from German, French and English. Among the authors he translated were Franz Kafka, André Gide, Villiers de l'Isle Adam, Hart Crane, T.S. Eliot, James Joyce, Rudyard Kipling, Herman Melville, Eugene O'Neill, Edgar Allan Poe, Carl Sandburg, Wallace Stevens, Rabindranath Tagore and Walt Whitman. He also translated from Old English: *Beowulf, The Seafarer*, etc. The anthologies to which Borges contributed contain texts in other languages translated into Spanish by other people.

21. *Antología de la literatura fantástica* (1940), *Cuentos breves y extraordinarios* (1955), *Libro del cielo y del infierno* (1960), *Libros de los seres imaginarios* (1967), *Libro de sueños* (1976).

22. All of whom appear in *Translators through History*.

23. According to Intersol Inc.'s *Global Advisor Newsletter*, Cameroon has 286 indigenous languages, 279 of which are currently living languages, which fall into 24 major African language groups (http://www.intersolinc.com/newsletters/africa.htm, accessed June 2011).

24. The *écrivain-interprète* was the forerunner of today's translators and interpreters. Among the most educated indigenous citizens of the time, they had considerable power and prestige, more perhaps than today's translators. In the colonial era, the role of the *écrivain-interprète* was not limited to translation and interpretation, but included administrative duties and creative writing in both African and European languages. The terms "secretary-interpreter" and "interpreter-secretary" have also been used in various contexts (see Chapter 9), but were not common in Cameroon.

25. Swahili is the official language of Tanzania and Kenya. While it has less than two million native speakers, it has become a *lingua franca*, spoken by an estimated 50 million people. After Arabic, Swahili is the most widely understood language in Africa, where it plays a crucial role in the economic, political, cultural and social life of the region, to the detriment of English in many cases (UCLA Language Materials Project, http://www.lmp.ucla.edu/Profile.aspx?LangID=17&menu=004 , accessed June 2011).

26. P'Bitek uses the spelling "Acoli", but "Acholi" is more widely used.

27. For example: *Bwanga-moi* is the title bestowed on "One who throws only one spear and puts the enemy to flight" and *Abel-moi* denotes "One who puts the enemy to flight" (p'Bitek 1974:176).

Figure 7. Okot p'Bitek

Figure 8. Matteo Ricci

CHAPTER 4

Translators and the dissemination of knowledge

Ever since the invention of writing, people have attempted to acquire the technical and scientific know-how of their neighbours. In their age-old quest for what has been perceived as "utilitarian" knowledge, they have translated extensively. There is no doubt that such a process of borrowing, or appropriating, the findings of others has led to the dissemination and development of science and technology. Yet the goal of translators has not been restricted to enriching their own nations with new information; they have often sought to further research itself. Acting as educators, and not simply as the educated, translators have used the knowledge gained from their work to contribute to the advancement of science in general. The translators of history should not be regarded as passive conduits of specialized information, but rather as agents fully implicated in the work they have reformulated in another language.

"Translation was the key to scientific progress", according to Henry Fischbach, "as it unlocked for each successive inventor and discoverer the mind of predecessors who expressed their innovative thoughts in another language" (1992: 194). Like any other mode of translation, and perhaps more so in some circumstances, technical and scientific translation is an instrument of cross-fertilization, transformation and progress. As Italian Renaissance philosopher Giordano Bruno (1548–1600) said, "From translation all science has its offspring". Translation is a source of inspiration, rather than an end in itself; it stimulates reflection and acts as a point of departure for further research. Consequently, translation and the commentary which accompanies it often merge, as do reproduction and creation in the work of the scientific and technical translators of the past.

Without translators, "the great pollinators of science" (Fischbach 1992), science would not have achieved the universal status that it now has. Through an examination of translation activity over the centuries, we can map the migration of knowledge and culture from major centres of learning in Asia (China and India) to Greece, from the Middle East to Europe, and then to the Americas. Since the time of ancient Greece, certain cities stand out as places where cultures converged, and where translators and scholars met. The torch of knowledge was passed through Athens, Alexandria, Rome, Byzantium, Edessa (Urfa in modern Turkey), Jundishapir (Iran), Baghdad, Cordova, Toledo, Salerno, Florence, Paris and London. From Antiquity to the present time, the language of science in the West and the Middle East has successively been Greek, Arabic, Latin and English. In the modern age, the work of past and contemporary researchers is disseminated the world over. No one country, however powerful, no one city, however prestigious, can claim to be the sole repository of human knowledge. The work of translators has resulted in the proliferation of centres of learning and their very proliferation continues to provide work to translators around the world.

In the earliest days of developing civilizations, the scarcity and cost of writing materials such as papyrus, vellum and parchment were obstacles to the advancement of science and hindered the production of translations, in general, and scientific translation, in particular. The invention of paper (c.105), attributed to Cai Lun (Ts'ai Lun)[1] of China, was critical for the circulation of translations. When the Arabs occupied Samarkand (in modern Uzbekistan) in 712, they, too, learned how to produce thin sheets from a pulp made of linen fibres. The first paper manufacturing plant was established in Baghdad in 794. The development of the paper industry led to an increase in the number of translations and a new demand for books. Paper was soon available throughout the Islamic world, which reached from the Indus Valley on the Indian Subcontinent to the Pyrenees. However, it took three centuries before paper reached Western Europe. It first appeared in Spain in the twelfth century, and the first paper manufacturers in France date from the middle of the fourteenth century. Printing, which was not possible until paper was readily available, developed over the course of the following century and stimulated both paper manufacturing and translation activity. Translations, after all, were the main products of the first printing presses.[2] The introduction of paper in the Arabo-Islamic empire had the same impact on the circulation of translations as printing presses in Europe did during the Renaissance. It was thanks to paper and printing that scientists and translators were able to have greater access to the scientific work of others and to build on it in the pursuit of knowledge.

The work of translators, which is never just a shift between two languages but between two cultures (Umberto Eco, quoted in Burke and Hsia 2007:7), led to a transfer of knowledge between China and Rome even before the Common Era (Needham 1954). The Alexandrian school, established in 322 BCE, was the site of exchanges between Europe, the Middle East and India as well as an important centre for Hellenistic studies in which translation played an important part. Nestorian Christians, expelled from the Byzantine Empire after their patriarch Nestorius was condemned for heresy by the First Council of Ephesus (431), settled in what is now southwestern Iran. There, they were responsible for translating the great authors of ancient Greece, along with Indian, and even some Chinese, medical texts. Ancient Greek and Syriac manuscripts were translated into Arabic in Baghdad in the ninth century. In the twelfth century, these Arabic translations, many of which had outlived their originals, were translated into Latin in Spain. Many of these Latin translations, medical works particularly, were subsequently retranslated into vernacular languages throughout Europe during the Middle Ages and the Renaissance.

During the Renaissance, there were two opposing tendencies: a renewed interest in classical languages and, with the emergence of nationalistic sentiment, an increasing use of vernacular languages. Starting with the Renaissance, but since the seventeenth and eighteenth centuries in particular, this democratization of knowledge and ever-expanding readership has given scientific and technical translation a didactic dimension. Translators became popularizers. Their mission was to explain, inform and instruct nonspecialists, such as laboratory assistants and apprentices who worked alongside their masters but did not understand Latin. In the fields of pharmacology, chemistry and physics, translators acted very much like teachers in that they introduced and explained the works they translated to a less enlightened readership. Two seventeenth-century translators, Jean Marcel de Boulenc and Nicholas Culpepper, were typical. De Boulenc translated a chemistry textbook by Oswald Croll into French, simplifying the material and describing the chemical processes step by step for a student readership. Culpepper, too, simplified the scientific documents he translated. In translating some of Galen's treatises for laymen, for example, he attempted to break the monopoly of knowledge held by the medical profession (Kelly 1979: 86–87).

This chapter begins in China, where translators were instrumental in the introduction of Buddhism and subsequently the Western knowledge of medicine, astronomy and mathematics. India is the next stage of the journey. From the nineteenth century onward, scientific translation there was a barometer of cultural exchange and a determining factor in progress and development. A study of Arab translators in the Middle Ages shows how translation can feed into scientific research and contribute to the development of a scientific language. The so-called Toledo School, a celebrated milestone in the development of scientific thought, is a further example of how translators disseminate existing information and also generate knowledge. An examination of translation in Scandinavia will shed light on how translators of some internationally known works have helped spread spiritual and human values. The chapter concludes with the appearance of machines in the working lives of translators, a development that by now has its own history and an ineluctable connection to the future of the profession.

China: importing knowledge through translation

The earliest translation activities in China date back to the Zhou (Chou) dynasty (c.1100 BCE). Documents of the time indicate that translation was carried out by government clerks, who were concerned primarily with the transmission of ideologies. It was not until the Han dynasty (206 BCE–220 CE) that translation became a medium for the actual dissemination of foreign knowledge. Buddhism, which originated in India and was unknown outside that country for a very long time, began to penetrate China toward the middle of the first century. Between 148 and 171, An Shigao, a Persian, translated some Sanskrit sutras, or precepts, into Chinese, and at the same time introduced some elements of Indian astronomy to China. In the fifth century, the Indian Buddhist monk Kumarajiva (c.350–c.410) lived in Kashmir and then in China, where he translated a large number of sutras. This initiated a school of translation that later flourished and enabled Buddhism to take root in China. From the time of Kumarajiva until the eighth century, the volume of translations increased and their accuracy improved.

Translating and importing knowledge became common practice during the Tang dynasty (618–907), a period of grandeur, expansion and flowering of the arts. Translation continued to be put to this use until the Song dynasty (960–1280). The invention of xylography (wood engraving) in the ninth century facilitated the spread of written material. In 718, the Indian army officer Xida Qutan translated an Indian almanac of astronomy which he published under the title *Jiu Zhi Li*. While the contribution of this book was not significant, given the advanced state of Chinese knowledge in the field, it did introduce a number of trigonometric functions and arithmetic symbols (Li 1993: 16–17). In addition, some twenty Indian books on pharmacology and medicine, ophthalmology in particular, were translated during this period.

One of the most famous monks of the Tang period was Xuan Zang (Hsuan-tsang) (c.600–c.664), a native of Henan province (Figure 12).[3] In 629, he left Chang'an (modern-day Xi'an), then capital of the empire, where he had gone in search of a spiritual master. He set out on a pilgrimage, on a quest for sacred texts in India (Watters 1904–05). He returned in 645, bearing relics and gold statues of Buddha, along with 124 collections of Sanskrit aphorisms from the "Great Vehicle" and 520 other manuscripts.[4] A caravan of twenty-two horses was needed to transport these treasures (Beal 1895: xviii–xx). The Emperor Tai Zong (T'ai-Tsung) gave him a triumphal welcome and provided him with every possible comfort.

At the request of the monk, the Emperor had the "Great Wild Goose Pagoda" built for him in Chang'an (Figure 22). Xuan Zang spent the rest of his life in this sumptuous pagoda, inspired by Indian design, and worked with his collaborators on the translation of the precious Buddhist manuscripts he had brought back. These translations helped to make Buddhism popular throughout China. "Team" translation was the method used for this large-scale undertaking: a foreign monk would recite the scriptures, which were then translated orally into Chinese by a native speaker; this was transcribed into written script and then polished stylistically. This tradition of team translation has been passed down ever since (Lin 2002: 161).

From the Yuan (1280–1368) to the Ming (1368–1644) dynasties, the translation of sutras took on less importance. As Yuan rulers directed their attention westwards, Arabs began to settle in China, becoming mandarins or merchants. Having learned Chinese, some erudite high officials translated scientific works from Arabic or European languages. The Arab Al-Tûsî Nâsir Al-Dîn (1201–74) translated Euclid's *Elements*, some works of astronomy including Ptolemy's *Almagest*,[5] and Plato's *Logic*. An Arabic pharmacopoeia *Al-Jâmiᶜ fi-al-Adwiya al-Mufradah* (Dictionary of Elementary Medicines), made up of thirty-six volumes listing some 1,400 different medicines, was translated toward the end of the Yuan dynasty. This was published during the following dynasty as *Hui Hui Yao Fang*. Later the Ming Emperor Zhu Yuanzhang ordered two mandarins of Arab origin, Ma Hama and Ma Sayihei, to translate two Arabic books on astronomy with the help of two officials, Li Chong and Wu Bozhong. Beyond satisfying the curiosity of a few scholars, these works are alleged to have had minimal scientific merit, given the already advanced state of knowledge in China.

The situation was to change toward the end of the sixteenth century. With the arrival of Christian missionaries, the Jesuits in particular, China came into contact with Europe, which had begun to overtake China in some scientific and technological fields. To facilitate their relations with Chinese officials and intellectuals, the missionaries translated works of Western science as well as Christian texts. From 1582, the year when Jesuits initiated work in China, until 1773, when the Society of Jesus was dissolved and the Jesuits left, seventy-one missionaries of various nationalities undertook this kind of work. They were Italian: Matteo Ricci (1552–1610) (Figure 8), Nicolaus Longobardi (1559–1654), Sabbathinus de Ursis (1575–1620), Julius Aleni (1582–1649) and Jacobus Rho (1593–1638), whose Chinese names were Li Madou, Long Huamin, Xiong Sanba, Ai Rueno and Luo Yagu, respectively; Portuguese: Franciscus Furtado (1587–1652), whose Chinese name was Fu Fanji; Swiss: Jean Terrenz (1576–1630), known as Deng Yuhan; Belgian: Ferdinand Verbiest (1623–1688), known as Nan Huairen; with a contingent from France, Germany and other places (Ma 1995: 377–78). The missionaries were often assisted by Chinese collaborators such as Xu Guangqi, a distinguished scientist and prime minister during the last years of the Ming dynasty, a period of intense scholarship and intellectual activity; Li Zhizao, a scientist and government official; Wang Zheng, an engineer and government official; and Zue Fengzuo, a scientist. Matteo Ricci was assisted by Xu Guangqi when he translated Euclid's *Elements* in 1607 and by Li Zhizao when he translated the *Astrolabium* by German Jesuit and mathematician Christophorus Clavius. For these scholars, translation was not confined to passive reproduction; instead, the translated text served as a basis for further research. Li Zhizao, for example, uses his preface to *Astrolabium*, the first work to set out the foundations of Western astronomy in Chinese, to make the point that the Earth is round and in motion.

With their translation of Clavius's *Trattato della figura isoperimetre* (Treatise on Isoperimetric Figures), published in 1608, Ricci and Li Dang introduced the concept of equilateral polygons inside the circle. In 1612, a six-volume translation by De Ursis and Xu was the first Chinese work on hydrology and reservoirs; it also dealt with physiology and described some of the techniques used in the distillation of medicines. As he translated, Xu performed experiments. Thus, he used the book he was in the process of translating as a kind of textbook, and translation was in turn a catalyst leading to new discoveries.

Translations were carried out in the fields of mathematics, astronomy, medicine, law, literature and religion. A 1613 translation by Ricci and Li showed how to perform written arithmetic operations: addition, subtraction, multiplication and division. They also introduced the Chinese to classical logic via a Portuguese university-level textbook brought in by a missionary in 1625.

In 1644, the Qing (Ch'ing) dynasty replaced the earlier, more scholarly Ming Dynasty.[6] Conflicts between the missionary order and the Pope, as well as between the Christians and the Manchu court, diminished the influence of the Church. Translation into Chinese all but stopped for roughly a hundred years with the expulsion of foreign missionaries by the Yongzheng Emperor in the eighteenth century. It resumed following the British invasion (1840–42) and the subsequent arrival of American, British, French and German missionaries. Foreign missionaries dominated scientific and technical translation initially, but Chinese translators, trained in China or at foreign universities, gradually took over the transmission of Western knowledge.

A leading figure during this period was the Chinese mathematician Li Shanlan (1811–82), who collaborated with the British missionary Alexander Wylie (1815–77) on a translation of a work on differential and integral calculus. The Chinese mathematician Hua Hengfang (1833–1902) and the British missionary John Fryer (1839–1928) translated a text on probability taken from the *Encyclopedia Britannica*. In 1877 Hua and Fryer translated Hymers's *Treatise on Plane and Spherical Trigonometry* (1858). This translation is a good example of how knowledge is both transmitted and generated through the translation process. It contributed to the dissemination of modern mathematical theory and, at the same time, stimulated the personal research carried out by the translators. Fryer and his collaborators also translated approximately one hundred chemistry treatises and textbooks. Many of these were published by the Jiangnan Ordnance Factory, where Fryer and Xu were the official translators.

The earth sciences, too, were introduced to China through translation. During the Opium War,[7] Lin Zexu, a Chinese official, translated part of the *Cyclopaedia of Geography* by Murray Hugh. Published in 1836, it was the most up-to-date work on world geography at the time. Wei Yuan (1794–1857) and Zi Jishe (1795–1873) made extensive use of this translation to compile their own book on world geography. By the end of the Qing dynasty, many medical books were available in Chinese. Ding Dubao (1874–1952), a physician and translator, was responsible for over fifty medical translations. He was awarded national and international prizes for his role in translating and disseminating works of medicine and pharmacology.

Just as translators helped open China to Western knowledge, they brought China to the attention of the West by reproducing classical Chinese works in foreign languages. These works of philosophy, politics, education and military science enabled Europeans to become acquainted with the long history and rich civilization of China. The translators, European sinologists living in China and working in close collaboration with Chinese scholars, included missionaries Martin Martini (1614–61), Antoine Gaubille (1689–1759), Jean Joseph Amiot (1728–93), Pierre Marchal Cibot (1727–80), and Ernst Faber (1839–99). Published in bilingual editions and accompanied by copious explanatory notes, these translations helped make the rest of the world more familiar with Chinese culture.

The missionary and sinologist James Legge (1815–91) was particularly distinguished. While abroad, primarily in Hong Kong, he applied himself to the study of the Chinese language and traditional writings. He translated and published a substantial body of work from Chinese into English, notably in collaboration with the scholar Wang Tao (1828–97). He believed it was his duty to be a "missionary to his own people and race […] to translate and explain the learning of the East to the scholars and missionaries of the West" (Ride 1970:10). Ultimately, he dedicated more of his career to his translations from Chinese than he did to his missionary work, leaving Hong Kong and going on to become the first professor of Chinese at Oxford University.[8]

After a series of sporadic periods of translation activity over its long history, China is currently experiencing what has been called a new "wave of translation". Dating from the opening to the outside world in the late 1970s, it is a comprehensive and intense movement encompassing all areas of knowledge (Lin 2002: 168). Connected with this surge in practical translation is a growing body of research by Chinese scholars working in the field of translation studies.

India: at the crossroads of translation

Translation has always been an important element in the intellectual life of India, a country with a strong tradition of multiculturalism and multilingualism. This section will highlight certain translations, scientific ones in particular, that were instrumental in the transmission of knowledge.

By the sixth century BCE, India had already established cultural ties with Mediterranean peoples, and toward the beginning of the Common Era also began to trade with Ptolemaic Egypt and Byzantium. This ushered in a period of fruitful cross-fertilization in both directions, eastward and westward. Indian thought influenced some of the medical theories found in Plato's *Timaeus*, in works by Roman physicians and encyclopedists, and in the writings of the Greek physicians Dioscorides and Galen (Filliozat 1964; Sen 1972).[9] In the year 150, a Greek astrological text, written in Alexandria a hundred years earlier, was translated into Sanskrit by Yavanesvara in Ujjain, in central India (Pingree 1963:229–246 and 1978). Astrology, in fact, emerged in India as a consequence of the study of Greek, and quickly achieved popularity (Filliozat 1963a:139). Indian scientific knowledge was transmitted to Tibet, from where it was passed on to the Mongols, as well as to some pockets of China, Japan, Indochina and Indonesia.

Between the third and the fifth centuries, as seen earlier, numerous Chinese and Buddhist scholars translated works of astronomy, mathematics, pharmacology and logic that had originated in India. For the most part, these translations have been lost, but the translation activity has been recorded and the titles listed in catalogues compiled during the Song and Tang dynasties (Sen 1972:45). From the seventh century onward, contacts with Arab traders along the Malabar coast resulted in the exchange of medical expertise between Indians and Arabs. A number of medical references of Indian origin can be found in the work of Rhazes (Al-Râzî, c.860–c.925), an Arabian physician and philosopher of Persian origin. The thirteenth-century translations of his work into Latin became standard texts in medieval Europe.

Cultural exchanges between India and other countries declined in the late Middle Ages and, as a direct consequence, the volume of translation also decreased. Indian scholarship became withdrawn and inward-looking. In the Middle Ages, the state of Indian science was comparatively advanced since learning had previously been imported from the Arab world into India by Muslims, as some studies have shown (Rahman et al. 1982). Translation was limited, however. In the sixteenth and seventeenth centuries, work in the fields of astronomy, mathematics and medicine took the form of commentaries on earlier research.

In the early years of the sixteenth century, Western science was introduced to India by travellers and merchants. The Portuguese were the first Europeans to arrive in India, establishing a colony on the west coast in 1510. They were followed by the Dutch in 1595 and the British, who formed the British East India Company in 1600. The presence of foreigners in India generated a new demand for translations. Jesuit missionaries, travellers and political envoys began to learn Sanskrit and other Indian languages. They gathered manuscripts in the fields of literature, religion, linguistics and philology, thereby laying the foundations for centres of Indian studies in Europe as well as in India itself. This activity resulted in a significant amount of translation from Sanskrit into European languages. In 1699, in the *Mémoires de l'Académie Royale des Sciences*, the French astronomer Jean-Dominique Cassini published his translation of an anonymous Hindu manuscript on astronomy, which had been sent to him by the French Mission of Siam (Sen 1972).

Translation also played a role in encyclopedic research. The English Orientalist and scholar William Jones (1746–94) produced an exhaustive compilation of Indian history, literature, science and religions, relying in part on translations. He was responsible for founding the Asiatic Society in London in 1784, initiating Oriental studies and the study of Sanskrit and actively promoting the translation of Sanskrit works into European languages. He also put forward the theory that Sanskrit was the source of Indo-European languages. Jones founded the journal *Asiatic Researches*, which published original contributions as well as new and old translations. Many translators took part in this vast enterprise, which spanned nearly two centuries, from 1690 to 1882.[10]

The work of Henry Colebrooke (1765–1837) greatly influenced later translators and historians of mathematics. His *Algebra with Arithmetic and Mensuration, translated from the Sanskrit of Brahmegupta and Bhascara* (1817) contained annotated translations from the *Brahmasiddhanta*, a work on astronomy and mathematics, and two treatises on algebra entitled *Bijaganita* and *Lilavati*. The latter was also translated into English by John Taylor in 1816. Written between 800 and 500 BCE, the *Baudhayana-Sulbasutra* is the oldest and most important work of Indian mathematics. It was published in 1874–75 by German Orientalist Georg Friedrich Wilhelm Thibaut (1848–1914), accompanied by an English translation, notes and excerpts of a commentary by Dvarakanatha Yajva, a sixth-century scholar who was the commentator and author of the *Sulba-Dipika*. From 1879 to 1888, Thibaut was director of the Sanskrit College in Benares (or Varanasi, a sacred city for Hindus in northern India). He founded the journal *Pundit*, which contained previously unpublished Sanskrit texts and translations of ancient Sanskrit manuscripts.

Beginning in the 1890s, a collection of ancient Sanskrit and Prakrit medical texts known as the "Bower Manuscript", named for the person who rediscovered them, was translated into English by Rudolph Hoernle (1841-1918), another

Orientalist (Hoernle 1987).[11] The nineteenth century saw the publication of many translations that had been completed long before but had remained unpublished. One such example was the work of Abul Faizi ibn-Mubarak (1547–95), an Indian Muslim poet of Persian origin, who had translated Bhaskaracharya's celebrated Sanskrit work on mathematics, *Lilavati*, into Farsi (Persian). He had also translated, or supervised the translation of, parts of the *Mahabharata*, a celebrated epic poem.[12] It is said that Faizi changed his name and went to Benares to study under a Brahmin scholar. He learned Sanskrit and studied the vedas for nearly ten years, with a view to translating them into Persian.[13] But he also fell in love with the Brahmin's daughter. The father was delighted to marry his daughter to his disciple, but when he learned that Faizi had concealed his identity, he forbade him to continue his studies and translations, as well as to publish what he had already translated.[14]

It is more difficult to evaluate the role that translation into Sanskrit or other Indian languages played in the transmission of knowledge, for lack of well-documented studies. The history of the migration of knowledge in the direction of India has yet to be written. Some fragmentary evidence does exist, however. As we have seen, the sixteenth century was a turning point for India as far as relations with Europe were concerned. One century later, European expertise in astronomy was introduced to India. With the help of astronomy texts from Arabia, Europe and India, Maharaja Sawai Jai Singh II (1699–1743), an astronomer in his own right, established five observatories and invented some of the optical devices used there. The astronomical tables he constructed were later found to be extremely accurate. His chief astronomer Jagannatha Samrat (1652–1744) translated Ptolemy's *Almagest* and Euclid's *Elements* from Arabic into Sanskrit under the titles of *Samrat-Siddhanta* and *Rekhaganita*, respectively. Jai Singh, known as the "astronomer prince", is credited with being the author of *Yantraraja*, a treatise on the design and construction of astrolabes, but this is possibly a translation from either Persian or Arabic (Sen 1972: 56).

The role of the translator in transmitting knowledge between linguistic communities and across generations of scholars is amply illustrated by a 1730 translation by Nayanasukhopadhyaha, entitled *Ukarakhya Grantha*. This Sanskrit geometry treatise was translated from a collective Arabic version, itself translated from a Greek original (Sen 1966). This kind of "relay" translation is not unlike the translations that found their way to medieval Europe, part of a chain in which the original had been Greek and its links Syriac, Arabic, Latin and vernacular European languages, successively.

In the early nineteenth century, the use of the vernacular in the teaching of science was gaining ground in Bengal and Delhi, following pressure from the intellectual elite, who called for greater accessibility to knowledge and opposed the cultural imperialism of Macaulay's educational system.[15] It was felt that translations should no longer be the exclusive province of a minority of scholars. Translation into the vernacular was a fundamental component of the campaign to popularize science, which had been taken up by various educational associations. The establishment of the Native Medical Institution in 1824 and courses in medicine at the Sanskrit College and Calcutta Madrassa (literally a "school") in 1826 required the translation of numerous European textbooks into Sanskrit, Bengali and other local languages. Between 1868 and 1910, at least ten scientific journals and forty-seven technical publications appeared in Bengali. The efforts to express modern science in Indian languages extended to other regions of India such as Madras, Bombay, the Punjab and the Oudh, a region in the modern-day state of Uttar Pradesh (Krishna 1991: 95).

The role of scholarly organizations in the popularization of knowledge was crucial. In 1843, an association for vernacular translation was founded in Delhi, under the auspices of Old Delhi College. Mathematician, author and scientific writer Yesudas Ramachandra (1821–80), a student and later professor at the College (Figure 9), translated Tate's *Elements of Mechanism* into Urdu under the title *Risala Usual Kalon ke bare main* (1863). Translation and creation went hand in hand for him. According to Syed Ahmad Khan, who founded a similar society in 1864, "Those who are bent on improving India should remember that the best way to do this is through the translation of all the arts and sciences into their own languages [...]" (quoted by Irfan Habib and Raina 1989: 605). Similar views were expressed by Maulana Imdad Ali, founder of the Bihar Scientific Society in 1868: "England, France and Germany would have never attained the exalted state of civilization which they now enjoy if works of science, originally from Rome and Greece, had not been introduced to the people in their own vernacular tongues" (Irfan Habib and Raina 1989: 605). In this context, translation is a determining factor in cultural development and an important component of identity politics.

A "multi-layered encounter", the transfer and acculturation of knowledge is complex; science and technology is seen as "Janus-faced: heralding economic prosperity, while presaging spiritual and cultural doom" (Raina and Irfan Habib 1993: 93–96). Indian scientists attempted to integrate Western scientific thought into their own culture – not without debate, however, as rationality came into contact with traditional ways of knowing. The scientific community was associated with the political elite in the process of decolonization (Raina and Irfan Habib 2004).

Baghdad: centre of Arabic translation

In the ninth and tenth centuries, the city of Baghdad in Iraq was the centre of a vast and ambitious translation enterprise: the aim was to translate the scientific and philosophical works of Ancient Greece into Arabic, the language of the new Muslim Empire. A large number of Syriac, Persian and Sanskrit texts were also translated. This project, which had a profound influence on the development of scientific and philosophical thought in the Muslim world, cannot be understood in isolation from the ethnic, cultural and intellectual upheaval that the region was undergoing at the time. There had already been a long tradition of studying the treasures of Ancient Greece and translating them into Syriac (ancient Aramaic). This tradition was perpetuated and translation encouraged by caliphs and other sponsors, who rewarded translators generously and even paid them salaries, as Arab chroniclers have reported.[16] The spread of writing throughout Islamic civilization also helped foster translation into Arabic.

By the mid-eighth century, the ᶜAbbâsids had become the ruling dynasty of the Islamic empire. In 762, the caliph al-Mansur built Baghdad and made it his capital. Under ᶜAbbâsid rule, many Persian practices were adopted, including that of translating foreign works. A palace library, modeled after the Sassanid (pre-Islamic Persian) Imperial Library, was established. Known as the *bayt al-hikma* or "House of Wisdom", the library was most certainly a storehouse or archive; it is also thought to have been the site of translation activity.

The extent to which the House of Wisdom or indeed the Baghdad movement as a whole, can be called a "school" has been debated, in much the same way as the qualification of Toledo as a "school" has been the subject of discussion, as will be seen in the following section.[17] "Much ink has been used unnecessarily on descriptions of the *bayt al-hikma*", writes Dimitri Gutas, "mostly in fanciful and sometimes wishful projections of modern institutions and research projects back into the eighth century". Gutas advocates a "minimalist interpretation" of what he believes was merely a library, where, moreover, translations were made, not of Greek manuscripts, but of Persian texts. He does concede, nevertheless, that the *bayt al-hikma* created a climate in which the Graeco-Arabic translation movement, described below, could thrive (Gutas 1998: 54–59).

As Islam began to spread toward the end of the seventh century, the new rulers set about creating certain structures and imposing Arabic as the official language. The first texts translated into Arabic were administrative: archival documents and registers. The translation of scientific texts occurred later. The appropriation of Greek culture, often via intermediate Syriac versions, reached its peak in the ninth and tenth centuries thanks to the Baghdad translators, the most celebrated of whom was Hunayn ibn Ishâq (809–75), also known by his Latin name, Johannitius. The Arabs were most interested in medicine and philosophy, but astronomy, too, was popular, reflecting contacts and trade with India. While the choice of texts was often dictated by the state (for purposes of Arabization of imperial structures, for example), the interests of individual caliphs and courtiers were equally important. Al-Mansur, who came to power in 753, was fascinated by astronomy; he apparently acquired many manuscripts on the subject from India and had them translated. Al-Ma'mûn, successor to Hârûn al-Rashîd, the hero of several stories in *The Thousand and One Nights*, was a follower of the Muᶜtazalite movement.[18] In an attempt to reconcile reason, in the Aristotelian sense of the word, and faith, al-Ma'mûn encouraged the translation of Greek philosophical writings and their commentaries into Arabic.

Hunayn and his many collaborators are credited with having translated a number of major works: Plato's dialogues and *The Republic*; Aristotle's logical treatises, known as the *Organon* and which included the *Categories*, the *Topics*, the *Analytics*, and the *Metaphysics*; *Isagoge*, an introduction to Aristotle's *Categories* by Porphyry, one of the principal founders of Neoplatonism; and *The Book of Causes* (*Liber de Causis*), attributed in medieval times to Aristotle, but in fact based on the *Elements of Theology* by the Neoplatonist and last major Greek philosopher Proclus. If the original Greek manuscripts were available and if translators with the necessary linguistic skills could be found, some of the translations were made directly from Greek into Arabic However, few translators were sufficiently proficient in both Greek and Arabic, particularly in the early years of this period. The Greek works were sometimes retranslated, either from previous Arabic or older Syriac versions, some of which had been produced by Nestorians expelled from Byzantium in the fifth century. Syriac was thus a frequent intermediary language.

What held the most appeal for the translators and their sponsors was the entire Hippocratic and Galenic corpus, along with such seminal works as Euclid's *Elements* and Ptolemy's *Almagest*. The earliest Arabic translators of scientific and philosophical texts date back to the eighth century: Yûhannâ Mâsawaih, Ibn al-Bitrîq and Ibn Jibrîl. In the following century the names of Al-Hajjâj ibn Matar (c.786–c.835), Ibn Lûqâ (820–912), Ibn Nâᶜima al-Himsî (c.835) and Ibn Qurra (834–901) figure prominently. In the ninth century, Ishâq ibn Hunayn and Hubaysh al-Aᶜsam, the son and nephew of Hunayn ibn Ishâq, respectively, worked under his supervision. Later Yahyâ ibn ᶜAdî and Mattâ ibn Yûnis undertook the revision of previous translations, seeking to improve both form and content. All this activity helped to enrich and consolidate Arabic as a scientific language.

The translators were often specialists in the field in which they translated, although the term is perhaps inappropriate for a time when knowledge was far less fragmented than it is today. Yûhannâ Mâsawaih and Hunayn ibn Ishâq were themselves established physicians. The high quality of Hunayn's translations, in fact, has been attributed to his medical expertise. He is credited with translations of Galen, and with original works: *Medical Questions, Treatise of the Eye* and *Treatise of the Teeth*. Furthermore, he laid the foundations for ophthalmology, on which Rhazes based part of his work.

During this particular period, the role of translators in the transmission of knowledge – and the volume of translation was indeed considerable – should not overshadow their creative activity. The translated text was not an end in itself, but a catalyst that stimulated original reflection and the production of knowledge. Translations were often accompanied by commentary, summaries or explanatory notes intended to make the original texts more intelligible and to complement them by answering some of the questions they raised. Drawing on their source texts, translators exercised their own inventive capacities, introduced fresh ideas and fuelled new debates. Thus translation helped establish a new system of thought that was to become the foundation of Arabic-Islamic culture – both on the conceptual and terminological levels. One or two centuries earlier, Syriac translators had inserted parallel commentary in their renderings of Greek philosophical works, adding a layer of their own Neoplatonic ideas. Later on, the twelfth-century philosopher Averroës (1126–98) would try to restore Aristotelian thought to its unadulterated state, retranslating the texts without the cumbersome additions of earlier Syriac and Arabic translators.

Translation is useful in the generation of new concepts, particularly when the translated text is integrated into a given system of thought. In his Arabic translation of a work by Proclus, Ishâq ibn Hunayn refers to "God Almighty", instead of using the Hellenistic concept of causation or the principle of "the One" (Badawî 1968:72). This approach can be compared with that of the Toledan translators, who avoided any references they considered "unorthodox" so as not to offend their Christian readers (Foz 1988).

Translators also exercised their creativity when it came to producing appropriate terminology. The early Arabic translators were frequently obliged to use transliteration, partly because their command of Arabic was not always adequate, but also because the language itself had not yet acquired the necessary philosophical and scientific lexicon. When these early translations were revised – sometimes only a century later – transliterated terms were replaced with neologisms that were more in keeping with the morphological structures of Arabic. In his revision of the Arabic translation of Dioscoride's *Materia Medica*, Hunayn recommended Arabic equivalents for the Greek terms which had been employed by the original translator, Istifân ibn Bâsil.

Translators contributed to the dissemination of knowledge in part through their quest for precious manuscripts. History contains repeated references to translators and their sponsors who went to great lengths to acquire Greek manuscripts and establish the authenticity of the texts before undertaking their translation.

The work of Arabic translators was not always addressed to a strictly learned readership. Although their work was usually commissioned by a patron or scholar, it was sometimes carried out with didactic intentions. Hunayn, for instance, sometimes translated for the benefit of his medical students, and he urged his collaborators to pay particular attention to intelligibility and clarity. Hunayn mentions in one of his *Epistles* that he had added an "explanation of difficult passages" in a Syriac translation of a commentary on the Hippocratic *Oath* (Hunayn 1925: 40). In his translations, he aimed for a style that could be understood by someone "who was not a medical specialist, or who was unacquainted with philosophy" (quoted by Ibn Abî Usaybiᶜa 1882: 191).

The flourishing translation enterprise that occurred in ninth-century Baghdad was a determining factor in the Arab assimilation of the cultural treasures of China, India, Persia and, above all, Greece. Intense translation activity continued throughout the empire until Arab dominance ended in the thirteenth century. The translated works acted as raw material that nourished the creative talents of Arab translators and furthered the development of science before being passed on to the Western world. The next significant step in the transmission of knowledge occurred in the twelfth and thirteenth centuries, as the hub of translation moved westward.

Medieval Spain: cultural exchange and rebirth

The term "Toledo School" has been used for nearly two centuries to designate the flourishing translation activity that took place in Spain during the twelfth and thirteenth centuries.[19] In recent years, some scholars have endeavoured to dispel, disprove or clarify the set of ideas associated with the city. The concept has been dismissed as a myth: "The notion of a 'School of Toledo' (in very capital-letter senses) has been mythologized in such a way as to make its historical coverage as broad as possible" (Pym 2000: 56). To begin with, translation activity extended beyond Toledo to reach other parts of the Iberian Peninsula, or Hispania. The idea of a school at which courses might have been given to translators has also been disputed: "There was no *foundation*, and consequently nothing was *founded*, by any archbishop; there was no *collège* […] no *courses* whatsoever […]" (Santoyo 2006: 33).[20]

The work of translating, compiling, annotating and spreading knowledge, on the other hand, was so vast and the individual accomplishments so difficult to evaluate, that it is perhaps understandable that such a concept was used to refer to the collective effort required. New perspectives in translation history have enabled scholars to more fully assess the far-reaching impact of the "Toledo" translators, not only for Spain but for Western civilization in general, and to take account of the complexity and ambiguity of relations among the three traditions, Arab, Jewish and Catholic, that came together in medieval Spain. Foz (1998) and Pym (2000) do just that, setting aside the now outdated and overly simplistic term "Toledo School" and providing a more nuanced narrative of the history of translation across two distinct periods, the twelfth and the thirteenth centuries.

This activity was centred on the philosophical and scientific achievements of the Greek and Arab world – in medicine, mathematics, astronomy and astrology, in particular. The so-called "school" was fundamental to the transmission of scientific and philosophical knowledge to medieval Europe. In the twelfth century, translations were essentially from Arabic to Latin, whereas in the thirteenth century they were from Arabic into the Spanish vernacular. There is no doubt that the translators of that period radically altered the state of knowledge in the West. The rediscovery of Aristotle through the commentaries of Averroës and Avicenna stimulated scholastic thought in the new universities. The introduction of key works of Arabic scholarship to Europe brought breadth of knowledge and a more comprehensive view of the world. The Western world became acquainted with the Arabic system of numeration and algebra, the Ptolemaic geocentric system in which the world is believed to be the centre of the universe, and the works of Hippocrates and Galen, along with an important body of other Greek and Arabic medical knowledge.

Historical research has shed some light on the significance of these translations. Translators themselves, however, have not yet been given sufficient credit for having served as the architects of this so-called "twelfth-century Renaissance", whose impact on intellectual growth and renewal was so great. They have remained what Antoine Berman labelled the "forgotten ones" (Berman 1989: 677). It is important, therefore, to investigate the role they played in generating, spreading and popularizing knowledge, and to identify the ideological and material constraints to which they were subjected.

The relationship between translation and creation is crucial in this particular case, as it was in the case of the Baghdad school, since the work took place at a time when there was a striking imbalance between the state of knowledge in the source culture (Arab Spain) and the receiving culture (Spain of the Reconquest).[21]

As an illustration of this situation, the library of the order of Cluny contained only a few hundred books (Haskins 1970: 43),[22] while perhaps as many as 300,000 Arabic manuscripts were kept in Toledo (Werrie 1969: 205). The involvement of the scholars who set about translating this huge stockpile into Latin was complex: they first discovered then assimilated new knowledge; at the same time, they had the task of communicating it to their own culture, in which access to knowledge was restricted to an extremely small educated elite. Difficult material conditions affected the work of translators, as did their relations with those who held power, as the next chapter will show.

This translation enterprise was undertaken in a social and cultural milieu which in the twelfth century was dominated by the Church and the set of *auctoritates* it imposed, the "authorities" being celebrated classical authors, scholars and theologians. However, by the following century, while scholars were in certain cases members of the ecclesiastical establishment, this affiliation was not a condition for practising translation. Alfonso X (1221–84), a deeply religious patron of learning, exercised control over translation in his time (Figure 14).[23] The change in status of Jewish translators between the twelfth and thirteenth centuries is particularly revealing. In the twelfth century, it was essential for translators to be associated with the Church. Those who did not convert to Christianity were employed as mere intermediaries, whose role it was to provide an oral version of Arabic texts in the vernacular. In the thirteenth century, Jewish translators assumed a more central role, practising their craft openly, even though they were in a situation of obvious allegiance to the king. This is reflected in the way in which they are often designated in prologues to works of translation: *nuestro iudio* (our Jew) or *nuestro físico* (our physician).

The approach to translation – the extent to which it was constructive and creative – depended largely on the translators' position in the power structure, and on the relationship between power and knowledge in general. Generally speaking, the translators of the twelfth century acted on behalf of the Church, actively engaged in recovering the legacy of the Greek and Arab worlds. In the thirteenth century, on the other hand, they tended to serve secular patrons. The knowledge to which scholars had access by virtue of their work as translators was put in the hands of their patron, then refined and "processed" in accordance with his requirements. At that time, learning was based on quotation and commentary, and creation consisted simply in emulating ancient models. Scholars were expected to refer to an authority, whether it be St. Augustine or Aristotle (Eco 1985: 499).

Translators adapted the texts they worked on. This was not simply a matter of individual preference, but rather a reflection of the material and ideological constraints related to writing in Latin or the Spanish vernacular. In the twelfth century, formal changes were made in accordance with Latin conventions of presenting information. In addition, certain historical and geographical references specific to the Arab tradition were judged to be irrelevant and were omitted. The constraints to which translators were subject varied considerably. This can be illustrated by comparing two different versions of the same text, or by examining critiques or admonitions expressed by certain translators with regard to the work of their colleagues. The difference in approach is evident, for example, in two Latin translations of Ablumasar's *Introductorium majus*. The first version, made in 1133 by John of Seville (John of Spain, 1110–80), is extremely literal and includes a substantial introduction (the equivalent of about sixty pages today) entitled *Tractatus primus*. The introduction to the second version, *Liber primus*, produced in 1140 by Hermann of Dalmatia (c.1100–c.1160) is only about twenty-four pages (Lemay 1962:24).[24] It is known that Robert of Chester (fl. 1150),[25] one of Hermann's closest collaborators, had warned him against cutting too much from the source text, a common pitfall among Latin translators of the time who were unaware of the Arabic tradition of historiography and rhetoric. The reason given for the omissions was the verbosity of the Arabic writings. But, as Robert of Chester pointed out, a translator could easily be discredited in the eyes of any reader in a position to refer to the original (Lemay 1962:21).

Under the patronage of Alfonso X in the following century, translators had less leeway. Emendations had more to do with the important task of creating and defining terminology for an emerging Spanish vernacular.

Translation was a creative activity based on a given text, but not limited by it. This resulted from some of the conditions under which the transmission of knowledge took place – copying as the sole method of manuscript reproduction, and an ill-defined concept of intellectual property. To an even greater extent, the political context of the quest for knowledge shaped the way in which translators approached original texts.

Dissemination of knowledge occurred in slightly different ways in the twelfth and thirteenth centuries. In the twelfth century, both the environment and working methods of translators favoured the spread of knowledge. For instance, many translators had to go in search of their raw material, or source texts, themselves. Some translators left their own country in search of Ptolemy's *Almagest*: Gerard of Cremona (1114–87) set off from Italy, Michael Scot (1175–1234) from Scotland and Adelard of Bath (c.1116–c.1142) from England. Others, like Mark of Toledo, returned home after having worked and studied abroad.[26] The Latin translators contributed to the circulation of texts through their travels, especially as they sometimes came home to teach what they had learned. In many cases, work was carried out by two scholars working in tandem. The team of Abraham bar Hiyya (c.1065–c.1136) and Plato of Tivoli (fl. mid-twelfth century) is a particularly interesting example of this phenomenon: like many others at the same time, they translated works from Arabic into Latin, and also translated Abraham's treatise on geometry, *Liber embadorum*, from Hebrew to Latin via vernacular Spanish.[27] This kind of undertaking was perhaps more an expression of personal interest, and the interrelationship between translation and research that existed at the time, than a result of any systematic policy regarding the dissemination of knowledge.

On the other hand, translation and creation can be differentiated in the works of one of the best known Latin scholars of the time, Adelard of Bath. His translations resembled rough versions, working documents intended for his own personal use or for specialists, probably students, while his own original works were more polished and definitive (Burnett 1990). This is also discernible in the work of other translator/authors of the period, such as Domingo Gundisalvo.[28] Translation from Arabic into Latin was used by scholars as a means of exchanging knowledge among themselves, rather than making it accessible to a wider audience, or, to use an anachronistic expression, popularizing it.

In the thirteenth century, greater emphasis was placed on dissemination of knowledge. This was related to changes in the practice of translation and its subdivision into separate functions (primary translators distinct from assistants, for example). Prefaces frequently alluded to the value of vernacular texts for the learned, or *omnes entendudos*. Behind these general declarations lay a more specific project: translation into Castilian Spanish. In the West, Alfonso was one of the first sponsors of translation on a large scale, commissioning a set of texts in the vernacular that came to be known as the *Book of the King*.

The translators of Spain were popularizers to varying degrees, although we must bear in mind that the concept of a mass readership is a modern one, with no real equivalent in medieval society. In this respect, translation carried out in the twelfth century differed the most from that of the following century. Latin, the language of the Church and of scholarship, was chosen as the target language during the twelfth century. Rather than seeking to communicate information in a clear manner, and to a broader readership, translators appeared to be far more concerned with enhancing their own knowledge. This is evident in the widespread use of the following translation strategies: transliteration (which led to the introduction into Latin of many unknown and incomprehensible words), semantic borrowings (which assigned specific scientific meanings to existing terms in the target language) and abbreviations (for which no explanations were provided).

In the following century, on the other hand, the adoption of the Spanish vernacular as the target language, together with Alfonso's insistence that texts should be *llanos de entender* (easy to understand), indicated a new desire to move beyond the ecclesiastical community and transmit knowledge to wider circles. The emphasis placed on "terminological" research (to use a modern expression) reflected efforts to extend the resources and reach of the target language.

The study of creation and popularization in relation to the work of the Toledo translators raises the issue of the appropriation of knowledge through translation. To begin with, Latin works of science and philosophy were scarce. The sponsors of translation (mainly clerics in the twelfth century and the king in the thirteenth), and the translators who worked under their patronage, sought in the twelfth century to incorporate foreign knowledge into a Latin framework, and in the thirteenth century to forge a Spanish culture on the basis of this storehouse of knowledge. As in the other examples examined, translation was carried out in a political context, one in which the development of a national language was associated with the affirmation of national identity.

The Nordic countries: breaking down the barriers of isolation

In the Nordic countries, translators introduced the Latin texts that were authoritative in the religious and legal spheres in medieval Europe. In addition, they preserved the oral tradition of northern European mythology, which took the form of Viking sagas and the Finnish *Kalevala*, by translating them into Latin or the vernacular. In more recent times, Nordic translators have played an important role in the transmission of works both to and from German, English and French. Since the nineteenth century, translators have introduced the rest of the world to works by the Danish author Hans Christian Andersen (1805–75) and philosopher Søren Aabye Kierkegaard (1813–55), the Norwegian playwright Henrik Ibsen (1828–1906) and the Swedish playwright and novelist August Strindberg (1849–1912).

Intermittently, translations into the Scandinavian languages have helped to break down the isolation characteristic of the northern region. This is as true for the period following Christian conversion which began in Denmark, Norway and Iceland in the tenth century, and in Sweden in the eleventh, as it is for the second period of cultural renewal that occurred in Scandinavia in the nineteenth century.

The Vikings were great travellers who traded as far afield as the Mediterranean basin and the west coast of Africa. Caches of medieval Arab coins found in Sweden are evidence of trade links between Arabs and Vikings. The Vikings, however, did not produce anything that comes close to the wealth of translations done by the Arabs, who played a similar role on the world scene at roughly the same time (800–1050). A possible explanation is the nature of the Viking alphabet: the use of the runic alphabet was confined to relatively short inscriptions on stone monuments. Translation in any nation depends on the availability of an effective writing system and a national language, as seen in previous chapters. Until the arrival in the tenth century of English Christian missionaries who encouraged the adoption of the Latin alphabet, literature in the region had been limited to orally transmitted folk ballads and sagas.

The first missionaries to arrive in Scandinavia played a dual role in cultural and religious communication. Their efforts to bring Christianity to the warlike peoples of the North first bore fruit in the tenth century, with the baptism of the Danish King Harald Blaatand ("Bluetooth") around 960. As was the case elsewhere, monasteries were not merely religious institutions, but centres of learning, where manuscripts were compiled and preserved. While they introduced Christian values, the missionaries were not blind to the cultural heritage of the people they were converting and sought to preserve the original culture at a time when it was threatened by change. The major early works of Scandinavian literature, the Eddas and the Icelandic sagas, were recorded in Latin by monks or by authors educated by missionaries. They would probably have been lost otherwise.

A striking example of the contribution of translators to the dissemination of knowledge is provided by St. Bridget's *Revelationes*. The Latin text of the *Revelationes* was established from a Swedish original and retranslated into Old Swedish around 1380. With the exception of the *Corpus Juris*, which was fundamental to the establishment of the Swedish system of legislation, the translation of the Brigittine Revelations is regarded as the first major translation into Swedish. It heralded the standardization of the Swedish language undertaken by the Reformers in the sixteenth century.[29]

A Norwegian translation of the Bible was begun during the reign of Haakon V Magnusson in the thirteenth century, but some secular literature was also translated from Latin. For example, the *Life of Merlin* by Geoffrey of Monmouth, who had introduced the legend of King Arthur into European literature, was put into verse as the *Prophecies of Merlin* by a monk in Thingeyrar, in combination with a translation of Monmouth's *Historia regum Britanniae*. In a fourteenth-century manuscript, this text was preceded by the *Saga of the Trojans*, a translation of a text attributed to Dares Phrygius, a Trojan priest, which was well known in its Latin version in the Middle Ages. Numerous French works were also translated at this time.

After the year 1000, the nations of northern Europe sacrificed national identity and language in favour of Latin. It was not until around 1500 that their own writing began to emerge in the vernacular. Translations of Martin Luther provided an impetus for Scandinavian nationalism, and his versions of the Bible were quickly translated from German into both Danish and Swedish. Luther's Bible – his 1522 *New Testament* and his 1534 *Old Testament* – was all the more influential because it appeared not long after the development of printing technology. Scandinavian translations were fundamental to the region's break from the universalism of the Catholic Church, and influenced the development of the written form of the languages for centuries.

Latin, the international *lingua franca* of science and culture, was introduced to Scandinavia at a relatively late date, and remained in use there for longer than in many other European nations. Some of the great scientists published in Latin. Danish astronomer Tycho Brahe (1546–1601) attempted to reconcile the Ptolemic and Copernican astronomical systems in a work entitled *Astronomiae instauratae progymnasmata*, later edited by his pupil, the German Johannes Kepler, and published in Prague in 1602–03. The Swedish botanist Carolus Linnaeus (Carl von Linné, 1707–78) is considered to have been the first scientist to introduce a systematic classification of the species, first in botany, then in zoology. He published the results of his research in Latin in *Flora Lapponica*, which appeared in Amsterdam in 1737.[30] In 1841, when Kierkegaard submitted his master's dissertation, he had to petition the king for special dispensation to submit it in Danish, since Latin was still normally used for all scholarly writing. Permission was granted, but he was nonetheless obliged to use Latin at his thesis defence and for documents appended to the thesis.

German (Low German in the Middle Ages, High German after the Reformation) was used in cultural, diplomatic and commercial communication between Scandinavians and their southern neighbours, and was the source of numerous translations. During the seventeenth and eighteenth centuries, French was also central to Scandinavian culture, particularly toward the end of the eighteenth century at the court of the Swedish King Gustav III. It was only in the early years of the twentieth century that these languages began to be eclipsed by English.[31]

The humanist Christiern Pedersen (1480–1554) was one of the first scholars to encourage the development of Denmark's literature in the vernacular. He studied in Greifswald and took holy orders in 1505. Three years later, he travelled to Paris where he developed an interest in translation and the relatively new phenomenon of printing. In 1514, working with the printer Jodocus Badius, he produced the first complete print edition of the *Gesta Danorum* (Danish Chronicles), which had been written three hundred years earlier by Saxo Grammaticus.[32] He later translated this work into Danish and also compiled a Latin-Danish dictionary. Upon his return to Denmark, he supported the Reformation and became secretary to Christian II, following him into exile in Holland in 1525. There, Pedersen translated part of the New Testament (1529) and the Psalms (1531) into Danish. He also contributed to the Danish translation of the Lutheran Bible, which was printed in 1550.

Saxo's *Gesta Danorum* was again translated into Danish by Anders Sorensen Vedel in 1575, Sejer Schousbolle in 1752, Nicolaï F.S. Grundtvig in 1822, Winkel Horn in 1879 and Jorgen Olrik from 1908 to 1912. The most influential of these translators was Grundtvig, who also translated *Heimskringla* (Sagas of the Kings of Norway) written six centuries earlier by the Icelandic historian Snorri (1179–1241). In 1820, he produced Danish translation of the Anglo-Saxon epic poem *Beowulf*. He is considered the architect of Scandinavian identity through his attempts to revive the memory of Viking heroes and Norse Gods, while also circulating knowledge among Danish farmers, the backbone of the country's economy.

The first Finnish author of note was Mikael Agricola (c.1510–57), Bishop of Turku, who imported Lutheranism from Germany. He produced a primer in 1540, and a number of religious and educational works. His translation of the New Testament was printed in 1548, and that of some books of the Old Testament in 1551–52. A complete Finnish Bible was published in Stockholm in 1642.

Swedish rule in Finland, which was formalized by the peace of Nöteborg in 1323 and which continued until annexation by the Russian Empire in 1809, was not favourable to the development of Finnish literature. But after 1809, a spirit of nationalism developed and Finns began to write in their own language. The first edition of the *Kalevala*, the pre-Christian epic poem that had been handed down orally for centuries, was published in 1835 by the scholar and physician Elias Lönnrot, who had scoured the country in search of material used by folk singers. Lönnrot was instrumental in the development of Finnish technical and scientific vocabulary, and compiled a Finnish-Swedish dictionary (1866–80). With the stature of such universal works as the Indian *Mahabharata*, Homer's *Iliad* and *Odyssey* and the Old English epic *Beowulf*, the *Kalevala* has been translated into many languages: German, English, French, Russian and Japanese, for example.

It was through translation that many Scandinavian authors became a part of world literature: Andersen's stories are widely known in some ninety languages, Kierkegaard has had an important impact on modern philosophy, and the innovative plays of Ibsen and Strindberg have contributed significantly to contemporary theatre. Translators not only helped to bring foreign culture to the often isolated Nordic nations, but also ensured that their rich cultural achievements would be shared with the rest of the world.

Machine translation: machines as translators?

Translation activities have intensified in response to the explosion of information in an ever-wider range of fields and the increasing circulation of ideas across the globe. A vast amount of translation is carried out as part of the day-to-day work of research institutes, universities, laboratories, documentation centres, and national and international organizations.

"The modern world is like a huge translating machine, spinning faster and faster", Edmond Cary observed over a half a century ago (1956:62). With the staggering volume of material to be translated quickly and effectively, which coincided with shifting political imperatives and speed-of-light changes in technology, it was natural that humans would seek ways to harness the power of machines.

The idea of mechanized translation can be traced as far back as the seventeenth century although merely in the realm of "dreams". While applications for patents had actually been filed by the mid-1930s, what came to be known as "machine translation" (MT) arose only with the appearance of the first computers (Hutchins 2011:1). The origins of MT are generally attributed to a letter dated March 1947 from Warren Weaver of the Rockefeller Foundation to cyberneticist Norbert Wiener. In 1954, the first public demonstration of machine translation was given. The fruits of collaboration between IBM and Georgetown University, the results were impressive enough to stimulate large-scale funded research programs in the U.S. and throughout the world. The pioneers of MT came from a variety of backgrounds: engineering, physics, linguistics, and philosophy – all with different motives and approaches (Hutchins 2000:1).

The limitations of the early systems, which were essentially bilingual dictionaries, soon became apparent. Syntactical analysis was introduced in keeping with new developments in linguistics. During the first decade of research, "optimism remained high" (Hutchins 2000:3), a reflection borne out by Émile Delavenay (1905–2003), director of publications for UNESCO and founder of an association for automatic translation and applied linguistics. Delavenay sums up the state of machine translation on a similar note: "The general conclusion is one of optimism. Machine translations today are still very imperfect. But the way to perfecting them is clear" (Delavenay 1960:123).

Despite the early enthusiasm and hopes for MT, the quality of the output was disappointing and the hurdles significant: computers were expensive, not widely available, cumbersome to use, and limited in storage and speed (Hutchins 2000: 3–4). A now-famous report of ALPAC (Automatic Language Processing Advisory Committee) was released in 1966, concluding that there was no need for further investment. Research came to a virtual standstill in the U.S. for the ensuing fifteen years. There were some exceptions: SYSTRAN translated from Russian to English for the United States Air Force during the Cold War; a system was developed for use by the Commission of the European Communities; and METEO was developed at Université de Montréal for translating weather reports. Often cited as one of the rare successes in machine translation, METEO was used by Environment Canada for twenty years until it was replaced by another product.

The context for the initial research was the onset of the atomic age, as Delavenay points out in his introductory chapter, when "vast potentials of industrial power [were] available to serve the political ends of great empires" (1960:2). During the 1960s a relatively small number of users in the U.S. and Soviet Union were content with the crude output of machines in exchange for rapid access to scientific and technical information. By the mid-1970s, multilingual communities, international trade, and evolving political circumstances spurred a new demand for machine translation, in a greater number of subject areas, in Europe, Canada and Asia.

During the following decade, the advent of microcomputers and text-processing software created a market for cheaper MT systems, produced by a range of companies in different countries. MT enjoyed a revival in the 1980s, when "Cold War incentives were replaced by more pressing political and commercial demands" (Hutchins 2000:4), with two notable examples: the multilingual Eurotra system, designed to translate the seven, then nine, official languages of the European Community, and the Japanese CICC project, which came about with collaboration from China, Indonesia and Thailand. In the 1990s, speech translation was introduced, and in the first decade of the twenty-first century, the use of MT and translation aids spread significantly, extending from large corporations to individuals, many of them non-translators making use of MT applications on their personal computers and hand-held devices. Automatic translation is used online, in applications such as web pages, which require fast, but not necessarily fully accurate, real-time translations. MT is becoming a "mass-market product, as familiar as word-processing and desktop publishing" (Hutchins 2011:4).

The emergence of localization, "the linguistic and cultural adaptation of digital content to the requirements and the *locale* of a foreign market" (Schäler 2010:209), has developed since the mid 1980s, coinciding with advances in both personal computing and machine translation. Translators working in the field of localization use computer-assisted translation tools such as electronic terminology databases and translation memories. The content is "multimodal", involving not only text but graphics, audio or video, too (Schäler 2010:210–211).

Since its resurgence in the 1980s, then, MT has continued to make its mark. It clearly has a future, then, as well as a history. Forcada identifies both the "challenges" and "limitations" of MT today and draws the conclusion that MT will never replace human translators: "On the contrary, in certain situations that should be clearly evaluated, one can expect a *good* MT system to free translators from the most mechanical part of the translation task, so that their productivity increases to match the increasing demand [...]" (2010:222).

Ray Kurzweil, the American futurist and author of books on artificial intelligence, among other topics, predicts that, by the year 2029, computers will have human levels of language understanding and will therefore be able to do the same level of translating. He makes this claim with a significant caveat, however: the best human translators are not perfect, he says, particularly as far as literary translation is concerned, because each language has "its own personality". "Same" is therefore not equivalent to "perfect". In his view, the "epitome of human intelligence is our ability to use language" and tools derived from innovations in machine translation will "increase our ability to use, create, manipulate and translate language" (Kelly 2011). In this, he does not differ a great deal from Delavenay's contention so many decades earlier that it was not a matter of a "robot brain" replacing the human mind, but rather a "tool at the service of the human intellect" (Delavenay 1960: 1).

The preceding pages have provided but a glimpse of the vast history of the transmission, production and dissemination of knowledge. Through the ages, translators have been agents of change, transforming the content of the works they have transposed from one language to another.

The language of the target culture benefits from the work of translators, who are required to forge terms to convey the new concepts and realities they encounter. In Baghdad, in Toledo and other cities of twelfth and thirteenth century Spain, and in medieval Europe, translators helped develop a scientific language, a learned register for the vernacular, through borrowings or by stretching the resources of their own nascent languages. And the more the translated texts were integrated into the linguistic system and cultural fabric of the receiving culture, the more widely they were disseminated. Knowledge moved beyond the narrow circles of specialists who had access to Hebrew, Greek, Latin and Sanskrit, the traditional languages of scholarship, as translators helped legitimize the use of vernacular languages. Closer to our time, the empires of the past were replaced by independent nations and autonomous peoples, paving the way for translations that would provide them access to knowledge in their own languages. These achievements also coincided with a certain democratization of education that necessitated further translation, popularization and localization.[33]

In specialized fields, the book is no longer the primary medium for diffusion of information: newsletters, internal communications, journals, archival documents and patents have become increasingly important. Much information is not even produced in printed form, but is made available electronically, via audio and video tapes, DVDs, computer databases, and a wide range of technologies and increasing number of digital devices – all requiring the attention of translators. As a vehicle and as a tool, technology helps satisfy our increased appetite and need for knowledge, for as one observer said at the dawn of the age of machine translation, "more than ever before, scientific intelligence is impossible without translation" (Delavenay 1960: 2).

Notes

1. Chinese names are spelled according to the Pinyin system of transliteration. The Pinyin system was officially adopted by the People's Republic of China in 1979 to standardize Chinese in Western languages, replacing the previous Wade-Giles system used by English speakers. In this case Cai Lun is the Pinyin version and Ts'ai Lun (Tsai Lun) the Wade-Giles spelling. Where appropriate, the traditional or historic spelling is provided in parentheses and in some cases multiple variations are given in endnotes. Family names appear first, followed by given names, according to Chinese usage.

2. As discussed in Chapter 2 with reference to William Caxton, in particular.

3. Some alternative spellings are: Suan Zhuang, Zuanzang, Hiuan-Tsang, Hiuen Tsiang, Hiouen Thsang, Yuan Chwang and Hsuan Tsang.

4. The doctrine of Buddhism is founded on the oral teaching of Buddha (sixth century BCE) and is divided into two main sects: earlier Buddhism or the "Lesser Vehicle", which developed mainly in the north of the region (Tibet, China, Japan), and evolved Buddhism or the "Great Vehicle", which is more open to new ideas regarding religion, mysticism and cult. The "Great Vehicle" led to the formation of a variety of sects.

5. The *Almagest* was the most important work of the Greek astronomer Ptolemy (100–170 CE). From the Greek *megiste* ("the greatest" treatise or compilation), the Arabic text was known as *Takrir al-majisti*, hence the Latin name *Almagest*. Comprised of thirteen books combining previous knowledge and Ptolemy's own research, the *Almagest* remained the standard work on astronomy until the time of Copernicus. See also Chapters 5 and 7.

6. The Qing dynasty (1644–1911) was established in China by the Manzhou (Manchu) clan after the defeat of the Ming Dynasty in 1644. Its twelve emperors reigned until 1911, when the Republic was founded.

7. The First Opium War (1839–42) was provoked by China's efforts to seize a large consignment of opium which had been illegally imported by the British. The British besieged Canton and forced the Chinese to cede Hong Kong. The Chinese were also forced to return the confiscated opium and open several ports to European trade.

8. Legge will be examined further in Chapter 6 in the context of his translations of sacred Chinese texts.

9. Dioscorides (c.20–70) was the author of the oldest surviving text on drugs and their uses; Galen (c.130–200) was noted for his work in the field of anatomy.

10. Some other translators worth mentioning include Jean Sylvain Bailly, Ruben Burrow, Joseph Tieffenthaler, John Bentley and Léon Réodet. See Sen (1972: 44–70).

11. Prakrit refers to a group of ancient Indian dialects that derived from Sanskrit or evolved alongside it. The relationship between Prakrit and Sanskrit can be compared to that between classical and vulgar Latin. It is still the sacred language of Jainism.

12. The *Mahabharata*, a great epic of 120,000 verses dating from the Vedic era (c.1000 BCE), was immensely popular. It was translated in all the countries that were in contact with Indian culture, and provided their literature and art with numerous themes.

13. The vedas are a collection of sacred and poetic texts written in Old Sanskrit and constituting the first Indian literary documents. Vedism is the early form of Brahmanism.

14. This legend is reported by Alexander Don, author of a 1770 English translation from Farsi entitled *Farishta's History*.

15. Thomas Babington Macaulay (1800–59) was a British historian and statesman. From 1834 to 1838, he served in India, where he tried to establish a British-style educational system. He is also responsible for having drafted a penal code that became the basis of India's criminal law.

16. In particular Ibn al-Nadîm (fl. 987) in his *Fihrist* (Index). The main translators of the time received about 500 gold dinars a month. It is said that the Caliph al-Ma'mûn paid Hunayn ibn Ishâq the weight of his Arabic translations in gold, and that Hunayn became a rich man by working on specially heavy paper (Makdisi 1990:245).

17. Santoyo makes this point after critiquing the use of the term "school" in reference to Toledo (2006:32), citing Salama-Carr (1990), Pym (2000) and Gutas (1998).

18. In opposition to orthodox Islamic doctrine, the Muᶜtazalite sect held reason to be a source of religious knowledge. According to them, the Koran, as a creation, could not be eternal. The belief was adopted by Al-Ma'mûn, who in 833 imposed it as an article of faith.

19. The term "Toledo School" or "Toledo School of Translators" originated with the historian of Aristotelianism, Amable Jourdain, who first noted the existence of a "college of translators" in 1819, in a work published a year after his death (Foz 1998:172). The notion was perpetuated by the German classicist Valentin Rose, who in an 1874 article wrote about a formal "Schule von Toledo" (Santoyo 2006:31). Georges Mounin described Toledo as the "first true school of translators" (Mounin 1965:35, quoted by Pym 2000:36) and the idea has continued to "trickle down" and find its way into a variety of texts.

20. Although the label "Toledo School" has been called into question, the designation persists, including in Spain itself, where on December 3, 1986 a stamp entitled *Escuela de Traductores de Toledo* was issued in the series *Patrimonio cultural hispano islamico* (Cover illustration for Foz 1998). It is interesting to note, furthermore, that in an article entitled "The Imperial College of Santa Cruz de Tlatelolco", published in the same collection as that in which Santoyo's 2006 paper appears, there is a reference to the "famous Toledo School founded by Bishop Ramon" (Arencibia Rodriguez 2006:263). One contributor may be setting the record straight, but the editors of *Charting the Future of Translation History*, Georges Bastin and Paul Bandia, have not taken a stand.

21. The Reconquest (*Reconquista* in Spanish) refers to the period of approximately 800 years during which Christians succeeded in regaining control of the Muslim-held areas of the Iberian Peninsula, ending with the defeat of the Moors in 1492.

22. This religious order, whose name came from the city of Cluny in France, occupied all the bishoprics in Spain at the time of the Reconquest.

23. Alfonso (Alonso) X, Spanish King of Castile and Leon from 1252 to 1284, was more of a scholar than a statesman. In addition to commissioning scholars to translate works of science from Arabic to Castilian, he had them compile a code of law and write a history of Spain. A writer, poet and astronomer in his own right, Alfonso, known as Alfonso the Wise, is also considered the founder of the Castilian language.

24. A cleric of Slavic origin, who had the Latin names Hermanni Secundi and Hermano quoque Dalmatia, as well as the French names of Herman de Carinthie and Hermann le Second. He should not be confused with another translator named Hermann, a monk of German origin who died around 1272, and who had the Latin names Hermannus Germanicus and Hermannus Teutonicus (Gil 1974).

25. The English cleric is referred to in several ways: his medieval names as they appear in various documents are Robertus Ketenensis or Reteninsis; in English, he goes by the names of Robert of Chester or Robert of Kent, although it is not certain where he was actually from; in French texts he appears as Robert de Rétines, Robert de Ketton and Robert de Chester; he is also known as Roberto Castrensis, Roberto Cestrensis, Roberto Retinensis, Roberto Ostiensis, Roberto Ketinensis, Roberto Astensis and Robertus Anglicus (Gil 1974).

26. See Chapter 7.

27. They are also known as Abraham bar Hiyya ha-Nasi, Abraham Judaeus Savasorda, or simply Savasorda, and Plato Tiburtinus. Abraham bar Hiyya did not live in Toledo; he grew up in al-Andalus, Muslim governed territory, and later worked in Barcelona. He served as an intermediary, translating from Arabic to the vernacular, which Plato of Tivoli would then translate into written Latin (Foz 1998:44).

28. This canon of the Toledo cathedral was also known as Gundisalvi, Gondisalve and Gonzalva. He produced translations from 1130 to 1170, and was one of the first to translate Avicenna.

29. See Chapter 2.

30. An English version of Linnaeus's work, entitled *Lachesis Lapponica*, was published in 1817.

31. The works of the Swedish chemist K. W. Scheele (1742–86) were translated into English by J. G. McIntosh in 1901 and again by L. Dobbin in 1931.

32. Saxo Grammaticus (c.1150–1220) was a Danish cleric and scholar. He is credited with writing the first full history of Denmark, a heroic epic that combines both history and mythology. Most of the original manuscripts were lost. Pedersen went in search of an existing copy, which he finally located in the collection of the Archbishop of Lund. In collaboration with Jodocus Badius (Josse Badius or Josse Bade) (1462–1535), a professor at the Sorbonne and eminent printer and scholar, he issued an edited version, in Latin, under the title *Gesta Danorum*. This version was the source of all translations, one of which was a translation into Danish made by Pedersen around 1540. Pedersen's translation was never published and was lost in the great fire of 1728, which destroyed the library of the University of Copenhagen. Vedel, however, had access to it when he carried out his re-translation of the work (Boserup 1981:9–11).

33. Translators, in fact, contributed to the circulation of certain theories of education. Veronese Guarino (c.1370–1461) translated a well-known work by Plutarch on the education of children in 1411, giving a powerful impetus to the development of modern pedagogical thought. Similarly, the 1564 Polish translation of a book on education by Pietro Paolo Vergerio, done by Marcin Kwiatkowski (d. 1585), stimulated the growth of humanist ideas on education in central, western and southern Europe. The public school movement in the United States, Canada and Latin America was inspired by the 1835 English translation of Victor Cousin's *Rapport sur l'état de l'instruction publique en Prusse* (Paplauskas-Ramunas 1956: 110).

Figure 9. Yesudas Ramachandra

Figure 10. Doña Marina

CHAPTER 5

Translators and the reins of power

Translators, it could be said, are subjected to power, relegated to a position of complete impotence. "They have no rights", wrote the translator Maurice-Edgar Coindreau, "only duties" (1974: 131). The anecdote that follows provides an interesting illustration and introduces the theme of this chapter.

The lawyer Eugène-Philippe Dorion (1830–72) was an important figure in official translation in Canada during the years preceding and following Confederation (1867). He was highly acclaimed by his contemporaries for his knowledge of ancient languages, as well as English, French and some native languages. Appointed head of the French translators' bureau, he improved the quality of language in French versions of legislation, but he sometimes had to bow to the will of politicians. One of the founding fathers of Confederation, Sir George-Étienne Cartier, exercised his authority and insisted that he translate the term "Dominion of Canada" as *Puissance du Canada* in the *British North America Act*, the constitutional legislation that created modern Canada. The translator found it pretentious for a non-industrialized colony of three-and-a-half million inhabitants to claim to be a "power". He was not alone in this opinion. However, his outstanding linguistic ability and authority in the field of translation were outweighed by the dictates of a minister. Common sense and a translator's judgment could not override the influence of a politician (Delisle 1984: 7). The expression endured until the 1950s, after which it fell into disuse until the Canadian *Constitution Act* of 1982 eliminated it definitively.

Translators are thought to have little alternative but to respect the powers that be – especially if those powers hold the purse strings. The translator's *droit à la parole* is, after all, the right to render someone else's ideas for the benefit of a third party. The translator is even more constrained by obligations to remain trustworthy, keep official secrets and remain employable for repeat performances. Thus, translators have power only by delegation, and only for as long as they can be trusted. Theirs is a second-hand authority that remains circumscribed. In the final analysis, translators are excluded from the power relationships that really matter.

This is most clearly demonstrated by the way interpreters are presented on television. They stand among the mighty of our time – heads of state, military leaders and captains of industry – whose words pass through them. They are the interpreters, literally, of power, but the power that makes them interpreters is not theirs to wield. When we watch these interpreters at work, we are forcefully reminded that they are not the ones initiating the conversation. The person they are to translate for greets the visiting interlocutor before the translator comes into the picture; interpreters do not greet their counterparts in the other delegation before the conversation is officially under way.

The television images are arresting and compelling. We are only too willing to visualize translators in this constellation of power because it exemplifies what we think of as the archetypal power relationship: power vested in one person, who is in absolute command.

Power initiates translation, or at least controls it. Translators may find themselves smitten with the beauty of a certain text, particularly if it is a literary text. Even if they are moved to transpose that text into their own language, they will find that they seldom have full control over the outcome. If their work is to have any impact at all, they will still have to persuade an institution of power – if only a publishing house, or an editor of a literary journal – to disseminate the translation.

Though this point seems quite straightforward, the situation is actually far more complex. The dynamics of power and coercion are rarely as simple as they appear. Power, as Michel Foucault has abundantly shown, can take many shapes and forms. This chapter will examine the history of translation in the Western world from the perspective of power, providing a series of examples of the diverse ways in which translators are connected with centres of power.

The case studies that follow are taken from different historical periods and different cultures. We start with an example from the twentieth century, a time of massive translation arising from internal requirements of bilingual or multilingual states and from increasing exchanges among states. In the modern age, the sources of power have not generally been involved in the production of translation. In this particular case, however, a translation problem came to the attention of those who held the reins of power, because it was linked to the very issue of power itself, stemming as it did from the formulation of the nature of the homeland.

We then move back in time to examine some major translation enterprises which developed in medieval times under the direct patronage of primary centres of power. We then go on to follow the gradual emergence of multiple centres of power and the shifting relations that translators have had with different agents. In a more recent example, translators constrained by the repressive cultural policies of fascist Italy and the former Soviet Union managed to exercise a certain power themselves in a subversive move to import values that ran counter to the dominant ideology. Further illustrations, drawn from the history of the Americas, link translators and power in the context of conquest and colonization. The chapter then focuses on the changing role of women translators, who have moved beyond their initial anonymous and undervalued position to one of relative strength. This is followed by a review of some of their more fortunate male counterparts who have, to some extent at least, influenced or even held the reins of power at different moments in history. The chapter concludes with an overview of how recent studies of translation shed new light on questions of power.

The Balfour Declaration: "homeland" or "national home"?

In a developed society, those who wield power do not usually exercise direct control over translation. While they may initiate or commission translations, they do not monitor the production of those translations and are not likely to be aware of details of that production. In this respect, the situation is not significantly different from that of sixth dynasty Egypt (third millennium BCE), when translators and interpreters (Figure 18) were under the supervision of the Princes of Elephantine, "overseers of dragomans", rather than of the Pharaoh directly (Kurz 1985).[1]

The central power of the State becomes aware of translation only when something goes wrong in the translation of texts that directly concern it. One striking example is drawn from the translation of the Balfour Declaration into French.[2] The English text reads as follows:

> His Majesty's Government view with favour the establishment in Palestine of a *national home* for the Jewish people, and will use their best endeavours to facilitate the achievement of this object, it being clearly understood that nothing shall be done which may prejudice the civil and religious rights of existing non-Jewish communities in Palestine, or the rights and political status enjoyed by Jews in any other country.

The French translation of the text reveals the misunderstanding. It reads as follows:

> Le gouvernement de Sa Majesté envisage favorablement l'établissement en Palestine d'un *foyer national* pour le peuple juif, et emploiera tous ses efforts pour faciliter la réalisation de cet objectif, étant clairement entendu que rien ne sera fait qui pourrait porter préjudice aux droits civils et religieux des communautés non juives en Palestine, ainsi qu'aux droits et au statut politique dont les Juifs pourraient jouir dans tout autre pays.

The problem lies in the translation of the term "national home" – not just from English to French, but also from Hebrew to English. Underlying the linguistic problem is the attempt on the part of the Jewish people to formulate the concept of "homeland" in the first place. The term "national home" was the English translation from Hebrew by journalist and translator Nahum Sokolov (1861–1936) (Sokolov 1919). During subsequent post-World War I negotiations aimed at implementing the Balfour Declaration, Sokolov was to act as the right-hand man of Chaim Weizmann, who later became the first president of the state of Israel. In 1916, Sokolov had arrived at the term *"Bayit Leumi"*, or "national home". Both *"bayit"* in Hebrew and "home" in English mean what in French is called *"foyer"* – something like "hearth" which, through metonymy, signifies a dwelling or house of one's own. But they can also signify what in French is expressed by the term *"patrie"*, or "fatherland". In Hebrew, *"bayit"* has an even broader connotation than in either English or French since it is also used to refer to the Temple of Jerusalem and even to the Jewish state as a whole. For Sokolov and the Zionist Commission that had helped to draft the Balfour Declaration, the use of the term "home" in no way indicated that the idea of the creation of a Jewish state, or fatherland, was being abandoned in favour of some vague *"foyer national"* that would be unprotected by any actual guarantees under international law, however idyllic and symbolic a place it might appear to be. When he coined the term in 1916, Sokolov did not anticipate that its connotational field might be reduced in this way. The term *"bayit"*, which had been used historically to refer to the first Jewish state founded by King David and to the second Jewish state that came into being after the Jews returned to Palestine from captivity in Babylon, naturally came to designate the State of Israel that was to be created in 1948.

The discrepancy between "home" and *"foyer"* led to acrimonious exchanges between Lord Curzon, then-British Foreign Secretary, and his French counterpart Berthelot. Curzon went by the English "home" and its connotations, whereas Berthelot maintained that the French government had only ever agreed to a *"foyer"* and the more limited connotations associated with it (Goodman 1943).

But things do not always go wrong in the way described above. In fact, power exercises its control over translators by means of institutions to prevent them from going wrong more often. In an earlier phase of Western civilization ending with the Reformation, the centres of power were relatively undifferentiated and central power (then usually one person) was more actively involved in the commissioning of translations, if not necessarily in the supervision and criticism thereof. In the Middle Ages, two centres of power commissioned translations: the State, represented by kings, caliphs, or princes; and the Roman Catholic Church, represented by the Pope himself, or by cardinals and bishops.

Medieval translation enterprises from Baghdad to Western Europe

In the Middle Ages, three main translation enterprises developed under the patronage of these centres of power. The first was the Baghdad School, which grouped together the second generation of translators of the ͨAbbâsid period

(813–33).[3] The school coalesced around the person of Hunayn ibn Ishâq (809–75), a philosopher and medical specialist who translated from Greek into Arabic or Syriac, and who occupied a privileged position at the court of the Caliph al-Ma'mûn (786–833).

The second enterprise was the so-called "Toledo School". There were two distinct translation movements in medieval Spain. During the first of these two periods, in the twelfth century, the scientific and philosophical heritage of the Greco-Arab world was translated from Arabic into Latin. For the most part, these translations were completed under the patronage of churchmen, such as Archbishop Raymond, one of the driving forces behind this movement. During the second period, in the thirteenth century, it was primarily scientific works that were translated, this time from Arabic into Spanish and, to a lesser extent, into French and Latin, under the patronage of King Alfonso X (Figure 14).[4]

The third important translation enterprise of the Middle Ages occurred in the second half of the fourteenth century, when a group of scholars translated the *auctoritates*. These central texts of the Greco-Latin tradition were translated from Latin into French. This particular "school" operated under the patronage of King Charles V, also known as Charles the Wise (1338–80).[5]

Throughout the Middle Ages, similar translation enterprises flourished elsewhere in Europe, although on a smaller scale. Toward the middle of the ninth century, Charles the Bald (823–77), King of France, commissioned translations from Greek and Latin. Around the same time, King Alfred the Great of England (849–99) instituted a program of translation from Latin into English, and even produced some translations himself. In Italy, translations of hagiographic texts were produced successively in Naples, Amalfi and Pisa. Translators were active in Sicily between 1230 and 1343. A first group translated from Arabic into Hebrew during the reign of Holy Roman Emperor Frederick (Friedrich) II (1194–1250) and his successor Manfred (1222–66). A second group, more significant in numbers and output, translated from Arabic into Latin during the reigns of Charles (1226–85) and Robert of Anjou (1275–1343).

In both France and Spain, the translation activities mentioned above were part of a linguistic policy developed by the monarchy. Until that time, Latin had been the only language considered suitable for the writing of scientific or philosophical works in Western Europe. It became crucial for translations to be made into French or Spanish so that Latin could be superseded by the increasingly important vernacular languages. The personal renown of the patrons of the different "schools" – Alfonso X and Charles V, for example – did much to attract the most talented translators of the time.

There were certain recognized and even well organized occupations and professions in medieval times, but translation was not among them.[6] The great majority of those who produced translations, therefore, did so under the aegis of the Roman Catholic Church, which acted as the ultimate guardian of knowledge. Some of them were called *diaconus, archidiaconus* and *canonicus*. Other translators operated under the sponsorship of a monarch. They had titles like *aulae imperialis protonotarius, notaire et escriven de monseignour le Roy*, or signed their works "*votre humble serviteur et subject*", *su físico* and *clerigo del rey*. In the case of schools patronized by monarchs, the correlation between the status of the translators and the conditions under which they worked was very strong indeed. Hunayn ibn Ishâq, as indicated previously, was paid the weight of his translations in gold before falling into disgrace.[7]

The translators who worked within the Church had more personal input and were able to pursue their personal interests to a higher degree. The best known and most prolific of the twelfth-century translators into Latin, Gerard of Cremona (1114–87), is listed as a canon of the chapter of Toledo from 1157 to 1176. He translated Ptolemy's *Almagest* because he wanted to secure a copy of it for himself.[8] When translators worked within the Church, their translations were protected by its authority, even when the translations were not commissioned by bishops and archbishops, who did not necessarily know what was available in Arabic, the source language.

The power relationship between monarchs and their translators is strikingly represented in the iconography of the time and in translators' prefaces. Miniatures usually represent translators humbly kneeling at the feet of a monarch, or some other royal personage, and presenting their work to him. The prefaces are essentially dedications, and they invariably follow a precise schema that emphasizes the central position of the initiator of the translation: the translator purported to have translated the text in question because the monarch had asked him to do so, even though he, the translator, was totally unprepared to undertake a task of such magnitude. That task, the translator would maintain, consisted in serving the interests of the patron, following his directions and recommendations and, obviously, singing his praises.

In certain cases, translators were able to obtain special remuneration for their talents. A letter written in the twelfth century by Peter the Venerable to Bernard of Clairvaux reveals that Peter had to "open wide his purse" – *multo precio conduxi* are his exact words – to convince Robert of Chester and Hermann of Dalmatia to collaborate on the translation of the Koran and other Islamic writings from Arabic into Latin. In the next century, Alfonso X of Spain distributed rich rewards among those members of the royal chancery who were entrusted with parts of the texts he wanted translated. In the fourteenth century, Charles V of France endowed Raoul de Presles (1316–83) and Nicolas Oresme (c.1320–82) (Figure 16), among others, with substantial riches for translating some of the major texts of Latin Antiquity into French.

All through the Middle Ages, patronage gave translators opportunities they would never have had otherwise. The power of royal and ecclesiastical patrons enabled them to pursue their personal interests, opening up spaces they could not have opened for themselves in the societies in which they lived. In the twelfth century, for instance, scholars interested in the writings of the Islamic infidels would have been burned at the stake had they not been protected by powerful patrons who wanted to have those writings translated.

The power of the patrons was counterbalanced by the very personal, albeit limited, power that individual translators possessed by being experts in their fields. In the context of medieval scholarship, translators had a power all their own. Scholarship, it will be remembered, consisted of commentary much more than creation in the Middle Ages. This tradition, combined with the theological view of the word as epiphany, or revelation of the nature of things, led to a dual definition of the task of translators. They had to respect the letter of the text (by translating literally, that is), but they were also entitled to "ornament" the translation in order to make it more accessible to their audience. They could therefore omit passages and insert commentaries to an extent never again equalled in the history of translation in the West.

Toward multiple centres of power: the case of France

As the organization of French society became more sophisticated and new centres of power emerged, the situation of translators changed. No longer personally controlled or supervised by monarchs, princes or the Church, translators had to learn to deal with new institutions that began to function with a certain degree of independence. The Académie française was the most illustrious example of this process, the culmination of efforts that had begun in the sixteenth century to free intellectual life from the influence of the Church and to confer prestige on the French language.

Perhaps the most striking feature of most of the new institutions was that they tended to outlive the powers that founded them at a particular moment in history, and to develop in their own way, thereby evolving into independent centres of power. The relatively autonomous authority that accrued to new institutions over the years and centuries was rarely questioned by superior powers as long as they were not provoked by the new institutions. And as a kind of institutional inertia set in, their prestige was even likely to increase as time went on because they were in a position to influence, and in some cases, regulate activities they had originally been created merely to oversee.

In France, as in most other European countries, the Renaissance was a period of intense translation activity. Continuing a tradition established by their predecessors, kings like Charles VIII (1470–98) and Louis XII (1462–1515) actively initiated and encouraged the production of translations. But with the advent of the Reformation and a gradual secularization of society as a whole, translations acquired the potential to act as instruments of subversion, and were in fact put to that use. As a result, the Church grew much less tolerant of translation, even to the point of suspicion. Concomitantly, the new-found pride in the French language (another phenomenon with parallels in the rest of Europe), which was now seen to be on a par with Latin, also tended to discourage the production of more translations, even though translations had contributed to the development of the French language in the first place.

The Roman Church was concerned that the faithful receive a "correct" interpretation of sacred texts, as prescribed by Roman Catholic biblical hermeneutics. Only clergy trained in this study were trusted to carry out biblical translation. It is hardly surprising that those who wanted to reform the Roman Church would use the weapon of translation against it, disclaiming the very value of its biblical hermeneutics, and that the Church itself would be ruthless in its attempted repression of such translations, not to mention the translators who produced them.

One of the most notable examples of the seriousness of purpose with which the Roman Catholic Church defended itself against translations it considered subversive was a set of regulations developed for precisely that purpose. As early as the fourth century CE, the Church had spared no effort to safeguard the purity of its doctrine, and had begun to verify the texts, original and translated, that were put at the disposal of both the clergy and the laity. It used the old Roman office of the censor as a basis for formulating these regulations, which is why the reprimands it addressed were (and are) known as "censures".9 These reprimands concerned purity of doctrine, theological acceptability, and judgments of accuracy. Once a censure had become definitive, those who incurred it could be refused permission to print their work (*imprimatur*). They might even see their works added to the index of prohibited books, or they could be excommunicated. These censures could (and can) be pronounced by the church hierarchy at all levels, from the bishops upward, and by the so-called "privileged" Catholic universities like Louvain (Leuven), Paris and Cologne.

Yet these regulations were not uniformly applied. Indeed, their application has varied considerably in space and time. They were most rigidly enforced in the Papal States during the Middle Ages, and in the various ecclesiastical states, or prince-bishoprics of Europe, during the same period. Catholic monarchies that derived their legitimacy from the doctrine of the divine right of kings enforced the same regulations to a much lesser extent, with the exception of France. Medieval rigidity was gradually replaced by a more liberal approach during the Renaissance, but returned in full force with the advent of the Reformation. Luther, for example, was considered a "diabolical translator", and, as a result of his activities, all translations of sacred texts grew suspect once more.

Church reformers throughout Western Europe advocated the translation of the Bible into the vernacular. They hoped to wrest power from the Church, which in their opinion had become corrupt, and place that power in the hands of the common people. Jan Hus (c.1372–1415), for example, translated the Bible into Czech. He managed to hold his own against the Roman Church as long as he enjoyed the patronage of one of its rivals, King Wenceslas (Vaclav) IV (1361–1419) of Bohemia, whose actions were also instrumental in changing the character of the University of Prague from a German-dominated to a Czech-dominated institution. Hus, later the first rector of the Czech-dominated university, lost the support of his royal patron when he denounced "Antipope" John XXIII, of the Pisan line, who sold indulgences to finance his campaign against his papal rival, Gregory XII. Since Wenceslas also stood to gain from the sale of indulgences, he dropped his support of Hus, and treacherously had him arrested and tried at the Council of Constance.[10] Hus was permitted to defend his cause before the Council, but it was a lost cause: despite a guarantee of safe conduct, he was condemned as a heretic and burned at the stake in 1415.

John Wycliffe (c.1320–84), known as the "Morning Star of the Reformation", is credited with the first complete translation of the Bible into English (1382). He was shielded by John of Gaunt (1340–99), Duke of Lancaster and fourth son of Edward III. When Wycliffe attacked the Roman Catholic Church and denounced the wealth of priests and monks, Gaunt promptly appropriated all its wealth, exploiting Wycliffe's pronouncements for his own gain.

Martin Luther (1483–1546), whose German Bible created literary German and became the model for translations in many other languages, also enjoyed the support of an alternative institution. Luther had galvanized the German nobility by addressing an open letter to them: "To The Christian Nobility Of The German Nation". The nobility provided him with an honour guard when he stood before the young Holy Roman Emperor Charles V at the Diet of Worms in 1521.[11] Refusing to retract, Luther was excommunicated, declared a heretic and banished. His protectors once again stepped in, giving him refuge in the Wartburg castle, near Eisenach, where he finished his translation of the New Testament and began work on the Old Testament. The motives of the German nobility were not unlike those of John of Gaunt, except that they also hoped to achieve greater autonomy for their own states and possessions.

With the success of the Reformation in France, both the spiritual and temporal authorities adopted a much stricter attitude to the circulation of ideas, and hence to translation. The most famous victim of this change in attitude was Étienne

Dolet (1508–46). Dolet started his career under the protection of the powers of his day. He travelled to Italy and stayed in the university town of Padua for many years, conforming to the image of the humanist prevalent at the time. There, he discovered new ideas that ran counter to the doctrines of Christianity. Later, at the University of Toulouse, he came into contact with the conservative wing of the Catholic Church and reacted against it. He established himself as a printer in Lyon and began to publish the works of Marot, Lefèvre d'Étaples, Erasmus and Louis Berquin. In the eyes of conservative prelates, these writers were suspect, the first on moral grounds, the three others on theological ones. It was inevitable that Dolet should incur the wrath of the ecclesiastical authorities. He was saved only by the intervention of King François I (1494–1547). Dolet kept publishing, however. He was arrested again and accused of spreading works of heresy, but this time the king could not save him.

The tenor of the times had changed fundamentally. The Counter-Reformation was spreading through France: the Church had become acutely conscious of the dangers of humanism and had begun to take action against it systematically. Dolet was tried by the Sorbonne on the basis of his translation of *Axiochus*, a work attributed to Plato. He was condemned for having added a few words in one passage. These words were seen to cast doubt on the immortality of the soul and were judged to have been "dictated by heresy" (Cary 1963a: 14). On August 3, 1546, Dolet was burned, as were his books, because his translation had been too free. His death can be regarded as a symbolic end to a period dominated by humanist thought. At the time, the centres of power were in a position to intervene directly, swiftly and effectively. They could thwart a person by putting him to death; if they considered his work dangerous, they could curb its impact by burning it, too.

Meanwhile, other centres of powers were developing in France. A group of young poets, led by Pierre de Ronsard (c.1524–85) and known as *La Pléiade*, gave a voice to the intellectuals and began to regulate artistic expression. In 1549, barely three years after Dolet's execution, Joachim du Bellay (1522–60) published *Deffence et Illustration de la Langue Françoyse*, which dealt a severe blow to translation. Translation, du Bellay argued, was not a "noble" genre, since it did not involve creation. Nor was it a patriotic or progressive one, since it imported foreign works, and in particular those of Antiquity. From that time onward, everything conspired to wean writers off translation and to promote creation in the French language instead.

The career of Jacques Amyot (1513–93) is a perfect example not only of the continuing interest the authorities had in translation, but also of the new directions it was to take. One of the last translators to be commissioned by François I, Amyot (Figure 4) was given the task of translating Plutarch's *Lives*, which was considered politically safe in that it had little to do with the doctrinal conflicts of the time. Enjoying the protection of Margaret of Navarre, the king's sister, Amyot obtained a chair of Greek and Latin at the University of Bourges, where he taught languages for ten years. Before undertaking his translation of Plutarch, he engaged in serious philological work to establish a satisfactory reading of the original text. He even travelled to Italy to compare his version with other manuscripts. He spent over four years in Venice and then went to Rome, where he was close to the influential Cardinal of Tournon, who entrusted him with a diplomatic mission to the Council of Trent. It is interesting to note that Amyot was also a tutor to Henri II's children (the future Charles IX and Henri III). He ended his career as Bishop of Auxerre. He was thus an important member of the ecclesiastical institution, whose rules he had scrupulously observed. His translation of Plutarch's *Lives* was hailed as a model of its kind, written as it was in elegant French. Not unlike Luther's translation of the Bible, this work was highly regarded for the quality of its language. Even though Amyot's translation was later criticized on other grounds – the Academician Claude Gaspar Bachet de Méziriac (1581–1638) pointed out 2000 errors (Bachet de Méziriac 1998:6) – no doubt was ever cast on its stylistic merits.

The movement against translation and in favour of French, to the detriment of Latin, was taken a step further in the following century. There was an increasingly apparent desire to create a language that would become the vehicle of neo-classical literature. François de Malherbe (1555–1628), court poet to Henri IV, undertook a revision of the French language. In particular, Malherbe sought to eradicate archaic expressions and foreign loan words. Throughout the Renaissance, translation had been regarded as a means of gaining access to the wonders of Antiquity, and was practised extensively. It was now relegated to second place and subjected to the rules of the French language and French taste. Political powers continued to commission some translations: Nicolas Coëffeteau (1574–1623), for instance, translated Florus's *Roman History*, and published it in 1621, on the king's orders. This mediocre compilation was considered a stylistic model and was admired by the grammarian Vaugelas. Secular power, which succeeded the power of the Church, established itself more firmly with Malherbe and became institutionalized with the creation of the Académie française.

The Académie was established in 1634 by King Louis XIII at the instigation of Cardinal Richelieu (1585–1642).[12] The creation of this institution was in itself an attempt to exercise some control over the group of literati that had begun to meet at the house of Valentin Conrart (1603–75). During the Académie's first years, Conrart was the originator of many works of translation produced by individuals and groups. He also gave instructions and advice. From Conrart's circle arose the man whose new way of translating was to become characteristic of his time – Nicolas Perrot d'Ablancourt (1606–64), who was elected to the Académie in 1637. The term "*belle infidèle*" (beautiful and unfaithful) was coined to describe d'Ablancourt's translation of Lucian's *True History*.[13] In his prefaces, he set out the

principles underlying his approach. He advocated censorship, additions, modifications or modernization of the original text in the name of taste and linguistic
and cultural differences. In addition, he expressed a desire to do more than merely
translate: his objective was to create and polish a language that had by this time
reached maturity. D'Ablancourt's translations did, in fact, hold a definite charm
for their French readers.

In seventeenth-century France, as elsewhere, translation developed in accordance with the wishes of those who commissioned it, but it also reflected changing attitudes. In the Renaissance, French translators turned to Antiquity just as
their kings turned to Italy, or foreign lands beyond, for inspiration and authority. France's attempts to dominate Europe, expressed in the policies of Louis XIV
(1638–1715), were reflected in the attitudes of French translators of the neoclassical period, who exercised considerable influence on the cultural level.

The tenor of the times was to change again, although the changes would not
have been perceptible to the founders of the Académie. The very term "*belle infidèle*" implies a form of criticism. Resistance to the new age's domesticating translations first appeared in the marginalized Jansenist subculture of Port Royal and
elsewhere. Religious conviction, meticulousness and pedagogical motives made
people like Le Maître de Sacy (1613–84) demand greater formal fidelity in translation. Pierre-Daniel Huet (1630–1721), Bishop of Avranches, most clearly formulated the importance of a certain literalism in translation in his treatise *De optimo
genere interpretandi* (On the Best Kind of Translating) (DeLater 2002). Ironically,
Huet's views were not widely disseminated because they were expressed in Latin.
Once the common language of learning in Europe, Latin had become accessible
to no more than a limited number of intellectuals.

Translation as subversion: Italy and the former Soviet Union

With the growing complexity of societies and the accompanying proliferation of
centres of power since the time of Huet, translators have had more masters to
serve and please. They have also become increasingly adept at playing these masters off against each other and finding grey areas in which the authority exerted
by different masters overlaps, and is therefore rendered diffuse and eventually
inoperative.

In fascist Italy, a period extending from the early 1920s to the end of World
War II, literary policy paradoxically succeeded in fanning the embers of an anti-
fascist culture, rooted in a utopian myth of America which was itself open to different interpretations, even among its closest adherents. Benito Mussolini, one
of the founders of fascism and leader of Italy for most of that time, wanted a *vita
nuova* in Italian literature (Hibbert 1975). Having been a writer himself, albeit

somewhat of a failed one, he was looking for a successor to prominent poet and nationalist Gabriele D'Annunzio (1863–1938). To that end, literary competitions were organized on themes such as "the battle for wheat", "the joys of fecundity and motherhood" and "the achievements of Italians abroad". But while there was some treatment of these themes in the films of the fascist period, no literary fascism emerged. The literary response to fascism was one of indifference, if not actual dissent.

There were good reasons why this should be so. By the 1930s, imprisonment, censorship and politically motivated firings had silenced many of the most significant writers living in Italy. Just as fascist jails had the unintended effect of providing Antonio Gramsci (1891–1937) with the time and resources to write the bulk of his critical work, so fascist censorship contributed to the creation of a translation industry. There were three important motives for translating. First, for a number of important and influential writers, translation became an economic necessity. Many of them had lost their earning power. They had either been dismissed from their jobs because they were ideologically suspect, or had found themselves in the position of not being able to contribute to newspapers or magazines for fear of censorship. Second, for writers who had serious difficulty publishing their own work, translation became a creative opportunity. Finally, translation was a form of political activity: it had the effect of giving expression to the cult of America.

From 1938 onwards, Elio Vittorini (1908–66) worked for the Milanese publisher Valentino Bompiani as a translator, editor and administrator, helping to organize the Italian translation industry. He promoted North American prose zealously and enlisted professional writers and translators to carry out the translations. Although Vittorini and Bompiani had to be careful in their choice of texts so as not to incur the disapproval of the state censor, they soon had an impressive list of American titles on the market, including work by William Faulkner, Dorothy Parker and John Steinbeck. For Vittorini, one of the criteria for selecting a book to be translated was its chances of commercial success in Italy. Bompiani, on the other hand, saw his role as publisher in a somewhat less commercial light.

All manuscripts had to be submitted to the Ministero di Cultura Popolare (ministry of popular culture, also known by its abbreviation Minculpop) for ideological vetting before publication. Vittorini had to deal with Minculpop if he was to accomplish his project, a two-volume anthology of North American literature (Vittorini 1984). The anthology was assembled in 1941, all the short stories and novellas having been translated by established Italian writers, including Cesare Pavese (1908–50), Alberto Moravia (1907–90) and Eugenio Montale (1896–1981). Vittorini divided the material into nine chronological sections and wrote introductory notes for each section. Minculpop considered Vittorini's editorial commentary provocative and the first edition of *Americana* was immediately seized.

After negotiation with Minculpop, Bompiani secured a compromise. In 1942, *Americana* was reissued without Vittorini's commentary. Instead, it had an introduction by Emilio Cecchi (1884–1966). Like Benedetto Croce (1866–1952), to whose generation he belonged, Cecchi was a liberal opposed to fascism, but he was baffled by much of the modern American writing that inspired Vittorini and Pavese. Cecchi and Vittorini expressed different types of opposition to fascism on the basis of the same set of texts. Cecchi made his introduction more of a reader's guide to North American literature. The emphasis throughout his essay is on the philological accuracy of Vittorini's collection of translations, as opposed to what he calls other "artless translations". Cecchi draws attention to Sinclair Lewis's (1885–1951) absence from the anthology and claims that it is justified not so much by the race laws – Lewis was a Jew – as on grounds of literary taste. He then goes on to give a condensed history of the depression years in America and the effect on narrative. He warns against Italian writers using Ernest Hemingway and O. Henry as their models. In short, Cecchi's introduction was an attempt to situate *Americana* in the context of high literature and good taste.

Such an attempt made good political sense. Literary culture in Italy was a minority interest in the hands of an elite. Minculpop did not consider it a threat to the regime, and saw no need to oppose it. This seems to be the most plausible explanation of why a set of translated texts seized one year could be published the following year, albeit without Vittorini's "political" commentary. It is important to point out that the actual translations remained the same throughout. Minculpop did not object to the translations as much as to their ideological packaging. An analogous fate had befallen Luther's Bible in Germany four centuries earlier. His text was read in many Catholic German states, as well as in Protestant ones, although in editions from which his introduction and glosses had been removed and replaced with those of Catholic theologians. Significantly, though, Luther's translation itself had remained virtually unchanged.

In 1940, Bompiani published Montale's translation of Steinbeck's great proletarian work *In Dubious Battle*. A novel dealing with class struggle, an unsuccessful strike and violent strike-breaking, *La battaglia* could not have been read as anything but a subversive text.[14] Yet Minculpop appears to have been placated by a cautious and anonymous introduction stating, among other things, that the novel's content might surprise Italian readers somewhat, since they lived in a country where the class struggle no longer existed, certainly not in the sense understood by Steinbeck. Minculpop may have been placated, but the readership, such as it was, could not have failed to appreciate the translation industry's message. Given Vittorini's contention that North American literature was a literature that dealt with universal themes, the political message of *La battaglia* was crystal clear.

For Vittorini, translation was a form of political activity because it gave substance to the myth of America. Pavese also saw translation as a means of performing a vital service for Italian readers, because it showed them that literature was not necessarily restricted to what fascism wanted it to be. The myth of America was an ideological deformation of perceived reality or even a lay religion whose sacred texts were contemporary American novels and short stories in translation. The translation industry was a subversive force, but the subversion was not of a direct variety. The myth of America, as a land embodying a harsh class struggle and at the same time utopian principles, posed a direct challenge to the fascist view of the world. It also fed quite directly into the postwar neorealist movement, which was to have such a profound influence on Italian literary narrative and cinema.

Fascist Italy is not the only case in which translators took a stand against repression. The former U.S.S.R. provides a further example. In his preface to a two-volume anthology of poetry in Russian translation, Efim Etkind (1918–99) made this fateful statement: "No longer in a position to express themselves fully in their own works, Russian poets [mainly from 1934 to 1956] communicated with their readers through the literature of Goethe, Shakespeare, Orbéliani[15] and Hugo" (Etkind 1977:50). Silenced by the regime in power, these poets exercised their poetic talents through the art of translation, which enabled them to borrow the voices of foreign poets. This was true, in particular, for Anna Akhmatova (1889–1966) and Leonid Martynov (1905–80), both translators of Victor Hugo; for Nicolay Zabolotsky (1903–58), translator of Georgian poets; for Boris Pasternak (1890–1960), translator of the great tragedies of Shakespeare, Goethe's *Faust* and the poetry of Verlaine; and for Samuel (Samuil Yakovlevich) Marshak (1887–1964), who produced Russian versions of Shakespeare, William Blake, Robert Burns and Heinrich Heine. Joseph Brodsky (1940–96), recipient of the Nobel Prize for literature in 1987, is one such poet/translator. He was convicted of having been a "social parasite". His crime? To have written poetry and taken advantage of others by making word-for-word translations from languages that he did not really know (Etkind 1977:122).

On the basis of his sentence concerning the poets he anthologized, Efim Etkind was judged "antisoviet". As in the case of Vittorini, his anthology was censured. All the books he had written were removed from libraries and burned, including works on translation theory, on the history of French, German and Russian literature, on stylistics and poetry. An old librarian, forced to burn Etkind's books, is reported to have returned from work in tears, telling her family: "Today, I acted like a fascist" (Etkind 1977:295).

In April 1974, Etkind was relieved of his duties, stripped of his university degrees, expelled from the Writers' Union and forced to leave his country. Such was the fate of someone who, in his courses on translation theory and history, had reflected on the cross-fertilization of cultures, on their mutual enrichment through translation and on the notion of translation as a concrete act of internationalism in the fields of science and literature.

Conquest and colonization in the New World

In the context of conquest and colonization, translators and power are inextricably linked. Translators who belong to the conquered people or culture find themselves confronted with one centre of power, although this situation changes again when colonial administrations are established. What does not change, however, is the goal of conquest and colonization. Indigenous translators consciously or unconsciously become the instruments of foreign domination over their own people, even though they may also try to engage in acts of resistance. Yet power relationships become so unequal that they often have little choice in the matter.

One of the most telling examples is the Spanish conquest of the Americas. From the documents of the period it is clear that the colonizers fully understood the importance of translators. Particularly revealing are the twenty-nine laws promulgated between 1529 and 1680: these laws placed greater emphasis on the translators' loyalty to the Spanish Crown and the moral nature of their personal life than on any linguistic knowledge. Translators were expected to help spread Christianity and consolidate Spanish rule. In the first stage of the actual establishment and consolidation of the new power structure, translation took the form of interpretation far more often than that of written translation.

Columbus's first Spanish translator-interpreter was Don Luis de Torres, a converted Jew with a knowledge of Castilian, Latin, Arabic, Hebrew, Greek and Aramaic, curiously deemed well-equipped, therefore, to communicate with the inhabitants of the New World. Columbus, understandably, could not get by with Torres alone, and needed to have recourse to indigenous translators.

The initial task of translators and interpreters in the service of the conquistadors who followed Columbus was to dissuade the Indians from resistance. The most famous of these was Doña Marina (la Malinche), whose work as interpreter to Hernán Cortés is highlighted in another chapter. The daughter of an influential chief, or *cacique*, Marina (Figure 10) was not merely Cortés's interpreter; she was also his adviser and concubine. She informed on spies and exposed conspiracies, and was most successful in persuading her fellow Indians not to resist the Spaniards.

Marina was subsequently condemned by her own people for having aided the conquering Spaniards (Cypess 1991). According to a popular Mexican legend, her ghost walks the site of the former Aztec capital of Tenochtitlán (modern-day

Mexico City), lamenting her fate, and unable to find rest in the afterlife because she betrayed her people during her life on earth. Her role has been seen in a new light in recent times, however, especially by feminist historians, who stress the constraints to which she was subjected as a woman and slave, and who look upon her as a model, a symbol of fruitful cross-cultural exchange rather than betrayal (Alarcón 1989).

Perhaps the most far-reaching act of "translation" in the New World was the destruction of the Maya codices, judged to be detrimental to the task of Christianization.[16] In 1562, Bishop Diego de Landa ordered that they be burned; only three codices survived, and they were not translated until much later. Not until 1688, when Spanish rule was firmly established in Central and South America, was a history of the Quiché Indians translated into Spanish, under the title *Empiezan las historias del origen de los Indios de esta provincia de Guatemala*. The preface to the translation states that it was undertaken in the service of Christianization. Texts of the native peoples had to be burned initially, but once the myths they contained had been reduced to mere superstition, they were no longer seen as dangerous. Some acquaintance with them was considered helpful in the final "mopping up" operations of Christianization.

Around 1573, schools of translators and interpreters were founded in Nueva España – for example, the Imperial College of Santa Cruz de Tlatelolco – under the influence of three "powers": the Crown, the Pope and the Franciscan Order (Arencibia Rodriguez 2006). These schools provided training to indigenous linguists, carefully selected from among Indians of noble birth. They learned to translate Christian sacred texts into native tongues, mainly Náhuatl, thereby contributing to the process of Christianization by "reconciling cultural spheres" (Arencibia Rodriguez 2006:264). On the one hand, the Catholic Church was responsible for the eradication of idolatries in the New World, including indigenous books and codices; ironically, the Church also impeded the intended work of these translation schools following the 1564 Council of Trent, which adopted restrictive measures regarding the translation of the Bible into vernacular languages (Arencibia Rodriguez 2006:271). The same powers, it would seem, can have conflicting views as to how to achieve their objectives.

Women translators: England, the Continent and North America

While translation was seen as one of the few socially sanctioned ways of writing open to women during the Middle Ages and the Renaissance, women operated differently from men within this sphere of activity, as in many other social and intellectual activities in the history of the West. In England, women were restricted to the translation of religious texts. In 1603, John Florio (c.1553–1625), the English translator of Montaigne, made the link between translation and the status of women explicit: since translations are always defective, he argued, they must be female (quoted in Hannay 1985: 9). It has been argued, on the other hand, that the disenfranchisement of women and their "distance from the most prestigious discourses of translation" have provided incentives for developing new modes of thinking and original ways of practising translation (Agorni 2005: 818).

When the work of a woman translator was published, it was often anonymous. If it was known to be by a woman, it was usually restricted to manuscripts disseminated within the family circle. Even powerful women, like Mary Herbert, Countess of Pembroke (1561–1621), who was the sister of the Elizabethan poet and courtier Philip Sidney, did not compose original works of literature. She translated Petrarch's *Triumph of Death*, among other works of poetry, but she is perhaps most justly remembered for *The Tragedy of Antonie*, her translation of Robert Garnier's *Marc-Antoine*. The first secular play ever to be translated into English, *Antonie* puts forward a positive evaluation of Cleopatra. Around the same time, Jane Lumley (1537–76) translated the first extant English version of Euripides's *Iphigenia* (Hannay 1985; Krontiris 1992).

Mary Herbert's translations are considered to have great stylistic merit, as are those of Sir Thomas More's daughter, Margaret More Roper (1505–44), who translated Erasmus's *Precatio Dominica* in 1524. However, most translations made by women during the Renaissance are more literal, not least of all because literalism afforded a certain kind of protection in that it allowed the translators to decline all personal responsibility.

Margaret Tyler (fl. 1580) proved to be an exception to both rules set out above. Not only did she translate a Spanish romance, Diego Ortúñez de Calahorra's *A Mirrour of princely deedes and knighthood* (1578), rather than a religious text, but she translated it in a nonliteral manner. In a vigorous and bold preface to her translation, she defended her choice of "manly" subject matter which enabled her to introduce positive images of women of action at a time in England's history when it was not considered seemly for women to be active. She also contested the prevailing patriarchal rhetoric and asserted her right to translate in the first place (Robinson 1995). Chivalry romances came into vogue as a result of her work, and continued to be translated from Spanish into English in the centuries that followed. She was the first woman in England to publish a romance, and the first English translator of Spanish romance to work directly from the original rather than from a French intermediary.

Women on the Continent enjoyed more freedom than English writers, and by 1600 European women had established a tradition of secular writing (Hannay 1985). Among the most notable was Anne Le Fèvre Dacier (1654–1720).[17]

It was with regard to Madame Dacier that *traductrice*, the feminine form of the French word for translator, was used for the first time (Garnier 2002:13). She spent some years translating and annotating Latin and Greek authors such as Plautus, Aristophanes, Callimachus, Anacreon and Sappho, authors that ran counter to the tastes of her time. Some of this work was done in collaboration with her husband, André Dacier, but she is recognized as the one who provided the impetus to introduce difficult and underappreciated authors to a wider French readership. She is credited with having developed a translator's "code of ethics" through her internalization of the relativity of cultures, respect of difference, and the kind of intellectual honesty that consists in conveying as much of the original text as possible to the audience (Garnier 2002:23). Madame Dacier's scholarly translation of Homer's *Iliad*, which stood at the opposite end of the spectrum from the poetic recreation of her male contemporary Houdar de la Motte (1672–1731), marked the beginning of the end of the "belles infidèles" in France (Cary 1963a) and placed her squarely in the midst of the French literary controversy between the "ancients and moderns". Her translations of the *Iliad* and *Odyssey* were the crowning achievement of her career. Although they were criticized, as was Homer himself who had many detractors at the time, there have been twenty-six editions and they remained the authoritative French versions well into the twentieth century.

Gabrielle Émilie Le Tonnelier de Breteuil, marquise du Châtelet – known as Émilie du Châtelet (1706–49) – was a French scientist and translator. The problematic nature of her work at the time and its reception since then are reflected in the observation that she "has gone down in history first of all as Voltaire's mistress and secondly as the only French woman of her time seriously to develop her talent for mathematics and physics" (Terrall 1995:283). Educated at home by enlightened and well connected parents, who also gave her the opportunity to meet the intellectuals and scientists in their *salons*, she became fluent in English, Italian, German, Greek and Latin. She displayed a keen interest in the abstract sciences and devoted herself to the study of mathematics. Through her relationship with the mathematician Maupertius, she was introduced to the revolutionary theories of English physicist Sir Isaac Newton (Whitfield 2002:91).

Once she began to live with Voltaire at the Château de Cirey, Émilie participated to an even greater extent in the scientific debates of the day and engaged in a voluminous correspondence with the leading scholars. She wrote scientific and philosophical essays, including an explanation of the philosophy of Leibniz. Translation formed only a part of her body of work. She translated the classics for both practice and pleasure; she worked on, but did not complete, a translation of Virgil's *Aeneid*. Her primary achievement was her translation, from Latin into French, of Newton's major work *Philosophiae Naturalis Principia Mathematica* (*The Mathematical*

Principles of Natural Philosophy). The translation was accompanied by commentary, left unfinished by her untimely death, and was published posthumously in 1759 by Voltaire. It remained the standard French version until the publication of a new one in 1985. As a woman without access to institutions of her time such as the university and the French Academy of Sciences, Émilie depended on her personal relations to participate in scientific deliberations. The approach she takes to translation, too, is determined by her gender: translating Newton and commenting on his theories were the means for her to gain access to the male world of science. Her purpose, depicted as a pedagogical or "maternal" one, was in reality more closely linked to her desire to do her own scientific research. Voltaire captures the ambiguity of her situation in a letter to his friend King Frederick II of Prussia in which he mourns the loss of "a great man whose only fault was being a woman" (Whitfield 2002).

Sarah Austin (1793–1867) was the first professional woman translator of note. She translated various travelogues and medieval poetry into English from French, German and Provençal, along with some works by the nineteenth-century German historian Leopold von Ranke. Among the most important woman translators of the nineteenth century working in English were Harriet Waters Preston (1836–1911) and George Eliot (Mary Ann Evans, 1819–80), both of whom were also writers. George Eliot translated Spinoza's *Ethics*, as well as works by German thinkers such as theologian and writer David Friedrich Strauss, philosopher Ludwig Feuerbach and theologian and translation theorist Friedrich Schleiermacher. An equally important figure was Constance Garnett (1861–1946). Garnett (Figure 23) single-handedly introduced English readers to over seventy volumes of contemporary Russians authors such as Chekhov, Dostoyevsky, Gogol, Tolstoy, Gorky and Turgenev (Garnett 1991; Simon 1996). At the end of the nineteenth century, the Irish dramatist and folklorist Lady Gregory (Isabella Augusta Persse, 1852–1932) translated from Old Irish; her translations were instrumental both in the literary and political spheres.

Contemporary scholars such as Susanne de Lotbinière-Harwood (1991), Barbara Godard (1990 and 1991) (Figure 11) and Suzanne Jill Levine (1991) have supplemented their practice with a feminist theorization of the act of translation, moving translation into the political arena via a new consciousness of the gendered nature of language. All three have framed their work as translators with a view to "recasting women's role in language" (de Lotbinière-Harwood 1991). Whether working on the texts of Latin American (Levine) or Canadian writers (Lotbinière-Harwood and Godard), they foreground the role of the translator, challenge traditional hierarchies of authority and seek to give new prominence to the gendered voice of the translator (Von Flotow 1997 and 2011; Simon 1996).

When translators wield power

Despite these examples of accomplished women translators, most women translators of the past were shut out or otherwise constrained by the society in which
they lived. Certain male translators, on the other hand, played an important part
in the history of translation and managed to wield a certain power though not
necessarily because of their translating skills *per se*. In twelfth and thirteenth century Europe, for example, a surprising number of Jewish physicians – court physicians, in particular – were also translators. Jewish doctors travelled from place
to place, bringing their knowledge with them. They mediated between centres of
power and performed the dual duties of curing and translating.

Power can use translators in more ways than one, and translators are related to
power by more than their translations. These interrelationships often depend on
how translators integrate into existing power structures and the extent to which
they are able to exploit contradictions within those structures.

St. Jerome (c.347–420), who will be discussed in greater detail in the next chapter, travelled widely and lived in the desert of Chalcis for some two years, indifferent to power. But then he was invited to Rome, where he became secretary and
adviser to Pope Damasus I (304–84). Jerome (Figure 20), also known by his Latin
name, Eusebius Hieronymus, acted as a spiritual leader to cultivated ladies and
began translating the Bible at the invitation of the Pope. He occupied a position of
extreme power at the time. In fact, he is said to have beeen a potential candidate
to succeed Damasus as Pope upon the latter's death in 384. But Jerome fell out of
favour and the new Pope, Siricius (334–99), made life difficult for him and for his
translations. He carried out most of his later work at a retreat near Bethlehem.

Leonardo Bruni (1369–1444), commonly called Aretino after Arezzo, his birthplace, marked an important turning point in translation history through his dis-
agreements with the Spaniard Alonso Cartagena (1384–1456). Translator of Plato
and Aristotle into Latin, Bruni argued that good taste in Latin was more important
than literalist fidelity to Greek. Cartagena defended the earlier fidelity paradigm,
even though he did not know any Greek. It was a powerful debate, heralding the
later discussions of the "*belles infidèles*". The participants were also quite powerful:
Bruni became chancellor of the Republic of Florence, and Cartagena was Bishop
of Burgos. Moreoever, their powers were connected. From the mid-1430s, Bruni
was a prominent member of the Florentine cloth importers' and wool merchants'
guilds, at a time when Florence was an important trading and manufacturing city.
Much of their wool came from Burgos, former capital of the Kingdom of Castile
and a wool exporting centre at that time. As Bishop, Cartagena had important
connections among the city's traders. Bruni and Cartegena certainly argued about

translation. Yet their relations as trading partners eventually helped them agree to disagree, remaining on good commercial terms despite translation.

William Caxton (c.1422–91) translated from French and is best known as the first printer in England (Figure 5). Yet his real power was gained from neither translation nor printing. He was for many years a rich and influential wool trader in Bruges, where he earned the title of "Governor of the English Nation of Merchant Adventurers" in the Low Countries.[18] His prestige among his fellow merchants enabled him to become financial adviser to Margaret, Duchess of Burgundy. By the time he began to translate and print literature he was already in a position of considerable intercultural power.

Alexander Fraser Tytler (1747–1813) is well known for his *Essay on the Principles of Translation*. But with what authority did he set out those principles? Tytler was writing only in his capacity as a lawyer, since his translations of Petrarch and Schiller were published after the famous *Essay*. Tytler was Lord Woodhouselee and variously held the titles of Judge-Advocate of Scotland in 1790, Lord of the Court of Session in 1802, Lord of the Justiciary in 1811. A fine position from which to hand down judgments about translation.

The final example of a translator holding the reins of power is John Hookham Frere (1769–1846) who translated the fifteenth-century Florentine poet Luigi Pulci. He was also a British Undersecretary for Foreign Affairs and staunch opponent of Jacobin ideas.[19] He was a diplomat whose career came to an ignominious end when he advised the British army against retreat from the French at La Coruña, Spain. Not all translators are infallible experts in intercultural matters.

Reframing translation in the twenty-first century

Translation is not, and perhaps never has been, an isolated activity carried out independently of the power struggles within and among societies. Most translators work well, and safely, within the perimeters drawn for them by the political powers of their time. The relatively rare translators who break with the norms of their society do so because they are able to make use of delegated power, because they are able to exploit their insertion between contradictory forces and because their multiple forms of employment sometimes allow them more social authority than is usual. But the history of translation is also populated with its martyrs, those who contravene the rules or overstep the bounds that have been defined for them by the powers that be, and who consequently suffer banishment, punishment and even death.

Scholars of translation studies have increasingly focused on the ways in which the translation process is linked to power, challenging earlier dichotomous views, including the one contrasting fluent, self-effacing translations with foreignizing strategies that oppose particular hegemonies. There are circumstances, they show, in which the translator may well have an ambiguous allegiance, playing the role of a "double agent in the process of cultural negotiation" (Gentzler and Tymoczko 2002: xix).

Those who have reframed translation from the perspective of postcolonial theory and practices have brought questions of power to the fore (Bassnett and Trivedi 1999; Simon and St-Pierre 2000, for example), so that the "cultural turn" in translation studies has become the "*power* turn". Beyond the field of translation studies itself, interestingly, scholars from other disciplines have appropriated the notion of translation. Thus postcolonial scholars, such as Eric Cheyfitz (1991), Tejaswini Niranjana (1992) and Vicente Rafael (1993), have turned to translation studies for the concepts and terminology to articulate their views. Homi Bhabha (1994: 212), in particular, has defined translation as *the* site for cultural production (Gentzler and Tymoczko 2002: xv). In this context, translation theory intersects with and enriches general theories of cultural and power relations.

Notes

1.   For more on the Princes of Elephantine, see Chapter 9.

2.   The Balfour Declaration was a statement of British policy contained in a letter, dated November 1917, from Foreign Secretary Arthur Balfour to Lord Walter Rothschild. The declaration, drafted in consultation with the Board of Deputies of British Jews of which Lord Rothschild was vice-president at the time, was incorporated into the 1922 League of Nations mandate for Palestine, which provided for the establishment of a "national home" for the Jewish people in Palestine. (See Neher-Bernheim 1969; Stein 1961; Weizmann 1949 and 1957).

3.   The ᶜAbbâsids were a dynasty of caliphs who ruled the Islamic Empire from 750 until the Mongol conquest of the Middle East in 1258. The name derives from al- ᶜAbbâss, the uncle of the Prophet Muhammad. In 750 the ᶜAbbâsids transferred the capital of the caliphate from Damascus to Baghdad, thus shifting the centre of the empire from Syria to Iraq. The ᶜAbbâsid period is known for its rich cultural and intellectual life.

4.   Translation in Baghdad and Toledo, and elsewhere in medieval Spain, is discussed in more detail in Chapter 4 and again in Chapter 7.

5.   See also Chapter 2.

6.   The translation profession has not yet been fully recognized in many countries even to this day, despite the efforts undertaken by a number of national translators' associations. There are some countries, however, in which the translation profession has been granted official status under the law.

7. Chapter 4, note 18. Hunayn was imprisoned by the Caliph in 856, for refusing to produce a poison at his request; he was authorized to translate again only after he had been pardoned.

8. See also Chapters 4 and 7. While a certain number of well-known figures appear elsewhere in the book – St. Jerome, Hunayn ibn Ishâq, Alfred the Great, Alfonso X, Nicolas Oresme, Charles V, William Caxton, Martin Luther, Doña Marina, Étienne Dolet and Jacques Amyot, to name a few – in this chapter they are examined primarily in the context of power relations. Other references are listed in the index.

9. In early Rome, the *censor* was one of two magistrates who took the census and scrutinized the morals and conduct of citizens. Cato the Elder (234–149 BCE) was one of the most famous censors.

10. The Council of Constance, the sixteenth ecumenical council of the Roman Catholic Church, was held 1414–18. The council brought to an end the Great Schism, during which the church had been divided by three claimants to the papacy: John XXIII in Pisa, Benedict XIII in Avignon and Gregory XII in Rome. The council elected a new pope, Martin V, and attempted to carry out church reforms, also taking action against the Hussites (followers of Jan Hus) and the Lollards (followers of John Wycliffe).

11. A "diet", deriving from the medieval *dieta*, meaning "appointed day", was a formal assembly held in certain European countries. The diet of the (German) Holy Roman Empire was held in different cities at the invitation of the Emperor. Originally, it brought together nobles, princes, church dignitaries and later representatives of the imperial cities.

12. See Chapter 2, note 11.

13. See Chapter 2, note 12.

14. The title "In Dubious Battle" is a reference to Milton's *Paradise Lost*, an allusion to Lucifer's rebellion against God: "[…] and Me preferring, / His utmost pow'r with adverse pow'r oppos'd / In dubious battel on the plains of Haev'n, / And shook his throne. […]" (Book I, v. 102–105). The association with *Paradise Lost* is lost in the Italian title "*La battaglia*".

15. Sulkhan-Saba Orbéliani was an eighteenth-century Georgian writer.

16. The Aztecs, Inca and Maya had produced thousands of illustrated books, or codices. The Spaniards systematically destroyed these manuscripts containing the thought and knowledge of ancient civilizations of the Americas.

17. There is disagreement about Anne Dacier's date of birth. Encyclopedias and library catalogues tend to give 1654, but primary sources would appear to support 1647. See Garnier (2002:41, n. 5 & 6).

18. See Chapter 2, note 3.

19. The English Jacobins were supporters of the French Revolution in the early years and included a number of writers such as Coleridge and Wordsworth.

Figure 11. Barbara Godard

Figure 12. Xuan Zang

CHAPTER 6

Translators and the spread of religions

From the viewpoint of translation, religions fall into two broad categories: those for which there exists one unique, sacred language and those for which the message of sacred texts can be expressed with equal validity in all tongues. In the first case (of which Judaism and Islam are the main models), translations have been considered mere adjuncts of the original text, while in the second case (which includes Christianity and Buddhism), they have come to replace the original.

Religious texts, also known as scripture, are the texts that various religious traditions consider to be sacred. All members of a community agree to confer mythic status on these writings, whose age and linguistic features set them apart from other kinds of discourse. Centuries of veneration have given them a thick overlay of meanings. The liturgical use of sacred texts encourages reverence and discourages change. In addition to scriptures per se, the major world religions have developed a set of auxiliary texts, such as hymns, lives of saints and commentaries, which have also been the object of translation.[1]

Although the theological status of translated texts differs from one religion to another – and can even vary within a particular religion – the major religious texts of the world have nevertheless been abundantly translated. Translation has not only been extensive in every case, but these translations have sometimes been decisive in bringing about important changes in religious thought and practice, or at least in channelling response to ongoing changes. The great cultural shifts that have punctuated the history of Western and Eastern traditions have been made possible by translations. The major translations of the Bible, for instance, were crucial to the transition of culture, first from a Semitic to a Hellenic world, and later to a Latin one. In a similar way, the translations of key Buddhist texts into Chinese and Tibetan contributed directly to the spread of Buddhism and a new world view into large areas of Asia.

This chapter will not attempt to exhaust the history of a subject to which entire libraries have been devoted. A few examples, however, will serve to illustrate how translators have contributed to the transformation and transmission of religious texts. There is extensive and well-known documentation on the history of translation in certain religions – the translation of the Christian Bible, in particular. Fewer studies, on the other hand, have examined the translation of sacred texts from a cross-religious perspective.[2] This chapter will provide references to the first category and will also open up new avenues for exploring the subject more broadly.

Within most religious traditions there have been conflicting attitudes toward translation, moments of history when translation has been encouraged and others when texts have been frozen into interpretive immobility. Paradoxically, translations undertaken in times of cultural transition sometimes acquired the status of originals, barring access to the source texts from which they emerged. This was certainly the case for the Greek-language Septuagint (c.250–130 BCE), which replaced the Hebrew Bible, and later became the Old Testament of the Christian Bible until the appearance of the Latin *Vulgate*. Likewise, the *King James Bible* or *Authorized Version* (1611) became the source text for subsequent Protestant translations into many non-European languages.

Translations of religious texts have reflected changing political, philosophical and ideological conditions; they have encouraged dialogue with foundational texts and provided new readings for different audiences. Also, translators have helped extend religious influence, often adding an ideological dimension to military conquest or colonial domination. Translation is an essential element of most evangelizing projects, as is clearly seen in the histories of Christianity and Buddhism. Charting the role of translators within the various religious traditions reveals the sometimes contradictory imperatives governing the relationship between divine and profane languages.

Translators of religious texts have generally perceived their task from the perspective of theology or philology, paying more attention to the letter of the text than to the adaptation of the religious message to a given target culture. Caught up in the controversies of the past, in the rivalries and conflicts that have divided one tradition from another, they have probably been more aware of the differences separating their respective cultures. It is only from our vantage point as modern-day translators that we are in a position to observe the similar doctrinal and historical difficulties that have arisen in translating Jewish scriptures and the Koran, or Christian sacred texts and the Bhagavad Gita.[3]

This chapter will examine the Judaic and Christian traditions, focusing on the different ways in which each of the two religions has historically envisaged Bible translation. The emphasis has been placed mainly, although not exclusively, on translations into English. Smaller sections deal with the translation of Islamic, Hindu and Buddhist sacred texts; they illustrate how translators have helped to make these texts accessible to an ever-expanding readership. Of a different nature are the translations of so-called "sacred" texts of the East – some of which may or may not be deemed "religious" *per se* – made by curious Westerners with various motives.

Judaism: the oral and written word from ancient to modern times

While Judaism has dedicated itself to preserving, transmitting and interpreting the Divine Word in its original Hebrew formulation – which remains the unique interpretive source – a strong tradition promotes the translation of these texts for pedagogical purposes.

From its earliest writings to the mystical tradition of Medieval Hasidism, Judaism has always emphasized the direct link between language and the Divine presence. Many texts affirm that since the world was created in Hebrew, and since the Torah was given in Hebrew, its full meaning can be expressed in Hebrew only. As Steiner has pointed out, quoting the Talmud: "To mutilate a single word in the Torah, to set it in the wrong order, might be to imperil the tenuous links between fallen man and the Divine presence" (1975:61).[4] However, such attention to the letter of the Hebrew text does not preclude the possibility of translation, once the original text is established.

The Talmud also speaks of the necessity and legitimacy of translation. It is said that the word of the All Highest, as addressed to Moses and to the people of Israel on Mount Sinai, "splintered into seventy languages".[5] A strong tradition of rabbinical interpretation underscores the necessity for interpreting and translating the Law so that it can be understood by all people. Translation for non-Jews was considered legitimate, and translation of the Bible for Jews who no longer spoke Hebrew was also permitted. However, until the twentieth century, it was widely assumed that Jewish translations of the Bible were to be used only in conjunction with the original text. Consequently, translators of the Hebrew Bible tended to opt for a bilingual, parallel translation, often accompanied by verse-by-verse commentary.

First oral and then written translations existed before the definitive canon, or officially accepted list of books, of the Hebrew Bible was even established. The Hebrew Bible is composed of twenty-four books collected over a period of 1000 years, the oldest portion being the Torah, also called the Pentateuch or the Five Books of Moses. The complete canon of the Bible was established about 100 CE, but not generally accepted until the latter half of the second century.

At different times in history, the experiences of the Jewish people have necessitated translation of the Hebrew Bible. By 538 BCE, when the Edict of Cyrus the Elder, King of Persia, allowed the Jews to return to Judea, marking the end of the Babylonian exile, many Jews had forgotten Hebrew. Around that time, Ezra the Scribe began the practice of publicly reading the Torah while Levite priests explained it to the people (Nehemiah 8.3 and 8.7–8). The Scriptures were always read in Hebrew during services in the synagogue, since this language alone had ritual value, but they were translated into the vernacular for the benefit of the worshippers.

For centuries, the distinction between the written original and the oral interpretation was given precise visual and aural representation in the synagogue. As the reader read from the Torah, an interpreter by his side translated the "portion", or the particular segment being read that week. The translation was made verse by verse into the common language of the people, usually Aramaic.[6] This ritual was particularly characteristic of the Talmudic period, from the second to the fourth centuries CE.

The text could be delivered to the followers only through reading because the Torah had been given to Moses in written form. The prominence of the Hebrew written text was highly dramatized. So as not to give the impression that he was improvising, the reader was not allowed to lift his eyes from the text; nor was he permitted to recite from memory in case he made a mistake or suggested that he was the author of what he was reciting. The *meturgeman*,[7] or interpreter, listened and translated orally, without even looking at the Torah so that he would not appear to be repeating what was written there. Likewise, the reader of the Torah could not assist the translator, because again there might be confusion as to whether his words were of written or oral origin. This is why there had to be two separate persons to accomplish these functions. The interpreter had to stand away from the Torah, and usually somewhat below the level of the Torah, to signify the subordinate status of the oral to the written text. In addition, the interpreter was never permitted to speak louder than the reader, and their voices were not to be heard at the same time (Kaufmann 2005).

The first significant written translation of the Hebrew Bible was the Greek version, known as the Septuagint, commonly designated LXX. The translation is said to have been commissioned in the third century BCE by Ptolemy Philadelphus (Ptolemy II), King of Egypt, on the initiative of his librarian Demetrius of Phalera, who wished to enrich the celebrated library of Alexandria. The story of the translation was told less than a century afterward by an Alexandrian Jew writing under the pseudonym Aristeas to his fictitious brother Philocrates (Pelletier 1962; Harl et al. 1988). In his letter, Aristeas reports how he was sent on a mission to Jerusalem to present the idea to the high priest Eleazer. He tells how the high priest then selected seventy (or seventy-two) scholars of great distinction who were wise, pious, familiar with the teachings of the Torah, and also steeped in Hellenic culture. Retold, with some variations, in the first century CE by two other Jewish writers, Philo of Alexandria and Flavius Josephus, the legend has been passed on through the ages. Although the translation was originally purported to be a collective effort, a later legend told that the translators were assigned to separate quarters and were not allowed to communicate with each other. Yet they produced identical translations, proof that they were divinely inspired. Philo adds that a festival was celebrated each year on the Island of Pharos, by Jews and non-Jews alike, to commemorate the miraculous translation of the Septuagint.

This early story of translation established a model of inspired biblical translation which was later adopted by Christianity. The phenomenon of identical translations produced by seventy-two scholars confined to their separate cells was considered proof of a direct link between each translator and the divine presence. Collective translation was also a way for institutional guidance and control to influence the translation process. While collective efforts in other fields of translation have generally been considered unnecessary or even detrimental to stylistic coherence, group translation was later to become the norm in Bible translation. Shared responsibility could to some degree shield the individual translator from oppression and mistreatment and help avoid the fate of translators such as William Tyndale, martyred in 1536 for his work on the Bible.

While apocryphal, the legend of the Septuagint is not without its grain of truth. The Pentateuch was in fact translated into Greek in Alexandria during the third century BCE,[8] but probably to meet the needs of the Jewish community, in which Hebrew was hardly spoken any longer, rather than to fulfil the wishes of the king. The 200,000-member community, of which 100,000 lived in Alexandria, was a heterogeneous group of mercenaries, merchants, farmers, artisans and intellectuals. They were mainly Greek-speaking and had a special status within the city. They remained attached to their homeland, Palestine, sent taxes and offerings to the Temple of Jerusalem, and continued to make pilgrimages to the Promised Land. They had a closer affinity for Greek culture, however, and had even begun to use the Greek language in some of the synagogue rituals. Translation of the holy books was necessary to replace imperfect oral translations made in the synagogue. It served not only to strengthen Jewish values among the Jews themselves but also to propagate them among the increasing number of sympathizers and converts to Judaism.

It is not known exactly how many translators were involved or precisely who they were. The other books of the Hebrew Bible were translated subsequently, the whole enterprise extending from approximately 275 to 100 BCE. Accomplished by different translators living at different times, with varying knowledge of Hebrew and Greek, the Septuagint is uneven in quality. However, it has been an invaluable text: in ancient times it made the Bible accessible and it served as the authoritative Old Testament for early Christianity. It was the basis for other ancient versions of the Bible (Ethiopic, Coptic, Slavonic, etc.), and it preserved the Apocryphal texts not included in the Hebrew canon. In modern times, its primary value is in biblical scholarship.[9]

Although widely used by Greek-speaking Jews initially, the Septuagint was eventually adopted by Christians, who used it in preference to the Hebrew original. This caused the Jews to reject the Septuagint. They gradually replaced it with newer versions, which eliminated certain ambiguities and took into account corrections introduced by the Masoretic text.[10] Nevertheless, the Talmud does not condemn the work of the Seventy (which it considers inspired) and authorizes the translation of revealed texts in all languages, particularly into Greek. It is only later that one finds Talmudic commentaries – such as the eighth-century *Masekhet Soferim*, for example – expressing outright opposition to the Septuagint: "It is said that five sages wrote the Torah in Greek for King Ptolemy and that this day was as black for Israel as the day on which Israel made the Golden Calf, because the Torah could not be translated adequately". These often-quoted words, it is believed, refer not to the undesirability of translation in general, but very specifically to the Septuagint (Orlinsky 1974: 383–386): the Bible of the Jews, which was perceived as having been "hijacked" by a new and adversarial religion. As the Christian Church "monopolized the Septuagint and increasingly used it in the controversies with the Jews", the Jews began to distance themselves from it and eventually condemned a translation they had originally held in such high esteem (Jinbachian 2007: 39).

As long as it remained an act of interpretation and explanation, on the other hand, translation itself continued to be encouraged by the rabbis. Translation was considered one of the modes of communicating and transmitting the divine word, but translated versions were nonetheless regarded as secondary to the original. With the exception of the Septuagint, Jewish translations of the Bible have traditionally been accompanied by the original Hebrew text. Only in modern times is the Hebrew text sometimes absent.

The Jewish translator must be familiar with the four levels of interpretation of the Torah and the rules of hermeneutics, or theory of interpretation: seven of the rules were established at the time of the scholar Hillel (30 BCE) and thirty-two at the end of the Talmudic period in the fourth century CE. Among the recommended procedures were reasoning by analogy – that is, detecting the use of a single word in different contexts and using one to explain the other – and deducing meaning through interpretation of contiguous biblical passages. The translator was advised to avoid both the excesses of literalism and the dangers of blasphemy.

The Talmud refers to two translations undertaken under the authority of famous rabbis, one by Onkelos (c.35–120 CE) into Aramaic and another by Aquila of Sinope (second century CE) into Greek.[11] Well known for his *targum* ("translation" or "interpretation" in Hebrew, generally referred to as the Targum Onkelos), Onkelos was considered by the medieval rabbi Rashi to have best assimilated the rules of interpretation and to have clarified many difficulties of the Hebrew text. It is said that Onkelos made additions that were divinely inspired; reference was made to his commentary whenever an obscure passage needed clarification.

While a product of the same school, the translations by Onkelos and Aquila were radically different. Onkelos did not hesitate to use interpretive paraphrases if necessary, whereas Aquila's text was extremely literal. Why this major difference in translation method? Written in Aramaic, a language similar to the original Hebrew, Onkelos's text was destined to perpetuate a long tradition of synagogue interpretation; it was not meant as a replacement text but as a commentary.

Aquila's Greek version, on the other hand, was addressed to Jews who were no longer able to read the Hebrew text. It was meant to replace the Septuagint for ritual and pedagogical uses. Stripped of formulations that had permitted Christianizing interpretations, it was intended to be a faithful mirror of the original, reflecting the state of the Hebrew text five centuries after the Septuagint, as well as the interpretation taught by the rabbis. Aquila believed he could convey the meaning of the text not by translating the words themselves but their etymological sense. He tried to translate short, long, feminine or masculine Hebrew words with short, long, feminine or masculine Greek ones. St. Jerome, the translator of the *Vulgate*, was later harsh in his assessment of Aquila's translation methods. As someone who himself placed greater emphasis on meaning than words, he was critical of this pursuit of meaning by slavishly imitating or borrowing from the original language.

Later Jewish translations of the Bible included versions in Judeo-Persian (1319), Judeo-Tatar (1836) and Judeo-Romance languages, such as the famous Ferrara Bible (1553) published by Abraham Usque, of which there were separate editions for Jews and Christians.[12] Especially influential were the Arabic translation of the Bible by Sa'adia ben Joseph (Sa'adia Ga'on) (882–942), and the 1780 German translation by Moses Mendelssohn (1729–86). All these translations used the Hebrew alphabet to phonetically transcribe the languages into which the text was translated. Only in modern times have Jewish translators used the alphabets of foreign languages.

Many Yiddish translations of sacred texts have been produced, reflecting a unique form of "internal Jewish bilingualism" (Shandler 2005: 93).[13] In fact, the earliest forms of Yiddish literature were versions of the Bible, legends and liturgy originally written in Hebrew, imitating, in print, the practice of translating the Torah orally in ancient times. The most popular of these, perhaps, was the *Tsenerene*, translated by Yaakov ben Yitzchak Ashkenazi (1550–1628) and published in the early seventeenth century. This work integrates translation of the biblical text with commentaries and even folklore, and was intended mainly as a woman's Bible (Shandler 2005: 94–95).[14]

Two outstanding Yiddish versions were published by leading modern poets, I. L. [Isaac Leib] Peretz (c.1851–1915), a Polish author and playwright, and Solomon Bloomgarden, an American who wrote under the pseudonym Yehoash (1870–1927). In his 1910 translation, in particular, Yehoash distinguishes himself from previous Yiddish translators by his efforts to demonstrate the "belletristic capacity of Yiddish" to do justice to this "foundational Jewish text" (Shandler 2005: 100).

The most important contemporary English-language Jewish translations were carried out in the U.S. (Orlinsky and Bratcher 1991). The Jewish Publication Society of America, representing both traditional and Reform Judaism, produced the first complete Bible in 1917, and the New Jewish Version – the Torah, the Five Megilloth and Jonah – was translated by an American Jewish team in the 1960s. Harry M. Orlinsky (1908–92) was co-translator of the five-volume English version of Rashi's commentary on the Pentateuch, and the only Jewish consultant for the Protestant Revised Standard Version of the Old Testament, published in 1952. Martin Buber (1878–1965) and Franz Rosenzweig (1886–1929) translated the Bible into German. Believing that the biblical texts derived from an oral tradition, Buber's German translation drew on the sensuous poetic form of the Hebrew language and reflected his view of the Bible as a record of Israel's ongoing dialogue with God. Initially undertaken in collaboration with Franz Rosenzweig, Buber's Bible was completed in 1962.

Contemporary translations of Jewish scriptures and prayer books have been undertaken to address issues of gender, making these religious texts gender-neutral or gender-sensitive, similar to the projects within the Christian religion to be discussed below.

The long history of translation within the Jewish tradition, accompanied as it was by reflection on the meaning of texts and their interpretation through translation, has culminated in abundant practical activity and a rich body of translation theory. Modern translation studies has been greatly enriched by the work of scholars steeped in the Jewish tradition.

Christianity: religious texts in the languages of the world

Rowan Williams, Archbishop of Canterbury since 2003, has said, "Of all the great world religions, it is Christianity that has the most obvious and pervasive investment in translation" (quoted in Noss 2007:3). When the Christian church came into being, it had as its sacred writings the Hebrew Scriptures – not, however, in their original language but in the Greek translation, the Septuagint. Thus, one of the two fundamental texts of the nascent Church, the Old Testament, was a translation. The other, the New Testament, was written primarily in Greek.

The Church's central message was that Jesus was the Messiah not only of the Jews, but of all peoples everywhere. It was inevitable that as the Christian faith developed and spread, it would begin to provide translations of the Scriptures, in particular the New Testament. Even before the canon of the New Testament was finally fixed late in the fourth century, the Gospels and the Letters of Paul were being translated from Greek into other languages. Christianity, perhaps more so than any other religion, has enthusiastically embraced translation as a means of disseminating its sacred writings. There have been moments, however, especially in the history of Catholicism, when translation was discouraged and even officially prohibited. The shifting attitudes toward translation will be examined in the pages that follow.

The cultural importance of Bible translation in the history of the Western world cannot be overemphasized: no other text has had such a pervasive influence on language, literature and beliefs. "No other book has been translated over such a long period of time as the Bible [...] and no other document is today the object of such intense translation activity as the Bible" (Noss 2007: 1). Translated into over 2,500 languages – either in whole or in part – the Bible is the most widely circulated book in the world.[15] The various translations of the Bible have been decisive in revitalizing its meaning and interpretation at pivotal moments in Western history. The efforts of translators have helped to foster and legitimize new vernaculars, resulting in the rise of national languages beginning in early modern Europe and the many languages of colonies and former colonies during the nineteenth and twentieth centuries.

As early as the second century, parts of the New Testament were translated into Syriac and Latin. Around 170 CE, Tatian (c.120–173), a convert and disciple of St. Justin Martyr, prepared in Syriac a running version of the four gospels, arranged to form a single narrative known as the Diatessaron. The earliest Latin translation, known subsequently as the Old Latin, was made in North Africa. In the third century, translations appeared in different dialects of Coptic.

The Gothic version of the Bible was the work of Ulfila (c.311–c.382). As discussed in Chapter 1, he invented an alphabet in order to translate the Scriptures and carry out his work of Christianization. The fragments of his translation constitute the oldest surviving literature in any Teutonic language.

St. Jerome (c.347–420) is undoubtedly one of the best known translators of all time, in the West in any case, where he has come to be considered the patron saint of translators (Figure 20).[16] Jerome is noted for having produced the *Vulgate*, or standard Latin Bible. Born of Christian parents in Stridon, located near modern-day Ljubljana in Slovenia, Jerome was sent to study in Rome. There he lived a life of dissipation, as he later said himself, enjoying the many attractions of the city, including the circus and theatre, as well as less honourable ones which were to weigh on his conscience all his life. He was nevertheless a brilliant student and an avid reader. During the years spent in the capital of the Empire, he acquired a knowledge of classical literature (Virgil, Horace and Cicero, in particular), pagan philosophy and the law, which he intended to practise. At the age of nineteen he was baptized.

He went to seek his fortune in Trier (a Germany city today, but then an important one in the western Roman Empire). It was there that Jerome first learned about the lives of Egyptian monks and chose to follow their example. When he returned to Rome, his religious vocation began to take shape. He abandoned his career in the Roman imperial civil service, gave up his worldly goods and left for the East. He discovered Christian literature as he was studying Greek in Antioch. Increasingly attracted by the asceticism of monastic life, he moved to the desert of Chalcis, in what is now Syria. He spent two years in penitence, living an austere life. During that time, he had the famous dream in which he was accused of being "a Ciceronian, not a Christian". Moved by this spiritual experience, Jerome devoted himself to the study of Christian literature and the Bible, and also to acquiring knowledge of the Hebrew language. On his return to Antioch, he was admitted to the priesthood and began to work on some of his celebrated scholarly writings.[17] He then spent some time in Constantinople, where he turned his attention to another literary pursuit, translating homilies on the Song of Songs and the Gospel according to St. Luke.

In 382, he returned to Rome and served as an interpreter at the synod of the Greek and Latin Churches. The synod proved unsuccessful, but Jerome remained there in the service of Pope Damasus I, acting as his secretary, interpreter and theological adviser and living a comfortable life. By this time, Jerome was a philosopher, rhetorician, grammarian and dialectician, familiar with Hebrew, Greek and Latin. The Pope, therefore, turned to him, requesting that he translate and revise the Bible. Jerome accepted this task and began by translating the New Testament and the Psalms, working from accepted Greek texts.

After the death of his protector Damasus in 384, Jerome left Rome and took refuge in Bethlehem, which he considered his "spiritual retreat", and continued his work as a translator. After completing one translation of the Old Testament from Greek, he translated it anew from Hebrew. He is credited with being the first to have translated the Old Testament into Latin directly from the original Hebrew (*hebraica veritas*), rather than from the Septuagint. Jerome left a substantial body of commentaries and other writings that have contributed to the tradition of biblical scholarship in the West. In over a hundred prefaces, numerous letters (Labourt 1949) and prologues to his translations of the Scriptures, he also articulated his views on translation. His letter to the Roman senator Pammachius (letter 57) is particularly instructive in this respect (Kelly 1976).

When Jerome completed his translation and revision of the Bible in the late fourth century, his work gave rise to considerable criticism. St. Augustine (354–430), Bishop of Hippo Regius in Numidia (modern-day Algeria), opposed the translation of canonic texts into Latin, except in the form of critical editions drawing attention to discrepancies between the Septuagint and the Hebrew text. Augustine favoured translation from the familiar Greek Septuagint rather than the Hebrew original. In 405, he wrote to Jerome complaining that his parishioners were dismayed at the disappearance of the familiar words they had come to expect during the liturgy:

> I do not wish your translation from the Hebrew to be read in the churches, for
> fear of upsetting the flock of Christ with a great scandal, by publishing something
> new, something seemingly contrary to the authority of the Septuagint, which ver-
> sion their ears and hearts are accustomed to hear, and which was accepted even
> by the Apostles.   (Augustine 1951, 1:95)

St. Augustine's initial reaction notwithstanding, the Latin *Vulgate*, comprising
Jerome's translation of the Old and New Testament, served the Western Church as
its sacred text for over a thousand years, "extending the influence of the Latin language through time and over geographical realms further than the Roman Empire
had ever reached" (Noss 2007: 16–17). Jerome played a pivotal role in bringing together classical culture and Christianity. As many others who have brought about
intellectual and spiritual revolutions, he was a controversial figure throughout
his life. He also had his admirers. One of the most notable was Erasmus, who
regarded Jerome as a "Christian Cicero" and published a nine-volume edition of
his work (Olin 1979).

Jerome was canonized in the eighth century and proclaimed a Doctor of
the Church (*Doctor doctorum*) in the thirteenth century, along with three other
fathers of the Roman Church, St. Ambrose, St. Augustine and Pope Gregory I,
known as Gregory the Great. The fact that he achieved sainthood for his work
casts a very special light on the translator's relationship with divinity in the eyes
of the Christian Church and its followers: Jerome is regarded as having worked
under divine inspiration and this in turn has secured protection for his version
of the Bible. After a period of neglect, the cult of St. Jerome was revived during
the Renaissance by Giovanni di Andrea, a celebrated jurisprudence expert at the
University of Bologna, who saw in Jerome the archetype of the humanist scholar,
devoted to the beauty of correct form and language. Jerome was a prominent
figure during the Renaissance. From the fourteenth to the seventeenth centuries,
in fact, he was one of the Christian saints who most frequently inspired painters
and artists in general, despite the fact that he was neither a miracle worker nor a
martyr to his faith.

In addition to the Bible, other types of religious texts were translated in Europe
throughout the Christian era and during the Middle Ages, in particular. This was
the result of a new readership that extended beyond the Latinate clerics, comprising mostly nuns and pious lay people, especially women (Pezzini 1991a). Also
underlying the translation activity was the growing self-confidence of vernacular languages; translation into the vernacular was both a sign of and an agent of
change. It had become necessary to translate *from* Latin in order to reach a wider
audience within a single national and linguistic community, and works originally composed in the vernacular were translated *into* Latin to ensure distribution

beyond the limits of a nation. Many religious texts, originally written in Latin, were translated into the vernacular only to be translated back into Latin (Barratt 1984). Some manuscripts, such as the *Imitation of Christ* by Thomas à Kempis (1380–1471), were translated as many as three times by different hands during the same century (Sargent 1984: 157).

The role of the translator depended not only on the new audience and possible new use of the translated work, but also on its genre. There were three principal types of work: liturgical hymns and religious poetry in general, narrative texts (lives of Christ and the saints) and texts used for religious instruction.

Latin hymns were translated in late medieval England to be quoted in sermons, used in private prayer or sung. Some of these translations – renderings by John Lydgate (c.1370–c.1450), a monk and prolific English poet, for instance – may even be regarded as experiments in vernacular liturgical writing (Pearsall 1977: 234). The methods used by the translators were governed by the purposes the texts were meant to serve. Preachers, for example, would tend to emphasize the iconic and emotional elements of the text they were translating by introducing concrete nouns and visual adjectives; they would also clarify certain words and simplify syntax (Pezzini 1991b).

Narrative texts abounded. The vast literature of *exempla*, tales used to enliven a sermon or reinforce a moral truth, illustrates the rather free hand which translators had. Tales of ten Latin lines could grow into stories running from fifty lines to three times that number. Oral delivery was responsible for the ever-growing elaboration of the *exempla*'s narrative features and dramatic detail. Changes were also brought about as translators adapted the texts to different audiences.

Of the medieval legendries, written accounts of the miraculous lives of saints, the thirteenth-century *Legenda Aurea* by Jacobus de Voragine (c.1229–98) was the best known. William Caxton (c.1422–91) (Figure 5) published the first English version of the *Golden Legend* in 1483. In the preface, he describes his approach to translation: he produced a "new" version by keeping an eye simultaneously on the original Latin and various contemporary translations, among which was an anonymous English translation published in 1438, commonly known as the *Gilte Legende* (Blake 1969: 117–120; Hamer 1978).

The primary method used by translators of instructional texts was adaptation. This was evident in St. Æthelwold's tenth-century translation of the Benedictine Rule into Anglo-Saxon. A combination of different versions of the Latin original is used as a source, and comments and glosses are inserted (Gretsch 1973).

Underlying all these translational practices was the conviction that what was produced in the field of religious literature was a common heritage, a quarry from which to excavate what was needed for the spiritual profit of the faithful. Indeed, the particular content and structure of religious texts made them relatively easy to adapt to different uses, and they were frequently and liberally "abridged, expanded, and rearranged" (Barratt 1984:427). Compilations were created by uniting unspecified passages from different works (Pezzini 1992). This was how old books gave rise to new ones, according to the medieval conventions evoked by Chaucer.[18] The translator often combined the roles of compiler, adapter, commentator and clergyman.

The end of the Renaissance coincided with the beginning of the Reformation, destined, as the name suggests, to transform the Catholic Church. Latent as early as the Middle Ages, the movement gained momentum during the sixteenth century, aided by the intellectual curiosity and freedom associated with humanism, the development of printing which enabled the reformers to disseminate their ideas and, in particular, the appearance of new versions of the Scriptures, which could be translated into vernacular languages from original texts.

Translation was so important to the new movement, in fact, that it has been said that the Reformation was fundamentally a dispute over the freedom to translate the Bible into the vernacular (Cary 1963b:9). The relatively tolerant attitude toward the translation of religious texts into vernacular languages, which had prevailed during the Middle Ages, did not necessarily carry over into subsequent periods. The position of the Roman Catholic Church was reflected in the 1546 decision of the Council of Trent to establish the *Vulgate* as the only "authentic" version, a decision which was not reversed until 1943 (Delisle 2005).[19] The authorization of the *Vulgate* gave the Church more power as "the only authority competent enough not only to select the right translation, but to understand it as well" (Pym 2007:209).

The Dutch scholar Desiderius Erasmus (c.1466–1536), also known as Erasmus of Rotterdam, was the most influential humanist in Europe of his day. Living at a time when medieval feudalism was disintegrating and the Church was in crisis, Erasmus attempted to reconcile reason and faith, and secular and sacred literatures. He studied in Paris and Oxford and went to Italy, where he learned Greek. He travelled through most of Europe and came into contact with the leading scholars of his time, including Sir Thomas More, with whom he became friends at Cambridge.

In 1516, Erasmus published an edition of the New Testament. This was the first Greek New Testament to be printed, and it was accompanied by an elegant new Latin translation. In his preface, Erasmus stressed the importance of returning to the Hebrew and Greek sources, and expressed the wish that the Bible be translated into all languages. In order to interpret the original texts correctly, he said, it was essential to be familiar with the original language, literature and rhetoric, and to be a grammarian rather than a theologian (Schwartz 1963). Erasmus thus set the tone for Bible translation during the Renaissance: the authority of theologians was questioned, translators returned to original sources and sacred texts began to be translated into vernacular languages.

Martin Luther (1483–1546), whose seminal work has been examined in Chapter 2, has become the symbol of the Reformation. In collaboration with a group of scholars, he produced a complete translation of the Bible in 1534. It is sufficient to point out here the extent to which Luther's Bible inspired foreign translators and served as a model for similar translations of the Bible: into Swedish (1541), Danish (1550), Icelandic (1584) and Slovenian (1584), to name a few examples.

The Reformation in France, too, was spawned by great humanist scholars and translators. Jacques Lefèvre d'Étaples (c.1455–1536) produced a French translation of the Old Testament in 1528, a complete Bible in 1530, and a new annotated edition in 1534; the poet Clément Marot (1496–1544) published a French edition of the Psalms in 1542. The highly influential Reformer Jean Calvin (1509–64) revised his cousin Olivétan's 1535 Bible, and later published in Latin, with his own French translation, the first work of theology in the French language: l'Institution de la religion chrestienne (1541).

Bible translation in England, linked as it was to the vicissitudes of politics, is particularly useful for our understanding of the role of translators in the propagation of new religious ideas. As early as the fourteenth century, the English crown had begun to distance itself from the Church of Rome. John Wycliffe (d. 1384) was a supporter of English royalty and a leader of the anticlerical and antipapal movement. He denied transubstantiation, condemned the practice of indulgences and advocated religious reforms and the separation of Church and State. Known as the "Morning Star of the Reformation" or the first "Protestant", Wycliffe was in favour of returning to the Bible to renew the faith. Together with a group of collaborators, he produced an English Bible around 1382. This was probably the most important translated work of the fourteenth century in England. It has been criticized for its repetitions, imperfections and excessively literal style, but this first complete translation of the Bible laid the foundations for English biblical language and contributed to the development of English prose. The translation was based on the Vulgate, since Wycliffe and his colleagues were not familiar with Greek or Hebrew, unlike the Renaissance humanists who succeeded them. The Church prohibited the use of Wycliffe's Bible. In 1428, forty-five years after his death, his body was exhumed by order of the Council of Constance (1415). His remains were burned and his ashes thrown into the Swift River.

William Tyndale (c.1494–1536) was the first Englishman to translate the Bible directly from the original languages (Figure 13). At Magdalen College Oxford, he studied languages, theology and the other liberal arts. He went on to Cambridge, not long after Erasmus had taught there and had promoted the Greek language and new ideas of the Renaissance. In 1523, Tyndale sought the support of the Bishop of London, Cuthbert Tunstall, for his project to translate the Bible into English. Having recently been to Germany as ambassador, however, Dr. Tunstall was suspicious of a potentially heretical venture. Failing to obtain patronage in England, Tyndale left in 1524 to continue his work in Germany, where he became acquainted with Martin Luther. Inspired by the example of Luther, Tyndale started translating the New Testament from the original Greek, from the text that had recently been established by Erasmus. Under the influence of the populist ideas of both Erasmus and Luther, Tyndale sought to produce an English Bible that would be accessible and intelligible to all people, even "a boy that driveth the plough" (Daniell 1989: viii).

By now the establishment was seriously alarmed by his activities. When publication was prevented in Cologne, Tyndale completed his work in Worms in 1525. Ports were watched, and copies of his English New Testament were burned as soon as they reached England. Its readers were persecuted, and there was a public burning of Tyndale's Bibles at Paul's Cross. So ruthless were the authorities that only one copy of Tyndale's first complete New Testament is known to have survived. His work was denounced by the Church hierarchy and others such as Thomas More, who demanded Tyndale's death as a heretic. Even in the face of such efforts to intimidate him, Tyndale was undeterred. In Antwerp, where he had taken refuge, he produced another edition of the New Testament. He also learned Hebrew and started on the Old Testament. Catholic authorities caught up with him in Antwerp in 1535 and he was arrested by agents of Emperor Charles V. Accused of heresy and condemned to death, Tyndale was strangled and burned at the stake on October 6, 1536. His final words are said to have been: "Lord! Open the King of England's eyes".

Only a few months after the execution of Tyndale, the tide turned in England. Having broken with Rome, Henry VIII ordered that a copy of the English Bible be placed in every church in his kingdom. Ironically, this Bible was in large part Tyndale's, but it did not bear his name, since he was regarded as an outspoken Lutheran heretic. Moreover, despite the fact that Tyndale had defended the supremacy of the king in the state, he had vehemently opposed Henry VIII's divorce. Tyndale's translations, stripped of their prefaces and glosses, were published again and again under other names.

In 1535, as Tyndale awaited execution, Miles Coverdale published the first complete English Bible, based largely on Tyndale's work. Coverdale himself was in exile on the Continent at the time. Under the patronage of Thomas Cromwell, the minister to Henry VIII responsible for drafting the legislation that severed

England from the Roman Catholic Church, Coverdale issued the "Great Bible" in 1539 in collaboration with Richard Grafton.

Another well-known edition of the Bible was produced around the same time by John Rogers (c.1500–55), under the pseudonym Thomas Matthew. Rogers was a chaplain to English merchants in Antwerp. There he met Tyndale and converted to Protestantism. He combined Tyndale's translations with those of Coverdale to produce a complete Bible known as the "Matthew's Bible" (1537). Rogers was later imprisoned and sentenced to death, the first Protestant to be martyred under the Catholic Queen Mary I, also known as "Bloody Mary".

The influence of William Tyndale's translation carried over into the production of the Authorized Version of 1611. It is said that eighty per cent of the Authorized Version of the New Testament is in fact Tyndale's prose. A scholar of Greek and Hebrew, Tyndale also seemed to possess a natural instinct for how those languages might be rendered in English. The words he forged and the phrases he constructed were so clear and imaginative that all subsequent translations have drawn on them (Daniell 1989 and 2003).[20]

The *Authorized Version*, also known as the *King James Version*, was the work of fifty-four scholars.[21] Commissioned by King James (1566–1625), these scholars drew up an elaborate set of rules for the work to be done. They worked in six groups, the work of each group checked by the others. The objective of the translators was not to produce a totally new version, but rather to preserve the best parts of existing ones. Thus, their "translation" consisted largely of a revision of previous versions and, to a significant extent, Tyndale's Bible. Celebrated for its elegant style and superb prose, the *King James Version* remained the standard Bible of the English-speaking world for nearly four hundred years.

Subsequent revisions would emulate the committee model, beginning with the "Revised Version" (N.T. 1881; O.T. 1885). Unlike the translators of 1611, the nineteenth-century revisers scrupulously followed the original Greek text word for word. Their goal was to offer an easy-to-follow translation, to catch the solemn repetition of words and phrases, to mark the subtleties of expression and to convey the strangeness of unusual forms of speech. When it was first published, however, the new translation was not enthusiastically received.

In their expeditions to the New World and other continents, Europeans encountered peoples who had never before been exposed to Christianity. As the Europeans sought to propagate their world view, including their religious beliefs, translations became a necessary tool. In the wake of the Reformation, Bible translation was often undertaken by scholars and missionaries who had acquired their knowledge of non-European languages for the express purpose of conveying their religious message. They all had a special interest in translation, but often no clear notions of translation principles or techniques.

In an interesting, but not unusual, convergence of commerce and proselytism, members of the Dutch East India Company, formed in 1602, produced one of the earliest translations of the Scriptures into a non-European language. John (Jan) Van Hasel, a director of the company, completed a Malay version of the gospel according to Matthew. Soon after, in 1612, another Dutch trader, Albert Cornelisson (Cornelisz) Ruyl, also translated Matthew. His version was considered preferable to Van Hasel's so he set out to translate the rest of the New Testament. He died before it was completed, but his versions of Matthew and Mark were printed, along with the Dutch versions, in Holland in 1629. Van Hasel, meanwhile, persevered and completed a Malay version of all four gospels, of which Luke and John were published in Amsterdam in 1646 (McClintock and Strong 1885:690).

John Eliot (1604–90), a Cambridge-trained Puritan minister, travelled to America, where he undertook a similar task. He arrived in the Massachusetts Bay Colony in 1631, just eleven years after the first pilgrims. After preparing an Indian catechism (1653), he translated the New Testament (1661) and then the whole Bible (1663) into Algonquian, the language of the Massachusetts Indians. This was the first Bible to be published in North America. It was the twenty-second language into which the whole Bible had been translated, and the earliest example of translation and printing of the entire Bible into a new language as a means of evangelization.

In Canada, Catholic translators and missionaries followed the waves of colonial expansion under the French regime (1534–1760). The first translations were undertaken by Pierre Maillard (c.1710–62), who translated religious texts into the Algonquian language of the Micmac Indians of Eastern Canada. Maillard devised a grammar for the Micmac language and invented a system of hieroglyphic symbols as well as a phonetic alphabet. He translated a number of biblical texts and other material for religious instruction, which have been preserved and handed down from one generation to the next (Johnson 1974; Gallant 1990).

The "conquest" of Canada by the English in 1760 ushered in a new period of religious translation, since the English were predominantly Protestant. Silas Rand (1810–89), a Baptist minister and missionary who also happened to be a philologist and ethnologist, translated several parts of the Old Testament and the entire New Testament into Micmac, which he published in 1875 in Halifax. He was largely unsuccessful in drawing the Micmac nation away from Catholicism, however. His anthropological interest in Micmac mythology drew him toward the alien culture and inspired him to preserve it through translation rather than to assimilate it through conversion. He translated from Micmac into English and collected 900 manuscript pages of legends, devoting as much time to this task as he had to his Bible translation and meticulously checking and rechecking each text with a Micmac storyteller. Silas Rand's *Legends of the Micmacs* was published in 1864 and remains key to understanding the Micmac oral tradition (Gallant 1990).[22]

The nineteenth century saw a dramatic increase in the number of languages into which the Bible was translated. During the first third of the century, there were translations into over eighty-six new languages, sixty-six of which were non-European languages: forty-three Asian, ten American, seven African and six languages of Oceania. Noteworthy English-speaking translators of the Bible were: Robert Morrison (1782–1834), the first Protestant missionary in China, who produced a complete Bible in 1823; Adoniram Judson (1788–1850), an American Baptist missionary serving in Burma, who produced a New Testament in 1832 and Bible in 1835; Samuel Robbins Brown (1810–80), an American missionary to China and Japan, who translated the New Testament into Japanese in 1879; John Ross (1842–1915), a Scottish missionary to China who is also known for translating the first Korean Bible in 1887; and Henry Martyn (1781–1812), an Anglican missionary to India and Persia, who translated the New Testament into Urdu, Persian and Judaeo-Persic between 1806 and 1812. William Carey (1761–1834), a Baptist minister, settled at the Serampore mission, near Calcutta, where he made Bengali translations of the New Testament in 1801 and the Old Testament in 1809, and then went on to translate parts of the Bible into thirty-four Indian languages or dialects with his companions William Ward and Joshua Marshman (Smalley 1991). By the end of the nineteenth century, the Scriptures had been translated into a total of 570 languages and dialects.

The missionary enterprise continues to this day. Operating in over 200 countries and territories, 146 national Bible societies came together under one umbrella organization, the United Bible Societies, in 1946. Together, these societies constitute the biggest translator, publisher and distributor of the Bible in the world, and are also involved in areas such as literacy training and humanitarian activities. Members have travelled to the most isolated areas of the globe in order to ensure that all linguistic groups, no matter how small, have access to the Christian Scriptures in their own languages. There are now more than 450 complete Bible translations with the Scriptures now available in 2,527 of the world's estimated 6,500 languages (http://www.unitedbiblesocieties.org, accessed October 2011).

Behind this far-reaching activity lies a considerable body of knowledge. The study of Bible translation continues in various forums, such as the Eugene A. Nida Institute, the research and professional development arm of the American Bible Society. Established in 2001 and named for renowned linguist and translation scholar Eugene Nida (1914–2011), the Institute has supported scholarship, conferences and publications in the field of Bible translation, among its other functions, with a view to strenghtening translation studies in general.

Missionary translators have exercised a very special kind of power. As representatives of a dominant foreign culture, translating texts of such stature, they are endowed with prodigious authority. The influence of their translation work has been augmented by the prestige of the source language and culture, generally American English. The translations have often initiated a dialectic of cultural tensions, which – in the case of some Amazonian tribes, for instance – have resulted in an accelerated process of assimilation into the dominant culture. From a postcolonial perspective, missionary translation is controversial. Viewed in a negative light, it stems from an aggressive mentality and a dual "mindset": "an arrogant claim that I/we alone know the truth or what is best for you, and a driving sense of duty to 'enlighten' the benighted 'heathens' or to 'civilize' the 'barbarous' other" (Wang 2008: 18).

At the same time, scholarship has yielded fresh perspectives on religious translation in a postcolonial context. Taking an Afrocentric, or "postmissionary", approach to translation in a world where there is an increasing shift in Christianity from North to South is seen as a step in the right direction: "As the struggle for political independence was rooted in the literary movement of Negritude, so African theology is rooted in an open dialogue with African culture" (Aroga Bessong and Kenmogne 2007: 380).

New insights into the historical and literary wealth of the original text have continued to inspire translators, and new readings and cultural adaptations have continued to emerge. Since the second half of the twentieth century, there has been an explosion in Bible translations. *The New English Bible* (1970), the expression of the most important bodies in the Protestant community of Great Britain, was unusual in having among its committee members a poet, T. S. Eliot. Criticized for excessive freedom in interpreting the Hebrew text, the NEB was revised and published in 1990 as *The Revised English Bible*. Ecumenical versions vie with "ordinary language versions", and interconfessional and intercultural texts like *The New Arabic Bible* (1992) compete with more obviously sectarian versions.

Efforts have been made to eliminate discrimination based on race and gender through the use of "inclusive" language. Feminist interpretations of the Bible have had a significant impact, originating with what is known as the first wave of feminism of the late nineteenth century.[23] Elizabeth Cady Stanton (1815–1902), one of the most prominent American suffragettes, produced *The Woman's Bible* in 1898, in itself not a new translation, but rather a compilation of texts, accompanied by commentary, aimed at correcting the masculine bias of previous versions. Her compatriot, Julia Smith (1793–1886), was the first woman to translate the entire Bible on her own, something she did from the Greek and Hebrew. She published her Bible in 1876 at her own expense (Von Flotow 2002). Changing ideologies inspire fresh interpretations: a feminist translation of the Bible's love poetry, *The Song of Songs*, produced by Marcia Falk in 1982, is a good example.

In 1997, the International Bible Society, the U.S. publisher of the New International Version (NIV), issued a new gender-inclusive edition in Great Britain.[24] This provoked a reaction from ultra-conservative groups in the United States, where it was never distributed. As one observer wrote in an editorial, "Don't give in to feminist pressures to rewrite the Scriptures" (quoted in Burke 2005: 129). Later on, in 2002, the International Bible Society did in fact publish a gender-inclusive edition of the NIV, to be called TNIV (Today's NIV) but it was made clear that this version was merely an "alternative" to, rather than a replacement of, the traditional New International Version (Burke 2005: 140).

The English Bible has also been published in versions intended for very specific readerships (Noss 2007: 18). One example, whose success is reflected in its numerous editions, is Clarence Jordan's *The Cotton Patch Gospel*, a series that began with a first volume in 1968; four volumes have been issued and reprinted several times and are now available in Kindle format. Also of note are Christopher Goodwins's *The New Testament in Limerick Verse* (2001) and a version by Kel Richards (2006) titled *The Aussie Bible (Well, bits of it anyway!)*, which was based on a similar one called *The Cockney Bible: Well, bits of it anyway...* (Coles 2001) and which was followed in 2008 by *More Aussie Bible*.

In addition, the Bible has been translated into artificially constructed languages like Esperanto (Noss 2007: 18). A particularly intriguing example is the Klingon Bible Translation Project undertaken by the Klingon Language Institute, which on its website proclaims that while its "goals do not include missionary work" the project is worthy for "purely secular reasons".[25] They have taken on the translation of the Bible, as they have the translation of Shakespeare, to elevate the status of the artificial language.

In post-missionary Africa, multimedia resources have been put into play in the context of the "Afrocentric approach to Bible translation" referred to above. Just as the Christian population of the past had access to Scripture through painting, iconography, songs and means other than the printed text, African dancing, dramatic representation and even television and film – all rooted in local cultures – can play a role in the process of "rectifying some of the serious mistakes of the missionary approach" (Aroga Bessong and Kenmogne 2007: 380).

Islam: the Koran, untranslatable yet abundantly translated

Unlike Christianity, Islam has not readily embraced translation as a means of propagating its doctrine. Just as Judaic texts underscore the role of Hebrew as the language of revelation, several Koranic verses explicitly state that Arabic, and no other language, was intended to be the vehicle of the Divine word. For example:

"Thus we have sent it down as an Arabic Qur'an, that you might comprehend" (12:2). Similarly, the Koran proclaims its own superb eloquence and unique style, which render it practically irreproducible in any other language: "This is a message brought down by the Merciful, the Compassionate: A Book of Revelations eloquently expressed" (41:2). The doctrine of the *inimitability*, and hence untranslatability, of the Koran is an element of general agreement in the Muslim community.

Why is the Koran considered untranslatable? For Muslim scholars, the answer lies in the belief that it is a "linguistic miracle with transcendental meanings that cannot be captured fully by human faculty" which accounts for titles of translated texts such as *The Meaning of the Qur'an* or *The Message of the Qur'an*, but not *The Qur'an* on its own (Abdul-Raof 2005:162). Throughout history, the Koranic text has been associated with the expressive quality of the Arabic language, reflected in the rich body of pre-Islamic poetry. Early Muslim scholastic tradition placed the debate about the inimitability of the Koran within a broader theological concern with the Divine Essence. Any attempt at translation is futile since eternal discourse, as embodied in the Koran, cannot be imitated or reproduced by any human.

And yet, the *World Bibliography of Translations of the Meanings of the Holy Qur'ân* (Binark and Eren 1986) lists 2,672 translations of the Koran, printed from 1515 to 1980 alone, into some seventy languages. As early as the ninth century, within two hundred years of the death of the Prophet Mohammed, translations from Arabic into other languages began to emerge, usually in interlinear form in order to preserve the original sacred text. The diversity of linguistic and religious groups for whom translations were made over the centuries reflects not only the wide interest of non-Arabic speakers in the Koran, but also the complexity of the very task of translating it. The fact that there are over 300 translations in Urdu alone, for example, indicates a lack of unanimity with regard to both the meaning and translatability of the Scripture. Considering that the Arabic Koran is commonly used for liturgical purposes, that the call to prayer is recited in Arabic and that learning the Koran in the original Arabic is still an essential element in the training of Muslims all over the world, one might well wonder at the existence of these myriad translations.

Historically, however, the expansion of the "Abode of Islam" (*dâr al-Islâm*) across non-Arabic-speaking communities has generated a variety of responses to the theological implications of language. The Koran has defined itself in universalistic terms as "an admonition for the whole world" (81:27). As the religion spread across a territory that was increasingly polyglot, there was a need to reconcile this dimension of the Koran with its semantic inaccessibility to non-Arabs. Several abortive attempts were made to use translations for liturgical purposes in languages other than Arabic (Binark and Eren 1986). More successful, and ideologically more acceptable, was the practice of "interpreting" or "commenting on" Koranic passages rather than "translating" them as such. Thus, emphasis was placed on the complementary nature of the translation rather than on its substitution for the sacred text.

In the Islamic tradition, three modes of reception of the Koran link the aural, visual and cognitive processes: oral recitation, writing (copying, or the art of calligraphy, is a sacred act) and reading (textual interpretation). This complex interaction between Muslims and the Koran, combined with the multidimensional nature of the text itself, make the function of the translator as a propagator of religious ideas appear rather ambiguous. As is the case for Judaism, translations have been undertaken, not to secure conversion to Islam but to accompany and reinforce integration of believers into the Islamic community.

Shal Wali Allah (1703–62), an Indian theologian and reformer, was the author of a controversial annotated translation of the Koran into Persian, the literary language of eighteenth-century Muslim India. He wanted to bypass religious scholars and make the Scriptures directly available to the literate public. The first Muslim to publish an English translation with explanatory notes of the entire Koran was Mohammed Alî Lahori (1874–1951), a prominent Muslim scholar. His version was published in 1917.

In the West, curiosity regarding the Orient was motivated by fear as well as fascination, and translations have sometimes been undertaken in order to refute the arguments of Islam, as the next chapter will show. The first translation into Latin of the Koran was done by Robert of Chester; it was officially commissioned by the Abbott of Cluny, who financed a team of translators working in Spain. The translation was completed in 1142–43 and later printed by Theodor Bibliander in Basel in 1543, with commentary by Martin Luther and Philipp Melanchthon, among others.[26] The Basel edition – adapted and re-translated – exercised considerable influence. Other translations followed in the seventeenth century, often accompanied by polemical material. A 1698 edition of Ludovico Marracci's Latin translation of the Koran, previously published in 1691, was accompanied by a *Prodromus ad refutationem Alcoran* (Preamble to a refutation of the Koran), which was an indication that the intended purpose of the translation was to counter the ideas of the Koran (Binark and Eren 1986).[27] In 1649, Alexander Ross (c.1590–1654), who did not know Arabic, translated the Koran into English from the 1647 French version of André Du Ryer (1580–1660). Ross warned his readers that while the Koran might be "a poyson, that hath infected a very great, but most unsound part of the Universe", his translation might also prove to be an "Antidote", which would confirm in the reader the "health of Christianity" (Arberry 1955:7).

Pope Alexander VII, pontiff from 1655 to 1667, renewed the Church's ban on publishing the Koran, both in the original and in translation. It was not until 1772 that a German edition of the Koran, translated directly from Arabic by David Friedrich Megerlin (c.1698–1750), was published in Frankfurt-am-Main. The best known English renditions of the Koran include those of Salé (1734) and Palmer (1880), as well as more contemporary translations by Bell (1939) and Arberry (1955). George Sale (1697–1736) was a solicitor, Orientalist and author of a ten-volume dictionary. Edward Henry Palmer (1840–82) was also an Orientalist, at Cambridge, familiar with Arabic, Persian and other eastern languages. He participated in expeditions to the Middle East and had some success in negotiations with the Bedouin on behalf of the British authorities, until he and his companions were ambushed and murdered in the desert. Richard Bell (1876–1952) was a British Arabist at the University of Edinburgh. Arthur John Arberry (1905–69) was a scholar of Arabic, Persian, and Islamic studies, who held various distinguished chairs and professorships; his is considered to be one of the most highly respected versions of the Koran produced by a non-Muslim scholar.

Noteworthy French versions include the 1647 translation by Du Ryer, the 1783 version by M. Claude-Étienne Savary (1750–88), a pioneer of Egyptology, and the 1847 critical edition of the Koran by Régis Blachère (1900–73), a French Orientalist and professor of Arabic in Morocco and at the Sorbonne.

The titles of some translations of the Koran have continued to reflect their particular status as companion texts, rather than substitutions for the original. A 1930 version by Marmaduke Pickthall (1875–1936) was entitled *The Meaning of the Glorious Koran*. Arberry called his translation *The Koran Interpreted*. In his view, "the Koran is untranslatable […] the rhetoric and rhythm of the Arabic of the Koran are so characteristic, so powerful, so highly emotive, that any version whatsoever is bound in the nature of things to be but a poor copy of the glittering splendour of the original" (Arberry 1955: 27).

This kind of translation, however, must be possible because it is happening, as Lynne Long points out in a collection of essays aptly titled *Translation and Religion. Holy Untranslatable?* "Whether it is permitted or not", she explains, "it is necessary and difficult and will never be satisfactory to everyone" (Long 2005: 15). An online tool offers "non-Arabic-speaking brethren" access to the holy text of Islam in thirty-eight languages from Albanian to Zulu with the following caveat: "We are aware that the translation of the meanings of the Glorious Qur'an, however accurate it may be, must fall short of conveying the wealth of meaning that the miraculous text of the original conveys" (http://alagr.com, Foreword to the English translation, accessed January 2012). In a world characterized by large-scale migration, practising Muslims find themselves in situations where they need the help of translations to understand their sacred text. In a post 9/11 age, moreover, curiosity, and perhaps fear once again, have given rise to translations addressed not only to those inside but also to those outside the Muslim community.

Hinduism: the case of the Bhagavad Gita

The Hindu tradition covers a period of four thousand years. The range of sacred texts is so wide that the history of their translation is best illustrated by selecting one particular text (Sharma 1993: 26–35). The Bhagavad Gita seems a particularly appropriate choice for several reasons: it is a widely known Hindu text with a long history of translation. Parts of the Gita were translated into Arabic as early as the eleventh century; it was translated into numerous Indian languages other than Sanskrit starting in the thirteenth century (Esnoul and Lacombe 1972; Bolle 1979; Callewaert and Hemraj 1983). After Sir Charles Wilkins (1749–1836), a printer and writer in the service of the East India Company, produced the translation of the Bhagavad Gita into English, it was translated into other European languages.

The role of the translator in circulating the Bhagavad Gita, and in extending and modifying it within the Hindu tradition, is best illustrated by focusing on two major translations of the Gita in modern times: a translation into Marathi by Bal Gangadhar Tilak (1856–1920) and another into Gujarati by Mahatma Gandhi (1869–1948).[28] Both translations are accompanied by commentary and both are available in English translation (Tilak 1965; Desai 1970).

The Bhagavad Gita, which means "The Lord's Song" in English, had always been an important text within Hinduism, but Tilak has been credited with having launched it on its trajectory of modern popularity, extending its role within Hinduism (Panikkar 1963). Unlike many Hindu scriptures, such as the Vedas in classical and medieval Hinduism, whose access was subject to caste and gender restrictions, access to the Bhagavad Gita has always been open to all. This undoubtedly helped Tilak, but he also broadened the influence of the Gita and modified the way in which it was understood. In the premodern period, the message of the Gita had been presented either as mystical or devotional in essence, and consequently other-worldly in orientation. Through his translation, as well his commentary, which he wrote while incarcerated by the British on charges of sedition, Tilak argued that the real message of the Gita was a call to action – to worldly, though selfless, action. It is easy to see why such an interpretation of the Gita would be favourably received by a people who had begun to feel restive under the British yoke and who yearned to cast it off. Tilak helped spread the word and the authority of the Gita. He made it yield a message of militant activism, to such an extent that some of his followers assassinated two British officers (Embree 1972: 301).

After Tilak's death in 1920, Mahatma Gandhi followed in his footsteps. Gandhi extended the Gita's importance within Hinduism even further by calling it his "mother" (Gandhi 1950: 157) and by offering his own translation (Sarma 1956). Gandhi agreed with Tilak that the thrust of the Gita was one of action. Whereas Tilak had translated the Gita to emphasize the message of *militant* action, however, Gandhi read into the text a message of *nonviolence*. Like Tilak before him, Gandhi both broadened the authority of the Gita within Hinduism and modified its message.

How could two prominent translators offer opposite interpretations of the same text? The answer lies in the way in which the Gita is related to the *Mahabharata*, the great epic of which it is a part. This epic, and especially the battle that is central to it – the conflict between the Pandavas and the Kauravas – may be understood either literally or allegorically. Tilak interpreted the context literally, as an actual battle between two armies, and he translated the Gita in his way, emphasizing militant struggle. Gandhi, on the other hand, understood the context allegorically as representing the fight between good and evil within the human soul. Accordingly, he translated the Gita to emphasize the nonviolent nature of the struggle. Both interpretations have the support of tradition (Sharma 1983: 44, 47).

The translator, then, plays a crucial role in the transmission and interpretation of Hindu texts. In fact, the translator determines the broad message of the text as much as its actual meaning. In this respect, the case of Tilak and Gandhi is not unique. The same type of manipulation is illustrated by the translation of another Hindu sacred text, the Rig Veda.[29] This collection of hymns dating from before the second millennium BCE was translated by Friedrich Max Müller (more commonly known as Max Müller) (1823–1900) and Swami Dayananda Sarasvati (1824–83), the former interpreting and translating the texts henotheistically, that is, in terms of the worship of several gods, and the latter monotheistically (Singh 1971).[30]

In a recent collection of essays, a "corrective hermeneutical lens" has been applied to the study of Hindu thought, beginning with the implications of applying the Western word and concept of "religion" to phenomena beyond the Western world (Sherma and Sharma 2008). It is misleading, according to one of the co-editors, to "lump together" the "widely disparate perceptions and attitudes that make up Indian religion" (Sharma 2008: 19). The Western concept of religion was introduced not only intellectually but administratively: the British colonial census in former times and the Indian census to this day identify one person with one religion. This has ignored the pluralism of India and has shaped Indian religious reality in a Western mould, whereas the situation in India might have resembled that of Japan, where several religions co-exist (Sharma 2008: 23–29). The volume also offers a postcolonialist critique of Max Müller's fifty-volume series, *The Sacred Books of The East*, the purpose of which was to select representative texts of the various Eastern traditions for translation into the English language (Sugirtharajah 2008). Not only were Müller's hermeneutics informed by Victorian evolutionary theories, historicism and comparative philology, but his project of "textual management" had the financial backing of the East India Company and the support of royal patronage. His work, as one of the foremost Orientalists of his time, served to further the intellectual conquest of India and assist missionaries in their work (Sugirtharajah 2008: 34). The "erudite scholarship" of Max Müller is acknowledged – the devil is "given his due" (Sharma 2008: 236) – albeit from a rebalanced perspective that provides for a broader, more inclusive view of Hindu traditions, understood as including both written texts and oral transmission.

Buddhism: the spread of the religion across East Asia

Unlike the Brahmanic tradition of Hinduism, which used Sanskrit as a scriptural medium, Buddhism has never known the concept of a sacred language.[31] Buddhist scriptures have been translated into a great variety of regional languages for centuries. Even Pali, the written medium of the oldest form of Buddhism, was not the language of the original canonical texts used during Buddhist sermons. Over time, however, the propagation of Buddhism led to the development and canonization of a "clerical literary idiom", such as classical Chinese in Japan and Korea, Pali in continental Southeastern Asia and literary Tibetan in Tibet.

The tremendous geographical spread of Buddhism from India through East Asia (first into China and northern Vietnam during the first century CE, then 500 years later to Korea and Japan, and in the thirteenth century to Tibet and Mongolia) gave rise to considerable translation activity, particularly in China. The missionaries who came to China during the first century were seldom fluent in Chinese and only a handful of Chinese are known to have mastered Sanskrit. Chinese versions of Buddhist texts were typically produced by a translation team, the foreign master reciting the text and, usually with the help of an interpreter, making a very crude translation. This version was written down and then revised and polished by Chinese assistants. This process accounted for the radical sinicization of Buddhism and its rapid assimilation into Chinese culture.

A more systematic programme of translation was undertaken by the prominent scholar Kumarajiva (c.350–410) at the beginning of the fifth century. Earlier translations had used notions and ideograms that were familiar to Chinese thought. As he translated the Buddhist canon, Kumarajiva created an extensive terminology aimed at replacing the Taoist terms that had formerly been used to express key Buddhist concepts. He employed large numbers of monks in the process and gave lectures on the texts he was translating to audiences numbering in the thousands.

The famous Chinese monk Xuan Zang (Figures 12 and 22) travelled to India in the seventh century, bringing back many Buddhist manuscripts which he spent the remainder of his life translating.[32] These translations contributed further to the spread of Buddhism in China.

The Sanskrit and other Indic texts introduced a wide range of linguistic forms that were unfamiliar to the Chinese: a complex grammatical configuration of nouns in three numbers and three genders, verbs in three persons and numbers, designations of past and present tense and so on. The Chinese did not have a corresponding syllabary and, when translating, had to employ a pictographic system of writing, which lacked the possibility of expressing case, number, tense, mood or voice. Despite these linguistic obstacles, the Chinese devoted themselves to the translation of the Buddhist canon and in the process preserved hundreds of texts that have since disappeared in their original form. Ironically, some of the Chinese versions may actually be closer to the Sanskrit *Urtext*, or original, than later Sanskrit versions produced in India and Nepal.

Translators were instrumental in spreading Buddhism in the Far East, in establishing literary languages and in laying the foundations for Chinese thought through a "comingling of and conflict between the exotic Buddhism and the native Confucianism and Taoism" (Lin 2002: 162–163). The work of missionary translators of the Buddhist faith is analogous to that of their Christian counterparts, but their impact on Eastern culture was more far-reaching as it occurred at a much earlier date.

Translating the sacred texts of the East

The sacred texts of major Eastern religions have also been translated into Western languages. From the eighteenth century on, in particular, European translations offered knowledge and understanding of the East to Western readers. The precise nature of this understanding, and the motives that lay behind the construction of a Western view of the East and its religions, have been the object of considerable debate over past decades.

The translations of Hindu texts by William Jones (1746–94), the first great Orientalist and Sanskrit scholar, had a significant impact on the West and were read by many eighteenth-century writers.[33] The French scholar A. H. Anquetil-Duperron (1731–1805) published a Latin translation of the *Zend Avesta*, a commentary of the Avesta in Pahlavi.[34] Eugène Burnouf (1801–52), a French Orientalist, published a Pali grammar and translated the *Lotus Sutra*, the sermons of Buddha, while Max Müller, mentioned above, produced his extensive series of Eastern texts.

While first praised for their scholarly contributions, these translators and their work are being revisited. The concept of "Orientalism" has been re-examined and critiqued as a tool of domination and discrimination (Said 1978). In this context, Orientalism is less about scholarship than empire. The work of missionaries, many of whom were translators, has been similarly re-evaluated. Some of the missionaries acquired a profound knowledge of the country in which they worked, along with familiarity with its language and religious practices. This "know thine enemy" or "martial" approach is thought to have been put into practice in order to better convert the "heathens" (Girardot 2002: 62; quoted in Wang 2008: 41). The situation is far from straightforward, however, as illustrated by the case of James Legge.[35]

James Legge (1815–91) is widely regarded as one of the most influential missionary-translators. His translations of *The Chinese Classics* (1861–72; second edition 1893–95) and *The Sacred Books of China* (1879–91) "continue to this day to be republished and employed by Western scholars" (Pfister 1995: 401). He contributed primarily to the translation of Confucian texts, but is also responsible for the translation of some Taoist and Buddhist material.[36] The (re)evaluation of his work by recent biographers and translation scholars is enlightening in that it reflects the critique of Orientalism triggered by Edward Said, which sparked the various currents of postcolonialist thought prevalent to this day.

Sent to the Far East in the service of the London Missionary Society for the purpose of converting the "heathens" to Christianity, Legge was far more than a missionary. He was subject to an "intriguing confluence of historical, cultural, intellectual and religious influences" (Pfister 1995: 401). During the thirty years he spent in Hong Kong, Legge set aside a significant portion of his time to intensive labours of studying, translating and publishing the Confucian canon, which he was the first to call the Chinese "classics", in English (Pfister 2004). So much so that, by 1873, he in fact resigned his duties as missionary entirely and returned to England to pursue strictly scholarly occupations. By the time he returned, his reputation as an Orientalist was such that private funding had been raised to create a chair in Chinese at Oxford University.

Legge occupied this chair and thus became the first professor of Chinese at Oxford University. He provided assistance to Max Müller in publishing *The Sacred Books of the East* series, which included his own work. Not unlike the monk Xuan Zang, he spent the last twenty years of his life dedicated to his labours as a translator, in a study surrounded by his books. Rising at three o'clock every morning, he would make himself a cup of tea, and then "work away at his translations while all the household slept" (*Pall Mall Gazette*, December 1897: 10).

James Legge is considered such a towering figure in the history of translation because of the sheer volume of his work, his meticulous method of translating and retranslating over the years, and his continuing influence. In the voluminous body of writing about Legge, his life, work and attitudes toward the Chinese have been analysed from different perspectives.

Legge has had his detractors: he has been characterized as a "missionary whose view of China was tinted (if not tainted) by his failure to see them on their own terms" and whose translations were "masterly but misguided" (Eoyang 1993:107). This point of view, however, misses Legge's "progressive transformation" from missionary to sinologist, and his movement toward a more "academic and secular Oriental scholarship" (Girardot 2002:62 and 687, n. 53).

Legge's life and life's work have been amply documented by Girardot (2002) and Pfister (2004), who have taken account of these complexities. While both are thought to have combined "cultural breadth and biographical depth", they are also considered "too sympathetic and trusting" in their assessment, in the opinion of a Chinese scholar, who undertakes a postcolonial reading of Legge that is "necessarily ideologically charged and critical, because it seeks to uncover the imperialistic violence underlying colonial discourse" (Wang 2008:17). Despite reservations of this nature, however, the translations of James Legge, accompanied by their scholarly apparatus – prefatory material, notes, and indexes – have been and continue to be standard editions, for the time being at least.

Each generation adds to our knowledge of the past and provides new motivation for translating religious texts. While the translation of religious texts remains tightly bound to institutions of religious authority, it has now become possible to bring to light the literary, cultural and documentary values of religious texts. And so today's translator is not necessarily a theologian; he or she might be a poet or a cultural historian.

In the twenty-first century, the displacement and migration of peoples around the globe are bringing cultures into contact with one another; sacred texts, too, are increasingly coming into contact with other cultures. Translation of these texts, therefore, however difficult, even "untranslatable" or "impossible", is indeed occurring. Heightened curiosity about world religions, a postcolonial openness to the other, and a need "to understand how other cultures work in order to live peacefully together" make the sacred texts of the world required reading for all and their "sympathetic translations crucial" (Long 2005:2).

Notes

1.   This chapter deals with religious texts in general: sacred texts, or scripture, as well as certain auxiliary texts used by the various world religions for liturgical, educational or other purposes.

2.   The authoritative and nonsectarian *Encyclopedia of Religion* (Jones 2005), for instance, has no entry on translation. Lynne Long, editor of the collection *Translation and Religion* (2005) takes both a cross-religious and cross-cultural perspective, bringing into play the writings of postcolonial critics, such as Homi Bhabha (1994) and Tejaswini Niranjana (1992), to provide a framework for discussing the translation of holy texts.

3. Koran may also be spelled Coran or Qur'ân. The most common English spelling, "Koran", will be used throughout this chapter, with the exception of quotations and titles in which other spellings have been used. Similarly, Bhagavad Gita is used without accents.

4. The Torah, which literally means "teaching", is generally translated as "Law"; strictly speaking, it refers to the five books of Moses, or the Pentateuch, but it refers more broadly to all twenty-four books of the Hebrew Bible. The Talmud, which signifies "learning" in Hebrew, is a compilation of Jewish law and lore. Together with the Hebrew Bible, it forms the basis of Jewish religious life. It is in two parts: the Mishna, written primarily in Hebrew around 200 CE, which is a codification of oral law; and the Gemara, written mainly in Aramaic between the third and fifth centuries CE, which is commentary on the Mishna.

5. The number seventy was used to designate humanity as a whole: the "seventy" nations and their "seventy" languages.

6. Aramaic was the *lingua franca* of large parts of southwest Asia from approximately 300 BCE to 650 CE, and it was the everyday language of Palestine.

7. *Meturgeman* is the Hebrew adaptation of the Aramaic *turgeman*, from which the English word *dragoman* derived via Arabic.

8. The language of the Septuagint was in fact what has been called "Koine" Greek. Koine was the popular form of Greek, the *lingua franca* for the eastern Mediterranean and Near East in the post-classical period (c.300 BCE–300 CE).

9. In the Eastern Orthodox Churches, the Septuagint is still regarded as the official ecclesiastical version of the Old Testament.

10. The Masoretic text, intended to establish a uniform and correct text of the Hebrew Bible, was elaborated by Hebrew scholars known as Masoretes. Their work extended from the fifth to the twelfth centuries.

11. Onkelos and Aquila were converts to Judaism. According to one theory, they are one and the same person, with the name "Onkelos" a variant of "Aquila" and applied in error to the Aramaic version of the Torah.

12. For example, the word "virgin" was used for the Christian version and "young girl" maintained for the Jewish one.

13. See Chapter 2 and note 27.

14. The title itself is evocative of its female audience: it is derived from a Hebrew verse of the Song of Songs (3:11), *Tze'nah u-Re'nah*, meaning "Go forth and see, daughters of Zion" (O maidens of Zion, go forth and gaze …).

15. Wikipedia gives 2,572 as of May 2011 (http://en.wikipedia.org/wiki/Bible_translations_by_language , accessed July 2011). The website of the United Bible Societies gives the number 2,527 (http://www.unitedbiblesocieties.org/?page_id=207, accessed October 2011).

16. Since 1992, FIT's annual celebration of International Translation Day (Journée mondiale de la traduction) has coincided with St. Jerome's feast day, September 30.

17. Jerome compiled an etymological dictionary of proper names and an index of place names mentioned in the Bible, and undertook a critical study of difficult passages in the book of Genesis.

18. See Chapter 3.

19. At the Fourth Session of the Council of Trent, April 6, 1546, the *Vulgate* was established as the only version "authentic for public lectures, disputations, preaching, and explanation". This decision was reversed on September 30, 1943 by the encyclical *Divino Afflante Spiritu* issued by Pope Pius XII, which opened the way for translation and biblical criticism (see Delisle 2005).

20. Tyndale is discussed in the context of the development of the English language in Chapter 2.

21. *The Authorized Version* is also commonly referred to as the *King James Version* (KJV) or *King James Bible*. The scholars were chosen from Oxford, Cambridge and Westminster. Some of the most noteworthy among them were Dr. Lancelot Andrewes, later Bishop of Winchester, who oversaw the project and who was familiar with Hebrew, Chaldaic, Syriac, Greek, Latin and at least ten other languages; Dr. John Overall, professor of theology and later Bishop of Norwich; William Bedwell, the greatest Arabic scholar of Europe; and Sir Henry Savile, the most learned layman of his time.

22. See also Chapter 3, which describes the work of German missionary Adolf Vielhauer, who translated the Bible into Mungaka, a Cameroonian language, and also compiled, transcribed and published indigenous oral literature.

23. "First-wave feminism" refers to the women's movement of the late nineteenth and early twentieth century in the U.K., Canada and United States. It focused primarily on gaining women's suffrage – hence the term "suffragette" – and, by extension, the right of women to be treated as equals to men. The term "first wave" was coined retroactively by feminists of the 1970s who recognized their predecessors by calling themselves "second-wave" feminists.

24. In 1973, the International Bible Society published the New International Version New Testament and, in 1978, the full NIV Bible. Today, there are more than 350 million copies of the NIV in print. Other NIV translations include a Spanish-language version, a simplified New International Readers Version, and the updated Today's New International Version.

25. See http://www.kli.org/wiki/index.php?Klingon%20Bible%20Translation%20Project, accessed July 2011. Klingons are a race in the fictional universe of Star Trek, featured in a long-running television series and several films. It is also the language spoken by the Klingon "people", and adopted by a large number of "Trekkies" or Star Trek fans.

26. Theodor Bibliander (1509–64) was a Swiss Orientalist, publisher, and linguist. He was familiar with Latin, Greek, Hebrew, Arabic and other languages from the East and became a professor of theology. He published the first printed edition of the Koran, based on Robert's earlier translation. The edition included a translation of the Arabic theological tract known as the *Book of a Thousand Questions*.

27. This translator goes by the following names: Ludovicum Marraccium, Ludovicus Marraccius and Luigi Marracci or Marraccio (Binark and Eren 1986).

28. Hindi is the official language of India, with English as a secondary official language. Marathi and Gujarati are widely spoken regional languages.

29. The Vedas (Sanskrit "knowledge") are the most sacred books of Hinduism. The term Veda applies to four collections of hymns, which eventually grew into larger books containing prose texts and commentaries: Rig Veda, Sama Veda, Yajur Veda and Atharva Veda. The four books are regarded as having been transmitted by divine revelation during the Vedic period and are looked upon as expressions of the fundamental genius of Hindu thought.

30. *Henotheism* is the worship of one dominant god by a society in which other gods are also present, in opposition to *monotheism*, the doctrine or belief that there is but one God, *polytheism*, the belief in a plurality of gods, and *pantheism*, a doctrine according to which the universe conceived of as a whole is God.

31. Buddhism was founded by Siddhartha Gautama, the Buddha (c.560–c.480 BCE); it was a sect derived from Brahmanic Hinduism but also a reaction against it. Buddhist sacred literature, a vast body of works, was transmitted orally and in written form in four principal languages: Pali, Sanskrit, Chinese and Tibetan. Pali is one of the more important dialects of Prakrit (c.450 BCE), in the Indo-Iranian branch of languages. See also Chapter 4, note 11.

32. The monk has also been discussed in Chapter 4.

33. See Chapter 4.

34. The Avesta is the sacred book of the Zoroastrian religion of ancient Persia. This collection of texts is written in the Avestan language, erroneously called Zend by European scholars. The term "Zend" really refers to the commentaries on the book written in Pahlavi, hence the name *Zend Avesta*.

35. Legge is also mentioned in Chapter 4.

36. Confucianism and Taoism, now classified among the "religions" of China, can also be considered ethical guides and philosophical systems; the "problematic nature" of the rubric "religion" has been raised (for example, by Girardot and Kleeman 2005: 1630). It was, in fact, by virtue of Legge's identification of the texts he translated as "sacred texts" that the Confucian and Taoist traditions were included, for the first time, in the "newly conceived and hierarchically ordered history of 'world religions'" (Girardot 2002: 12).

Figure 13. William Tyndale

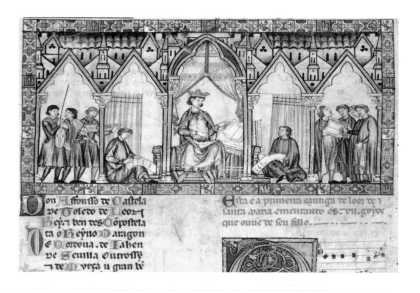

Figure 14. King Alfonso X

CHAPTER 7

Translators and the transmission of cultural values

This chapter is an invitation to travel, to follow the trail of translators on their exploration of foreign cultures. The term "cultural values" could apply equally to high culture, which generates knowledge, or popular culture, which transmits dreams. There is the kind of culture acquired through learning, and the kind that permeates our memory and actions. Both high culture and popular culture produce myths, stereotypes and symbols. The concept of "values" itself could include the idea of models or norms – aesthetic, stylistic, rhetorical, ethical or ideological ones. Some values are dominant, legitimized and reproduced through schooling. Others are subject to domination, sometimes perceived as deviant or marginal. All values are affected by relations of power, caught up in contradictions and tensions that are sometimes productive, sometimes inhibiting.

Cultural values are embedded in discourses that are canonized to varying degrees in different societies, some of which are distant in time, space and tradition. When translators encounter these values, they are not just prospecting for differences, not merely exploring unknown cultural territories. Through their recognition of the Other, they also change the perspectives of their own communities, upsetting the "words of the tribe" to use an expression that the French poet Stéphane Mallarmé used in his 1877 tribute to the American writer Edgar Allan Poe, whose poetry he translated. Translators do not simply import values, carrying out a unilateral transfer from a so-called source language or culture to a so-called target language or culture. Whatever they take hold of, they then put into circulation. Their work includes and induces transformations and manipulations. Beyond the prerogatives of patrons, clients and editors, beyond the materiality of texts, beyond the cost of their labour, translators cross and blur the lines between foreign cultural values and those of their own society. Boundaries, after all, are more fluid and less circumscribed than they are thought to be.

Such are the ambiguities underlying this chapter, which delves into several distinct periods, languages, genres and cultural situations. From the twelfth century through to the twentieth, the route by no means follows a straight line. We propose instead to meander through the past, evoking the diverse functions that translators have fulfilled through history. We are continually stimulated by scholarly discourse and exposed to new theoretical studies in an ever-expanding range of fields – some of which are brought to bear on the act of translating itself. We have access to this new knowledge either directly, or else through translations or popularizing reformulations. Very often the translator acts as a mediator in this process of cultural exchange.

This chapter is broken down into eight sections, or brief excursions. The first is to twelfth-century Spain and to nineteenth-century Paris, two periods when intellectual commerce moved in opposite directions. The following section examines how Christian Europe came into contact with the Islamic Orient during the period extending from the twelfth to the seventeenth centuries. We travel to Elizabethan England, a sixteenth-century culture profoundly interested in all that was foreign, and then to eighteenth-century England to see how Pierre Coste, translator of the philosopher John Locke, exemplified the way in which translation can help forge a new consciousness. The fifth excursion takes us to French Revolutionary times. The next focuses on a particular literary genre, the Gothic novel, which brought about a transformation of sensibilities when it came into fashion toward the beginning of the nineteenth century. This is followed by a leap to China, where Yan Fu stimulated debate at the turn of the twentieth century by translating great English thinkers. Our journey ends in the 1950s, when translation was an agent of change in the field of science fiction.

The translator's letter home

Translators generally live in cities, especially in large cities or capitals, at the major crossroads and locations of cultural exchange. Roads, railways, telephone lines and communication networks converge in cities and, at the same time, extend urban areas. When translators explore, they tend to seek values that might sooner or later be of benefit to their cities. They can do this in different ways. They can travel outward and have their translations move back to the larger urban centres, as was the case of foreign translators in twelfth-century Spain. Or they can venture into the central cities themselves in order to benefit from the influx of new values, as was the case in late nineteenth-century Paris. These two opposite examples, briefly explored, will suggest a few general hypotheses about the ways in which translators and translations can move.[1]

In the twelfth century, certain translators set out in search of protoscientific texts written in or translated into Arabic. In Tarazona, located in Aragon in northeastern Spain, a certain Bishop Michael commissioned at least ten translations from Arabic into Latin (Lemay 1963). He took some pains to locate the manuscripts himself, as reported by his translator, Hugo of Santalla: "*In Rotensi armario et inter secretiora bibliotece penetralia*" (quoted by Haskins 1967:70). The Bishop was entering "secret libraries", probably in the Moorish town of Rota (present-day Rueda Jalón), which had passed into Christian hands when Saragossa was captured in 1118. Yet the term *armarium*, used here to describe the hidden library, could also refer to a secret or sacred place (dictionaries give *sacrarium, locus occultus*) as well as, more interestingly, an arsenal or cache of weapons (*armamentarium*). The great books of the greatest writers could be hidden and used as weapons. But who sought after such arms? The same translator, Hugo of Santalla, tells us in a preface addressed to Bishop Michael, "What the modern astrologers of Gaul most bemoan their lack of, your benignity may now bestow on posterity" (quoted in Thorndike 1923 vol. 2:87). While Hugo the translator is of Hispanic origin, Bishop Michael, or Michel, was no doubt French. The translations were headed northward, to Chartres, perhaps to Cluny, and quite possibly toward the future centre of European learning, Paris.

The translators in twelfth-century Spain came from all over, as their names indicate, even in Anglicized versions: Adelard of Bath (English), Hermann of Dalmatia (a Corinthian, probably trained at Chartres), Plato of Tivoli (Italian), Robert of Chester (English), Rudolph of Bruges (Flemish), John of Seville or John of Spain (yes, Spanish, but quite possibly a Mozarab[2] or converted Jew), Hugo of Santalla (in all likelihood Spanish) and the most eminent of them all, Gerard of Cremona (Italian). All these scholars were in Spain seeking knowledge. If they had a symbolic Grail, it was undoubtedly the *Almagest*, the work in which Ptolemy had set out his geocentric description of the universe.[3] Unable to track down the Greek manuscript, the translators went in search of the Arabic version of 827. Desire for this text, *amor almagesti*, was said to be the reason why Gerard of Cremona (1114–87) ventured to Toledo around 1157. This quest will be discussed below.

The translators may have been from all over, but their patrons had significant, and more mundane, links to France. Archbishop Raymond of Toledo, presumed to be the founder of a "school" of translators in that city, was certainly French, as was Bishop Michael of Tarazona. So was Peter the Venerable (c.1092–1156), abbot of Cluny, whose role in this story is too commonly overlooked. In 1142, Peter travelled to Spain to collect tribute (a form of fund raising) for Cluny. While in recently conquered lands he nevertheless had the opportunity to explore a different kind of value. To gain knowledge that would provide arguments against Islam, he sponsored the first Latin translation of the Koran and explanatory documents.

The Koran itself was tackled by Robert of Chester, whose translation was to ricochet down through history. Robert was part of an elaborate translation team that also rendered a small collection of documents on Islam. Together with Hermann of Dalmatia, he worked with Peter of Poitiers, the Mozarab Peter of Toledo and a native informant anonymously named Mahomed. Included in the collection of documents accompanying the translated Koran was a text called *Liber contra sectam*, in which Peter the Venerable himself explains how and why the translation had been undertaken. This text is unusual in that it is addressed to "the Arabs" yet written in Latin: the ultimate purpose of the work, Peter explains, is not to inform a Christian readership about Islam but rather to provide arguments that could be directed against Islamic readers. The values to be propagated were Christian ones. Knowledge was supposed to come into Cluny (that is, France) and then move outward and eastward toward the periphery, to the Orient, which for a long time had included Spain. "My translators have penetrated into the depths of your [the Muslims'] libraries", he writes, "finding many things concerning your humanistic and scientific studies". Like Bishop Michael, the translators of the Koran explored conquered libraries. And the abbot was not above punning on the term *armarium* in this connection. He notes that even if his arguments are not translated into Arabic, they will at least be stored in Christian libraries/arsenals awaiting future use against the enemy: "*Habetit saltem Christianum armarium etiam aduersus nos hostes arma*". A well-supplied library was like a well-stocked arsenal. Thanks to a quirk of historical justice, the manuscript providing these details (through the research of d'Alverny 1994; Daniel 1960 and 1975; Kritzeck 1964) is now in Paris, in the Bibliothèque de l'Arsenal.

The translation of the Koran was completed in 1142–43 and the translators turned to other tasks. In 1143, Hermann was in Tolosa, where he produced a planisphere, based on an Arabic version of Ptolemy's Greek original, which he dedicated to Thierry of Chartres. Robert, for whom the translation of the Koran had been a mere "digression" compared to his real interest in mathematics and astronomy, went to Segovia in 1145, where he translated the *Algebra* by the famous scholar al-Khwârizmî, whose Latinized name, Algoritmi, has given us the term "algorithm". In 1149, Robert established astronomical tables for London. Whereas the Church sought arms against Islam, the translators continued their search for the wisdom of the *Almagest*.

The Koranic collection, it would seem, was not the only translational enterprise inspired by Peter the Venerable. Peter travelled to Salamanca where he met Archbishop Raymond of Toledo. Quite possibly as a result of this meeting, Raymond commissioned John of Seville (c.1110–c.1180) to translate a Greek text from Arabic into Latin. The Archbishop's successors would apply this policy consistently, with the result that Toledo gradually became a centre for foreign translators. Thus it was in Toledo that Gerard of Cremona undertook the translation of the *Almagest*, probably with the help of some kind of team. Once the texts were turned into Latin, they moved northward, like letters sent home.

In the network formed by translators and translations in movement at the time, Toledo was certainly a flourishing crossroads on the cultural border with the Islamic world.[4] But many translations were also produced elsewhere – in the major trading cities of Italy, in Palermo and in Constantinople. An example might illustrate these complex exchanges. Byzantine Emperor Manuel Comnenus had presented a Greek manuscript to the Norman King of Sicily as part of the peace negotiations in 1158. The text was none other than the *Almagest*. The scholar, soldier and translator Henricus Aristippus was serving as an envoy to Constantinople at the time and brought the manuscript back to Sicily. The Greek text was translated into Latin by an anonymous translator, helped by a certain Eugene the Emir of Palermo (Haskins 1967: 164). All this took place around 1160. Gerard of Cremona had travelled from Italy to Spain in search of this same text in about 1157, exploring in entirely the wrong direction, and translated it in Toledo in 1175. History has its ironies. Although not the first, and although produced not from the original language but rather through a long Arabic detour, Gerard's translation was to dominate the Latin reception of Ptolemy (see also Pym 1998 and 2000).

Within this twelfth-century network, translators tended to travel outward, toward peripheral towns and cities, and then have their translations move toward the new central cities, notably to Paris, London and Bologna, where the first European universities were founded. Scientific translation of the twelfth century was situated, in fact, on the borders of the old and new centres. As new centres, which would now be labelled cosmopolitan cities, became established, they attracted scholars and translators inward, participating in the intercultural production of knowledge. The great professors of thirteenth-century Paris were Roger Bacon, Albert the Great and Thomas Aquinas: an Englishman, a German and an Italian. The role of frontier points consequently declined; relatively few thirteenth-century translators went outward in search of new values. Their network was already different. Instead of a sending periphery and a receiving centre, they now worked between a sending centre and a receiving periphery.

The kind of network that existed in the late nineteenth-century could be considered the result of this transformation. The centres were not so different: Paris and London were still sites of intellectual production, although cities like Berlin, Munich and Vienna were also making their mark. All served as intersections and marketplaces, where texts from all directions were traded. Translators tended to be either in the central cities or travelling toward them. Their translations, once again letters sent home, were moved outward, toward the peripheries that various translators had left. Within this second network, to explore is to travel toward the centre.

Evidence for this pattern is easily gleaned from the "Notes from Abroad" that appeared in numerous periodicals around the globe at the end of the nineteenth century. The authors of these accounts, whether published in central cities or along the periphery, were very often translators earning their living from the circulation of news, scandal and fashion of one kind or another. But where were they when they wrote their "Notes from Abroad"? In the French and British periodicals, they were usually in Paris or London. In periodicals published in Germany, Russia or Mexico, they were often in Paris or London, too. Thus established in the centres, they sent their news and translations, frequently done from intermediary versions, toward the peripheries (Pym 1992).

After several centuries of literary exchange, the intellectual arsenals of these centres had grown full and rich and these cities grew increasingly multicultural. Artists from Britain, Germany, Scandinavia, Greece, Spain and many other countries converged on Paris, the capital of capitals. The poet Stéphane Mallarmé (1842–98), for example, who translated the poetry of Edgar Allan Poe, was famous for his Tuesday-night *salons*, held at his apartment on the rue de Rome. The group that gravitated around Mallarmé included writer-translators like Stefan George (1868–1933), a German, and Arthur Symons (1865–1945), an Englishman. Many of the foreigners living in Paris actually wrote in French: Oscar Wilde (English), August Strindberg (Swedish), Téodor de Wyzewa (Polish) and Oscar Milosz (Polish-Lithuanian), Stuart Merrill and Francis Vielé-Griffen (American). These writers were able to translate both into and from the central linguistic arsenal, working in two directions yet materially located at the centre of the network. Even those who opposed the values of *fin de siècle* Paris tended to do so from within the city: Max Nordau (1849–1923), the Hungarian-born, German-speaking critic of modernist decadence, lived on the avenue de Villiers, as reported in certain "Notes from Abroad" written by a French-speaking Guatemalan translator called Enrique Gómez Carrillo (1873–1927). Carrillo also lived in Paris; he visited Nordau and spoke to him in Spanish, since Nordau was Sephardic, his family having originated from the Jews who once traded across the frontiers of medieval Spain.

These centralized translators of the late nineteenth-century differed from the travelling translators of the twelfth century in at least two ways. First, they no longer sought foreign cultural values in ancient texts. Whereas the tendency during the scholastic period was to translate – or pseudo-translate – classical religious, philosophical and protoscientific texts that had acquired authority through time, modernist translators were attracted to literary novelties. Whereas scholastic translation paid tribute to classical texts through literalism often carried to an extreme, modernist translators tended to churn out texts that were quickly produced, quickly read and often quickly plagiarized. Zola, for example, was published in Spanish the same year as his works appeared in French (1885). Such speed was not necessarily hampered by geographical distance. In Sydney, Australia, Christopher Brennan (1870–1932) wrote a parodic version of Mallarmé's *Un Coup de dés jamais n'abolira le hasard* just a few months after the original was published in Paris in 1897.

Second, the foreign values entering the large central cities tended to circulate at such a pace that they had little time to coalesce around any one work. There was no more *Almagest*, no single great text to translate. Most of the translators were contemporaries or near contemporaries of their authors, with whom they established family-like ties rather than paying any sustained homage to source texts. There were of course multicultural debates about the relative merits of figures such as Baudelaire, Rimbaud, Wagner, Nietzsche, Ibsen or Tolstoy, all of whom were discovered and celebrated in French periodicals with echoes on the periphery. But such discussions came and went and greatness was a short-lived phenomenon. With few exceptions, translators tended not to approach their sources in excessive awe.[5] Translation became one method among others for the creation of new values.

What happens when "home" is not just a geographic location but rather an entire civilization? When Christian Europe, for example, encountered the Islamic East from the twelfth to the eighteenth centuries? The way in which the Koran has been transmitted illustrates the links between translation, scholarship and reception, thus emphasizing the role of translators in interpreting what they import.

The Koranic Orient and religious pluralism

The first culture that Christian Europe saw as being truly "different" was certainly that of the Islamic Near East, the land of Crusades and conversions. The religious texts of Islam were translated in an effort to learn about the doctrinal and intellectual strengths and weaknesses of a people looked upon as the enemy. The translations were intended to serve apologists or defenders of the Christian faith. Some of these texts nevertheless exerted considerable influence on Western literature from very early on. The *Kitâb al-mi'râj*, for example, was rendered into Latin (*Liber scalae*), French (*Livre de l'eschielle de Mahomet*) and Castilian (*La escala de Mahoma*) in the thirteenth century, and it is possible that Dante was familiar with these versions.

The first Latin translation of the Koran, as previously shown, was produced by Robert of Chester in the twelfth century. The thirteenth century saw a further Latin translation by Mark of Toledo; more faithful than Robert's, it had rather limited success and has remained in manuscript form to this day. Robert of Chester's version, on the other hand, influenced scholars such as Richard Fitzralph (fourteenth century), Simon Simeon (sixteenth century), Denys le Chartreux (fifteenth century) and, in particular, the Renaissance statesman and philosopher Cardinal Nicholas of Cusa. It was printed in Basel by Theodor Bibliander in 1543, when an abridged version was also produced by the Catholic humanist Johann Albrecht Widmannstetter. Bibliander's Koran was reprinted in 1550 and adapted in Italian for the printer Andrea Arrivabene in 1547. The Italian text was then the source for Salomon Schweigger's 1616 German version, which was in turn the source for an anonymous Dutch version of 1641. This single chain of translations and editions reveals a genuine interest in the text, along with a desire to go beyond popular legend and conjecture about the foreign religion.

With the seventeenth century came renewed interest, as seen in the preceding chapter. André Du Ryer (c.1580–c.1660), a diplomat in the Orient, rendered the Koran into French in 1647. Working from the original Arabic, Du Ryer sought to translate the text as exactly as possible. Despite its shortcomings (errors, verbosity, monotonous style and absence of critical scholarship), the French version was reprinted many times. It served as the source for the 1649 English translation by Alexander Ross and the 1658 Dutch version by J. H. Glazemaker, which was itself the source for the 1688 German edition by Johannes Lange. At the same time, various scholars were editing, translating and annotating parts of the Koran. Between 1650 and 1665, Dominicus Germanus, a Franciscan monk from Silesia, worked on a Latin translation of the Koran and numerous Islamic commentaries, producing a text that, despite its high quality, still remains in unpublished form (Devic 1883). Oriental studies were carried out with increasing rigour. These developments bore fruit toward the end of the seventeenth century. Abraham Hinckelmann published the Arabic text in 1694. Ludovico Marracci published the Arabic text with a Latin translation, accompanied by abundant commentaries and refutations in 1691 and 1698. Marracci's extraordinary work of scholarship opened the way for new translations from the original,[6] and his Latin translation was rendered into German by David Nerreter in 1703. To this series should be added the fragments and summaries that appeared in polemical works by writers like Heinrich Leuchter (1604), Michel Baudier (1625) and Johann Andreas Endter (1664). In sum, the Koran had established its place on the bookshelves of educated Europeans.

Europeans gradually became aware of passages in the Koran that referred to other religions, especially those likely to enjoy a privileged status in societies under Islamic control. The early translators were unsure about the groups concerned and hence used inaccurate terminology. The "Magians" (*majûs*) (Masson 1967: xxii, 17) were rendered as "gentiles" or "pagans" by Robert of Chester and were omitted by Du Ryer and those who followed him. The "Sabeans" became "Samaritans" in Du Ryer, while Robert of Chester turned them into "those who worship angels instead of God", or "those who change religion", which is actually one of the dictionary meanings for *Sâbî'ûn*. Despite their inaccuracies, these translations were responsible for encouraging Europeans to regard other religions in a less negative manner and to recognize a certain form of religious pluralism – an anachronistic term, perhaps, but useful in this context – if not in heaven, at least on this earth.

Of course, the values that are found (or perceived to be found) in a given text are one thing, and the way in which they are received by a readership in a new culture is another. There was no reason why the first Western readers of the Koran should have been more open to the concept of pluralism than to any other part of Islamic doctrine. Christian apologists relegated the idea to the level of "infinite absurdities, heresies and impieties", and criticized the concept because it contradicted other passages in the Koran that reserved eternal salvation for those who believed in Islam. Such was the reading put forward by Nicholas of Cusa (Book III, Chapters 2 and 10), who drew attention to what he considered to be a fundamental inconsistency in the book he was opposing. Marracci would later do the same.

It would have been unthinkable at the time to suggest that religions were in some way equivalent. Such an idea would have opened the door to confusion, annulling rival claims to possession of the one true religion. Not surprisingly, when similar ideas were formulated in Christian Europe, as for example by the fourteenth-century monk Uthred of Boldon, they were systematically censored by the church authorities (Daniel 1975: 249). Intermediaries like Arrivabene (1547) and Marracci (1691), therefore, did not hesitate to criticize this aspect of the Koran.

Through their translations and personal statements, the translators of the Koran nevertheless contributed to a fundamental debate about the possible equality of religions, an idea that had long been regarded as untenable. As late as the beginning of the eighteenth century, the Dutch Orientalist Adrian Reland wrote a book in which he denounced the lies and false ideas that had been circulated about Islam (Reland 1717). He was later helped by his translator David Durand (c.1680–1763), who used the opportunity to criticize the indifferentism prevalent in the Europe of his day (Reland 1721: 71–72).[7] Although Reland denied that the Koran proclaimed religious pluralism, he was full of praise for the tolerant attitudes of Muslims, which had been reported by numerous travellers.[8] The Islamic world appeared more positive when compared with Europe (Reland 1717: 162).

Pierre Bayle made essentially the same observation when he stated that "the Sara-cens and the Turks have treated the Christian church with more moderation than the Christians have had for the pagans, or indeed for one another" (1702: 1981).[9]

Bayle's intellectual heirs were the Enlightenment thinkers who struggled against religious intolerance in Europe. Writers like the Encyclopedists and the *Philosophes* frequently made the distinction between doctrine (the nonequiva-lence of religions) and actual practice (tolerance). Examples can be found in Diderot, Helvétius and Voltaire, in particular.[10]

When texts of another culture are read and interpreted, meanings are fre-quently read into them which they do not necessarily have. This is done through ignorance and naivety, as well as some measure of partisanship and manipula-tion, and has continued to our day. Nevertheless, well before Europe was aware of Buddhist tolerance, the familiarity with certain passages from the Koran led European intellectuals to question religious exclusivity, in general, and the exclu-sivity of Christianity, in particular. While it is no doubt true that "the Orient" was a European construct, as Edward Said suggested in his influential work *Oriental-ism* (1978), it was the reflection on Oriental texts that allowed European culture to re-examine itself, to resituate itself and, in some cases, to redefine its attitudes. Thus the West discovered arguments in favour of pluralism and tolerance, and it was through their participation in ideological, educational and ethical debates that translators played a role in bringing about this new consciousness.

Elizabethan England: translating with a purpose

Early Renaissance England had seen much religious translation and, to a lesser extent, some secular translation activity (Bennett 1952; Gray 1990). It was not until the second half of the sixteenth century, which coincides roughly with the reign of Elizabeth I, that translation of nonreligious texts into English developed in response to an expanding, essentially monolingual, readership. The European scholarly community, England included, continued to write in and translate into Latin. Various works originating in ancient Greece, along with contemporary ones from England and the Continent, were translated into Latin in Elizabethan England (Binns 1990: 215–216). This section, however, focuses on translations into English, which accounted for about twenty per cent of all works published in the country.[11]

Among the main sources of this cultural enrichment were classical Antiq-uity (Conley 1927; Lathrop 1967; Nørgaard 1958) and Renaissance Italy (Einstein 1902; Scott 1916; Rossi and Savoia 1989). The motivation for translating was in part utilitarian: translators tackled treatises on subjects such as warfare, education and health. But translation was also viewed as a means of enriching the English language, primarily its lexicon, as it was for other languages discussed in Chapter 2. Up to the mid-1570s, English was considered ineloquent in comparison to classical languages and contemporary Italian, French or Spanish (Jones 1953: 3–31; Barber 1976: 65–105). However, these considerations were overshadowed by repeated emphasis on the need to provide moral, political and social instruction to a new readership unschooled in classical languages, who came from what was not yet called the middle class – from the merchant class, in particular – and to whom reference is specifically made by some translators (Wright 1935: 339–372). This can be illustrated by this excerpt from the preface to the reader from the first English translation (1579) of Plutarch's *Parallel Lives* by Sir Thomas North (1535–c.1601): "[...] there is no prophane studye better than Plutarke. All other learning is priuate, fitter for universities than cities, fuller of comtemplacion than experience, more commendable in the students them selues, than profitable vnto others" (Matthiessen 1931: 54–102; Denton 1992b and 1993).

Translators wrote dedications addressed to their patrons and prefaces for their readers, which are a useful source of information about attitudes to translation that prevailed at the time (exploited notably by Conley 1927). Following the practice of classical rhetoric, in which they would have been well trained, translators presented the moral purpose of their task in metaphorical terms such as letting in light or opening a casket to reveal its precious contents (Hermans 1985b; Denton 1992a). These metatexts, or writings having to do with translation, reflected a universally accepted view of language and linguistic transfer (Rener 1989). In addition to this prefatory material, Elizabethan England also contributed a fundamental treatise on translation by the influential Puritan Laurence Humphrey (c.1525–89), *Interpretatio lingvarvm: sev De ratione convertendi et explicandi autores tam sacros quam prophanos* (1559), which has yet to be thoroughly studied (Binns 1990: 209–212).

When texts were selected and commissioned for English translation, choices or preferences for specific genres were motivated by a certain view of education. This was true not only of scholars, who believed they were at the service of the unlearned, but also of less-experienced translators seeking the protection of a powerful patron for a future career (Rosenberg 1955: 152–183; Bennett 1965: 30–55). Of course, choices were also dictated by the authorities, who were always only too willing to censure documents considered to be subversive from a moral, religious or political point of view. One result was a rather narrow range of classical works translated in Elizabethan England compared with work made available in other European languages (Highet 1949: 104–126; Bolgar 1954: 508–541). In England, preference was given to Roman writers and Greek ones living in the Roman Empire. Among genres, attention was devoted to moral and political philosophy, epic poetry and, in particular, history, which was viewed as "a storehouse of examples rather than processes" (Pocock 1985:146). This emphasis on the didactic value of studying individual actions of the past, especially in ancient times, meant that translators were attracted to history (Wright 1935:297–338; Martindale 1985:35–37) and to its subgenre, biography (although the distinction between biography and history was not as clear-cut as it is today). The supreme master here was Plutarch, and his *Parallel Lives* of eminent Greeks and Romans was regarded as an arsenal of examples of mostly virtuous political behaviour. Plutarch's *Lives* exerted considerable influence throughout Renaissance Europe (Burke 1966:142–143), including England (Shackford 1929). One of the most eminent "unlearned" readers of North's translation of the *Lives* was Shakespeare, who drew heavily on it for his three great Roman plays: *Julius Caesar, Antony and Cleopatra* and *Coriolanus* (Highet 1949:194–218; Serpieri 1988).

Among contemporary European works, great importance was attached to those providing advice on social behaviour, especially when they originated in what were held to be more "advanced" societies, such as certain states of Renaissance Italy. One example is *Il libro del cortigiano*, written in 1528 by Baldassare Castiglione. It appeared in English as *The Courtyer* in 1561, translated by Sir Thomas Hoby (1530–66) (Matthiessen 1931:8–53; Nocera Avila 1992). Castiglione and Plutarch demonstrated the need for loyalty to the highest authorities and for active participation in public life. They provided a model for the combination of intellectual and physical prowess required of any gentleman or citizen who intended to play a prominent role in society. In his preface, Hoby indicates that he is addressing a readership extending beyond aristocratic circles to include the gentry and higher merchant class (Nocera Avila 1992:35–37). The translations of Castiglione and Plutarch were thus addressed to very much the same kind of reader.

Writing for these new readers, who had little knowledge of the societies in which the source texts had been produced, entailed a set of problems related to the rhetorical concept of *perspicuitas*, or the need for clarity (Rener 1989:217–233). The primary obstacle faced by translators of the time was the inability of their own language and culture to express the cultural diversity embedded in the source texts. Translators could either expand the target-language stock of words by means of borrowings, or else look within the target culture for equivalents or near-equivalents that would express the foreign cultural phenomena. A preference for the second of the two options resulted in a significant naturalization or "Elizabethanization" of source texts.

Two brief examples will serve to illustrate these two translation strategies. The first comes from North's Plutarch and illustrates the problem of translating a phenomenon specific to Roman civilization – gladiator fights. Following a fairly

widespread practice of his time, North chose as his source text the French translation from the Greek published in 1559 by Jacques Amyot (1513–93), a version
highly regarded at the time for its philological value, despite the fact that Amyot
had added some explanatory glosses. In the following excerpt from *La Vie de
Coriolan*, the glosses are in bold: "[*V*]*n autre de la mesme famille, qui fut appellé
Celer, c'est à dire, prompt, à cause qu'en bien peu de iours apres la mort de son pere
il fit voir au peuple des combats de Gladiateurs, c'est à dire d'escrimeurs à outrance
[…]*" (Sturel 1908; Aulotte 1959, 1965, 1980 and 1986; Balard 1986). The target
readership is presumed to be ignorant of gladiators and so Amyot uses the unfamiliar words, adding an explanation expressed in contemporary terms. North's
translation of the passage shows a different approach: "One other of his owne
familie was called Celer: the quicke flye. Bicause a fewe dayes after the death of
his father, he shewed the people the cruell fight of fensers at vnrebated swordes
[…]". An ancient institution is modernized, depriving readers of the opportunity
to become familiar with it. Furthermore, the neutral stance of the French scholar
is replaced by the moral disapproval of the English translator, reflected in the use
of the adjective "cruell". A comparative study of the two translations would reveal
many similar examples.

The second example is taken from Hoby's translation. How can the refined
behaviour of an Italian court be communicated to a less advanced society? How
can the precise meaning of *sprezzatura* be expressed? This new concept had a very
positive connotation in Castiglione's treatise, where it refers to the art of making
studied behaviour appear effortless, a concept that would be translated nowadays
by "nonchalance" (Nocera Avila 1992: 183–187): "[*P*]*er dire forse una nuova pa-
rola, usar in ogni cosa una certa sprezzatura, che nasconda l'arte e dimostri ciò che
si fa e dice venir fatto senza fatica e quaso senza pensarvi.*" Hoby's translation reads:
"[…] and (to speak a new word) to use in euery thyng a certain Recklessness, to
couer art withall, and seeme whatsoeuer he doth and sayeth to do without pain,
and (as it were) not mynding it". The English translator's choice of a lexical item
with a rather negative connotation – "recklessness" as an equivalent for "*sprezzatura*" – suggests Puritan disapproval of deceitful behaviour.

Translation strategies are thus dependent on the purposes for which translations are undertaken in the first place. In late sixteenth-century England, education was a fundamental objective, and the role of translation was to help achieve
this goal. The translators filtered foreign texts accordingly. This by no means ruled
out a certain resistance to new values imported from other cultures, and translators were consequently caught up in a web of contradictions between ideological
renewal and the established morality. This once again illustrates that the circulation of texts and ideas involves a series of changes extending from the transfer process to the subsequent reception. On the eve of the cultural, political and

religious changes that were to sweep Europe during the second half of the eighteenth century, there were numerous instances in which translation was an act of both dissemination and transformation.

A Huguenot in England: the emergence of European consciousness

Pierre Coste (1668–1747), a French Huguenot who took refuge in England after the revocation of the Edict of Nantes in 1685, played a leading role in the dissemination of ideas and transmission of values (Rumbold 1991).[12] Coste's work went both ways. Not only did he bring English thought to the attention of the French; he also published French writers such as Racine and works of his own such as *L'Histoire du Prince de Condé* (1693) and introduced Montaigne, La Bruyère and La Fontaine to England. Translators like Coste and his contemporaries (Jean Le Clerc, Daniel Mazel and Pierre Desmoizeaux) were important links in the chain of French-English exchanges, sparking new political, moral and social debates and providing sources of inspiration for the Encyclopedists and economists. Journals or gazettes, many of which were produced in Holland, had a substantial impact in this context; they commented on recent texts and new translations, took part in the discussions of the day and contributed to the popularization of new forms of knowledge.

Pierre Coste first became known for his translations of John Locke, one of the first British empiricists. Locke opposed the despotic theories of Hobbes and the Cartesian doctrine of innate ideas, and argued strongly in favour of tolerance. In 1695, Coste translated *Some Thoughts Concerning Education*. His French version, *De l'éducation des enfants*, was the source for the 1735 Italian version. This work had a determining influence on Rousseau's *Émile*; it was soon well-known throughout western Europe, where it contributed to the development of modern education theory (Bonno 1955:219). Many scholars like Pierre Bayle, Jean-Baptiste Du Bos, Pieter Guénellon and Nicolas Toinard, who had little or insufficient knowledge of English, acknowledged their indebtedness to Coste. Locke's influence was to increase further with Coste's translation of *The Reasonableness of Christianity* (1696), which argued that religion was closely related to reason. Coste achieved even more success with his translation of Locke's foremost work, *An Essay Concerning Human Understanding*, which he completed in 1700, ten years after the original was published. Coste's *Essai sur l'entendement humain* was very widely read and reviewed, giving rise to a series of publications that drew increasing attention to Locke. The influence of this translation cannot be underestimated. It had an impact, for example, on Gottfried Wilhelm Leibniz, who completed his *Nouveaux essais sur l'entendement humain* between 1704 and 1709; on Pierre Bayle, who had just produced his famous *Dictionnaire historique et critique*

(1695–97); and on Jean-Baptiste (l'Abbé) Du Bos, who introduced Locke's *Essai* to the French royal court. Yet Coste was not only the initiator: he continued to facilitate the reception of Locke's work through his correspondence with various scholars, through his clarification of some of Locke's ideas – the result of frequent visits and discussions with Locke himself over a period of eight years – and through the corrections and revisions he made to his translation. This process was not limited to France.[13] Priests, philosophers, mathematicians, poets and critics all over western Europe discovered Locke through the French translation, especially as the use of French was widespread at the time.

Locke continued to exert influence in the second half of the eighteenth century. His authority can be attributed mainly to translations of his works, even if those who read the translations later went on to look at the English texts. His reputation, however, was not confined to the sphere of abstract thought. In breaking with a certain kind of metaphysics, Locke established the relevance of experimentation, observation and careful analysis, not unlike scientists such as Newton. It so happened that Coste also translated Newton, notably *Opticks*, first published in 1704, then issued in French under the title *Traité d'Optique* in 1720. It was no coincidence that Locke and Newton, partly translated by the same person, had a combined impact on writers like Voltaire, Condillac, d'Alembert, La Mettrie, Helvétius, d'Holbach and Condorcet (Rumbold 1991:106–115). It is not surprising to detect traces of Locke in Montesquieu's *De l'Esprit des lois*, in Diderot's *Lettre sur les aveugles* or of Newton in works by Fontenelle, Buffon, Maupertius and Mairan.

Coste's work continued to bear fruit when he translated some works by the third Earl of Shaftesbury, which made an impression on the young Diderot (who would later translate Shaftesbury's *Inquiry Concerning Virtue*), as well as on Fontenelle and other European writers. As a translator and intermediary, Coste contributed to the contact of ideas and dissemination of writings in which these ideas were expressed. He did this through his French translations of English thinkers, his French editions rendered into English, his own works translated into several languages and the readings and interpretations presented in his prefaces and letters. In sum, his work contributed to the emergence of a European consciousness and the development of a new conception of freedom. And yet, like his friend and protector Jean Le Clerc (1657–1736), also a free-thinking Huguenot writer (Barnes 1938), Pierre Coste has been all but forgotten. No more than a few notes on him have appeared in recent decades, not without errors or omissions (Rumbold 1991:124–126). Coste might thus epitomize the translator as an inquiring but self-effacing figure, honest and modest, studious and indifferent to fame. Yet his importance is underscored by the example of Germany where, in contrast, there was no translator of Coste's stature to import ideas from abroad and generate debates at that crucial moment in history.

Revolutionary France: serving the cause

The revolutionary period in France, roughly the decade from 1789 to 1799, does not correspond to any major upheaval in the history of French translation. There were few changes in the attitudes toward translation and translation techniques, or even in the choice of source texts, themes or genres. Yet the historical events certainly had repercussions, albeit subtle at times, on the course of translation history in France. Many a work of literature was transposed in the wake of the Revolution, perceived in either a positive or negative light by the translators or readership. When François-René de Chateaubriand (1768–1848), for example, was stranded in London in 1793, he translated long passages from Ossian as a way of reflecting on the nature and virtues of primitive man, meditating on the vagueness of passion, which for Lamartine and the writers of the next generation was to become a passion for vagueness. Another example is Friedrich Schiller's play *The Robbers* (*Die Räuber*), which was adapted as a melodrama by Jean La Martellière (1761–1830) and performed in Paris in 1792 under the title *Les Brigands*, enjoying great success with the populace. Neither of these cases reflects ideas directly for or against the Revolution. Yet both translators, consciously or unconsciously, were immersed in the sea of ideologies, aesthetics and sensibilities of the day. Both have been credited with having introduced new ideas, just as the 1798 translation of the *Psalter* by the philosopher Jean-François de Laharpe (1739–1803) has been recognized for its role in the early nineteenth-century religious revival in France.

Translators rarely thought of their work as being specifically revolutionary or counter-revolutionary. The many factors in play can be illustrated by a further example: when the *émigré* Charles de Villers (1765–1815) abandoned his version of the *Critique of Pure Reason*, undertaken around 1798, it was not directly as a result of the Revolution. De Villiers found Kant's thought impossible to express in the current French philosophical discourse, which had been profoundly marked by the sensualists and the ideologues. He would have had to forge new terms and syntactic forms in order to convey effectively Kant's German idealism, a philosophy so radically different from the brand of empiricism that had given rise in revolutionary France to institutions like the *Écoles Normales* and the *Institut National*.

While translation was not directly central to the debates about the new values of French society, it was present and influential in fields like literature, religion and philosophy. Translation was thus linked to a powerful but unformulated set of common opinions or beliefs, or *doxa*. An exploration of this connection will shed light on the relation between translators and the Revolution. Two significant cases will be considered: the rendering of political decrees from French into other languages, and the translation of Greek orators into French.

An essential element of the language policy in effect from 1790 to 1792 was the translation of official decrees into the various languages of France, and into the languages of neighbouring countries that were influenced by Republican thought (Germany, Flanders, Spain and Italy). The Revolution's message had to reach all citizens, not just the educated minority. A decree of January 14, 1790 required that all decrees be translated "into all the languages [*idiomes*] spoken in the various parts of France" (Brunot 1967:25). The term "*idiome*" is not to be confused with the term "French dialect", at least not in the opinion of regional parliamentarians. It referred to the spoken language of common people in the countryside, which many revolutionaries considered preferable to the written language of the urban bourgeoisie. This desire to inform the people as accurately as possible and in a language they could understand is related to arguments of such people as Mirabeau, who advocated the simplification of the French used in legal proceedings. The translation of these decrees was, for a short time at least, doubly revolutionary. It informed all citizens about political decisions, and it applied a principle of equality by elevating all languages to the rank of the French language itself:

> Let it not be thought that the various languages [*idiomes*] of southern France are no more than mere jargon: they are true tongues [*langues*], just as old as most of our modern tongues, just as rich, just as abundant in noble and bold expressions, in figures of speech and metaphors as any of the languages of Europe.
>
> (Document dated December 18, 1791, quoted by Brunot 1967:28)

Who actually translated these decrees? How were the translators recruited? According to the rare accounts scattered in archives, the translations were probably carried out by teams working in *ad hoc* translation bureaus. Unknown or forgotten, these translators, nevertheless, performed a considerable task, the importance of which neither they nor their political patrons fully realized.

Their criteria for producing a good translation were unequivocal and to the point. They sought to reproduce meaning faithfully and accurately, with a view to ensuring that their audience would fully understand the message. The results, however, do not appear to have met the expectations of their Parisian patrons. There were various reasons for this. First, the target languages, whose orthography was not yet standardized, did not lend themselves to the translation of these legal texts, since terminology in the field of law was itself in a state of flux. Secondly, the translators did not necessarily have an adequate command of these languages and, lastly, the public showed little interest in the decrees anyway. "The translations will only be of use to the uneducated class; and very few of the citizens of this class can and want to purchase the decrees [...]" (quoted by Brunot 1967:523). The issue of language thus resurfaced quickly and led to a more radical solution: the decision to impose a single "national" French language on the entire population. At the same time, primary schooling was made more widely accessible, in a measure indirectly aimed at repressing local languages.

Attitudes toward translation nevertheless became more moderate after the Thermidorean reaction, which put an end to the Terror and coincided with the victories of French Republican troops.[14] The practice of translation in the occupied territories extended to new genres like civic chants and anthems. Further translation bureaus were established, particularly in the occupied areas along the Rhine, and would later be of use in the Napoleonic campaigns.

Translation was carried out by the society producing the source texts, a situation that could perhaps be associated with propaganda. If the traces of the translators have been covered over, is it not because translation was a mere cog in the dominant political machine, operating in the service of a state ideology? Comparative study suggests that there is no simple answer to this question. Although some political regimes have used translation when trying to dominate others, translators have helped many alternative movements seek recognition beyond their frontiers. In such cases, translators operate as explorers who bring their own values to foreign cultures. From the fifteenth to the seventeenth centuries, to take just one example from the past, the Czechs translated religious and historical texts into Latin in order to promote awareness of their cause, namely the Hussite movement and its consequences. In our times, similar examples are not uncommon: Estonian demonstrators carry banners written in English; advertising campaigns aimed at attracting tourists are multilingual. However, at the end of the eighteenth century, this practice was still quite new; it was far less frequent than translation into one's own language, which will be examined in the following section.

The French Revolution aroused a passion for classical Greek and Roman culture, considered to be the ultimate expression of liberty. The influence of Greece on historians and moralists was reflected in the art and drama of an age of well-defined forms and idealistic morals. The art of public speaking was grounded in classical oratory, transmitted once again through translation. In 1792, Hérault de Séchelles, one of the architects of the Revolution, gave a speech in praise of the translator Athanase Auger (1734–92), who had translated the orations of Demosthenes and Aeschines in 1768. He set the tone from the very beginning: "Now that the Revolution has developed our political ideas, it has given us a measure that we lacked, in order that we might appreciate the works of some of the Ancients and take pleasure in all their genius; and so, let us no longer separate the names of Demosthenes and Auger" (Hérault de Séchelles 1970:208). Hérault de Séchelles believed that Auger had restored Demosthenes's "true face", revealing his "proud and sensitive soul, which bears all the dignity and all the suffering of the *patrie*", and the "general movement without which there is no eloquence among the people" (208–209). The political climate of the time made oratory so important that it was indirectly responsible for the changing attitudes toward the translator vis-à-vis the original author.

In was in this way that the function of the translator came to be so highly regarded. In Hérault de Séchelles's view, translation was of great importance, often "presenting an occasion for creation" (213). The same observation was made with respect to Joseph-René Dureau de la Malle (1742–1807), who translated Latin historians like Tacitus. Translators were seen to reflect the light of their models, but also to serve as models of oratory themselves in the prefaces they wrote to their translations. It was entirely natural and effortless, as Hérault de Séchelles writes, for Auger to indulge, in his day and age, in the pleasures that his imagination had so often savoured in history, delivering speeches in which the love of wisdom and the love of the new laws were intertwined (214–215). The transition from translator to author was made smoothly; the close association of translation and creation, in fact, was the best guarantee of truth.

On the one hand, a group of anonymous translators formed the indispensable link between the State and the often illiterate public of the new France. On the other, a revered and celebrated translator could combine translation and authorship, producing texts that embodied the ideological and moral values of Greek Antiquity rearranged to suit the exigencies of the revolutionary age. In both cases, the events of history worked to alter the practice of translation.

France's infatuation with the Gothic novel

Political and military relations between France and England were very tense at the end of the eighteenth century. Despite this hostility, literary commerce continued and even flourished, notably with the massive export of the English Gothic novel to the other side of the Channel (Prungnaud 1994 and 1997). The genre dominated the book market for nearly fifty years, until 1830 or so, and exerted a lasting influence on French aesthetics. After an initial period of systematic translation, which took place primarily between 1790 and 1800, the Gothic novel gradually began to affect French taste and sensibility, particularly at the time of the Restoration of the Bourbon monarchs (1814–30).

The translators of these novels played an important but ambiguous role. Beginning as importers of texts by such writers as William Godwin, Ann Radcliffe, Matthew Gregory Lewis and Mary Shelley, they slowly took to adapting and distorting the genre.[15] This phenomenon will be examined by taking into account the attitudes and translation strategies of translators, rather than sociological factors such as attitudes of publishers and the reading public, or the history of the publication and reprinting of both famous and minor titles (Lévy 1974: 150–176 and 1978: 363–375). This will shed light on the status and function of translation at the time.

Whatever the reasons behind France's initial infatuation with the Gothic novel, it was published with increasing frequency at the height of the fad. The chronological gap between the English originals and their French translations appears to have diminished as time went on. Two translations of M. G. Lewis's *The Monk* were published in 1797, less than a year after the original, and Ann Radcliffe's *The Italian* (1797) and William Godwin's *St. Leon* (1799) were translated the same year as the originals were published. Some of the bestsellers were even reproduced in different translations for rival publishers: Godwin's *Caleb Williams*, for example, was rendered three times between 1795 and 1797, Anna Maria Mackenzie's *Fratricide* appeared in two separate translations in 1798 and 1799, and *The Monk* and *The Italian* were both translated twice in 1797.

This intense translation activity cannot be attributed to commercial considerations alone. Other factors – ideological or psychological – came into play. The foreign texts imported through translation embodied subtle values like Anglican opposition to papist Catholicism, which fueled anticlericalist tendencies in France. The demonic violence in these novels also provided distraction from the political tensions of the period, as did their preoccupation with the supernatural and terror. The Gothic novel expressed atavistic fears and taboos like sadism and incest; it both unleashed and checked the imagination. Yet the tastes to which it appealed were not always the same on both sides of the Channel, and the novels that were most appreciated in France were not always the ones that had enjoyed the most success in England. Walpole's *The Castle of Otranto* (1764), for instance, was reprinted several times in England but only four in France (1767, 1774, 1797 and 1798). Lewis's *The Monk*, on the other hand, went through twenty-five editions in France, was immediately adapted for the theatre and opera and met with little opposition to its immorality. Lewis, of course, gave credit to his European sources, citing German and French models such as Cazotte's *Le Diable amoureux*, and this undoubtedly helped matters. Consequently, Lewis's work was more accessible and familiar to French readers than Walpole's, which was considered too grotesque and disturbing.

As the book market rapidly responded to the demands of the public, translators appear to have followed in the tradition of the "*belles infidèles*", swimming against the tide of literalism that was beginning to sweep through Europe at the beginning of the nineteenth century. They did not hesitate to change titles, delete entire pages and introduce new elements with a view to pleasing the reader and conforming to sensibilities that were dominant at the time. When Bernard de la Mare translated Sophia Lee's *The Recess* (1783–85) as *Le Souterrain, ou Mathilde* (1786), he had no qualms about abridging the work, arguing that some of the events were "more bizarre than interesting". Mary Gay-Allard adjusted the title of Ann Radcliffe's *The Italian; or, The Confessional of the Black Penitents*, making it *Éléonore de Rosalba, ou, le Confessionnal des Pénitents noirs*, since one of the main characters is a murderous monk, and the reference to Italy might therefore be considered "insulting to an entire nation". She preferred instead to make use of the heroine's name in the title. Such corrections and modifications were designed to make the novels more acceptable to the reader. In domesticating the English texts, the translators effaced their foreign origin but did not eradicate all traces of exoticism. Many of the changes were justified by the target-culture value system. For example, the word "God" appearing in Sophia Lee's *The Recess* was replaced by "*l'Être suprême*" (the Supreme Being) in the French translation; Lewis's monk Ambrosio became "le Jacobin espagnol" (the Spanish Jacobin) in the French version of 1797; and the term "miser" in Charles Robert Maturin's *Melmoth* was rendered as "Harpagon" (the main character of Molière's *The Miser*) when "freely translated" by Jean Cohen in 1821.

Through such approximations, abridgements, additions and even inaccuracies, the translators in effect became censors and revisers, and did so with the encouragement of the critics and public. The adaptations went beyond anything required by the criterion of readability alone: translations were intended to suit the habits of the readership, to achieve what was considered "good" style or the "genius of the language" and to conform to existing literary canons. Under such conditions, translators were not mere importers of values; they were also the guardians of target-culture norms. Their work bordered on rewriting the original. In keeping with such appropriation, many booksellers' catalogues actually listed the translators as authors. For example, the *Dictionnaire des romans* by Alfred Marc (1819) lists Jean Cohen as an author although the list of titles includes only his translations and none of his original compositions. The translator's creativity was signalled by expressions like "Gothic novel translated *freely*" or "Gothic novel *imitated* from the English", used to present the two French versions of Clara Reeve's *The Old English Baron* issued in 1787 by two different publishers.

This large-scale importation of transfigured texts influenced the development of translation practices. Two tendencies are worth mentioning. First, foreign works generally attracted so much attention that there was a growing desire to present everything as a translation. This was a time of pseudotranslations and literary spoofs. Second, English texts, in particular, enjoyed special prestige in France. Around 1815, the "myth of England" became fashionable once again (Reboul 1962), bringing back the positive image of English society that had been projected by eighteenth-century philosophers. The English language and other cultural products from across the Channel were in vogue among the elite. Three types of British novels were in particular favour among French readers: the sentimental novel, the Gothic novel and the historical novel. The notation "translated from the English" became a mark of prestige, and the false attribution of texts to English authors was a common hoax. Baron Étienne-Léon de Lamothe-Langon, a prolific writer from 1815 to 1825, used the names of Radcliffe and Lewis to promote texts he had written himself in 1816 and 1819, respectively. Imitation then became more important than any actual exploring or prospecting for foreign values. Translation became free adaptation, open imitation or a trick played by authors in search of recognition. The Countess du Nardouet, for example, falsely claimed that her novel *Barbarinski, ou les Brigands du château de Wissegrade* (1818) was "imitated from the English of Ann Radcliffe", whereas it was a work of fiction that did not owe anything to anyone else. The notion of translation was displaced to such an extent that the source text lost its importance. The ultimate result was pseudotranslation, a convenient literary subterfuge in which the source text was merely an imagined presence, a pretext for writing or getting one's works into print. In his preamble to *L'Hermite de la tombe mystérieuse, ou le fantôme du vieux château* (1816), Lamothe-Langon even went so far as to anticipate his readers' incredulity, thereby suggesting just how common a practice these literary masks and masquerades were at the time.

In the space of a few decades, translation took many forms: from free translation to conservatism, from the creation of copies to the creation of originals posing as translations. One of the most interesting phenomena is the retranslation of texts that travelled backward and forward between France and England. For instance, Madame Louise Marguerite Brayer de Saint-Léon's *Alexina, ou la vieille tour du château de Holdheim* (1813), originally presented as an imitation of an English work, was translated or domesticated into English in 1821 by Margaret Campbell, who called it *The Midnight Wanderer; or a Legend of the Houses of Altenberg and Lindendorf. A Romance.* This English version was then translated into French by a certain Duval and attributed to Ann Radcliffe, under the title *Rose d'Altenberg, ou le Spectre dans les ruines, manuscrit trouvé dans le portefeuille de feue Anne* [sic] *Radcliffe et traduit de l'anglais par Henri Duval.* A further case is Count William Beckford's *Vathek*, originally written in French and published anonymously. It was translated into English by Reverend Samuel Henley and published in 1786, without Beckford's name, as *An Arabian Tale, From an Unpublished*

Manuscript, claiming to be translated directly from Arabic. It was in this form that it was retranslated back into French and published in Paris in 1819.

The Gothic novel was eventually weakened by this inflation of forms and excess of literary exchanges, which led to a degradation of the original literary model. The compelling works that had initially held the attention of readers gave way to dull clichés. The enthusiastic admiration with which the new genre had been heralded was followed by disparagement, parody and rejection. Baudelaire, for one, expressed his indignation at the poor quality of translations of Maturin's *Melmoth the Wanderer* in 1821. The publishing industry of the time, increasingly subject to economic constraints, rather than the translators, was largely responsible for this state of affairs. Literature was gradually becoming industrialized, an object of mass production, as evinced by Balzac's beginnings in 1821–26.

The proliferation of translations of uneven quality did not just have negative effects, however. Although in the short term the result was the publication of rather mediocre books, things were quite different in the longer term. This mass-produced literature contained a wealth of new situations, plots and settings that would serve to stimulate the imagination of young readers like Théophile Gautier and Victor Hugo. The Gothic novel provided the novelists of the future with a rich source of inspiration. The aesthetics of terror – a legacy of the Gothic novel – became a common thread in French Romanticism. The role of translation in this transition was by no means negligible. In multiplying contacts between English and French cultures, translation helped provide readers with new images and contributed to the evolution of literature.

The impact of translated thought: a Chinese example

At various times in its history, China has been open to Western ideas. This openness has had different causes at different periods, but it has affected most disciplines and spheres of activity to one extent or another. In the world of ideas, translation has undeniably functioned as a means of discovering and apprehending knowledge developed in the West. For over three hundred years, many Christian missionaries introduced works of natural science, mathematics and astronomy to China. At the beginning of the nineteenth century, the Yangwu group, comprised of highly placed Foreign Affairs officials, initiated the translation of technical documents dealing with subjects like shipbuilding and the manufacture of weapons, and even established a number of translator-training institutions. This section will focus on one figure, from a slightly later period: Yan Fu (or Yen Fu, 1854–1921). His is the case of a cultural intermediary who, at a critical moment in history, sought to make European works of political and social science accessible to his people.

From a poor family in Fuzhou (Foochow), a port in the province of Fujian (Fukien), Yan Fu (Figure 15) attended a naval college and served on warships which took him to places such as Singapore and Japan. He chose the School of Navigation, where the language of instruction was English, and this would ultimately give him access to Western ideas (Sinn 1995: 429). He then went to Portsmouth and Greenwich, England, where he had been sent with a group of naval officers who would later serve in the Sino-Japanese war of 1894–95. In England, he read philosophical and scientific texts voraciously. Upon his return to China in 1879 he was appointed director of the Northern Chinese Naval Academy, becoming vice-president of the institution in 1889 and president in 1890. After 1896, he supervised several translation institutes operating under central and local government authority. After the fall of the Qing (Ch'ing) or Manzhou (Manchu) dynasty in 1911, he became the first president of Peking University (now Beijing University). He soon resigned to take charge of the translation bureau for the Navy and in 1913 was appointed foreign affairs adviser to the President of the new Chinese Republic.

Yan Fu's work was politically rather than culturally oriented and, as such, can best be understood in terms of the power relations of the time (Lin 2002: 177). He was profoundly shocked by the humiliating Treaty of Shimonoseki of April 1895, which sealed China's defeat by Japan. A patriotic and liberal intellectual, well aware of the risks that threatened the entire nation, he founded a newspaper in 1896, in which he published articles and editorials defending his political views. In particular, he advocated drawing on Western ideas, culture and values to strengthen a weakened China. The impact of his articles was "explosive" (Sinn 1995: 430), but it was through his translations, particularly his 1898 translation of Thomas Henry Huxley's *Evolution and Ethics* (1893), that he truly established a reputation throughout the country (Wong 2004: 245–246).

His list of accomplishments would go on to include Adam Smith's *Wealth of Nations* (1776), published in Chinese in 1901–02; Herbert Spencer's *The Study of Sociology* (1872) and John Stuart Mill's *On Liberty* (1859), both published in translation in 1903; writings by Edward Jenks published in Chinese in 1904; Montesquieu's *The Spirit of the Laws* (1748), which appeared between 1904 and 1909; J. S. Mill's *A System of Logic* (1843), translated in 1905; and William Stanley Jevons's *The Theory of Political Economy* (1878), translated in 1909. Five of these translations were distributed by a publishing house that had been established with the specific aim of promoting new scientific knowledge. The publishing company reprinted the titles listed above in 1931, at a time when Japan was once again a threat for China, and later in 1981–82, as China began to adopt a new policy of openness.

In the space of just ten years, several of the major landmarks of European political thought had been translated into Chinese. The impact of Yan Fu's work is well illustrated by the reception of Huxley in China. A biologist and supporter of Darwin, Huxley had applied the theory of evolution to society as a whole. His concepts of "struggle for life" and "natural selection" seemed, in Yan Fu's view, to be appropriate in portraying his country at that time. In his translator's notes, he declared that the powers that had invaded and exploited China were morally and intellectually "superior", and that China had become "inferior" as a result of relentless international competition. If China did not fight for its own existence, it would succumb to ineluctable domination or genocide. The translation of Huxley's *Evolution and Ethics* set off a heated debate throughout the country, involving scholars, conservative bureaucrats, the Manzhou aristocracy and the schools, where the text was frequently used for instructional purposes and the "survival of the fittest" became a favourite essay topic.

This was the first systematic effort since the Jesuits to present contemporary Western thought to Chinese intellectuals (Sinn 1995: 431). Yan Fu was soon highly regarded, known for his ability to grasp and communicate the essence of Western knowledge. Two other factors account for Yan Fu's success as a translator: his choice of source texts and his excellent style. Many of his translations are accompanied by translator's notes in which he sets out his methods and approaches to his craft. As he said himself, good translators must have a thorough understanding of the source texts, but they must also be aware of the needs and expectations of their compatriots so they can select works appropriate to their time. Yan Fu's choice of language and style also won him many readers. He wrote in classical Mandarin, which had developed in the Zhou (Chou) (1000–200 BCE) and Han (mainly 200–100 BCE) dynasties to become the language of the elite, and which was still in use in all publications, official or otherwise. He also rearranged chapters and paragraphs so they would be consistent with the presentation and organization of ideas in the Chinese classics. As a translator, Yan Fu was thus able to appeal to influential government officials and win their support.

Credited with having achieved both fidelity and stylistic beauty, Yan Fu is still considered a master and model for today's Chinese translators, who continue to quote and debate the preface he wrote to his translation of *Evolution and Ethics* (Wong 2004). He is well known for having formulated three principles of translation: *xin*, *da* and *ya*, or faithfulness, lucidity (fluency, clarity or comprehensibility), and elegance, which have been compared to the translation principles articulated by Alexander Fraser Tytler in 1791, but which may in fact be more deeply rooted in Confucian doctrine and traditional Chinese theory (Lin 2002: 164–165).

Yan Fu changed, however. At the close of a career spent opening China to new cultural horizons and importing modern ideas into China, he became disillusioned with the West and contemporary ideas:

> In my old age, I have seen the Republic during the seven years of its existence and an unprecedented bloody war of four years in Europe. I feel that the evolution of their [Western] races in the last three hundred years has only made them kill one another for self-interest, without a sense of shame. Today, when I reconsider the way of Confucius and Mencius, I feel it is broad enough to cover the whole cosmos and to benefit the entire world.   (Quoted in Sinn 1995: 446)

American science fiction and the birth of a genre in France

The emergence of the American nation at the end of the eighteenth century created a new international power whose influence gradually supplanted that of Britain and France. The struggle for international dominance eventually played out not only in the diplomatic, military and economic spheres, but also in the production of symbolic goods (Bourdieu 1979 and 1992). Of the literature the French chose to translate from American English certain kinds of texts stood out. They were selected for translation precisely because of their text type or genre, and then massively imported into French culture. Science fiction is the focus here, although detective novels could also be cited as an example of this trend.

When Hugo Gernsback launched the magazine *Amazing Stories* in 1926, he declared himself to be a follower of Jules Verne, many of whose works he published in serial form, although he was also an admirer of Edgar Allan Poe and H. G. Wells.[16] From the outset, science fiction was in many respects linked to translation. First of all, Poe had been translated into French by Baudelaire. Second, Verne had imitated Poe and attempted to follow in his footsteps, inspiring Gernsback and creating models for science fiction based on technical and scientific adventures.[17] Third, Gernsback's background itself was intercultural: he had spent his childhood and adolescence in Luxembourg before emigrating to the United States. This example serves to illustrate one of the functions of translation, which can serve to redistribute certain elements geographically. As source texts are handled in different ways by different translators, they are cast into a wide range of sociocultural contexts. Translations that are imported and domesticated can influence target-culture ideas and models. Something dormant in one culture can flourish once it is transplanted – through translation – to more fertile ground or a more favourable climate in another culture. Once strengthened in the target culture, the new models can then return to enrich the original source culture.

Verne's brand of scientific adventure stories was not to re-enter French culture until the end of World War II. Some sixty-six years had elapsed since he had first published his unique stories.[18] Previous efforts to promote the genre and its values had been unsuccessful: Maurice Renard had tried at the beginning of the century, Régis Messac in the 1930s and Georges-Hilaire Gallet just before World War II.

Boris Vian, Raymond Queneau and Michel Pilotin are credited with having successfully imported American science fiction into France in the 1950s. Vian first translated Frank M. Robinson's "The Labyrinth", published in the periodical *Les Temps modernes* in 1951 along with the first article on science fiction by Vian and Pilotin. Four further translations/adaptations of stories by Wallace West, Ray Bradbury, William Tenn and Murray Leinster were published in *France-Dimanche* in 1952 under the heading "Français, Attention! Voici la science fiction!"[19] Three of the four stories were in a humorous vein, which was reinforced in Vian's adaptation. In June 1953, the *Mercure de France* published "Tout smouales étaient les borogoves", a translation of "Mimsy were the Borogoves" by Lewis Padgett, the collective pseudonym of Henry Kuttner and Catherine Moore. The same year, Hachette-Gallimard published Vian's translation of Van Vogt's novel *The World of Null-A*, and in 1957 released the French version of the sequel, *The Pawns of Null-A*. Vian chose these texts because they were light stories that nevertheless contained a sharp social critique. These translations were prompted by a desire to circulate, legitimize and promote the genre. Translation was a part of the strategy, but the strategy went beyond translation. The version of "The Labyrinth" published in *Les Temps modernes*, for example, was accompanied by an article meant to be read in conjunction with the translation. A comparison of the discourse of translated fiction with the critical discourse of their translators, reveals just how consistent the themes are: the appeal of novelty, the challenge to established values and the constant call for lucidity.

The critical articles written by Vian and Spriel (Pilotin's pseudonym), as well as by Spriel and Queneau, endorsed science fiction as a new genre because it brought together two cultures, one scientific and the other literary. For Vian, the ideal reader of science fiction was "the mathematician, the physicist or educated people like Raymond Queneau, who know what is being done in literature, mathematics and physics. These are people who do not cut themselves off from whole areas of knowledge" (*L'Écran* 1958). American science fiction gave a nonspecialized image of modern man, an image that Vian boldly associated with Renaissance man. In his 1953 piece "Un robot-poète ne nous fait pas peur", he wrote, "They want to turn us into specialized workers [...]. We must refuse [...]. We must know everything. [...] The future belongs to Pico della Mirandola", referring to the Italian Renaissance author of the "Oration on the Dignity of Man".

Vian chose to translate *The World of Null-A* and *The Pawns of Null-A* in the hope that they might bring about some kind of breakthrough. The plot of these novels is based on Alfred Korzybski's widely contested general semantics. Korzybski argued that human language need not depend on the Aristotelian principle of identity and noncontradiction, and that the study of mathematical language could show this. Such a theory is obviously rich in possibilities for science fiction. The two Van Vogt novels translated by Vian show a society of human beings who are able to live on Venus in accordance with a non-Aristotelian logic applied through pure mental discipline. Korzybski's theories were also a point of reference for Lewis Padgett's story "Mimsy were the Borogoves", the title of which is a quotation from Lewis Carroll's *Through the Looking-Glass*. In this case, general semantics are used to define madness and normality according to non-Aristotelian criteria. These texts by Van Vogt and Lewis Padgett are examples of the poetics of discontinuity which characterized American science fiction. They radically questioned established values, using narrative modes that were noncanonical in the French society of the time.

Vian's interest in American science fiction also stemmed from its ability to appeal to the reader's powers of reasoning without diminishing the pleasure of reading. Science fiction, he claimed, combines emotional excitement with a very special kind of intellectual intoxication (Vian and Spriel 1951). Yet Vian did not advocate a purely cerebral or overly serious kind of science fiction.

The modernity of American science fiction went beyond the commentaries of Vian, Queneau and Pilotin. The genre showcased science and technology, extraterrestrial otherness, mutation and metamorphosis (Gouanvic 1994 and 1999). Science fiction developed these themes in a contradictory way. In the twentieth century, as in the nineteenth, the United States was divided by conflicting ideological tendencies, some of them conservative and others more liberal. Science fiction came in both conservative and liberal flavours, with the balance between the two varying according to the period. Nevertheless, spurred on by Gernsback, science fiction emerged in the 1920s and 1930s as a genre in its own right, offering the American middle classes something they could not find in other literature: the construction of a new world order based on the primacy of science and technology. This was a world in which research no longer involved the pursuit of pure knowledge of natural phenomena but the direct industrial application of that knowledge to meet the needs of government, military, business and academic sponsors (Stover 1972). This was the dawn of R&D, the cornerstone of American social progress and the basis of "people's capitalism". American science fiction transmitted all these values. In bringing the genre to France, Vian and Queneau imported a world view whose centre was the United States. As indicated by the above reference to Pico della Mirandola, however, they rejected the excess of pragmatism and specialization associated with such a vision. In actual fact, there would be so many translations of American science fiction that the bad was brought in with the good. On the negative side, there was a claim to represent universal values and a tendency to see the future in terms of American destiny alone, in line with the founding myths of the American nation (Marienstras 1976). Science fiction conveyed the frontier spirit of America's founding fathers, substituting cosmic unknowns for the uncharted land that settlers conquered in the West. The goal, now secularized, remained essentially the same: to impose the American way as the only legitimate world view – by force if necessary. On the positive side, science-fiction writers like Ursula K. Le Guin, Philip K. Dick and, more recently, Samuel Delany and Octavia Butler were attracted to all forms of otherness, including a wide range of nonanthropocentric, or nonhuman, forms of life and egalitarian social relationships.

Around 143 novels and collections were translated in the 1950s, along with approximately 200 stories published in the French periodicals *Fiction* and *Galaxie*. These works were integrated into the structures that produced and distributed French science fiction, a genre openly identified as an offshoot of the American movement. Most of the French translators were little-known but versatile writers, translating realist fiction belonging to "high" literature, as well as detective novels and science fiction. Jean Rosenthal, for example, translated John Dos Passos, detective novels by Harry Grey and science fiction by Isaac Asimov.

This is a case where translation helped to import and launch a new genre. It gave science fiction a certain legitimacy, albeit within the restricted field of popular literature. Of particular importance in this regard was Hachette-Gallimard's "Rayon Fantastique" series, which set translation standards for virtually the whole field except the periodical *Galaxie*. The translators who published in this collection considered that they were fulfilling a duty to introduce an exotic genre. Adaptations were rare; instead, translators retained traces of foreignness originating from the source culture (not to be confused with science-fiction themes like extraterrestrials). This sometimes came at the price of a certain obscurity. The texts they translated contained references to American experience of the 1940s or 1950s, particularly everyday activities like eating, sex and personal hygiene. The values of American society were inscribed just as much in these practices as in the actual science fiction themes. The translators went to some lengths to convey these day-to-day occurrences accurately. Elements that were merely banal and trivial in the source text would then take on a new role in the target text, remaining banal and trivial but also drawing attention to the text's foreign origin.

Foreignness was also preserved through references to the literary and biblical canons of the source culture. Literary references are not lacking in American science fiction: both American authors *per se* and certain English-language authors like Shakespeare, Milton and Kipling whose actual identity is not mentioned. Such cases presented no real problem for the translators, since these authors had previously been translated into French and were reasonably well known to the French public. Unlike French writers of science fiction such as J.-H. Rosny aîné, Maurice Renard or Jacques Spitz, American science-fiction writers also referred to the Bible when conceptualizing natural disasters or catastrophes brought on by humans. In American scenarios, destruction is followed by a new beginning, whether the result of nuclear holocaust or natural cataclysm. One leitmotiv of American science fiction is purifying destruction, as in the Apocalypse of John, which acts as a condition for reconciliation with God and rebirth in a regained Eden (Ketterer 1974).

In general, American science fiction defended established American values, particularly the claims of the white Anglo-Saxon Protestant majority to represent a universal model of humanity and act with the approval of God. The translation of these texts, however, did not bring about a wholesale importation of such values. American science fiction also expressed an attraction for the Other, for that which is different in time and in space. It created tension based on a movement that went forever outward, toward a nonanthropocentric alterity, and toward human relationships based on new social conditions. The translators of science fiction performed contradictory functions, and continue to do so, in fact. On the one hand, they have served the interests of American propaganda; on the other, they have participated in the search for a modern utopia, a vision of heterogeneous places and possibilities, expressed in the works of some American science-fiction writers.

One of the oldest meanings of translation is "to pass contraband". In "Translation as Creation", Canadian literary translator Philip Stratford (1928–1999) describes the translator as someone who smuggles foreign goods across borders.

> Paradoxically, although for his own purposes he has decided that frontiers do not exist, and although he works in a sense to eliminate boundaries, he depends on them absolutely; he trades on the existence of frontiers and his own facility in crossing them. He is by necessity a man of divided allegiances, neither flesh nor fowl, a lonely, shadowy character, mistrusted by everyone. And probably envied a little in a covert way, too, for, more positively, he stands for freedom, risk, excitement and adventure. An aura of envy has always hung over the smuggler, and a lot of this is also due the translator. (Stratford 1978: 10)

This chapter has presented eight different cases in which translators have facilitated the importation of foreign cultural values, either consciously or unconsciously. The term "exchange" includes "change": the trajectory is never linear, transmission is never a literal transfer. The limits and stakes of translation as a "trans-action" have come to light in the different examples provided. Translators can fertilize target-culture values through the authors and texts they translate, or through their work as critics, commentators or participants in debate, as seen in various contexts. Translators import and transmit values. They do so by taking part in the creation of values and the circulation of certain aesthetic and intellectual options. Whether immediate or delayed, the effects of translation are undeniable.

Do translators go exploring and prospecting for foreign values? Translators can indeed be regarded as explorers, but only as long as they move beyond the perspective of convertibility, which is the ideological prelude to pure and simple appropriation. They are prospectors, as long as they do not remain within the essentialist and homogenizing vision of two presupposed cultural territories with well-defined borders, a vision in which translation would merely serve as a medium for unilateral or bilateral communication. Translation is not simple transfer, where the only failures would be the result of mistranslations or dubious equivalents. The translated version of a text is a subversion. It subverts the initial conditions for the production of meaning, just as it subverts the norms and values of the place where it is received as a new text. Translation is a symbolic act of violence. This might explain why there are societies that do not translate, and places where translation is prohibited.

The transfer of texts, ideas, concepts and ways of speaking almost always meets with resistance. One way of dealing with the unknown is to associate it with something one already knows; the new is mapped in terms of established norms, analogies are forced, differences are reduced and conventional associations work to deconstruct. Translators explore, interpret and sometimes anticipate the reception or use of their work. Their procedures involve a certain filtering, a constant oscillation between radical invention and blatant domestication of the Other. Not all historical situations are equally suited to the meeting and mixing of cultures. Modes of social organization, doctrines, ideologies, literary systems and categories of thought are not always open or malleable. They tend to close in on themselves when seeking to establish or maintain their domination, or their illusions of purity or homogeneity. The mixing of cultures is a long process. Sometimes smooth and continuous, it often works through sudden jolts. It is sometimes fertile, but often perverted. And yet it is present from the very moment the Self looks at the Other, when the act of importation is prefigured. Since they do not merely reproduce whatever was there before them, since they do not bring about brutal assimilation, translators can cause disturbance, either through the personal traces they leave in their texts (Folkart 1991) or through the long-term effects of their work.

When grappling with texts that are indeterminate, with multiple and shifting meanings, translators take part in the generation of values, traditions and exchanges. The acceptance and recognition of their activity has gone through highs and lows, since all societies have only a relative and variable tolerance for that which is problematic. Yet if translators were to cast off their image as anonymous or intruding explorers, they could become self-respecting traitors, carefree smugglers untroubled by borders or passports, double agents in a history that could not unfold without them. Translation, then, would no longer be substitution but cross-fertilization, resulting in the hybridity of cultures.

Notes

1. Sherry Simon (2006 and 2011) has examined the idea of "divided" or multilingual cities such as Montreal, Calcutta, Trieste, and Barcelona, where both separation and contact inspire and provoke translation and linguistic plurality within the cities themselves.

2. During the period of Muslim domination of Spain (eighth to fifteenth centuries), Mozarabs were Iberian Christians who pledged allegiance to a Moorish ruler in exchange for the right to practise their own religion.

3. See also Chapters 4 and 5.

4. But too much can be made of Toledo in this context. The designation of this particularly fertile period of translation as a "school" has been discussed in Chapter 4. See also Pym (2000).

5. One very notable exception was the introduction of Edgar Allan Poe to France, first by Baudelaire who translated the short stories, then by Mallarmé who translated his poetry, and finally by Paul Valéry – a participant in the *mardis de la rue de Rome* – who translated and commented on selected *Marginalia*. In each case, translation was seen as a way of paying tribute to a great author, even portrayed by Baudelaire as a spiritual brother ("*un frère spirituel*") (Woodsworth 1988 and 2000).

6. In particular, versions by George Sale (1734), David Friedrich Megerlin (1772), Friedrich Eberhard Boysen (1773) and Claude-Étienne Savary (1783).

7. Indifferentism is a consciously nurtured attitude or philosophy of indifference toward religion.

8. Reland is referring primarily to Guillaume Joseph Grelot and Jean Chardin, but many other travellers could also have supported his claims: from Pietro della Valle to François Pétis de la Croix, from François de La-Boullaye-le-Gouz to Joseph Tournefort, from Paul Bellon to Paul Ricaut, Islamic tolerance had become a leitmotiv in travellers' accounts of the Orient.

9. Pierre Bayle had reason to be critical of fellow Christians: he was a French Protestant and took refuge in Holland, where he spent most of his career as a scholar and philosopher.

10. Diderot (1976, 8:309, art. "Schooubiak"); Helvétius (1973:1986); Voltaire (1961:578; 1963, vol. 1:275 and 1963, vol. 2:770).

11. See Bennett (1965:87–111); Ebel (1967:125); Watson (1974:2165–94), listing translations between 1500 and 1660.

12. The Edict of Nantes was decreed in 1598 by King Henri IV, granting the Huguenots, or French Protestants, religious freedom in a primarily Catholic country and bringing to an end the religious wars which had ravaged France in the previous half century. The Edict of Nantes was later revoked by Louis XIV, leading to the departure of French Protestants, mainly to neighbouring European Protestant nations.

13. In Holland, Philippus van Limborch's objections to Locke began to gain ground and in the German states, Jean Barbeyrac's observations were used in the second edition of the *Essay*. Theologian Johann Christian Fabricius was influenced, as was Friedrich von Schiller, who taught history before he was acclaimed as a poet and dramatist. Coste's work reached scholars such as the Swiss Johann Jakob Breitinger, Johann Jakob Bodmer and Jean-Pierre de Crousaz, the Italians Ludovico Antonio Muratori and Paolo-Matteo Doria, and so on.

14. The Thermidorian Reaction was a revolt against the Reign of Terror, ending the most radical phase of the French Revolution. The name refers to the month of "Thermidor" in the French Revolutionary Calendar; the date in current terms was July 27, 1794.

15. The following are some examples of the work produced by these authors. William Godwin wrote *The Adventures of Caleb Williams; or, Things as they are* (1794), translated in 1795 by Samuel Constant; the same novel was translated again in 1796 by Count Germain Garnier as *Les Aventures de Caleb Williams, ou les Choses comme elles sont*, then once again in 1797 by "country people" as *Les Choses comme elles sont, ou les Aventures de Caleb Williams*. Godwin is also known for *St. Leon* (1799), published in French the same year as *Saint-Léon, histoire du XVIe siècle*. In 1797, five novels by Ann Radcliffe were published in French translation including *The Mysteries of Udolpho*, translated by Victorine de Chastenay as *Les Mystères d'Udolphe*, and two versions of *The Italian; or, The Confessional of the Black Penitents*, as *Éléonore de Rosalba, ou, le Confessionnal des Pénitents noirs*, translated by Mary Gay-Allard and *L'Italien, ou le Confessionnal des Pénitents noirs*, translated by André Morellet. M. G. Lewis was the author of *The Monk* (1796), which was also translated twice in 1797: as *Le Moine*, by J. M. Deschamps et al. and *Le Jacobin espagnol, ou Histoire du moine Ambrosio et de la belle Antonia, sa sœur*. Mary Shelley was of course the author of the celebrated *Frankenstein; or The Modern Prometheus* (1818), translated and published only once by Jules Saladin.

16. Hugo Gernsback (1884–1967) was born in Luxembourg. Noted in particular for *Amazing Stories*, the first periodical to deal exclusively with the nascent genre, he is considered to be the father of the genre about to be named "science fiction". The award for achievement in science fiction, the "Hugo", bears his name. Verne, who wrote his popular works in France beginning in the 1860s, had been systematically translated into English and published in the United States from 1873 on.

17. Verne had written an article on Poe prior to the publication of *Five Weeks in a Balloon* (the first of the "Extraordinary Voyages") in 1863, and his *Sphinx des glaces* was written as a sequel to Poe's *The Adventures of Arthur Gordon Pym*.

18. Meanwhile, Jules Verne was being translated and retranslated into English over a period of well over one hundred years. See O'Driscoll (2011).

19. Wallace West's "Sculptors of Life" was published in French under the title "Les Vivisculpteurs" (286:12–13); Ray Bradbury's "The Veldt" was rendered as "Le Veldt dans la nursery" (288:6); William Tenn's story, translated into French as "Pas Bêtes, les gars de Bételgeuse" (289:10), was no doubt based on a story called "Betelgeuse Bridge", although this has not been confirmed; and Murray Leinster's "If you was a Moklin" was translated into French as "Si vous étiez un Moklin" (292:9).

Figure 15. Yan Fu

Figure 16. Nicolas Oresme

CHAPTER 8

Translators and the production of dictionaries

The relationship between translators and dictionaries can be analysed from different perspectives. Translators are consumers of dictionaries; they have also contributed to their production. While dictionaries have long been part of the translator's arsenal, history shows that translators have done more than simply use these books as tools. They have also actively compiled words or terms. Translators have been lexicographers just as lexicographers have served as translators, as was the case of Émile Littré for the French language and Samuel Johnson for English. How did this alliance between translators and dictionaries originate? How far back does the encounter go? In short, what role have translators played in the trajectory of dictionaries through history? This chapter will illustrate the important contribution of translators to lexicography and their association with dictionaries.

Monolingual dictionaries: from clay tablets to paper dictionaries

Dictionaries are as old as writing itself, and stand out as one of humanity's greatest intellectual achievements. This revolution in the world of ideas took place in Mesopotamia around 3500 BCE. Writing first emerged as a means to document practical information. With urbanization, it became necessary to record the nature of the goods that were exchanged and to ensure that economic transactions were recognized by all parties involved. Once it met administrative needs, written language was improved upon and used for sacred and scholarly purposes. It was then put to secular and intellectual uses, in the service of literature, narratives and epics, for example.

Dictionaries followed close on the heels of writing, once durable materials were found to support them. From clay tablets to papyrus, parchment, paper and small plastic disks (diskettes, CDs and DVDs), USB keys, as well as websites – many different materials have been used in the production of dictionaries. Beyond this observation, though, how is a dictionary different from a novel, an essay or a catalogue of parts or products? To be considered a dictionary, a book must above all constitute or contain an inventory of words arranged in a certain order (alphabetical, thematic, or a combination of both), set out in independent paragraphs known as "entries". In addition, each entry must contain a series of set, formal categories that provide one or more items of information of a pragmatic nature (e.g. spelling, part-of-speech label, pronunciation, definition, illustrative examples). This formal architecture is the microstructure, providing a blueprint for each entry. The pragmatic statements add up to a linguistic portrait of the headword. Thus, the entry summarizes all of the word's functions both in language and in discourse.

The first dictionaries made their appearance in Sumer toward the end of the fourth millennium BCE.[1] They were lists of terms compiled on small clay tablets. By 3000 BCE, perhaps even as early as 3300 BCE, tabular records came into use. These first catalogues listed the names of objects such as receptacles, fabrics or tools; they also enumerated plants (e.g. trees, fruits and vegetables), minerals, animals, proper names, names of professions, academic subjects (e.g. mathematics and economics), and so on. By around 2700 BCE, scribes were producing the first encyclopedic compilations, summarizing the body of knowledge of their time. Lists produced during this period had two attributes: they were monolingual and conceptual.

Between 3000 and 2600 BCE, the Akkadians inherited Sumer's prosperity. Midway through the third millennium, the Akkadians imposed their own culture, substituting it for Sumer's, with the exception of the Sumerian language, which was assimilated and maintained by the Akkadians for their own communication purposes. Toward 2340 BCE, the Akkadians also adopted Sumer's cuneiform writing system to transmit their language. This transition from one language to another gave rise to a need for translation and the development of linguistic tools, including dictionaries. However, it was not until the end of the third millennium, around 2000 BCE, that bilingual lexical tablets appeared. These were the work of Semitic authors. The production of Sumerian-Akkadian bilingual lists can be attributed to two factors: the symbiotic relationship between the two cultures and the replacement of the Akkadian language by the Sumerian one. The entire cycle spanned several centuries.

The dictionary across cultures

Dictionaries were thus among the earliest illustrations of how languages work. Taken in its broadest sense, the term "dictionary" refers first of all to monolingual compilations, which preceded all other forms of recording the mysteries of language. This type of monolingual work made perfect sense in the case of the great civilizations of the past with a written language, which were primarily inward looking.

In the fourth millennium BCE, the Syrio-Mesopotamian region, or the so-called Fertile Crescent, was the birthplace of a double intellectual revolution: a system of writing was created, and all kinds of inventories of words and terms, including dictionaries and early versions of encyclopedias, were produced.

In Egypt, the earliest accounts of lexicography date back to the third millennium BCE, but remain scarce until the middle of the second millennium. At first, the lists were monolingual and documented the names of people and places. Scribes would use these nomenclatures as teaching tools. As was the case in Mesopotamian culture, bilingual records would only come later.

Once their language fell into decline, the Copts turned to bilingual glossaries to preserve their ties to Pharaonic Egypt. Coptic was in fact the last stage of the Egyptian language. By the eighth century, it had replaced Greek in Egyptian administrative documents. From the ninth century on, however, the importance of the Coptic language diminished as Arabic gained ground, and it disappeared entirely by the eleventh century. Competition among languages was one of the reasons for creating bilingual glossaries. As early as 580, there were Greek-Coptic lexicons. One example is the *Glossary* created by Dioscorus of Aphrodito.[2] Coptic was subsequently associated with other languages such as Latin and Arabic. The Copts' desire to prevent their language from disappearing explains the proliferation of bilingual vocabularies, including the *scalae*, or scholia, which were marginal notes or explanatory comments, made by grammarians on classical texts.

In Greece, the first dictionaries were *léxeis* or *glôssai*, monolingual compilations that listed sayings or explained obscure, archaic and dialectal words found in the writings of Homer, Alcman, Solon and other ancient authors. The earliest of these compilations, such as those produced by Protagoras of Abdera, date back to the fifth century BCE. But it was in Alexandria that the Greek dictionary truly flourished, between the late fourth and early third centuries BCE. It was there that Ptolemy I Soter (c.367–283 BCE) founded the Library of Alexandria, which housed a school of lexicography. Construction of the library began around 288 BCE. Four years later, Zenodotus of Ephesus (fl. third century BCE) was named its first superintendent. Engaging in a subject popular for two centuries, Zenodotus listed and explained the obscure terms in Homer's works. The greatest and most famous head librarian of the Library of Alexandria was Aristophanes of Byzantium (c.257–180 BCE). Aristophanes established a school of philology and lexicography. He was also the author of a large work entitled *Léxeis* (Words).

Glossaries and lexicons on every subject appeared throughout Antiquity, until the beginning of the Common Era. Homeric scholarship continued, as understanding his work remained a priority. There was an interest in everything: specialized terminologies, lists of verbs, features of dialects, inventories of objects such as kitchen items, etc. These glossaries often took something of a philological approach. From the first century to the sixth, lexicographic production both intensified and diversified. Methodological principles were formulated, in particular the classification of words in alphabetical order. Some key works stand out during this period of prolific production: the comprehensive lexicon of Pamphilus of Alexandria in the first century, and Diogenianus of Heraclea's lexicon in the second century, which inspired Hesychius of Alexandria to produce his *Synagoge pason lexeon kata stoicheion* (*Alphabetical Collection of All Words*) late in this period (fifth to sixth centuries). The collection is, as the title suggests, in alphabetical order; it includes words borrowed from other languages and dialects that were commonly used in Alexandrian Greek, as well as words taken from the writing of Homer. The work is particularly useful in shedding light on the history of the Greek language. In the middle of the sixth century, Hesychius of Miletus published his *Onomatologos*, or *Biographical Dictionary of Learned Men*, a comprehensive listing of celebrated Greek and other non-Christian writers.[3]

In Rome, great Latin thinkers drew inspiration from Greek works, particularly those in the field of philosophy and technical terminology. More practical in nature than the Greeks before them, the Romans initiated encyclopedic works, resulting from compilations of their own scientific research and those of the Greeks, to which they had access. Many authors published such works, for example Cato, Varro, Pliny the Elder and Aulus Gellius. The Romans also followed in the Greek dictionary tradition, producing simple compilations that served to differentiate terms. Marcus Terentius Varro (116–27 BCE) produced *De lingua Latina*, a massive encyclopedic work on the Latin language. It enjoyed widespread distribution and was very influential. From the start of the Common Era to the sixth century, many authors devoted themselves to lexicographic endeavours: Marcus Verrius Flaccus (c.55 BCE–20 CE) wrote *De Significatu Verborum*, a great dictionary of obscure words; Gaius Plinius Secundus (23–79 CE), better known as Pliny the Elder, authored *Historia Naturalis*, a scientific encyclopedia; Julius Pollux (fl. second century CE) wrote the *Onomasticum graece et latine*, a dictionary useful to writers; and Sextus Pompeius Festus (fl. second century CE) created an epitome or abridged version of Flaccus's *De Significatu Verborum*. Bilingual glossaries were also produced, and became more common by the sixth century. Philoxenus of Mabbug (c.440–c.523), to give one example, a Syrian bishop, theologian, and translator of the Bible, is also credited with having compiled a Latin-Greek Glossary, generally, if incorrectly, known as the "Philoxenus Glossary" or "Pseudo-Philoxenus Glossary".[4]

Lexicography in Ancient Greece and Rome was characterized by an interweaving of often diverse material. Standard dictionary content, with respect to general language and terminology, for example, existed alongside grammatical information, encyclopedic statements and commentary of all kinds. These works did have the merit, on the other hand, of establishing a "trivium" of sorts, or three modes of analysing words and things in Western Europe throughout the Middle Ages: the dictionary, the grammar and the encyclopedia.

The Middle Ages, or the dawn of structured lexicography

The Middle Ages, particularly in the East, where Byzantine civilization came into contact with a rising Islamic culture, was a productive time for dictionaries. In the ninth century, the Byzantine Patriarch Photius I (c.820–c.891) produced *Bibliotheca,* also known as *Myriobiblon* (*Ten Thousand Books*), a compilation of excerpts from the great texts of Antiquity. This collection was followed by his *Lexicon,* a collection of noteworthy terms from early Greek texts.[5]

During this time, Arabic lexicons and encyclopedias proliferated. The philologist Ibn Durayd (c.837–933) wrote a large Arabic dictionary and a work on etymology. Between 975 and 997, the Persian philosopher al-Khwârizmî wrote an encyclopedia entitled *Keys to the Sciences,* in which he explained scientific terminology.[6] The most methodical and influential encyclopedia was issued by the Ikhwân al-Safâ, (Brethren of Purity or Brethren of Sincerity), a secret society from the second half of the tenth century. The work takes the form of fifty-two epistles capturing all the existing knowledge of Baghdad and Basra of their era. They are credited with publishing the first multi-authored encyclopedia.

The development of dictionaries in the western regions of Medieval Europe was influenced by both the Latin culture and Christianization, along with three other specific factors: the imitation of great works of Antiquity, the conservation of ancient texts and the rise of national languages. The first two resulted in the production of Latin dictionaries, while the third led to an increase in bilingual glossaries. The age of bilingual production was to last nearly 1,000 years, stretching from the *Reichenau Glosses* of the eighth century to the first completely monolingual French dictionary, the *Dictionnaire françois,* published in 1680 by César-Pierre Richelet (1626–98). Throughout the Middle Ages, lexicography was used for biblical exegesis. The Bible was translated and/or glossed from a Latin version – the explained language – into vernacular or vulgar Latin, and then national languages – the explaining languages. This work was grounded primarily in the exegetical and historical preoccupations of grammarians, philologists, rhetoricians and writers. Translators can also be added to the list, given the close contact between Latin and the emerging vernacular languages.

There was a wide range of bilingual works at the time, even leaving aside the Latin dictionaries, from Isidore of Seville's seventh century *Etymologiae* – a sort of encyclopedia of medieval knowledge with a large section devoted to language and an alphabetical dictionary – to Papias the Lombard's eleventh-century *Elementarium Doctrinae Rudimentum*. Other works include Huguccio (Hugh) of Pisa's twelfth-century *Liber derivationum*, William d'Aubigny (Brito)'s *Expositiones difficiliora verborum de Biblia* and John of Genoa's thirteenth-century *Summa quae vocatur Catholicon*. In the thirteenth-century, Alexander Neckam, Bartholomew of England and Vincent of Beauvais produced encyclopedic works.

The scholarship of Vincent of Beauvais (1190–c.1264) deserves particular mention. His *Speculum Maius* (*The Great Mirror*) was a seminal work that offered humanity a mirror in which to see itself and sought to incite people to act better both individually and collectively. This was the first true medieval encyclopedia. Its scope was monumental: covering God, humanity, creation, nature, education, art, science and history, it provided a record of knowledge in the Middle Ages and a didactic panorama of humankind and its future. It enjoyed remarkable success. It was the first work printed in Strasbourg in 1460 and it was reprinted repeatedly until 1879, serving as a valuable reference work for many translators for centuries.

The earliest European medieval glossaries date back to the fifth and sixth centuries, and more often than not, these works focused only on Latin, as evidenced by their titles: *Liber glossarum* (seventh–eighth centuries), *Abavus* (eighth–ninth centuries), *Glosas Emilienses* (ninth century), to name a few. These works, such as those by Priscian and Donatus, provided the first written evidence of the *lingua romana* and the *lingua germanica*, by glossing important foundational Latin, and sometimes Greek, texts.

The appearance of these glossaries can be attributed to the widening gap between Vulgar Latin and the burgeoning Romance and Germanic languages. Latin texts were becoming difficult to understand everywhere and new tools were needed to decode and interpret them. The new dictionaries proved the otherness of Latin (the interpreted language) and the existence of European vernaculars (the interpreting languages). The scriptures remained the focus of most of the glossaries. In the earliest ones, notations in the margins and between the lines of manuscripts were in simplified Latin first, and then in a Romance or Germanic language, depending on the place of publication. Some examples are *Endlicher's Glossary* (fifth century), which explained Vulgar Latin words of Gaulish origin using other Vulgar Latin words; the *Reichenau Glosses* (eighth century), comprising both a glossary of the Vulgate Bible and an alphabetical glossary listing words from various sources; and the *Kassel Glosses* (ninth century), a compilation of often Latinized Romance words with the corresponding Germanic words (in Bavarian).

The first Latin-French lexicons appeared in the thirteenth century. Among them were the *Abavus* (late thirteenth to early fourteenth century), with 262 entries, and the *Aalma* (latter half of the fourteenth century), a voluminous dictionary with 13,680 entries that formed an abridged, bilingual Latin-French adaptation of John of Genoa's *Catholicon*. The *Aalma* emerged as a reference point for dictionaries during the second half of the Middle Ages, and, in 1485, it received the distinction of being printed in Paris. Not only was French present in these glossaries to provide equivalents for corresponding Latin terms, but it was also used to define Latin words for which there was no match in the vernacular.

As bilingual glossaries thrived, so did monolingual ones. These were often inventories of technical language: for example, bestiaries (a series of fables featuring animals as characters), *computi* (publications showing how the Catholic Church calculated the dates of moveable feasts for the religious calendar), lapidaries (treatises on the magical and medicinal qualities of precious stones), herbaries (catalogues of plants and their symbolism) and volucraries (catalogues of birds and their symbolism). Brunetto Latini (1220–94) produced a summary of encyclopedic knowledge of the day. Although he was Florentine, Latini wrote *Li livres dou tresor* in French prose for two principal reasons: he was living in France and he is said to have found the language more delightful and more widespread.

In the following century, Charles V's private tutor, Nicolas Oresme (c.1320–82), was an important figure in the promotion and development of the French language; he was also a great translator (Figure 16).[7] He questioned the privileged and strategic position of Latin as the sole vehicle for all knowledge and wisdom. Even though he believed it would take patience and time for French to establish itself permanently as a scientific language, Oresme pursued the goal of providing French with the internal mechanisms to convey all things scientific. His many translated works included those of Ptolemy and Aristotle. Commissioned to translate Latin versions of Aristotle's *Ethics* and *Politics* (1372), he explained why he chose to use French instead of Latin when translating texts pertaining to science and philosophy, and he gave insights into his methodology. Oresme sought to lead by example, to show that through his efforts, "this noble science [of philosophy] will be better understood and turned by others in the future into clearer and more perfect French" (Menut 1940: 100) He saw the use of neologisms and loan translations as a means of building up the resources of the French language. Of the neologisms that Oresme coined to shore up the French language, some did not survive (*accidental, colligance, signation, tardiveté*), while others did (*abrogation, angulaire, conjonction, hexagone, longitude, sphère*).

Oresme also drew attention to numerous specialized terms that he felt were necessary and could enrich the French language, often adding appendices. *Le livre de ethiques*, for example, contained a glossary at the end in which he defined and explained fifty-three words, such as *aristocratie, contingent, fortitude, économie*, and *rectitude*. At the end of his *Livre du ciel et du monde* (c.1375), he listed 121 French terms he had coined.

In the Middle Ages, translators played a role in the development and evolution of French, and they helped to establish the language's status alongside Latin. The terminological and lexicographic impact of their work is tangible to this day. Linguistic creation in the vernacular paved the way for compilations that took the form of glossaries and then dictionaries. The dictionary became an important social tool and also became central to linguistic undertakings.

The dictionary in Europe: from the Renaissance to the present

With the Renaissance, a period when Western lexicography made great strides, translators became increasingly involved in the production of dictionaries, for a number of reasons. First, the enthusiasm for Antiquity resulted in a renewed interest in Latin and Greek. Secondly, the religious upheaval associated with the Reformation led to the study of ancient biblical languages such as Hebrew and Syriac, a dialect of Aramaic. At the same time, European vernaculars were being strengthened with formal grammars. Such was the case in Spain (1492), Italy (Florence, 1495), France (1527) and Germany (1535). This intense linguistic activity was reflected in lexicographic advances, too, with the publication of several monolingual dictionaries devoted to classical languages.

In the case of Greek, the most remarkable work was the *Thesaurus graecae linguae* (1572) by the printer Henri Estienne (1531–98). He was the distinguished translator of such works as the *Odes* of Anacreon, the *Preceptive Moral Poem* of Phocylides and the works of philosopher and physician Sextus Empiricus. Latin already had its masterwork with *Dictionarium, sue latinae linguae thesaurus*, produced in 1531 by another member of the Estienne family, Robert (1503–59, Figure 17). Robert Estienne was also known for having written the *Dictionnaire françois-latin* [...]. Its publication in 1539 marked the first time the word *"dictionnaire"* (dictionary) was used in the title of a French work of this kind. He was also a translator, having penned a version of the *Bible* (1551) and the *Psalms* (1552).

While the seventeenth century saw its share of new dictionaries of ancient languages, including *Etymologicum linguae latinae* (1662) by Holland's Gerardus Vossius (1577–1649), translator of *El Conciliador* by Rabbi Manasseh ben Israel (1632), lexicograpahers were more preoccupied with modern languages. In Spain, Sebastian de Covarrubias (1539–1613) wrote *Tesoro de la lengua castellana o española* (1611). The Accademia della Crusca, founded in Italy in 1583 in order to purify the language, published its *Vocabolario* in 1612, the first great European dictionary in a national language. In France, the Académie française was created in 1634. Four years later, in accordance with the mandate it had been given, the

Académie began work on the production of a dictionary. The first edition was published in 1694, titled *Le dictionnaire de l'Académie françoise, dedié au Roy*. In England, meanwhile, many dictionaries were devoted to explaining difficult words. Among these, *Glossographia* [...] (1656) by Thomas Blount (1618–79) reflected substantial progress in lexicographic methods.

The eighteenth century, characterized by an explosion of ideas, science and technology – all of which needed to be synthesized – became the century of the encyclopedia. In England, Ephraim Chambers (1680–1740) published *Cyclopaedia* (1728); across the Channel, Denis Diderot (1713–84) and Jean le Rond d'Alembert (1717–83) translated part of Chambers's work and enriched it with original ideas. This gave rise to the *Encyclopédie* (1751–72), an immense 35-volume inventory, to which five extra volumes would later be annexed. Diderot had already made a name for himself through his work as a translator: Shaftesbury's *An Inquiry Concerning Virtue and Merit,* which he translated as *Essai sur le mérite et la vertu* in 1745; Edward Moore's *The Gamester,* which he translated as *Le joueur* in 1760; and Salomon Gessner's *Idyllen,* which he translated from the German and published along with his own stories as *Contes moraux et nouvelles Idylles* in 1773.

A proliferation in language dictionaries was also under way. In France, Nicolas de Chamfort and Joseph-Nicolas Guyot co-authored the 30-volume *Grand vocabulaire français* (1767). It was published by Charles-Joseph Panckoucke (1736–98), who was also known for having translated *De rerum natura* (*On the Nature of Things*) by Lucretius, *La Gerusalemme liberata (Jerusalem Delivered)* by Torquato Tasso and *Orlando Furioso* (*The Frenzy of Orlando*) by Ludovico Ariosto.

In Great Britain, Nathan (or Nathaniel) Bailey (d. 1742) published his impressive *Dictionarium Britannicum* in 1730, which formed the basis for the famous *Dictionary of the English Language* (1747–55) by Samuel Johnson (1709–84) (Reddick 1990). In addition to his work as a lexicographer, Dr. Johnson was a translator. In 1735, for example, he published *A Voyage to Abyssinia* by the Portuguese missionary Father Jerome Lobo and, in 1738, the *Third Satire* of Juvenal.

In Germany, philologist and translator Johann Christoph Adelung (1732–1806) published his *Grammatisch-kritisches Wörterbuch der hochdeutschen Mundart* (*Grammatical-Critical Dictionary of the High German Dialect*) (1774–86), a work that had a great impact on German grammar and spelling of the day.

For several reasons, the nineteenth century gave rise to important lexicographic undertakings. The Romantic movement was behind some of this interest, with a number of its key players in favour of enriching the lexicon of their respective languages. Other factors were the emergence of new disciplines such as historical linguistics and comparative grammar, as well as the discovery of Sanskrit by Europeans in the late eighteenth century, which fuelled interest in Oriental studies.[8] The *Vergleichendes Wörterbuch der indogermanischen Sprachen*

(*Comparative Dictionary of Indo-European Languages*) (1868) by linguist August Fick (1833–1916) is a good illustration.

The French language, too, benefited from the publication of several important texts, notably the *Nouveau vocabulaire français ou Abrégé du dictionnaire de l'Académie* (1801) by grammarian and Latinist Noël-François de Wailly (1724–1801). De Wailly produced revised versions of Caesar's *Commentaires* (1767) and Cicero's *Orations* (1772), and also undertook to translate other classical authors such as Quintilian and Sallust. It was Émile Littré (1801–81), though, who was responsible for the most celebrated work of what can be considered the century of the dictionary. First published in thirty instalments from 1863 to 1873, his *Dictionnaire de la langue française* was reissued as a four-volume edition in 1873, with a final supplement added in 1877. Émile Littré was also an eminent translator, having tackled Homer's *Iliad*, Hippocrates's *Complete Works*, Pliny the Elder's *Natural History* and Dante's *Inferno* (Delisle 1996).

Littré's contemporary, Pierre Larousse (1817–75), published his *Grand dictionnaire universel du XIXe siècle* […] in fifteen volumes (1866–76), with supplements issued in 1878 and 1888. The *Grand dictionnaire* was at once a dictionary of the language, containing new terms and slang, and an extensive alphabetical encyclopedia. In England, James Murray (1837–1915) became the editor of *New English Dictionary on Historical Principles* in 1878. The publication, which became a model for works of this kind, was renamed *The Oxford English Dictionary* in 1895. In Germany, the most significant work of the nineteenth century was the *Deutsches Wörterbuch* (*German Dictionary*). Grounded in etymology, this dictionary was directed by Jacob Grimm (1785–1863), and was written from 1852 to 1858. Credited with having founded German philology, Grimm is best remembered for the famous *Grimm's Fairy Tales*, which he wrote with his brother Wilhelm.

By the beginning of the twentieth century, most major European languages had their own major dictionaries. Parallel to these seminal works, which focused primarily on general language and which were often based on the latest discoveries in the field of linguistics, there were numerous other kinds of publications. Some were more encyclopedic in nature, while others consisted of inventories of specific features of the language (e.g. scientific or technical dictionaries, dictionaries of synonyms, or scholarly dictionaries).

As they became increasingly abundant, dictionaries contributed to the process of democratization. Mandatory schooling made it necessary for everyone to have ready access to educational tools, in particular to dictionaries in the mother tongue. This led to the creation of works for different target groups, ranging from primary school children to adults. The monolingual and general lexicography of the first half of the twentieth century was a field of activity to which philologists, linguists, terminologists, educators and sometimes whole teams of specialists dedicated themselves. Although they had had some involvement in scientific and technical dictionaries, translators, on the other hand, did not devote their attention to this field until the 1970s, when they began to achieve greater visibility through their work on specialized dictionaries.

Bilingual and multilingual dictionaries

Bilingual lexicography extends as far back as the Sumerian era and spread under political, military and social circumstances, in particular when the Akkadians assimilated the Sumerian culture and language. Around 2000 BCE, bilingual lists were frequent, and interaction between different peoples gave rise to the development of multilingual lexicography.

In Mesopotamia and Egypt, multilingual records were produced in order to facilitate the interpretation of foreign languages. There is evidence of trilingual lists in Sumerian, Akkadian and Hittite. There were also lists of terms from four languages, for example the Sumerian-Akkadian-Ugaritic-Hurrian dictionary discovered in Ugarit, dating back to the fourteenth to thirteenth centuries BCE. This was the work of scribes. While many of these scribes – specialists in writing and languages – also performed translation tasks, it is impossible to know with certainty if the authors of the dictionaries were translators.

During the Middle Ages, Latin was the language of knowledge in Western Europe, under the influence of the Church. Those who set out to evangelize non-Christians, however, needed equivalencies between classical and vulgar Latin. They drew up lists of the most important words required to read the scriptures and liturgical texts. This was the beginning of the bilingual glossaries of the Merovingian period, which extends from Clovis's conversion to Christianity in 496 CE to the deposition of Childeric III and the crowning of Pépin le Bref (Pippin the Short) in 751. Bilingual glossaries, of which the eighth-century *Reichenau Glosses* are an eloquent example, are regarded as the ancestors of bilingual dictionaries.

Well versed in Medieval Latin, the first secular translators to work on Greco-Roman literature encountered difficulties and voiced their lexicographical concerns when translating classical Latin texts. When commissioned by King John II of France (John the Good) to translate Livy's *Ab Urbe Condita*, or *History of Rome* (1355–1356), for example, the Benedictine Pierre Bersuire (1290–1362) prefaced his translation with a lexicon to explain the Latin terms he felt he had to keep. Likewise, when Nicolas Oresme was commissioned to translate Latin versions of Aristotle, he explained why he chose French as the target language for texts pertaining to science and philosophy, subjects that were traditionally restricted to

Latin. Oresme, as seen previously, also added glossaries of specialized terms and appendices with lists of French terms he had coined.

The Renaissance was characterized by a rebirth of interest in Greek and Roman civilization while the religious controversies of the Reformation rekindled the study of ancient languages such as Hebrew, Syriac and Greek. Antiquity was much admired, once again conferring on the Greek language a status equal to that of Latin. Fascination for travel and international relations created a need for textbooks and lexicographic works to help understand foreign languages. The Renaissance thus became the first golden age of multilingual dictionaries. Latin, which remained the language of the literary and scholarly class, was often one of the languages in these works, either as a source language or as a target language. The *Dictionarium latino-graecum* was produced by German humanists Philipp Melanchthon (1497–1560) and Johann (Johannes) Lonicer (c.1497–1569), who were both known for translating works from Antiquity. Melanchthon had translated the works of Ptolemy, Homer, Hesiod, Euripides, Aeschylus, Thucydides, Sophocles, Xenophon and Terence, whereas Lonicer had focused on Pindar's *Odes* (1535). Pairing Latin with French, the prolific Robert Estienne is responsible for some significant dictionaries: for example, the *Dictionarium latinogallicum* (1538) and the *Dictionnaire françois-latin* [...] (1539). The first genuine Latin-English work, *The Dictionary*, was compiled in 1538 by Sir Thomas Elyot (Eliot) (c.1490–1546). This title marked the first use of the term "dictionary" in the English language. A humanist and translator, Elyot did much to popularize the classics through his versions of Plato, Isocrates, and Galen and other physicians of Antiquity. In Northern Europe, the humanist Christiern Pedersen (c.1480–1554) published the first Latin-Danish lexicon in 1510. Pedersen translated such works as Saxo Grammaticus's *Gesta Danorum* (1514), *The New Testament* (1529), *The Psalms of David* (1531) and Luther's *Bible* (1550). In 1534, Pedersen published *Kong Holger Danskes Krønike*, a free adaptation of the fifteenth-century French work *Ogier le Dannoys* (*Ogier the Dane*).

Toward the end of the Middle Ages and especially during the Renaissance, lexicographers and printers, who were also involved in translation, began to produce bilingual dictionaries in which Latin was entirely absent. The first of its kind was the *Vocabulary in French and English* (1480), published by the famous printer William Caxton (c.1422–91, Figure 5), who also translated numerous works.[9] John Florio (1553–1625) compiled a substantial Italian-English dictionary, *A World of Words* (1598), translated Montaigne's *Essays* (1603) and authored the first English version of Boccaccio's *Decameron* (1620).

From the seventeenth century onward, a growing interest in foreign languages, motivated by political, commercial, educational or other considerations, led to a proliferation of dictionaries focusing on national languages. French and

English were primarily used in many language combinations, although Spanish and Dutch came close because of specific political circumstances. A case in point is *Nuevo diccionario, o tesoro de la lengua española y flamenga* (1659) by Arnold de la Porte, the first chaplain of the Castle of Antwerp (Bakker & Dibbets 1977:222). Likewise, the Ottoman Empire played an important role in international relations during that time, as illustrated by the *Dictionnaire turc-français et français-turc* by François Pétis de la Croix (1622–95), interpreter to the king and translator of *Histoire de France* into Turkish.

The eighteenth century was famous for its encyclopedists, who were moved by a spirit not unlike the one behind the inventories of the languages of the world. It is not surprising, therefore, that multilingual dictionaries flourished alongside monolingual works. French was paired with other European languages (German, English, Italian, Spanish and Dutch) in bilingual dictionaries, and the first French-Russian dictionary was published in 1786. Giuseppe Marc'Antonio Baretti (1719–89), a friend of Samuel Johnson and translator of Pierre Corneille's works (1747–48), wrote a *Dictionary of the English and Italian Languages* (1760) and a *Dictionary of Spanish and English* (1776).

Lexicography took a new direction in the nineteenth century with the interest in Sanskrit, to which linguists turned their attention in their search for an original common language. Dictionaries of Sanskrit, Assyrian and Persian appeared. The *Sanskrit-English Dictionary* was published in 1819 by Orientalist Horace Hyman Wilson (1786–1860), who translated the works of the Indian poet Kalidasa and published *Select Specimens of the Theatre of the Hindus* (1827), a three-volume survey of Indian drama. Wilson is the author of the first complete translation of the *Rig Veda* into English, which was published in six volumes from 1850 to 1888. Other examples are Émile Burnouf (1821–1907), translator of the *Bhagavad Gita* (1861), who is responsible for the *Dictionnaire classique sanscrit-français* (1863–64), and Edward Henry Palmer (1840–82), author of a version of the *Koran*, who produced the *Short English-Persian Dictionary* (published posthumously in 1883).

Although classical Greek and Latin were dead languages, they were kept very much alive by lexicographers, who combined them with the principal European languages and sometimes with non-European languages, as in the *Lexicon arabicolatinum* (1830–37), by the German Orientalist Georg Freytag (1788–1861), translator of the Persian author and philologist Farouz-Abadi.

At the same time, production of dictionaries devoted exclusively to living languages increased steadily. A remarkable encyclopedic dictionary of French and German (1869–80) was produced by Karl Sachs (1829–1909), a German who specialized in Romance languages, and Césaire Villate (1816–95), a French professor. It was a translator who produced a new Turkish-French dictionary

(1885): Casimir Barbier de Meynard (1826–1908), known for his translation from Persian of *Meadows of Gold and Mines of Gems* (published in French as *Prairies d'or*, 1861–77), by Abul Hasan Al-Masu'di (Masoudi) and *The Fruit Garden* (1880) by the famous poet Saadi, in collaboration with Abel Pavet de Courteille (1821–89).

British lexicographers were also enticed by exotic languages. Edward Lane (1801–76), for example, translated *The Thousand and One Nights*[10] (1838–40) and also authored an extensive *Arabic-English Lexicon* (1863). German was paired with traditional languages as well as with many other European languages and languages from other continents. Examples include the 1839 Czech-German dictionary by Joseph Jungmann (1773–1847), and the 1858 German-Turkish dictionary by Hungarian Orientalist Ármin Vámbéry (1832–1913), who discovered the relationship between the Turkish and Hungarian languages. An example of a dictionary combining German with a non-European language is the Manchu-German dictionary published in 1864 by Hans von der Gabelentz (1807–74), who also translated the *Geschichte des großen Liao* (*History of the Great Liao*) from Manchu, which came out three years after his death.

Increased globalization of trade from the twentieth century on has stimulated continued growth in the field of lexicography. While such activity was modest before World War I, it did result in the *Langenscheidt's Encyclopaedic Dictionary of the English and German Languages* (1908) by Eduard Muret (1833–1904) and Daniel Sanders (1819–97), which was long considered the most complete English-German dictionary. French, which had dominated diplomatic relations in the West before the war, had to share its monopoly with English after 1918.[11] This situation gave impetus to a French-English dictionary project, which resulted in Jean Edmond Mansion's (1870–1942) acclaimed *Harrap's Standard French and English Dictionary*, published from 1934 to 1939.

The profound political upheaval triggered by World War II fuelled even further developments in bilingual lexicography, including previously unheard-of language combinations. The creation of an Eastern Bloc under Soviet domination gave new importance to the various languages of the satellite nations. This was particularly true in East Germany, which was drawn into the Soviet Bloc. The German language was prominent: a 1966 inventory documented approximately forty general dictionaries pairing German with such languages as Russian, Polish, Czech, Bulgarian, Romanian, Hungarian and Albanian (Bäse 1966: 160). Just as evangelization and colonization had once required familiarity with a number of foreign languages, Russia's interest in developing countries gave rise to dictionaries for the languages spoken in those countries. A multilingual state such as the former USSR had to find ways to facilitate communication among the many ethnic and linguistic communities living within its borders, too. In addition, several

European nations have had to address linguistic challenges arising from the presence of large numbers of immigrant workers.

All of these factors, added to the internationalization of political, economic, scientific and cultural relations, intensified translation activity while also generating a need for lexicographical tools. In pairings of English and Nordic languages alone, for instance, a 1981 bibliography listed thirty-five English-Swedish, nineteen English-Danish, nineteen English-Norwegian and five English-Icelandic dictionaries (Gullberg 1981: 138).

Terminological dictionaries: from specialized glossaries to computerized term banks

A terminological dictionary is a work that catalogues the vocabulary of a specific area of human knowledge. It can be referred to as a technical or scientific dictionary, specialty language dictionary and language for special purposes (LSP) dictionary. This kind of inventory of terms can be monolingual, bilingual or multilingual. Judging from historical documents and testimonials, it would appear that monolingual technical works predated bilingual ones (Boulanger 2003: 65–96).

During the first or second century CE, the Greek physician Herodotus is said to have published a glossary of Hippocratic terms. Hippocrates, considered to be the father of Western medicine, would later become the subject of numerous studies. During the second century, for example, the Alexandrian grammarian Herodian also drew up a specialized lexicon based on Hippocratic terms.[12] Many other works of this type would appear across cultures throughout history, from Antiquity to the Middle Ages. For example, in the medieval Arabic world, the Spanish-Arabic geographer and historian Abu Abdullah al-Bakri (1014–94) produced a dictionary of geography. During the thirteenth century, historian Abû-l'ᶜAbbâs Ahmad ibn Khallikân (1211–82) wrote *Wafayât al-Aᶜyan* (*The Obituaries of Eminent Men*), a biographical dictionary of the key figures of Islam, which would later be translated by British Orientalist William McGuckin de Slane (1801–78) and published as *The Biographical Dictionary*.

Technically oriented bilingual and multilingual lexicons appeared as early as the Sumerian era. During the Greco-Roman era, specialty works became commonplace, as did their translation. For instance, Galen was translated into Syriac by the sixth century, since Syrian scholars were interested in medicine and compiled true bilingual dictionaries of medical terms. There were numerous works in this field. The physician Hunayn ibn Ishâq (809–75) was considered "the master of all Islamic translators".[13] An important translator of Hippocrates and Galen, he also wrote a study explaining Greek words in Syriac. Another noteworthy work is

Liber de medecinis simplicibus (*The Book of Simple Medicine*) by the tenth-century Arab physician Yahyâ ibn Sarâfiyûn, also known as Serapion the Younger, to avoid confusion with his ninth-century namesake, Serapion the Elder, who may actually have been John of Damascus, or John Damascene.[14]

The Greek, Syriac, Arabic, Persian, Berber and Spanish languages coexisted in the territory through which Islam spread, prompting Arabic authors to draw up lists of equivalents for different words designating the same object or concept. As early as the ninth century, the physician al-Razi, known by his Latin name Rhazes (865–925), enumerated organs and diseases in Greek, Syriac, Persian, Hindi and Arabic in a work called *Liber Continentis* or the *Comprehensive Book*. When Stephanus Antiochenus translated ᶜAli ibn al-ᶜAbbâs's *Liber Regius* in the twelfth century, he included a Greek-Latin-Arabic glossary titled *Medicamentorum omnium breviarium* (1127). Similarly, the Cordovan physician Maimonides (1139–1204) wrote a glossary listing 405 plant names in Arabic, Greek, Syriac, Persian, Berber and Andalusian.

The first real specialized glossaries did not appear in Western European culture until the Renaissance. The Italian physician and Orientalist Andrea Alpago (1450–1522) included an Arabic-Latin glossary with his translation of Avicenna's *Canon of Medicine*. When Charles de l'Escluse (Clusius, 1526–1609) translated the 1554 *Cruydeboeck* by Flemish doctor and botanist Rembert Dodoens as the *Histoire des plantes* [...] *qui viennent en usage en médecine* (1557), he added French to the Flemish-Latin glossary that was part of the original version.

In the seventeenth century, new disciplines emerged, reflected in new compilations. The Catalan Friar Miquel (Miguel) Agusti (1560–1630) wrote a popular work called *The Book of the Secrets of Agriculture*, which appeared in 1617 with a glossary of terms in six languages: Latin, Spanish, Catalan, Italian, Portuguese and French. In 1674, the French scholar and translator Louis Moréri (1643–80) published his *Grand dictionnaire historique*, a vast encyclopedic, though monolingual, dictionary of historical and mythological names. In England, the critic and theologian Jeremy Collier (1650–1726) adapted Moréri's dictionary, publishing it beginning in 1688 as *The Great Historical, Geographical, Genealogical and Poetical Dictionary*. John Harris (c.1666–1719) published the *Lexicon Technicum: Or, An Universal English Dictionary of Arts and Sciences* (1704).

The eighteenth century was a time of scientific and technological explosion. Lexicographers quickly set to work generating terminology for the new concepts. Robert James (1703–76), an English physician, perhaps not coincidentally a friend of Samuel Johnson, is known for his work *A Medicinal Dictionary*. The dictionary was translated in France by Denis Diderot as *Dictionnaire universel de médecine* (1744–48). Among Diderot's collaborators on this project were François Toussaint (1715–72), who translated the fables of Christian Fürchtegott Gellert

(1768), and Marc-Antoine Eidous (c.1724–c.1790), the prolific translator of philosophers Adam Smith and Francis Hutcheson, theologians George Campbell and Alexander Gerald, and historian William Robertson (Lanson 1931: 586–594).

In the nineteenth century, international relations improved in a wide variety of fields and international organizations were established, bringing more speakers of different languages into contact. At international conferences, participants would choose to speak in their mother tongue. Translators and dictionaries became essential during this age of unabated scientific and technological progress for which new vocabulary had to be defined and translated. One notable monolingual French work was the *Dictionnaire des sciences médicales* (1812–22), by François-Pierre Chaumeton (1775–1819) and François-Victor Mérat de Vaumartoise (1780–1851); it was published and distributed by Charles-Louis-Fleury Panckoucke (1780–1844), who published a translation of Tacitus's works in 1831.[15] Although Latin was still included in numerous bilingual and multilingual dictionaries, particularly scientific ones, works covering the multiple aspects of the Industrial Revolution were devoted primarily to modern languages.

Technological advances continued throughout the twentieth century and beyond. Improved transportation and communications resulted in what was referred to as the "global village". The taming of the atom led to the discovery of new energy sources and space exploration opened new horizons. These developments left their mark on specialized lexicography, leading to the production of increasingly specialized dictionaries to keep pace with new discoveries. In the years prior to World War I, there was a general consolidation and updating of terminology in many of the fields already covered in existing monolingual and multilingual dictionaries. Among the fields that emerged in the twentieth century were electronics, the petroleum and automobile industries, aeronautics, telecommunications and photography. One noteworthy multilingual series was the *Illustrierte technische Wörterbücher*, a remarkable set of illustrated technical dictionaries by Alfred Schlomann (1878–1952), published in 1908 by the Oldenbourg publishing company. Using a generic title, the dictionaries set out terminology in German, English, French, Spanish, Italian and Russian, and covered most technological fields and their industrial applications.

During the war years, 1914–18, most of the dictionaries produced were military ones. Once the war was over, terminological production once again thrived in all fields of science and technology. Medical specializations emerged, such as dentistry and sexology. Other developments were radio or the "wireless" as it was called at the time, and the graphic arts, associated with the increasingly important cinema and media industry. In the years between the wars, many more lexicons were issued by official agencies and numerous glossaries were published in journals or in the form of appendices to specialized works.

This was also a time of prodigious terminological and lexicographic growth for the Soviet Union. The central government faced considerable problems communicating with its republics, which were in varying stages of development. The USSR had therefore started producing dictionaries in which specialized terminology was translated into the languages of the various republics.

When World War II broke out, lexicographers naturally began to concentrate on military matters once again, compiling dictionaries on warfare, weapons, transportation and military administration. In Canada, for instance, the Bureau of Bilingual Publications of the Canadian Army released their *English-French, French-English Military Dictionary* in 1945 under the direction of military translator Colonel Joseph-Henri Chaballe (1876–1952).[16] Translator and lexicographer Pierre Daviault (1899–1964) served as general editor for the 1,000-page work, which covered the full range of military life. In his foreword to the dictionary, Lieutenant-General and Chief of the General Staff J. C. Murchie said: "every effort has been made to include in this book the very latest terms, phrases and words that have resulted from the development of new weapons, equipment and methods used during the present war"; he also expressed the hope that the dictionary would be of "value to other members of the British Commonweath, to the United States, France and many other countries" (Chaballe and Daviault 1945: iii).

With the return of peace in 1945, attention shifted to rebuilding, restoring communications and stimulating the economy. These concerns were reflected in the many dictionaries published on the subject of business and the economy, as well as international law governing the power relationships in a newly configured world. LSP lexicography also reflected the most recent scientific and technological advances, as humanity entered into the atomic age, and an era of outer space, rockets, computers, electronics and microchips, with the worldwide web and internet on the horizon. Television became the subject of lexicographic study in the *Dictionary of Television, Radar and Antennas* (1955), a work in six languages by W. E. (Willem Elbertus, or Wim) Clason (1898–1990). A former translator with Philips in the Netherlands, Clason was the first to record the terminology of radar. As one of the first to work for the Elsevier publishing house on the series of multilingual dictionaries for which it was to become famous worldwide, his name became very familiar to users of specialized dictionaries between 1950 and 1960. Clason was responsible for a *Dictionary of Electronics and Waveguides* (1957), a *Dictionary of Nuclear Science and Technology* (1958), a *Dictionary of Automation, Computers, Control and Measuring* (1961) and many other reference works.

The proliferation of new technologies affected applied sciences as well as the natural, pure and social sciences. In 1951, John Edwin Holmstrom's *Bibliography of Interlingual Scientific and Technical Dictionaries* listed 550 works published after 1949 alone. By the fifth edition, published in 1969, this figure had jumped to 2,491. Publishing companies such as Eyrolles and Dunod in France, Bailey Press and Pergamon in England, Brandstetter and Oldenbourg in Germany, and Elsevier in the Netherlands – to mention just a few – began to cater to the specialized needs of translators.

During this time, the language services of international organizations such as the United Nations (UN), the World Health Organization (WHO), the European Coal and Steel Community (ECSC), and the European Economic Community (EEC)[17] published many glossaries pertaining to their respective spheres of activity.[18] This was the practice in an increasing number of organizations, in an ever-wider range of subject areas: the International Chamber of Commerce,[19] the Union Européenne des Experts Comptables, Économiques et Financiers (UEC),[20] the International Council on Archives[21] and the International Union Against Cancer.[22]

As more and more glossaries were produced, they spread beyond the specialized treatises and trade journals where they had customarily been housed. They were included in publications intended for linguists, terminologists and translators: *Lebende Sprachen* published in the former Federal Republic of Germany (or West Germany) and *Fremdsprachen* published in the former German Democratic Republic (or East Germany), *Meta* (Canada), *Traduire* (France), *Le Linguiste* (Belgium) and *Le langage et l'homme* (Belgium). It was also common for technical translators to share their professional experiences in these publications. The Munich publishing house Dokumentation included these new resources in its bibliography of science, technology and business in foreign languages (*Technik, Wissenschaft und Wirtschaft in fremden Sprachen*). The number of titles listed in the bibliography had increased from 1,202 in the first edition (1960) to 6,231 in the fourth (1969). The sixth edition, produced by Helga Lengenfelder and Henri Van Hoof, was published in 1979 by K. G. Saur as the *International Bibliography of Specialized Dictionaries*. Even though it catalogued only post-1970 works, the bibliography still contained an impressive 5,700 entries. Progress in this field was striking: the number of publications, which had not surpassed twenty or so titles annually between 1914 and 1940, was now upwards of 500 a year. These examples highlight the diversity of the fields of study. They illustrate the international nature of the production of terminological dictionaries and provide a frame of reference that allows us to understand their origins in time and place.

Specialized dictionaries reflect the rapid growth in scientific and technical vocabulary. Computers have been a boon to translators and lexicographers, helping them deal with this explosion by making it easier and quicker to process the immense volume of lexical data. Since the late 1960s, computerized terminology banks have been created to collect, classify and disseminate monolingual and multilingual terminology covering a broad range of fields of expertise. Of historic significance are the following: TEAM (Siemens) and LEXIS (Federal Language Bureau) in Germany, TERMIUM (Secretary of State, Ottawa) in Canada, the Banque de terminologie du Québec (Office québécois de la langue française) in Quebec – now called the *Grand dictionnaire terminologique* – and EURODICAUTOM (European Commission). Although these data banks are the responsibility of specialized professionals now known as "terminologists", many of the banks were originally built up from terminological records provided by translators, and to this day translators continue to add to them.

Translators and terminologists have collaborated in this way to enhance these valuable reference tools, which are, in most cases, made accessible via the internet. These electronic dictionaries are constantly updated to quickly keep pace with new areas of interest. While some fields are booming, others are splintering into very specific subfields: for example, the environment (greenhouse gases, freshwater reserves and global warming); medicine (aging, new diseases and nutrition); economics (globalization of markets, alter-globalization and neoliberalism) and communications (high-definition television, digital radio and webification). All these areas of specialization require terminological research, leading to glossaries and lexicons that must be continually updated.

The dictionary's journey

It took thousands of years to go from clay tablets to parchment. The transition from parchment to paper took hundreds of years more. It would be a few more centuries before other formats appeared alongside of paper. In the computer age, the hard drive emerged as a means of storing data, along with portable offshoots that evolved from large floppy disks, to diskettes, to CDs and DVDs. Few major dictionaries now exist solely in print form; most have corresponding electronic versions which are either available online, or burned onto small, flat disks that are reminiscent of the clay tablets bearing the etchings of the Mesopotamians. Storage capacity and durability have increased considerably with the invention of the USB (Universal Serial Bus) flash drive or memory key, which is removable, smaller than the various disks, and with a much larger capacity. It would appear that only material, shape and thickness have changed – although now the advent of "cloud" technology is signalling a new era in which records are taking a less tangible form. Only time will tell where the road leads next.[23]

Notes

1. See also Béjoint 2000 and 2010; Considine 2008; Hartmann 1986.

2. Flavius Dioscorus was a Byzantine official, lawyer and Copt poet of the sixth century. He was born in Aphroditopolis of Egypt and is hence more commonly known as Dioscorus of Aphrodito.

3. The term *"onomatologos"* was used in later Antiquity to refer to lexicographers such as Hesychius as "collectors of words"; this dictionary was arranged according to classes (poets, philosophers, etc.) rather than alphabetically.

4. This glossary was probably composed toward the end of the sixth century, long after the death of Philoxenus in 523 or 525, which is why it is sometimes referred to as the "Pseudo-Philoxenus" Glossary. Only one copy survives: a ninth-century manuscript located at the French Bibliothèque Nationale (Lindsay 1917: 158).

5. Photius I, also spelled Photios or Fotios, was Patriarch of Constantinople; he is recognized in the Eastern Orthodox churches as St. Photios the Great. It is not known for certain whether his *Lexicon* preceded or followed *Myriobiblon*.

6. Muhammad ibn Ahmad al-Khwârizmî; not to be confused with Muhammad ibn Mûsâ al-Khwârizmî, the famous ninth-century Persian mathematician.

7. See also Chapter 2.

8. See the references to the work of Orientalist scholar William Jones in Chapters 4 and 6.

9. See also Chapters 2 and 5.

10. Often known in English as the *Arabian Nights*, from the first English language edition (1706), which rendered the title as *The Arabian Nights' Entertainment*.

11. See Chapter 9.

12. The nationality of Herodian is unclear; he might also be from Syria.

13. Hunayn is discussed in greater detail in Chapter 4.

14. Some sources place Serapion the Younger in the late eleventh or twelfth century.

15. Charles-Louis-Fleury is the son of the writer and publisher Charles-Joseph Panckoucke mentioned earlier.

16. The Bureau of Bilingual Publications of the Canadian Army was established in 1942 and staffed by translators of the parliamentary debates who were employed by the federal Translation Bureau. In 1944, when it undertook the translation of foreign languages, Russian in particular, this unit became known as the Army Language Bureau (Chaballe and Daviault 1945: vii).

17. Also known as the "Common Market" in the English-speaking world, the EEC was re-named the European Community (EC) in 1993. The European Coal and Steel Community (ECSC), established by the Treaty of Paris in 1951, had laid the foundation for supranationalism and this supranational organization.

18. For example, the UN published *Atomic Energy: Glossary of Technical Terms* in five languages (1953); the ECSC released a glossary of transportation and customs terms in five languages (1958); and the WHO issued the *Terminology of Malaria and Malaria Eradication* in four languages (1963–64).

19. *A dictionary of advertising and distribution in eight languages: English, French, German, Spanish, Italian, Dutch, Portuguese, Swedish*, 1957.

20. *Wörterbuch des Rechnungswesens* (Accounting Dictionary) in four languages, 1961.

21. *Lexicon of Archive Terminology* in six languages, 1964.

22. *Illustrated Tumor Nomenclature* in five languages, 1965.

23. Henri Van Hoof (1994) was the author of Chapter 8, "Translators and the Writing of Dictionaries", published in the 1995 edition of *Translators through History*. This chapter, written by Jean-Claude Boulanger for the revised French edition of *Les Traducteurs dans l'histoire* published in 2007, expands on the earlier version, broadening its perspectives and adding a considerable amount of new material.

Figure 17. Robert Estienne

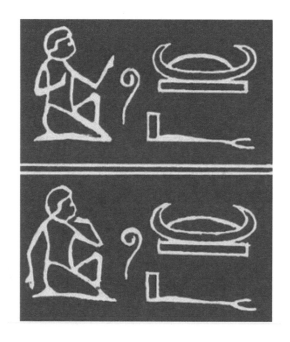

Figure 18. Hieroglyph depicting interpreting

CHAPTER 9

Interpreters and the making of history

Whatever their spheres of activity, the interpreters of the past have served not only as witnesses to events but also as participants in the unfolding or making of history. Without interpreters, relations among different peoples or nations and communication across linguistic and cultural boundaries would have been quite different.

Interpreters don't have a lasting legacy; translators do. These are the words of Andrew Dawrant, the only native speaker of English ever to be accepted as a Chinese-language interpreter for the United Nations. A Canadian who learned Chinese languages through a combination of television, formal studies and waiting on tables in a dim sum restaurant, he now interprets for prime ministers, diplomats, CEOs, and Nobel Prize laureates. He is said to be a "phenomenon", the world's top Chinese-English interpreter. Yet he feels:

> destined to be little more than an interesting side note when the history of China's Western relations during the early twenty-first century is written [...]. You translate *War and Peace* and if it's the best translation ever, people will read that for posterity. We leave no legacy. Our work is ephemeral. It is words in the air.
>
> (Hoffman 2011)

The spoken word is evanescent. Therein lies the paradoxical nature of understanding orality, leading to the "minoritization" of interpreting, or interpretation studies (Cronin 2002: 46). Our knowledge of the past performance of interpreters tends to be derived from such written sources as letters, diaries, memoirs and biographies of interpreters themselves, along with a variety of other documents, many of which were only marginally or incidentally concerned with interpreting. Given the absence of reliable written records, some blanks will probably never be filled in. Even with ample documentation, however, oral practice could never be fully accounted for through the "explicative apparatus of chirographic and typographic translation", as Michael Cronin has suggested, proposing instead that we recast our studies using "categories of power, culture, gender, and race" (Cronin 2002).

For the most part, interpreters and their craft have not found their way into the history books, which traditionally held the stories of momentous events, illustrious men and great achievements, all catalogued in the archives of literate societies. One explanation is the primacy of the written text over the spoken word. Those who have left written documents or worked on written texts, as translators have, are more likely to be chronicled by historians than those who have practised the art of oral communication, as have interpreters. The social status of interpreters may also account for their position in history: they are ethnic and cultural hybrids, often women, slaves or members of a "subcaste" such as the Christians, Armenians and Jews living in British India, for example (Roditi 1982:6). Interpretation has often been practised by the displaced and dislocated – victims of kidnappings, conflict and political upheaval – who have become bilingual or multilingual through their movement across cultures. While these cultural intermediaries and go-betweens have played an important role, they have not always been accorded the place they deserve by the generations of scribes, chroniclers and historians who selected what was to be recorded and what was not. Instead, anecdotes about interpreters were handed down from one storyteller or writer to another, and varied from one narrative to the next, the most extreme example of which is perhaps Sacajawea, whose story will be evoked later.

Research on the multiple aspects of the history of interpreting is relatively new. More traces than were previously thought to exist have been uncovered. As early as 3000 BCE the Egyptians had a hieroglyph signifying "interpreter" or "interpreting" (Figure 18) (Gardiner 1969). Ingrid Kurz (1986:218–219) has carefully documented the various references to interpreters in classical works: five in Livy and numerous others in the writings of Caesar, Cicero, Aulus Gellius, Horace, Pliny, Sallust and Valerius Maximus. Hans J. Vermeer, too, shows how references to interpreters in the literature of ancient Greece and Rome or the Middle Ages are both implicit and explicit (1992, 1:168–174). Drawing on his examination of Xenophon's *Anabasis*, for instance, he concluded that the Greeks and Persians each brought their own interpreter for their negotiations.

At various periods in history, a *lingua franca* would emerge as a medium of communication between people speaking different languages. This was the case for Latin, in particular, which was not only the language of the Church, science and letters, but also of diplomacy in Europe until the seventeenth century. To some extent, Italian and later French, played a similar role in Europe, as did Arabic in Africa, and English, French, Portuguese and Spanish in the colonial empires. However, these vehicular languages were used within specific geographic areas or social groups. As soon as armies, traders, explorers or missionaries went beyond these confines, interpreters were needed. The Romans, for example, used interpreters in the administration of their conquered territories and in campaigns on the frontiers of their empire (Van Hoof 1962; Roditi 1982:2).

Interpreting is mentioned with increasing frequency in Late Latin and medieval Arabic literature. The need for interpreters both grew and came to be recognized during the Middle Ages: French chroniclers, for example, tell about interpreters during the Crusades. This was true to an even greater extent during the Renaissance as humanism kindled an interest in foreign languages, then as Europeans set out on expeditions of exploration, conquest and empire-building. References are found in archives of the Venetian Republic dealing with trade, as well as in diplomatic archives from the late Middle Ages through the seventeenth and eighteenth centuries (Roditi 1982). With the birth of nations and the concomitant development of national languages, recourse to interpreters became more common and references to their work more explicit. The memoirs and correspondence of politicians and diplomats, and other raw material of history, contain information that has only begun to be mined. Interpreters themselves, particularly over the past hundred years, have left us with useful reminiscences.

However inconsistent the annals of history have been on the subject of interpreting, however piecemeal the records, there is now ample testimony to the interpreters who devoted their lives to the profession, as well as to those who took it up as the occasion warranted. Whether they chose the profession or were chosen by it, interpreters have helped shape history. Before examining the specific achievements of interpreters, we shall present a brief survey of the various modes of interpreting through the ages, showing how they have been linked to some important moments in history.

Evolving forms and methods of interpreting

In contemporary society, we have grown used to technology. For those who have had the opportunity to follow an international conference with the aid of headphones or have watched world leaders on television conversing with each other with apparent ease, simultaneous interpreting, or simultaneous "translation" as it is sometimes referred to by lay people, has become the norm. It has even come to be taken for granted as a technical achievement rather than a human accomplishment. However, interpreting has been and continues to be complex and demanding, with a variety of functions and forms.

Until the introduction of equipment designed specifically for simultaneous interpreting, consecutive interpretation was predominant. This form of interpreting involves listening to relatively large segments of speech, generally while taking notes, then repeating what was said in the other language. The length of the utterance to be interpreted can vary considerably, as can the degree and type of note taking.

Some of the finest moments in consecutive interpreting occurred at the time of the Paris Peace Conference and in the multilateral meetings that were to follow.[1] It is perhaps ironic that Paris should be the location at which French lost its privileged status as the language of diplomacy, as Jean Delisle has suggested in his preface to Baigorri Jalón's history of conference interpreting (2004: x). This did not occur without a "language battle", however. It was precisely because the victors of World War I came together on French soil and were hosted by French Prime Minister Clemenceau that England and the U.S. felt that there should be some accommodations made with respect to language. Thus both English and French became the official languages of the conference itself and the documents emanating from it. Margaret MacMillan, in her much acclaimed account, *Paris 1919*, summarizes the debate as follows:

> The French argued for their own language alone, ostensibly on the grounds that it was more precise and at the same time capable of greater nuance. French, they said, had been the language of international communication and diplomacy for centuries. The British and the Americans pointed out that English was increasingly supplanting it. Lloyd George said that he would always regret that he did not know French better (he scarcely knew it at all), but it seemed absurd that English, spoken by more than 170 million people, should not have equal status with French. The Italians said, in that case, why not Italian as well? [...] In that case, said Lloyd George, why not Japanese as well? The Japanese delegates, who tended to have trouble following the debates whether they were in French or English, remained silent. Clemenceau backed down, to the consternation of many of his own officials.   (MacMillan 2002: 55–56)

The outcome of this particular battle, namely the decline of French, in the wake of the much larger one they had convened to resolve, opened the door to multilingualism in the various organizations that were created thereafter, necessitating much work on the part of interpreters and translators (Baigorri Jalón 2004: 12–16).

At that time, and during subsequent international negotiations, consecutive interpreting was carried out by many highly skilled practitioners, some of whom will be highlighted further in this chapter. Among the pioneers were Paul Mantoux (1877–1956) and Gustave Henri Camerlynck (1870–1929), considered the most notable of the twelve interpreters appointed to work at the Paris Conference (Roland 1999: 121). Antoine Velleman (1875–1962), who founded the School of Translation and Interpretation (ETI) at the University of Geneva in 1941, is another example. Jean Herbert (1897–1980) became a prominent consecutive interpreter for the League of Nations, and later chief interpreter of the United Nations interpretation service in New York. Others included Robert Confino (1903–69), André Kaminker (c.1877–c.1961) and his brother George Kaminker (c.1890–c.1969).

Salvador de Madariaga (1886–1978), writer, diplomat and chief of the Spanish delegation to the League of Nations, mentions a certain Madame Angeli with admiration: she could "take in a whole speech in English, French or Italian and repeat it in the other two languages without ever taking a note". Interpreters with this kind of ability, Madariaga goes on to say, were best suited for the Assembly, while others, more used to shorter speeches and swift repartee, were better for committees, and "when endowed with tact and political acumen", for the Council (Madariaga 1974: 107). The Madame "Angeli" in question was in fact Madame Rossetti Agresti, as Baigorri Jalón has pointed out (2004: 92 and 116). Olivia Rossetti Agresti (1875–1960) was a British author and interpreter. A member of the well-known Rossetti family of artists and writers, a niece of artist, writer and translator Dante Gabriel Rossetti, she was involved in anarchist politics, then Italian fascism.

Numerous other consecutive interpreters, working in different eras and in highly different circumstances, have likewise been hailed for their ability to repeat long segments of discourse in another language, presumably with accuracy – from Doña Marina (c.1500–c.1530) working for conquistador Cortés in sixteenth-century Mexico to Vernon Walters (1917–2002), who served several United States presidents in the twentieth century.

Axis interpreter Eugen Dollmann (1900–85) reports a different kind of experience. In his memoirs, Dollmann tells of the first speech he had to interpret for Hitler. The speech was held outdoors and addressed to a group of about one thousand visiting members of Mussolini's youth organization. Intended to be very brief, it lasted more than half an hour. Dollmann, who had not yet mastered the technique of note taking, says that he made "an Italian speech which had nothing whatever to do with Hitler's words" but which was greeted with wild applause (Dollmann 1967: 13).[2]

Under certain circumstances, interpreters have specifically been asked to proceed in a sentence-by-sentence fashion. This was requested of Arthur Ferguson (1859–1908) at the 1898 Paris Peace Conference that ended the Spanish-American War. As the treaty was being drafted, texts were presented in writing. When these written documents were being read aloud, the delegates preferred that the interpreters provide a sentence-by-sentence rendering (Morgan 1965: 104).

A question that arises repeatedly is how faithfully the speaker's words and tone should be reproduced. Colonel Stephen Bonsal (1865–1951), U.S. President Woodrow Wilson's interpreter at the Paris Peace Conference, advocated a certain amount of editing or adaptation. He was allegedly asked by one of the Big Four to suggest to Lawrence of Arabia that he "soften the impact of some of [Emir] Faisal's words that were giving offence in influential quarters", thus following the precedent of Paul Mantoux, who "smoothed out so many rough places in the impassioned appeals of the nationalistic speakers".[3] Lawrence declined:

> Perhaps he is right; but I cannot follow his suggestion. You see, I am an inter-
> preter, I merely translate. The Emir is speaking for the horsemen who carried the
> Arab flag across the great desert from the holy city of Mecca to the holy city of
> Jerusalem and to Damascus and beyond. He is speaking for the thousands who
> died in that long struggle. He is the bearer of their last words. He cannot alter
> them. I cannot soften them.　　　　　　　　　　　　　　　　(Bonsal 1946: 33–34)

Some of those who observed Colonel Lawrence's interpreting style felt he did not always live up to these high principles (Keynes 1949). It is also rumoured that Faisal, "in white robes embroidered with gold, a scimitar at his side [...] merely recited the Koran while Lawrence extemporized" (MacMillan 2002: 391). Anecdotes of this kind abound. While many are from credible sources, others may well have been exaggerated in the telling.

Consecutive interpreting has on occasion been viewed as too time-consuming, although it does have its advocates. Interpreter and theorist Danica Seleskovitch (1921–2001), for one, maintained that consecutive interpretation can help focus a discussion because it allows the participants of a meeting additional time for thinking. Because of this, she has argued, "consecutive interpretation actually saves time" (1978: 124–125). This view was shared by many a delegate in the past. British Prime Minister Lloyd George and other delegates at the San Remo Conference, for example, agreed that it was easier to conduct negotiations through the medium of an interpreter than by means of direct speech, since the breaks would give more time for thought (Riddell 1933: 189).[4]

What is referred to as "whispered" interpreting has undoubtedly been practised for centuries although it was sometimes known by other names. This is a form of simultaneous interpreting, in which the interpreter whispers the translation to another individual. When an interpreter conveyed Latin verse in German to King Frederick of Prussia during a theatrical performance at the Jesuit College of Gross-Glogau on September 14, 1747, he was in effect using this technique (Barthel 1982: 143). These days, whispering is still used for meetings when only one or two persons do not understand the language of the majority.

Its advantages notwithstanding, consecutive interpreting began to be considered too cumbersome, especially when more than two languages were involved. During the League of Nations years, new solutions were already being sought. Special equipment for simultaneous interpreting, which allowed the interpreter to talk at the same time as the speaker by means of a system of earphones and microphones, was developed by International Business Machines (IBM) and introduced to the League of Nations by three Americans, Edward Filene, a businessman, Gordon Finlay, an electrical engineer, and Thomas Watson, the president of IBM. The possibility of selecting any one of the working languages by simply turning a knob seemed a marvel of technology at the time, but the system posed many technical problems because of the amount of wiring required. The International Labour Office in Geneva was the only agency of the League of Nations that decided to adopt it. The Filene-Finlay-IBM system was first put into use in 1927, in combination with consecutive interpreting, at an International Labour Conference in Geneva. Simultaneous interpreting was first used for a conference in 1935 at the 15th International Congress of Physiology in Leningrad: the inaugural address given by Nobel laureate Ivan Pavlov was simultaneously translated from Russian into French, English and German (Van Hoof 1962:19–20). However, as the activities of the League of Nations were curtailed in the years leading up to World War II, simultaneous interpreting, too, temporarily vanished from the sphere of international relations.

When IBM's simultaneous interpreting equipment surfaced again at a 1944 conference in Philadelphia, however, conditions were far from ideal. The interpreters sat in a basement beneath the speakers' platform, and the shuffling of feet overhead, combined with the inadequacy of the now twenty-year-old equipment, made interpreting difficult (Roditi 1982:10). Despite its perceived disadvantages, consecutive rather than simultaneous interpreting was used one year later at the historic San Francisco Conference, at which the United Nations charter was drafted.

The reappearance of simultaneous interpreting coincided with the War Crimes Trial of the International Military Tribunal in Nuremberg, held from November 1945 to October 1946. The tribunal was established by the victorious Allies to try the surviving Axis leaders. The Allies were the United States, Great Britain, France and the U.S.S.R., and the war criminals on trial principally German Nazi leaders. The languages of the tribunal were English, French, Russian and German. The proceedings were of immediate interest not only to the countries directly concerned, but to the world at large (Conot 1983). The time was ripe, therefore, to put simultaneous interpreting into practice once again (Figure 19).

The chief of interpreting and translation services at Nuremberg was Colonel Léon Dostert (1904–71). An American of French extraction with remarkable organizational abilities, he recruited interpreters among students and teachers of the School of Translation and Interpretation at the University of Geneva, along with people who happened to be familiar with several languages through family circumstances or the vicissitudes of the War. Only two interpreters, Édouard Roditi (1910–92) and Haakon Chevalier (1902–85), had previous simultaneous experience. Born in Paris of American parents, Roditi had inhabited a number of cultural spaces and gained proficiency in several languages; he was a poet, art critic and translator. Chevalier had been a professor of French at the University of California from 1929 to 1946 and had done a number of book-length translations of major French authors such as Stendhal, Malraux and Aragon. Dostert's team had to handle a wide variety of subjects under difficult conditions.[5] Nevertheless, the new method of interpreting appeared to be the way of the future. The technical system was perfected by a Canadian, a former Royal Air Force bomber pilot and audio engineer named Antoine (Tony) Pilon, whose research had led to the invention of radar. He designed the complex network of wires linking microphones and earphones that ultimately made simultaneous interpreting workable (Delisle 1990: 335).

Just as the League of Nations had grown out of peace negotiations following World War I, the United Nations came into existence at the close of World War II.[6] The requirements for interpretation grew more complex as the number of languages increased. Whereas the League of Nations had used English, French and Spanish, the UN was to have six official languages.[7] Once United Nations officials had the opportunity to witness the effectiveness of the new interpreting system, Colonel Dostert was awarded a contract to form a team of simultaneous interpreters, which was put into operation in 1947 at a Tariffs and Trade Conference held in London (Roditi 1982: 15). Resolution 152 (11), adopted on November 15, 1947, made simultaneous interpretation a permanent service, to be used either as an alternative to, or in combination with, consecutive interpretation.

This resolution in effect marked the end of consecutive interpretation in the Assembly, although this form of interpreting did not go out without its moment of glory. Lord Paul Gore-Booth, editor of the fifth edition of the *Guide to Diplomatic Practice* by Ernest Satow, to whom we will return later, recounts the following anecdote: "The noted Latin-American statesman and orator, Señor Fernando Belaúnde of Peru, made at the General Assembly a long political speech in Spanish which was translated into French by one of the famous brothers Kaminker. M. Kaminker reproduced every significant phrase, every telling pause, every emotional tone and even every dramatic gesture, and, having used no notes at all, sat down amid a thunder of applause" (Satow 1979: 511n).

Despite initial opposition by the experienced interpreters of the now defunct League of Nations, simultaneous interpretation was fully accepted by 1950, by which time equipment had improved. Consecutive interpreting continues to be used, particularly in the context of court and community interpreting. For the most part, however, simultaneous interpretation, greatly enhanced by sophisticated technology, is now widespread in most intergovernmental agencies and at multilingual conferences around the world.

Many a successful interpreter of the past was introduced to the profession in an entirely fortuitous manner. Roditi, for example, became an interpreter after a chance encounter on a train with Hans Jacob, an interpreter for the Foreign Ministry of the Weimar Republic, who persuaded him to sit an exam in Geneva

(Roditi 1978). Andrew Dawrant, referred to above, is another illustration, having found his calling after a similar meeting, this time on a plane, with Jean Duval, Canada's leading Chinese interpreter of the 1980s and 1990s (Hoffman 2011: F7).

The growing need for interpreters and hence for programs dedicated to their training is the result of significant changes in international relations at several levels – political, economic, cultural and scientific. During the second half of the nineteenth century, the Industrial Revolution gave rise to international organizations in such fields as railroads and telecommunications. By the end of the nineteenth century, there had been over 1,400 specialized conferences (Van Hoof 1962: 15). Greater social mobility brought to the conference table many experts and diplomats whose education had not included practice in foreign languages. Interpreting – in its consecutive form – emerged as a distinct activity performed by a body of professionals who were visible to larger international groups.

However, the assumption that "interpreters are born, not made" was fairly prevalent until modern times. Whereas language training had been available all through history in one form or another, the teaching of interpreting techniques as such began only in the early part of the twentieth century. The Foreign Offices of several countries began to organize examinations to fill specific needs in diplomatic interpreting: there are references to "student interpreters" in old personnel files of the U.S. Department of State (1904), as well as indications that both the British and Germans were building up specialized language services. Nonetheless, interpreters learned how to interpret on the job – by trial-and-error or, at best, through special programs offered by their employers. University programs aimed at training professional interpreters, distinct from language and literature programs, are a creation of the 1940s: University of Geneva, 1941; Vienna, 1943; Mainz/Germersheim, 1946; Saarland, 1948; Georgetown, 1949; Heidelberg, 1950. The number of schools has grown since that time.[8] Language combinations have multiplied, beginning in the 1970s with the successive enlargements of the European Community, now the European Union.[9] The introduction of special equipment for simultaneous interpreting has been a major factor in the development of the profession, necessitating specific training. Improved technology has also provided the means to monitor the student's progress, analyse the interpreter's performance and, more recently, to provide rapid access to specialized terminology.

As in the case of translation, the development of formal interpreter training has led to the emergence of a field of studies in its own right, in other words the articulation of a set of theoretical principles on the basis of which the discipline can be taught, observed and described. Interpreters, like translators of the written word, have begun to reflect, too, on their history and their multiple functions across religions, cultures and political entities.

Interpreters in the service of religion

All the major world religions have spread beyond the territories in which they originated. For this reason, both translation and interpretation have been influential in the religious lives of many peoples, although they have served different purposes, depending on the nature of the religions involved.

Judaism is not a proselytizing religion and hence has not led to the kind of missionary work associated with Christianity. Yet the Jewish faith relied on interpreters for centuries, primarily because Hebrew ceased to be the vehicular language of the Jewish people. After the Babylonian exile (586–538 BCE), a large number of Jews spoke Aramaic, which was also the diplomatic language of the time. This created a need for interpretation services for a mixed public. Between the fifth century BCE and the sixth century CE, indeed even up to the tenth century, interpreters were at work in Palestine and Babylonia, in courts as well as in Talmudic schools and academies. They would often work with the rabbi under whom they had studied and whose thinking and teachings they knew well. Some also seem to have been what we would call freelance interpreters, called in for important occasions. One example would be the investiture ceremony of a new judge in the Sanhedrin, the ancient Jewish court system. Interpreters were also employed by the synagogues to re-express the sermons and teachings of the rabbi. History has preserved the names of a few famous interpreters, such as Chutzpit HaMeturgeman (meaning Chutzpit the Interpreter), one of ten martyrs who were tortured and put to death by the Romans for having violated the prohibition against teaching the Torah.[10]

Some interpreters became rabbis themselves, or at least decision-makers, with laws and exegeses actually attributed to them. But it seems that the function of interpreters was mostly pedagogical. It was not so much a matter of translation from one language into another as the eloquent and clear re-expression of the words the rabbi whispered into their ears, sometimes in the same language. The Talmud, a compendium of rabbinical teaching and Jewish law and lore, refers to the necessity of translation and even contains a long exposition of the rules applying to interpretation for the synagogue (Kaufmann 2005).

As we have seen in Chapter 6, it was toward 538 BCE that Ezra the Scribe instituted the practice of having the Torah read in public in the synagogue – on Mondays and Thursdays (market and court days) and especially on Saturday (the Sabbath). Until the twelfth century, and to this day for Yemenite Jews, the reading was rendered consecutively, verse by verse, into the vernacular – initially into Aramaic, then also into Greek or Arabic. Only the Hebrew written text had ritual value, and it was hence forbidden to set down in writing and distribute any definitive version of the oral interpretation in the vernacular languages.

Interpreters also played a key role in the Islamization of Africa. West Africa, for example, had commercial relations with the Arab world as early as the seventh and eighth centuries CE. Arabic, the language of the Koran, was gaining prestige but was not necessarily understood in distant regions of Africa. Interpreters facilitated the spread of Islam by translating preachers' speeches orally into the local languages (Niang 1990: 34).

In the thirteenth century, William of Rubruck of the Franciscan Order of Friars Minor set out on a mission to Asia, at the behest of King Louis IX (Saint Louis). He was received at the Court of Mangu, or Mongka, Great Khan, the predecessor of Kubla Khan (Dawson 1966: 157). Rubruck started his journey from the Black Sea on May 7, 1253. He travelled through Southern Russia and across the Ural River, following the nomadic Mongols' camps as far as Karakorum and then turned back through Persia. He returned in May 1257 to Cyprus, reaching Antioch in June that year and Tripoli in August. Unlike earlier travels to the Mongol empire, such as the fact-finding mission undertaken for the Hungarian King Béla IV in 1237 (Jackson 1990: 26), this was a purely religious one. Rubruck was accompanied by another Franciscan, Bartholomew of Cremona, a clerk named Gosset, who was in charge of the King's presents to the Khan and an interpreter – *turgemannus*. This interpreter, whom William referred to as *Homo Dei*, meaning "man of God", a literal translation of the Arabic *Abdullah*, proved to be inefficient and unreliable, a "man of neither wit nor eloquence" (Dawson 1966: 109). All along the adventurous journey among the Tartars and then the Mongols, Rubruck felt his mission was hampered because his interpreters were not equal to the task. It was not only a question of his interpreters' competence, but also of their loyalties. As William of Rubruck reported, he suspected that the message conveyed by his Armenian interpreters was distorted out of "loathing" for the Saracens, and in order to "do them harm" (Dawson 1966: 149).

Europeans set out for the far-flung corners of the world from the fifteenth century on. They carried out their missions of exploration and conquest with a sense of conviction and superiority. The source of their confidence was in part the complex and mobile "technology of power" they possessed, which included writing, navigational instruments and weaponry. But, as was the case for the Turks, who had attempted to impose Islam with fire and sword, the superiority of the Europeans also resided in the Christian conviction that they "possessed an absolute and exclusive religious truth" and this played a major part in nearly all their cultural encounters (Greenblatt 1991: 9). For this reason, as Europeans moved through the world, Christianity also spread south to Africa, east to Asia and across the Atlantic to the New World. Christian missionaries of all denominations used interpreters to win converts.

By the time of the so-called discovery of America, Europeans were well aware of the importance of having adequate interpreters to assist them in communicating with the radically different peoples they encountered. When Cortés set out to conquer Mexico in 1519, he relied on interpreters to assist him not only in his conquest *per se*, but also in his efforts to convert the Indians. Cortés came across a slave named Jeronimo de Aguilar and bought his freedom. Aguilar had been shipwrecked off the coast of Yucatán and had learned the Mayan language during his eight years of slavery. Through Aguilar, who had received minor orders before being stranded among the Mayas, Cortés exhorted the Indians to give up their idols and embrace the Christian faith. The interpreter's familiarity with Catholic doctrine undoubtedly enhanced his effectiveness. In Tabasco, the Spaniards built an altar with the Blessed Virgin and a large cross, symbols of Christianity which were accepted by the Mayan inhabitants, at least according to Bernal Díaz del Castillo (c.1496–1584), a soldier in Cortés's army, who published a chronicle entitled *Historia Verdadera de la Conquista de la Nueva España* (*The True Story of the Conquest of New Spain*) around 1575.

With the people of Cholula and with Montezuma, the reaction was not so immediate. In communicating with the Aztecs, the crucial link was the recently baptized Marina (who will be profiled more fully in the next section). Marina and Aguilar performed what would be called "relay interpreting" today: anything said in Spanish would be rendered in Maya by Aguilar, then into the Aztec language of Náhuatl by Marina and vice versa.

In Tlaxcala, the next stage of their advance, Cortés again appealed to the people to abandon their gods, as he had done so effectively in Tabasco. According to Díaz del Castillo, it was very well explained "because Doña Marina and Aguilar, our Tongues, were already very well experienced in it" (Díaz del Castillo 1983:132). Cortés himself reported on these events with confidence in his letters home to King Charles (Carlos) V. In his fifth letter, he told of an Indian chief who "easily understood" a sermon that had been preached by one of the Franciscan friars and then translated by the interpreter. The chief, he reported, understood the "error of his sect" and "declared that he wished to destroy his idols immediately" (MacNutt 1977, 2:272). The true response of the natives has been forever lost, and we can only suppose, as Salvador de Madariaga has done in his biography of Cortés, that however adept the interpreters may have been, the religious and cultural values were not transmitted so smoothly. Madariaga comments on the Tlaxcala episode described by Díaz del Castillo:

> We can but surmise the waves of mutual incomprehension and misunderstanding that the sudden meeting of the two civilisations raised in both Indians and Europeans. Granted that Aguilar and Doña Marina, gifted as they both were,

succeeded in rendering a tolerably adequate transfiguration of the Christian faith
and dogmas not merely into the language but into the idiom of the Tlaxcatecs,
but how could these Indians' minds assimilate the dogma of the Virgin Birth [...].
(Madariaga 1942:202–203)

Interpreters helped priests and friars with their work, and this included interpreting
for executions. During the expedition to Honduras, Cortés ordered Cuauhtemoc
(Guatemoc), the last Aztec emperor, to be hanged along with his cousin the Lord of
Tacuba. Before they were hanged, the Franciscan friars commended them to God
through the interpreter Doña Marina. Pizarro's secretary, Pedro Sancho, noted
that an interpreter was used at the execution of the Inca ruler Atahualpa in 1533.
While Atahualpa was tied to the stake, a friar was sent to "console and instruct
him through an interpreter in the articles of our Christian faith". Allegedly moved
by these arguments, Atahualpa requested baptism, and as an apparent reward was
garrotted first instead of being burned alive (Hemming 1970:78).

The Roman Catholic orders at work on the newly "discovered" continent were
the Franciscans, then the Dominicans and Augustinians. By the end of the sixteenth century, Jesuits and others joined them. All the orders were intent on learning the language of the native population as quickly as possible. Fray Bernardino
de Sahagún (c.1499–1590), a Franciscan, went further. Realizing that the success
of missionary work hinged on a knowledge of the way of life of the Indians as well
as the language they spoke, he studied the Aztec religion and culture. With the
help of trilingual (Náhuatl, Spanish, and Latin) students under his supervision,
Sahagún left behind a history of New Spain known as the "Florentine Codex".[11]
Over a period extending from 1545 until his death in 1590, Fray Bernardino and
his students documented the culture, worldview, ritual practices, society, economics, and natural history of the Aztec people. Its 2,400 pages are organized into 12
books, with over 2,000 illustrations drawn by native artists. Despite the obvious
problems related to the fact that these colonial materials have been passed down
"through the filter of a European Renaissance mind" (Qiñones Kleber 2002:14),
the Florentine Codex is considered to be "one of the most remarkable accounts on
a non-Western culture ever composed" (Nicholson 2002:34).

The French Huguenot expedition to Brazil benefited greatly from a group
of interpreters who were already well integrated into the native culture. From
the early sixteenth century onward, Portuguese and French traders had been
travelling up and down the coast of Brazil. It is believed that Norman navigators anchored at the mouth of the Amazon even before Columbus reached the
shores of the New World. Some Frenchmen, referred to in the French accounts
as *truchements de Normandie* (although some Bretons were involved as well), had
moved into the villages, learned the language, cohabited with the women and

had children by them, and allegedly adopted all their practices, even cannibalism.[12] While these *truchements* were an embarrassment to the French missionaries, they were viewed as valuable to them as liaison agents (Léry 1990: xix). The Norman interpreters were familiar with the customs of the indigenous people, the Tupinamba Indians, and hence served as cultural intermediaries. Unlike the conquistadors, these interpreters inspired confidence in the local inhabitants, and were therefore indispensable to the transactions of French merchants throughout the sixteenth century (Delisle 1977b).

Jean de Léry (1534–1611), a Huguenot pastor, recorded his experience of the New World in his *History of a Voyage to the Land of Brazil* (1578).[13] Léry had been preceded in Brazil by Nicolas Durand de Villegagnon. Fleeing growing opposition to the Reform movement, Villegagnon had left France with six hundred followers in 1555, settling on an island off the shore of Brazil, where he built Fort Coligny. Among the difficulties encountered by Villegagnon in the New World were his efforts to impose strict moral standards on the *truchements*, who by this time lived according to another set of customs. Villegagnon demanded, for example, that they marry the Brazilian women whom they had taken as concubines. Within a short time, the interpreters rebelled and deserted the Protestant missionaries. In losing the support of the interpreters, Villegagnon also lost his influence over the native population (Delisle 1977b: 3). Villegagnon wrote to Geneva, requesting that preachers be sent out to help him accomplish his mission. Léry was one of those who set off to do so. Among the company were ten young boys, who were taken along "to learn the language of the savages" (Léry 1990: 6–7). However, the efforts of Léry and his companions to evangelize had little effect, and he returned to Europe in 1558. The Calvinist settlement in Brazil would last only two more years.

Baptist minister Joseph Merrick arrived in coastal Cameroon in the mid-nineteenth century.[14] He was accompanied by another Jamaican missionary, Joseph Jackson Fuller (1825–1908) (Nama 1990a: 359). One of the earliest slaves to be freed in Jamaica, Fuller was well-educated and well-travelled. He was a preacher and public speaker, and also translated books such as John Bunyan's *Pilgrim's Progress* into one of the local languages. These early missionaries were motivated by the requirements of evangelization. They paved the way for the work of Alfred Saker, considered one of the most influential missionaries in West Africa. The Africans who worked closely with the missionaries learned their European languages; they became interpreters and facilitated communication between the two communities.

Formal training of translators and interpreters in Cameroon was initiated by German missionaries. André Mbangué was one of three young boys from Douala who were sent to Germany in 1888 to be trained as bakers. The first Roman

Catholic baptized in Cameroon, he later served as a catechist, preparing Christians for the sacraments and interpreting religious dogma to them. Realizing the importance of bilingual catechists in disseminating the gospel, the German Palatine Fathers opened a seminary at which language instruction was provided along with ecclesiastical training (Nama 1990a: 362).

Exploration and conquest

Religious conversion, of course, was carried out in a larger context. In fact, religion was only one of several motives for the many expeditions from the Old World to the New; missions were also carried out for the purposes of commerce, power and territorial expansion. In the contact between Europeans and indigenous peoples in the Americas, contact that involved communication, cultural and commercial exchange, conquest and conflict resolution, interpreters were crucial. Only in recent years have studies from a variety of perspectives done justice to the complex lives of those who have come to be called "cultural brokers" or "go-betweens".[15]

Interpreters were critical, but not readily available. They were recruited, according to the mores of the time, from among Europeans and natives alike: "abducted Amerindians, captured and redeemed Castilian castaways, foreign prisoners, youthful catechists and missionaries, acculturated Indian *caciques* and *cacicas*, and Spanish garrison soldiers". For the most part, these individuals did not choose to perform their role as cultural mediators, but were compelled to do so (Luca 1999: 1).[16] In the sixteenth century and beyond, a favoured method was to kidnap natives of the new region and teach them the language of their abductors. However, the natives who were taken from their homelands to be displayed as curiosities in the conquerors' country and later turned into interpreters often did not relish the experience. Most of Columbus's recruits from San Salvador Island (also called Watlings Island, in the Bahamas), who were to be taught Castilian so they could serve as interpreters, escaped by jumping overboard. Having learned from this experience, he later had the captives' wives brought aboard the *Santa Maria* to make sure the men would not leave (Kurz 1990: 2, 11).

When Francisco Hernández de Córdoba sailed from Havana to Yucatán in 1517, he captured two Indians, who were baptised Melchior and Julian. They were brought back to Cuba where Julian died. Melchior, who had learned some Spanish, was taken on the next expedition, headed by Cortés. However, leaving the Spanish clothes he had been given by his captors hanging in a palm grove, Melchior ran off with the people of Tabasco and advised them to attack the Spaniards (Díaz del Castillo 1983). For his pains, Melchior is believed to have been offered as a sacrifice by the Indians.

On his first voyage to Canada in 1534, Jacques Cartier captured two Iroquois, Dom Agaya and Taignoagny, and took them back to France to learn French. On the second voyage (1535–36), the two Indian interpreter-guides were used to help Cartier venture further up the St. Lawrence River. These interpreters served their masters only up to a point, as long as their own people's interests were not opposed to those of the French (Delisle 1977a).

Other examples of this type can be found in the history of the colonization of the New World. Tristán de Luna y Arellano travelled to La Florida in search of riches in 1559. Even before sailing from New Spain (Mexico) he asked the viceroy, Luis de Velasco, for permission to take one or two female Indian servants along as interpreters. It is not known whether these women actually sailed with him (Luca 1999: 5). Later, his captains returned from a trip inland with an Indian woman called Lacsohe who served as an interpreter (Priestley 1971, 2: 303). De Luna and the Dominican vicar, Fray Pedro de Feria, were involved in a dispute over this practice of abducting indigenous men and women, requiring that the Viceroy step in and take a stand in de Luna's favour (Priestley 1971, 1: 65–67; also quoted in Luca 1999: 5).

Instead of training new "recruits" from scratch, it was sometimes possible to find servants or slaves from established settlements who had already learned the language of their masters by a method that would be called "immersion" today. This is illustrated by a letter dated May 6, 1560, written by Luis de Velasco to Tristán de Luna: "You say that the Indian whom my niece, Doña Beatrice, has would be useful as an interpreter, as would the other married woman of Tlaxcala whom my sister-in-law has" (Priestley 1971, 1: 121). This practice reoccurred when European countries built their colonial empires in the nineteenth century: "People who were at the service of the colonial master (e.g., houseboys) and were smart enough to speak his language, even in a broken way, were promoted to the rank of interpreter and offered official status in the colonial administrative system" (Niang 1990: 35).

Motivated by strategic and commercial considerations, Samuel de Champlain, colonizer of New France and founder of Quebec City (1608), set out to produce interpreters in a more deliberate manner, creating an institution of resident interpreters (*interprètes-résidents*) in the new colony. Young French adventurers were placed with the Indian tribes with whom the French traded; they lived among the natives, dressed liked them, hunted, fished and took part in their everyday lives. Through daily contact with the Indians, the interpreters became familiar not only with their language but also with their way of thinking. They were highly effective intermediaries between the native population and the European settlers and merchants, serving as guides, explorers, diplomats and traders (Delisle 1977a).

Étienne Brûlé (c.1592–1633) was one of the most colourful figures among these pioneering interpreters. He arrived in Canada with Champlain in 1608 and by the winter of 1610–11 was sent to live among the Algonquins. Brûlé became known as an interpreter of the Huron language and he helped write a Huron dictionary. He became so much a part of the Huron people that he was accused of having abandoned his own faith. But he also turned against his compatriots. In 1629, he allied himself with another interpreter to guide the English when they attacked Stadacona (Quebec City). After serving his new masters for a time, he returned to live in Huronia. Canada was returned to France in 1632 by virtue of the treaty of Saint-Germain-en-Laye and Champlain came back to New France the following year. Brûlé was killed by the Bear Nation, a Huron tribe, apparently for "political" reasons: they did not wish to compromise their alliance with Champlain by appearing to be accomplices to Brûlé's treason. Other resident interpreters of that era, from Normandy like the interpreters in Brazil before them, included Nicolas Marsolet, Jean Nicolet, Jean and Thomas Godefroy, Jacques Hertel and François Marguerie (Delisle 1977a).

In other cases, key interpreters for conquerors of the New World were produced by happenstance. Shipwreck survivors would learn the language of their new environment, also by immersion, and later serve as intermediaries between natives and Europeans. This was the case for two shipwrecked Spaniards who had lived as slaves for eight years (1511–19) in Yucatán. Jeronimo de Aguilar, as we have seen, agreed to become Cortés's interpreter, whereas the second man, Gonzalo Guerrero, who had an Indian wife and three children, refused to do so (Greenblatt 1991:140). Cortés used Aguilar as his interpreter for Maya, the Yucatec language, but for Náhuatl, the Mexican language spoken by the Aztecs, he had recourse to Marina.

Doña Marina (Figure 10), also known as Malintzin or la Malinche, is one of the most illustrious native interpreters to have served conquerors, invaders or discoverers.[17] In accounts dating as far back as the century in which she lived, as well as in the subsequent rewriting of history, she stands out as "one of the chief figures in the conquest" (Madariaga 1942:117).

Marina is mentioned in several sources, but is acknowledged very little by Cortés himself. In the five long letters Cortés wrote to Charles V, she is referred to as the "Indian woman" in the second letter (MacNutt 1977, 1:217) and as Marina by name only once, in the fifth letter, which deals with the 1524 expedition to Las Hibueras (Honduras) (MacNutt 1977, 2:273).

Marina is referred to most frequently in Bernal Díaz del Castillo's *True History of the Conquest of New Spain* (1575), in which she appears as "the most important go-between" (Greenblatt 1991:141). Díaz del Castillo sometimes gives the impression that he is quoting her verbatim, although he wrote from recollection, not from a diary. He started writing in 1558, when he was about sixty, about events that had taken place between 1519 and 1524. He always gives her the honorific

Doña. Clearly, he was writing from the point of view of the Spaniards, stating that the Lord had sent her to them to further their cause.

Marina's work is also documented in the Florentine Codex, Friar Bernardino de Sahagún's monumental history of Mexico referred to earlier. Bernardino mentions Marina less often and not as approvingly as Bernal Díaz del Castillo, but not in the derogatory way she was sometimes treated by the Mexicans after independence. Like Díaz del Castillo's account, the Florentine Codex was written in retrospect. What distinguishes the two versions of history is that Bernardino de Sahagún presents the other side's story using oral accounts by native informants old enough to have witnessed the events. In the section dealing with the conquest of Mexico, the illustrations of the Florentine Codex feature Marina less prominently than the *Lienzo de Tlaxcala*, an Indian picture history dating from around 1550 and painted under Spanish influence. Not only does Marina appear in every important scene of the chronicle, but she is customarily drawn larger than any of the other actors, including Cortés (Brandon 1988:84–85). This is in marked contrast to other pictorial representations of interpreters, one of the earliest of which (Figure 1) is in the Memphian Tomb of Horemheb (1333–1306 BCE), where the interpreter's figure is much smaller than that of the interpreter's master (Kurz 1986).

Cortés's interpreters and Marina, in particular, were more important to Cortés than the Tlaxcalan soldiers and other allies with whom he eventually conquered Mexico (Gargatagli 1992). Marina was crucial to the "circulation of cultural representations" precisely because she herself had moved from one culture to another (Greenblatt 1991:142–143).

Marina's biography is controversial; many of the facts, including the year of her death, have never been clearly established. She has been regarded as both an outcast and a great lady. Born around 1505, she was of noble lineage. Her father was *cacique* (chief) of the province of Coatzacoalcos, but died when she was a child. She was given away, apparently sold to Mayan merchants, when her mother remarried and bore her new husband a son. Marina herself may have been responsible for the mystery surrounding her early years (Herren 1992:37). She may have been sold several times before she was given to Cortés, one of twenty slaves presented to him and his men in Tabasco (Díaz del Castillo 1983:58). Cortés had the twenty women baptized and then presented them as gifts to his captains. Marina spoke the language of the Aztecs from whom she was descended and Maya because she had lived among the Tabascans. She is said to have learned Spanish quickly, although just how quickly is a matter of mere speculation. While only fourteen years old at the time, she stood out for her beauty and intelligence, and was given to Alonso Hernández Puertocarrero, an important gentleman. When

Puertocarrero returned to Spain, Marina became Cortés's mistress and bore him a son. During the ill-fated expedition to Honduras, Cortés married her off to Juan Jaramillo, thereby leaving himself free to marry someone of higher social status when he returned to Spain (Díaz del Castillo 1983; Greenblatt 1991).

As Cortés's "tongue" and "ears", Marina occupied a position of considerable power. And yet, she remains an ambivalent figure, seen as both a saviour and traitor (Greenblatt 1991:143). While indicted in post-independence Mexico as the "mother of a bastard race of *mestizos* and a traitress to her country" (Mirandé and Enríquez 1979:24), she has since been "rehabilitated" by feminist scholars, who portray her in a more favourable light and view her as the herald of the culturally hybrid societies of the future (Del Castillo 1977; Mirandé and Enríquez 1979; Alarcón 1981).

In the United States, Sacajawea (Sacagawea or Sakakawea) (c.1788–1812?), is a well-known figure. She served as an interpreter to the Lewis and Clark expedition, a journey of 4,000 miles overland to the Pacific Ocean which lasted from 1804 to 1806. Captured as a young girl by Hidatsa raiders, Sacajawea was purchased (or won while gambling) by the French-Canadian interpreter and *coureur de bois* Toussaint Charbonneau. She became his wife and accompanied him when he signed on as interpreter for the Lewis and Clark expedition. She helped form the chain of interpreters by which Lewis and Clark communicated with Nez Percés and other indigenous peoples, in particular her own tribe, the Shoshone, who supplied the expedition with horses. In the journal he kept, Meriwether Lewis referred to her as the wife of Charbonneau or else the "squaw", a derogatory Algonquian Indian word meaning prostitute, which was used by both Indians and Whites when referring to Indian women (Butterfield 2010). Gradually, however, Lewis and Clark came to appreciate the multiple roles she played as a linguistic, cultural and geographic guide and, as a woman with a child, as a sign to adversarial tribes that the expedition was a peaceful one.

Sacajawea's death from a fever in 1812 has been documented, although in some of the records she is again referred to simply as Charbonneau's wife; since he was polygamous, there could have been confusion about who had actually died. She is also reported, according to tribal oral tradition, to have returned to her people and to have died on the Wind River Reservation in 1884. This second scenario was disseminated through a 1933 biography written by a University of Wyoming professor, and was perpetuated as monuments to Sacajawea were erected (Butterfield 2010). This is an extreme example of an interpreter whose identities and loyalties are double and whose life story, too, has been conveyed in two different narratives.

War and peace

Armies have always needed interpreters to perform a variety of functions: determining the enemy's positions and plans, overseeing conquered territories, making and keeping allies, and negotiating with the enemy. Last but not least, interpreters have been required for communication within the same, but multilingual, army: think, for example, of the legions of Imperial Rome, the Byzantine troops who fought the Ostrogoths in Italy, the Swiss mercenaries in the service of numerous European Renaissance princes, or the patchwork of nationalities in the Austro-Hungarian army. In some cases, these interpreters were members of the military themselves. More by chance than by design, soldiers who knew the languages needed for communication would be thrust into the role of interpreter. In other cases, civilians – sometimes foreigners – would be recruited for the purpose. And as fighting came to a halt, the same interpreters often helped to negotiate the cease-fire, surrender or peace agreement. Some of the most exceptional cases are set out below.

Inscriptions dating back to the third millennium BCE provide the earliest indication of the use of interpretation (Kurz 1985). These inscriptions were found on the tombs of the princes of Elephantine, at the border between Egypt and Nubia. Living in a bilingual border region, the princes were acquainted with the language or languages of the tribes with which the Egyptians were in contact, and hence became "overseers of dragomans". Despite the fact that the Egyptians had little regard for foreign languages, the work of the princes was considered sufficiently important to merit special mention and inclusion in the enumeration of their other titles. These early interpreters could be considered military interpreters, at least in part, since some of the Egyptian expeditions to Nubia involved fighting as well as diplomatic and trade relations.[18]

The earliest clear references to military interpreters are found in Greek literature pertaining to Alexander the Great's campaigns in Asia, which took him as far as India. In the course of these campaigns, he had to rely time and again on interpreters to communicate with the various peoples he conquered or who became his allies. The Romans later used interpreters for similar purposes.

In 1248, Louis IX of France, or Saint Louis, as he is known, led a crusade to the Middle East where he found himself in need of interpreters. While the French were in Egypt, Baudouin (Baudoin) d'Ibelin (d. 1266) interpreted the words of attacking Saracens, according to the chronicle of Joinville (1963: 252).[19] Another interpreter, Nicole d'Acre, a priest familiar with the language of the enemy, is also mentioned in the chronicles of Joinville (1963: 254).

Accounts of a later French expedition to the Middle East – Napoleon's ill-fated campaign in Egypt and Palestine – contain numerous references to the work of translators and interpreters capable of handling both French and Arabic (Roditi

1982: 7). Jean-Michel Venture de Paradis (1739–99) was one such interpreter: educated at Louis-le-Grand school and the Constantinople dragoman school, he was appointed interpreter-secretary in 1785 and assigned to accompany Bonaparte as first interpreter of the Orient Army. He died during the expedition and was succeeded by Pierre Amédée Jaubert (1779–1847), who served as the emperor's personal interpreter-secretary before being sent on a mission to Persia (Gaulmier 1950; Degros 1984: 80). Jaubert was a French diplomat, academic and translator. He became Napoleon's "favourite Orientalist adviser and dragoman" (de Groot 2000: 230).

During his early career as a surveyor and map-maker and throughout much of his service in the army, George Washington relied on a number of self-styled interpreters. In October 1753, as an officer in the colonial army, Washington was ordered to proceed into the wilderness, to establish contact with friendly Indians and to carry a letter to the French while gaining intelligence on their positions and strength. He appointed Jacob Van Braam (1725–84) as a lieutenant and interpreter. Van Braam was a native of Holland who had advertised himself as a French teacher in the *Maryland Gazette* upon his arrival in 1752. In 1754, he was assigned to negotiate the terms of the surrender of Fort Necessity with the French. Some controversy arose over the meaning of the terms, owing to the fact that, since it had been raining heavily, the written record was reduced to notes on "wet and blotted paper" not legible to the other officers who had to rely on Van Braam's "word of mouth" account. There was speculation that, as a Dutchman, his grasp of the subtleties of English was insufficient, but he was also accused of having deliberately mistranslated the articles of capitulation, and was omitted from the list of officers commended for their service (Grizzard 2002: 320–321).

Washington enlisted Christopher Gist (1706–59) to help him with relations with the Indians and guide him in wilderness travel. Gist had been a leading explorer, surveyor and Indian trader by the early 1750s. He was with Washington at the surrender of Fort Necessity and in 1757 was appointed deputy superintendant of Indian Affairs, sending Washington "flying reports" or rumours with his own eyewitness accounts from the frontier (Grizzard 2002: 132). This appointment, however, was said to have been of limited success: while well acquainted with Indian customs, Gist apparently knew little of their language (Flexner 1965: 59).

During the American Revolution, the Prussian military expert Friedrich Wilhelm von Steuben was brought in to reform the Continental Army. Steuben did not know English, but he did know French and it was in that language that he negotiated the terms of his American assignment with Benjamin Franklin, who at the time was the American representative in Paris. When Steuben left for America in September 1777, the seventeen-year-old Pierre-Étienne Duponceau

(1760–1844), also known as Peter Stephen Du Ponceau, accompanied him as military secretary and interpreter. Duponceau, who later devoted himself to the study of indigenous languages, remained on his staff until nearly the end of the Revolution in 1783. Duponceau did not always live up to Steuben's expectations, however: full of curiosity, he was frequently reprimanded for "conversing on his own account without due regard to his subordinate role as interpreter" (Palmer 1937: 117). At Valley Forge, while carrying out inspections of the American army, the Baron was greatly handicapped by his ignorance of English. Duponceau continued to act as his interpreter, but the young Frenchman had little knowledge of military affairs or American customs.

To help matters, George Washington gave him the assistance of two young aides-de-camp, John Laurens (1754–82) and Alexander Hamilton (1757–1804), both of whom could speak French. Laurens, an American who had been educated in London and Geneva, later served as a special minister to France and worked with Lafayette's brother-in-law in drafting the terms of the British capitulation of Yorktown, the last major battle of the revolutionary war (Grizzard 2002: 180–181). Hamilton went on to command a regiment in Lafayette's division and became Washington's first secretary of the treasury (Grizzard 2002: 144–145).

Steuben brought to America his experience with Frederick the Second's infantry, the most highly trained corps of the time. Described by George Washington as "sober and brave [...] high in his ideas of subordination, impetuous in his temper, ambitious" (Washington memo dated March 9, 1792; quoted in Grizzard 2002: 387), he produced the Regulations for the Order and Discipline of the Troops of the United States, which were to remain in use by the army from 1779 until the War of 1812. Steuben wrote these drill regulations down in French. Duponceau translated them into literary English, and then Laurens and Hamilton edited Duponceau's version, introducing correct military terminology and phraseology. The Baron did not understand his own text once it was turned into English and had to learn the drill commands by heart. He is reported to have frequently lost his temper, "sprinkling his broken English with selections from his rich vocabulary of French and German profanity". On one of these occasions, the memorized drills did not do the trick and the men began to move in two directions at once. As the Baron began to swear in French and German, a young officer stepped out of the crowd and came to his rescue (Palmer 1937).

During World War I, and particularly during the negotiations to end the war, beginning with armistice talks in 1918 and culminating in the Paris Peace Conference of 1919, interpreters played a critical role, as we have seen.

The armistice was negotiated in Marshal Ferdinand Foch's railway-coach headquarters on a siding at Compiègne. Foch was Supreme Commander of the

Allied Armies, and was made Marshal of France after August 1918. Interpreters were required for the three languages involved: English, French and German. The Allied delegation listed Commander Bagot and Officer Interpreter Laperche as interpreters. Foch had his chief of staff, Maxime Weygand, read out the armistice conditions in French, clause by clause, so that the interpreters could translate them (Rudin 1944: 338 n. 36), and it was Laperche who "repeated the crushing conditions in German" (Weintraub 1985: 54).

The German delegation was headed by Matthias Erzberger, a Catholic civilian, who had advocated for a negotiated end to the war. Considered by some to be more acceptable to the Allies than a Prussian military officer might have been, he was appointed armistice commissioner. Despite his suitability for the negotiations, Erzberger needed to rely on the services of the interpreters, although this was also perceived to be an advantage: "Because he did not understand French, Erzberger had an opportunity to observe the demeanor of his adversaries" (Rudin 1944: 339). He signed the armistice ending World War I on November 11, 1918, a role that later proved to be fatal: in August 1921, he was murdered by two former German army officers, who were not prosecuted until the end of World War II.

Gustave Henri Camerlynck, mentioned earlier as one of the pioneers in the post-war years, had been a professor of modern languages. In collaboration with his wife, Gabrielle Jeanne Camerlynck-Guernier, he published several English and French language textbooks, which are in use to this day. A Frenchman born in Algiers, Camerlynck had spent the war as an interpreter to a British artillery regiment. Afterward, he became an interpreter for the French Ministry of Foreign Affairs. He succeeded Paul Mantoux as chief interpreter at the League of Nations and served as an interpreter and translator for a series of conferences (Baigorri Jalón 2004: 25–26; *Time Magazine* 1929).[20]

Paul Mantoux's work is amply documented and he is hence among the best known interpreters of the Paris Peace talks. Not only did he compile the only complete record of the deliberations of the Council of Four based on his own "notes of the official interpreter" (Mantoux 1992), but his work has also been described in the memoirs and testimonies of American delegate Robert Lansing and others.[21]

Born and educated in Paris, Mantoux wrote a thesis on the Industrial Revolution in England and went on to become a professor of French history at University College and at the School of Economics and Political Science in London.[22] When World War I broke out, he was mobilized as a second-class private and sent to the front to dig graves. His menial duties did not last long, however, and in January 1915 he was detailed as an interpreter officer. A few months later, he was sent to London to help David Lloyd George, then Minister of Munitions, to prepare for a meeting of English and French representatives. In 1917 and 1918, he served as the principal interpreter for talks between the British and French (Salomon 1993: 126). Mantoux was called back to France in 1918 by French Premier Clemenceau to serve as interpreter to the Supreme War Council in Versailles. He was a key interpreter throughout the Paris Peace talks. After the Council of Ten failed to make progress, and the smaller group of four began to meet, it soon became apparent that an interpreter would be necessary:

> Signor Orlando did not understand English, and President Wilson and Mr. Lloyd George had but an imperfect knowledge of French. M. Clemenceau was therefore the only one thoroughly familiar with both languages, and had to act as interpreter. This was found to be unsatisfactory; so Professor Mantoux was admitted [...].
>
> (Lansing 1921a: 61)

Mantoux had mastered both French and English and is said to have been blessed with an exceptional memory. He was able to translate the deliberations of the peace talks with utmost accuracy, as well as faithfulness to the individual rhetorical styles of the various speakers. As official interpreter among the Four, he interpreted from French to English and vice versa, "throwing himself into each speech with such verve that one might have thought he was himself begging for territory" (MacMillan 2002: 54).

After the peace talks ended, Mantoux was appointed Director of the Political Section of the League of Nations, a post which he held from 1920 to 1927. He then became director of a graduate institute of international studies (Institut Universitaire de Hautes Études Internationales) in Geneva (Mantoux 1992: xiii–xviii; Salomon 1993: 121–141).

Less scholarly or academic than either Camerlynck or Mantoux, the American journalist, essayist and diplomat Stephen Bonsal was nonetheless an equally important figure. He had studied in Germany and had traveled widely. He was a war correspondent for the *New York Herald* from the time of the Bulgarian-Serbian War of 1885 until 1907, and was then foreign correspondent for *The New York Times*. From 1893 to 1897, he held various diplomatic posts in Korea, Japan, and China. During World War I, Bonsal served in the American Expeditionary Forces (AEF) at the rank of lieutenant-colonel. He became an interpreter for the talks at the end of the war as a result of a favour he did, by chance, for President Wilson's adviser and representative in Europe. One day in Berlin, Bonsal had come upon a lost Colonel Edward House and had helped him find his way by interpreting for him. Later, when House was assigned to initiate Armistice negotiations, he specifically requested that Bonsal serve as an interpreter for President Wilson and himself (Bonsal 1946: 6–7).

Bonsal, too, kept diaries, which formed the basis for two books published many years later. *Unfinished Business* (1944), describing his experiences dur-

ing the Paris negotiations, published, interestingly, on the eve of the next peace
conference "to frame terms of reference with the same defeated enemy" (Bonsal
1946:8), earned him the Pulitzer Prize in 1945. He also published *Suitors and Suppliants* (1946), in which he recounts how the smaller nations came to plead their
cause. He cites a number of other wartime interpreters, such as a certain Colonel
Boyd, a "brilliant military secretary", who interpreted for General John J. Pershing
in his contacts with French officials (Bonsal 1946:9–10).

Described as "House's ubiquitous eyes and ears" (MacMillan 2002:306),
Bonsal was admired not only for his linguistic abilities, but also for his talents as
an adviser. In his introduction to *Unfinished Business*, Wilson Harris, also present
at the talks, reminds us how much House appreciated his interpreter:

> [Bonsal] knew the world from North to South and from East to West, and spoke
> many alien tongues. When delegates came from unfamiliar lands they were placed
> under his intelligent and sympathetic care. His interpretations and observations
> were invaluable and there was no man upon whom I leaned more heavily.
>
> (Bonsal 1944:7)

Harris also sheds light on Bonsal's method of interpreting. Bonsal's role, he says, was
to sit close to both Wilson and House and whisper to them "running translations of
all the speeches made in French". This was very demanding, he adds, since the President was against summarizing and insisted that "every sentence must be translated
in extenso as it fell from the speaker's lips – no simple achievement, for it meant in
effect taking in the next sentence while giving out the last" (Bonsal 1944:8).

Demanding as it was, this was not the most difficult task that awaited Bonsal
at the talks. At one point, he recalls, he was advised by Colonel House that he
was to interpret for the non-English-speaking members of the League of Nations
Commission:

> the great men of some seventeen nations assembled [...] for the first meeting of
> the Parliament of Man [...] did not want to lose the meaning of a single word that
> fell from the President's lips [...] the winged words and the message of the one
> whom they regarded as their Messiah. [...] I was catapulted to the other end of the
> table, where I was beset on all sides by inquiries [...]... in Cretan French [...]...
> in Roumanian French [...]... in Polish French [...]... in the French of Belgrade.
>
> (Bonsal 1944:29)

Bonsal felt he had no choice as a man in uniform but to follow orders, but in the
end survived the session. The difficulty of dealing with multiple languages was
reflected in the written text that emanated from the talks, the Covenant, or charter, of the League of Nations. In response to a comment on the poor quality of its
language, Bonsal notes that the Covenant was the "product of many minds and
not a few pens. Every sentence had to be translated into several languages and

then retranslated back a dozen times, and each time every word was subjected to [...] suspicious scrutiny [...]" (Bonsal 1944: 249).

General Vernon A. Walters (1917–2002), too, enjoyed a long career of public service. Born in New York, he lived and attended school in Europe from ages six to sixteen. He became proficient in several foreign languages, including French, Italian, Spanish, Russian and German, although family circumstances prevented him from completing high school. Walters enlisted in the army in 1941. He thought that his language skills would get him a job in intelligence, but they did not initially. Instead he ended up driving a truck. He was later sent to officer candidate school, then to Army Military Intelligence School, where he took classes in French, German, Italian, and Arabic. Shipped overseas to French Morocco, he was involved in prisoner-of-war interrogation, something he was well suited to because of his knowledge of languages.

In *The Mighty and the Meek*, reminiscences published not long before his death, Walters points out that, at each turn, he stood out for his linguistic skills. This led to his role as an interpreter and, eventually, to a career as a diplomat, too. "This is in many ways a name-dropping book," he says, "but I cannot help it for that is the way in which my life has been lived, because of my knowledge of a number of foreign languages" (Walters 2001: xi). He does indeed drop names: he lists, in fact, ten U.S. presidents from Roosevelt to George Bush Sr., several postwar leaders such as Churchill, De Gaulle, Castro, Thatcher, and Mitterand, popes from Pius XII to John Paul II, along with some of the "meek", a London taxicab driver, for example, and some of those he rescued through international diplomacy.

Not only did Walters translate for these people, he also kept careful records of their historic conversations. He made important – often clandestine – arrangements, provided advice on defence matters, and even carried out diplomatic missions in his own right. Known for his diplomatic skills, or more precisely a special brand of behind-the-scenes diplomacy, Walters also entered the memories of world leaders through his facility for languages. Henry Kissinger, with whom Walters worked during the Vietnam peace negotiations, refers in his memoirs, *White House Years*, to the "genius" of this "masterful interpreter". As he says, "His skill at translating was phenomenal; he was also a great actor, able to render not only the words but the intonation and attitude of the speaker" (Kissinger 1979: 279).

According to Walters, it was General Dwight Eisenhower, for whom he had interpreted when NATO was being set up, who thought he had gone as far as he could go as an interpreter and steered him toward other duties (Walters 2001: xxi). After serving as deputy director of the Central Intelligence Agency, Walters became a diplomat. He was appointed ambassador-at-large in 1981 by President Reagan and visited 108 countries. In 1985, he became U.S. ambassador to the UN, and from 1989 to 1991 served as ambassador to Germany where he witnessed the fall of the Wall and the reunification of Germany.

When he interpreted, Walters almost never took notes. In *Silent Missions*, he describes Richard Nixon's visit to Rome in 1970. During a lunch with President Saragat, Nixon delivered a very long toast without pausing for translation. When he had finished it, Walters translated it even though he had not taken notes. When asked by the President whether the speech had been too long, Walters replied, "No sir, but it shouldn't be any longer" (Walters 1978: 568–569).

Léon Dostert, mentioned earlier for his role at the Nuremberg Trials, was another illustrious army officer turned interpreter. Born in Longwy, France, he went to the United States in 1920. He was educated in Pasadena, California, and later attended the Georgetown School of Foreign Service. He taught French at Georgetown University from 1930 to 1942, and then entered the U.S. army as a major. During World War II, he served as French interpreter for Eisenhower. He was promoted colonel in 1945. After the war, Dostert became the chief interpreter of the Nuremberg Military Tribunal. He continued to perform his duties at the war trials until 1948, when he was appointed director of simultaneous interpretation at the United Nations. He also served as administrative counselor to the International Telecommunication Union in Geneva. Dostert was then appointed director of the Institute of Languages and Linguistics at Georgetown University. He was one of the first to have experimented with machine translation of scientific texts. He developed methods of teaching foreign languages to blind students, pioneered language laboratory instruction at Georgetown, set up language training centres in foreign countries and launched a literacy program in Turkey.

A. H. (Arthur Herbert) Birse (1889–1981), reports in his memoirs that, like many an interpreter before him, his introduction to high-level interpreting was "unexpected and fortuitous", his only qualification being his thorough knowledge of Russian (Birse 1967: 106). A British subject who was born in St. Petersburg and raised in Russia until the Revolution of 1917, Birse became a banker in Amsterdam and London. When war seemed imminent in 1939, he registered in the Officers' Reserve. Transferred from Cairo to join the newly created British Military Mission in Moscow in 1941, he was called upon, as a result of the illness of a Foreign Office interpreter, to serve as an interpreter for Winston Churchill at his first meeting with Stalin in 1942. He spent three years working as an interpreter for the Anglo-Soviet Commission, where V. N. Pavlov, the personal interpreter of Stalin and Molotov, was his counterpart (Birse 1967: 113). As Churchill's interpreter, Birse worked at many historic conferences, including Teheran, Yalta, San Francisco and Potsdam (Figure 24).[23] After the war, Birse returned to his former occupation as a banker while also teaching interpreting courses at Cambridge (Roland 1999: 160). Things

Russian continued to punctuate his quiet career in banking, however. In 1953, he became involved in the breaking of a Soviet spy ring in Australia, an incident known as the Petrov case (*Gale Biography in Context* 2011).

In the German army, interpreters held the rank of officers. This was not necessarily an advantage if the interpreter became a prisoner of war. Eugen Dollmann, the interpreter between Hitler and Mussolini, Himmler and Italian Chief of Police Bocchini, and diplomatic envoy of the SS in Italy (Dulles 1947:9), referred to earlier, took great pains to point out that he was made a member of the SS without having been consulted. "I woke up one morning, the morning of 9 November 1937, to find myself in the SS" (Dollmann 1967:76). Erwin Wächtler (1903–89), son of a French father and an Austrian mother, had worked as a conference interpreter during the 1930s. When he was called up, he was assigned interpreting duties with the rank of officer in the German Army. After the war he became known as the dean of Viennese conference interpreters and for some years taught translation at the University of Vienna.

Robert Brainerd Ekvall (1898–1978) served as an interpreter during World War II while assigned to Peking for the Marshall mission. Ekvall had been a missionary in Tibet from 1929 to 1934 and again from 1939 to 1941. Because of his familiarity with East Asian languages, including Tibetan and Chinese, Ekvall was later recalled to active duty in 1953 to act as an interpreter at the Panmunjom negotiations to end the Korean War. Since the English, Chinese and Korean languages were on an equal footing at the meetings, the Panmunjom negotiations were particularly hard to staff. At the time, Ekvall was busy working on a book on Lamaism, a form of Buddhism prevalent in Tibet. As he wrote in his memoirs, "The road to Panmunjom which I had followed, unaware of both road and destination, had meandered through the years. At road's end the powers-that-be designated me an interpreter [...]" (Ekvall 1960:45).

Interpreting diplomats – diplomatic interpreters

Interpreting and diplomacy have tended to overlap, as we have seen in some of the cases examined thus far. The further back we go in time, the more difficult it is to draw a clear line between the two. Since diplomatic relations were usually the responsibility of the upper classes, which had a certain level of education, there were long periods when a common language could be used (Greek, Latin, Italian, French or English). Latin, the written language of the Roman Empire and its successor the Holy Roman Empire, as well as the Roman Catholic Church, was "not unnaturally the written language of all early European diplomacy" (Satow 1979:38). Latin was also the language of conversation among diplomats throughout Western and Central Europe until the time of the Renaissance, when other languages came into use, particularly French. As the use of Latin in negotiations began to decline sometime before 1600, except in Eastern Europe, international negotiations through interpreters became common practice. The prestige of the French court of Louis XIV contributed to the acceptance of French as the principal language of European diplomacy (Roditi 1982:4–7), although by the nineteenth century it also became acceptable for the representative of a nation to use the official language of that nation (Satow 1979:40).

When Cardinal Thomas de Vio Cajetano (1469–1534) was sent by the Pope to promote the idea of a crusade against the Turks, he needed an interpreter for negotiating with Louis II, the young King of Hungary and Bohemia. Baron Támas (Thomas) Nádasdy (1498–1562), whom the Cardinal had encountered during Nádasdy's time as a student in Italy, was on hand for the task. As a result of the Cardinal's recommendation, Nádasdy became the King's confidential secretary, then his envoy to the Diet of Speyer. After the battle of Mohács, which represented the beginning of the Ottoman domination of Hungary (1526), he became the widowed Queen's envoy to King Ferdinand of Austria (Wurzbach 1869). Nádasdy promoted education; he founded a school and set up a printing press.

Power relations can affect the extent to which common languages are used. Holy Roman Emperor Leopold I of the House of Habsburg, for example, preferred to use Italian at his court rather than French because of a long-standing enmity with the kings of France. The Ottoman rulers, who posed a major threat to their neighbours for over two centuries, did not readily consent to using Latin or French with European monarchs such as the Habsburgs, with whom they had to negotiate peace repeatedly, or with Louis XIV, who sought their alliance. Both European courts endeavoured, with varying results, to train their own interpreters or *dragomans*. Prince Eugene of Savoy, a successful military commander who rose to the highest offices of state at the Vienna court, received Efendi Mustafa, the Special Envoy of the Ottoman Porte on June 11, 1731. Heinrich von Penkher, the Imperial Court's interpreter-secretary, was the star of the day in the glittering cortège through the city to the Prince's castle. The Prince spoke German, Efendi Mustafa Turkish, and Heinrich von Penkher is said to have interpreted "fluently" from one language to the other (Stradal 1982:82).

In 1754, Empress Maria Theresa founded the Oriental Academy, which became the Diplomatic Academy of Vienna. Considered the world's oldest school of international relations, it produced numerous Orientalists and interpreters for the imperial court over the years and exists to this day. The most famous was Joseph von Hammer-Purgstall (1774–1856), who became an official of the court and state archives and also held the title of court interpreter. His verse translations of the famous Persian poet Hafiz paved the way for other work in the field of Near

Eastern studies, although he is said to have covered so large a field that he lay himself open to the criticism of specialists.

A century earlier in France, Colbert had also provided for training of official interpreters.[24] From that time on, in a project that was to continue for three centuries, the French Court arranged to train French-born youngsters, "the language children", to become interpreters for Turkish, Arabic and Persian. The highest title for the graduates was "King's interpreter-secretary" (Degros 1984). These interpreters were assigned to ambassadors and consuls. In 1833, after a period of decline, the Constantinople school was closed and students from the Louis-le-Grand and Michelet schools in Paris were sent directly to the embassy in Constantinople. After 1880, the renowned School for Oriental Languages in Paris took over and replaced what was left of the original program.

Andrew Dickson White (1832–1918) is another example of a prominent public figure whose multiple occupations and accomplishments also included interpreting. White is known principally as the first president of Cornell University, a position he held for twenty years and which he regarded as his "crowning achievement" (White 1939: vii). He was also a distinguished historian and diplomat. Like some of the others we have just examined, White left an extensive autobiography in which he provides useful insights into the education and experience that paved the way for the interpreting and diplomatic roles he assumed on occasion.[25]

After completing studies at Yale, with an interest in history and politics in particular, White went abroad for three years. In Paris, he learned French not only by taking courses at the Sorbonne and at the Collège de France, but by living with the family of a French professor where not a word of English was spoken (White 1939: 31). It was at this time that he became acquainted with the American minister to Russia, Governor Seymour of Connecticut, who in 1854 invited him to be an *attaché* of the American Legation in St. Petersburg, where French would have still been the language of communication in diplomatic circles. It was the time of the Crimean War (1853–56), and during his six months in Russia, White accompanied the American Minister as an interpreter, not only at court, but in his discussions with Foreign Minister Karl Nesselrode and his successor Alexander Gorchakov, as well as with others in power at the time. As he notes in his autobiography, this provided him with an opportunity to make his "historical studies more real" by observing the men who were making history (1939: 34).

Afterward he enrolled at the University of Berlin, and learned the German language, again by immersion, by living with the family of a very scholarly professor (White 1939: 35). He continued to study history, as well as art and literature, and continued his travels through Austria to Italy. He returned to the United States to occupy roles in academia, but remained active in American political life at the same time. In the course of his career, he encountered all American presidents from Buchanan to Taft, notable European kings and statesmen, authors, scientists, and men of letters (White 1939: xi–xii). During his presidential years, he took up opportunities to avoid becoming "a mere administrative machine". He was assigned such public duties as commissioner to Santo Domingo, minister plenipotentiary in Berlin, and commissioner at the Paris Exposition – positions that enabled him to draw on his knowledge and linguistic abilities and, at the same time, provided material for his university lectures (White 1939: 219). At the conclusion of his term as university president, he occupied a series of diplomatic posts: minister to Russia in 1892; ambassador to Germany in 1897; and head of the U.S. delegation to the first Hague Peace Conference, held in 1899.[26]

At the Hague Peace Conferences, French was still the only official language and the U.S. delegations to the conferences included members who didn't know the language. Ellery C. Stowell (1875–1958) joined the delegation at the second conference. A young American working on his PhD in international law at the University of Paris, Stowell proved most useful, since he spoke Russian and French in addition to his native English (Davis 1975: 168). Stowell surfaced again in 1908 at the London Naval Conference, where he was a secretary with the U.S. delegation, sitting, ready to translate, behind Rear Admiral Charles H. Stockton and Professor George Grafton Wilson, who did not understand French well (Davis 1975: 309). He was later an associate professor of international law at Columbia University, and a widely known writer and speaker on U.S. foreign relations. He resigned from his position at Columbia when criticized for taking a stand in favour of war, resenting what he considered to be an attempt to interfere with his "academic freedom" (*The New York Times* 1918).

Occasionally, high-ranking officials would serve as interpreters. Baron Sidney Sonnino (1847–1922) was born in Italy to a Welsh mother and an Italian father of Jewish heritage, who converted to Anglicanism. He was a newspaperman and then held several government positions, including Prime Minister. As the Italian Minister of Foreign Affairs, he assisted President Vittorio Orlando at the Paris Peace Conference (Lansing 1921a: 106). Hans Luther (1879–1962), then Chancellor of the Weimar Republic, interpreted for confidential talks between Gustav Stresemann and Aristide Briand, the foreign ministers of Germany and France, respectively, held at Ascona, Switzerland.[27] However, this crossover between diplomatic and interpreting duties can have its disadvantages, as Vernon Walters reminds us in an anecdote dating back to 1946:

> General (George) Marshall arrived and had with him a rather senior ambassador
> who was to serve as his interpreter. As he went around calling on the various for-
> eign ministers, this ambassador, who knew many of the ministers from previous
> meetings, became involved in lively conversation with them. General Marshall
> did not like this and I was soon commandeered as General Marshall's interpreter.
>
> (Walters 1978: 144)

The career of Ernest Mason Satow (1843–1929), whose writing has already been
referenced, is another illustration of the close links between interpreting and diplomacy. In his articles on Satow, Brian Harris (1992 and 2003) offers an explanation for why interpreters have the potential to become diplomats. Linguists,
particularly those with a command of "problematic" languages (far removed
from their own culture and hence more difficult to master), are at an advantage
in diplomacy. It is not merely a question of language itself, but an issue of "the
intimacy that language allows with the peoples and cultures" (Harris 1992: 13).
As examples of gifted interpreters who have risen to important diplomatic posts,
Harris mentions Jean-Michel Venture de Paradis, the eighteenth-century French
interprète du Roy mentioned above, and two important diplomatic protagonists
in Japan of the 1860s: Sir Harry Smith Parkes (1828–85), named Her Majesty's
Envoy Extraordinary and Minister Plenipotentiary and Consul-General in Japan
after considerable service in China, and Léon Roches (1809–1902), Consul General of France in Edo, Japan,[28] who had previously served in North Africa. Satow
followed in this tradition (Harris 1992: 13).

Born in England, Ernest Mason Satow was the son of a Swedish merchant
and an English woman. He first became interested in Asia as a student at University College, London. In 1861, he won first place in a competition for a student-
interpretership in the Far East. After an initial stay in Peking, where he studied
Chinese, Satow went to Japan. Less than ten years after the opening up of the country by Commodore Perry, this was a time when foreign residents were still in constant physical danger.[29]

When Satow arrived in Japan, the incumbent linguist at the British legation
was still an English-Dutch interpreter. The interpreters worked in relay to convey messages to their Japanese interlocutors. In early 1865, Satow was promoted
from student-interpreter to interpreter. By the end of 1866, he was given a further promotion and transferred from the Yokohama consulate to the legation
at Edo (Harris 1992: 7). Satow worked both as an interpreter and translator. He
was sent on further assignments to Siam (1884), Uruguay (1888) and Morocco
(1893). When he returned to the Far East, it was to occupy the position of Minister and Head of Mission: in Edo, which had become Tokyo by then, from 1895
to 1900, and in Peking from 1900 to 1906. In 1907, he represented Britain at the
Second Hague Peace Conference and subsequently served for a six-year term as

British member of the Court of Arbitration. He wrote a number of studies on international law and history. He is most renowned for his *Guide to Diplomatic Practice*, originally published in 1917. Considered of such value that it has been revised and reprinted several times, Satow's *Guide* is still used as a textbook for budding diplomats.

Interpreting is a most human activity, involving a direct, immediate and highly personal act of mediation between individuals, who are nonetheless subjected to the political imperatives of the situation they occupy in the spaces between cultures. The history of interpretation, therefore, is one that is problematic, one in which the ambiguities – not the least of which are those that derive from the inadequacy of written records to take full account of the act of interpreting – are bound up in a web of conflicting ideologies, divided loyalties and relations of power.

Existing written and oral accounts, imperfect as they are, enable us to trace elements of a history of interpreters. Many questions arise but the answers remain incomplete, particularly for those of the more distant past. However, interpretation, like translation, has come into its own since the later twentieth century. Enhanced professional status and the creation of professional interpreters' associations from the 1950s onward have led to the formulation of ethical standards and professional guidelines. Training programs, professional associations, research and publications, and a move toward writing its own history have all advanced the art and science of interpreting. Theoretical approaches to translation studies in general, formulated over the past two to three decades – the cultural turn, the postcolonial turn, the "power" turn and others – have contributed to a reframing and deeper understanding of some of the issues and complexities in the field of interpreting.

Notes

1. The Paris Peace Conference was convened in January 1919 to resolve matters arising from World War I. The Supreme Council, having conducted the war, took responsibility for the peace talks. Commonly called the Council of Ten, it included the five principal Allied and Associated Powers: France, the U.S., Great Britain and Italy, which were represented by their heads of state, Georges Clemenceau, Woodrow Wilson, David Lloyd George and Vittorio Orlando, respectively, accompanied by their secretaries or ministers of foreign affairs, and Japan, which had two delegates of ambassadorial rank (Lansing 1921b: 213). The Japanese delegation, unlike those of the other great powers, was not headed by a prime minister or president (MacMillan 2002: 307).

2. The Axis refers to the alliance between Nazi Germany and Fascist Italy; the name was given by Mussolini in 1936 to the German-Italian friendship agreement signed by Count Galeazzo Ciano and Adolf Hitler. Dollmann recounts his career in a work entitled *Dolmetscher der Diktatoren* (Bayreuth: Hestia-Verlag, 1963). The work was published in French as *J'étais interprète de Hitler et de Mussolini* (Paris: Éditions France-Empire, 1965) and in English as *The Interpreter,*

Memoirs of Doktor Eugen Dollmann (London: Hutchinson & Co., 1967). This episode is reported in the original German version only; like many others, it was not included in the English translation.

3. Thomas Edward Lawrence (1888–1935), known as Lawrence of Arabia, was an English military officer, adventurer, writer and translator. He studied archaeology, architecture and history at Oxford. He also learned Arabic and worked in the Middle East as an archaeologist after graduating. In addition to *Seven Pillars of Wisdom*, an autobiographical account of his exploits in the Arab Revolt of 1916–18, he published a translation of the *Odyssey* in 1932 under the assumed name of T. E. Shaw. In the translator's note, he points out that his was the twenty-eighth English version of the Homerian classic. J. L. Borges, as we have seen in Chapter 3, was interested in Lawrence and in 1936 wrote an article about his translation of the *Odyssey*.

4. The Conference of San Remo took place in April 1920; French, British and Italian heads of state met to discuss the implementation of the Treaty of Versailles, which had been negotiated at the Paris Peace Conference.

5. For more information on interpreters at the Nuremberg trials, see Baigorri Jalón 2004, Chapter 5.

6. In 1945, representatives of 50 countries met in San Francisco to draw up the United Nations Charter. Original membership was 51 nations, a number that has increased to 193 as of 2011.

7. English and French were originally established as working languages at the UN. Later, Arabic, Chinese, Russian and Spanish were added as working languages in the General Assembly and in the Economic and Social Council. Arabic, Chinese, English, French, Russian and Spanish are the working languages of the Security Council (Official web site of the UN: http://www.un.org/en/aboutun/languages.shtml, accessed October 2011).

8. Information on the establishment of interpreting schools is taken from the 1985 edition of the *Guide des Établissements proposant des cours en interprétation de conférence*, published by the Geneva-based International Association of Conference Interpreters (AIIC, Association Internationale des Interprètes de Conférence). AIIC listed twenty-six schools in its November 1993 publication. By 2004, the number of schools had increased to 178. This number is expected to change once the results from a 2011 survey have been compiled (www.aiic.net/schools). At last count, AIIC had 2,965 individual professional conference interpreter members in 101 countries, representing 51 languages (www.aiic.net/database/, accessed September 2011).

9. As of December 2010, the European Union had 23 official and working languages (http://ec.europa.eu/education/languages/languages-of-europe/doc135_en.htm, accessed September 2011).

10. Chutzpit was the interpreter to Rabban Gamaliel II, head of the talmudic academy at Yavne. He died along with the High Priest and Rabbi Akiba, one of the famous scholars of the time, during Emperor Hadrian's persecutions in the second century.

11. The work originally entitled *The General History of the Things of New Spain* is commonly referred to as the "Florentine Codex" because the best manuscript has been preserved in archives in Florence. A 1978 edition provides a modern English translation (Sahagún 1978).

12. The word *drugement* entered the French language via Arabic in the twelfth century and later became *truchement*. The same word yielded *dragoman*, which came to refer more specifically to interpreters of the Near East (Balliu 2005). See also references to *turgeman* in Chapter 6, specifically p. 182, note 7.

13. Jean de Léry journeyed to Brazil in 1556–58, but he did not publish the first edition of the *History* until 1578; four other editions appeared during his lifetime (1580, 1594, 1599 and 1611). A 1972 version was edited by Michel Contat, who modernized the spelling; another French version was published in 1975, edited and annotated by Jean-Claude Morisot; and the most recent French edition is from 1995. The English edition referred to in this chapter is a 1990 translation by Janet Whatley.

14. See also Chapter 3.

15. History "from below", subaltern studies and postcolonial studies, among other approaches, have shed new light on migrant and hybrid peoples. On interpreters, specifically, see Karttunen (1994), Szasz (1994), Cronin (2002) and Luca (1999 and 2004).

16. Luca's article (1999) focuses on the conquest of La Florida. He covers the topic of go-betweens more broadly in an as-yet unpublished Ph.D. dissertation (2004).

17. Malinalli Tenépal was her original name. She was christened Marina and given the title *Doña* by the Spaniards out of respect for her nobility, although none of Cortés's men – or even he for that matter – was referred to as *Don*. The Indians gave her the name *Malintzin*, derived from Marina (the sound *r* being unknown to the Mexicans, who imitated it with *l*) and the suffix *-tzin*, signifying rank or nobility. She enjoyed the unique distinction of having her own name used also for her master, since the Indians began to refer to Cortés himself by the name Malintzin, which the Spaniards turned into *Malinche* (Madariaga 1942: 151–152; Del Castillo 1977: 146n).

18. Some doubt has been raised in other quarters about whether the inscriptions even refer to interpreting at all (Vermeer 1992, 1: 64–65).

19. Jean, Sire de Joinville (c.1224–1317), who accompanied Saint Louis on the Seventh Crusade (1248–54), was a chronicler of medieval France. He is known for his biography of King Louis, *La Vie de Saint Louis*, completed in 1309.

20. According to an obituary published in *Time Magazine*, Feburary 25, 1929, he was born in "French Flanders of bourgeois parents" (http://www.time.com/time/magazine/article/0,9171,880475,00.html, accessed September 2011).

21. Mantoux had published an unannotated version of the transcripts in two volumes in 1955. The 1992 English-language edition provides a translation of these records with annotation and additional documentation used in discussions by the Four. The Council of Four had originally decided not to keep records, to the consternation of the British secretary to the Conference, Sir Maurice Hankey. Later on, to facilitate the proceedings, Hankey began to take notes once again. Every day, meanwhile, Mantoux would dictate his recollections of the previous day's meetings in a confidential memo to Clemenceau, based on the handwritten notes he had taken in the course of his interpreting work. He kept a copy of the transcripts for himself, which he left behind when the Germans entered Paris in 1940, but it survived the war and was the basis for this subsequent publication (MacMillan 2002: 274).

22. First published in 1927 and reissued several times, it was published in English as *The industrial revolution in the eighteenth century: an outline of the beginnings of the modern factory system in England*, trans. Marjorie Vernon and ed. T. S. Ashton (New York: Macmillan, 1961). It was released once more as recently as 2005 by Routledge.

23. The Teheran Conference was a meeting of The Big Three Allied leaders – Winston Churchill (Great Britain), Franklin D. Roosevelt (United States) and Joseph Stalin (U.S.S.R.) – held November 8–December 1, 1943. The Big Three met again in the Crimean city of Yalta, February 4–11, 1945, to plan the final months of World War II. The San Francisco conference opened April 25, 1945 to prepare the charter for the United Nations. The Potsdam Conference, July 17–August 2, 1945, was the final Allied summit meeting of World War II.

24. According to Colbert's decree of 1669, dragomans could no longer be foreigners, but had to be French by birth. Two schools were to be opened for training these interpreters, one in Constantinople and the other at a Capuchin monastery in Smyrna. The Smyrna school failed, but the Constantinople school became well known. However, it soon became apparent that students in Constantinople needed to be sent to Paris, and in 1721, ten *"enfants de langues"* were sent to study at the Jesuit *Collège Louis-le-Grand*.

25. Andrew Dickson White's *Autobiography*, published in 1905, was in two volumes, 1,200 pages. In 1939, a condensed version was published, focusing mainly on his contributions to Cornell University: *Selected Chapters from the Autobiography of Andrew D. White*. Ithaca, N.Y.: Cornell University Press, with an introduction by F. C. Prescott.

26. The Hague conferences were held in 1899 and 1907, called by the Tsar of Russia, Nicholas II, for the purpose of promoting disarmament. The most important outcome of the conference was the establishment of the Hague Tribunal, which ultimately became the International Court of Justice.

27. In 1925, Stresemann and Briand negotiated the Locarno Pact, which was intended to stabilize relations in Europe. It was at this meeting that Briand first communicated to a German his dream of European reconciliation (Kelen 1963:155). The following year they received the Nobel Peace Prize for their efforts.

28. Edo, which literally means "estuary", also Romanized as Yedo or Yeddo, is the former name of Tokyo, and was the seat of power for the shogunate that ruled Japan from 1603 to 1868. The name was changed to Tokyo when the city became the imperial capital in 1868.

29. After 1639, the Japanese had pursued a policy of almost total isolation from the outside world. Nagasaki, where the Chinese and Dutch were allowed to trade, was the only point of contact with foreigners. U.S. Commodore Matthew Perry is credited with the "opening" of Japan in 1854, when he led a naval mission to Japan and set in motion a process by which Western ideas and commerce were gradually accepted. At the time of Satow's arrival, a violent struggle was still going on between the Shogun, or chief of government, and the Emperor.

Figure 19. Nuremberg Trials

Figure 20. St. Jerome

Description of illustrations

1. Double Egyptian interpreter (c.1350 BCE)

This image evokes a theme that survives to this day: interpreters and translators, in general, are perceived as "double agents", with a dual allegiance – to two masters and two cultures. This ambiguity and negotiation across cultural spaces is rich in consequences and forms the background for much of the portraits of the translators and interpreters in this book.

This scene is part of a bas-relief carved on the tomb of Horemheb, who succeeded Tutankhamen as Pharaoh. Horemheb is shown, while still viceroy to Tutankhamen, receiving Syrian and Libyan emissaries seeking assistance to relieve a famine. The social status of the interpreter is indicated by his size in relation to Horemheb. At left, the interpreter listens to the entreaties of the visitors, who are in a position of supplication to the viceroy. The right-hand image shows the interpreter relaying the visitors' message to Horemheb.

Source: Rijksmuseum voor de Oudheid, Leiden; courtesy of Ingrid Kurz.

2. Mesrop Mashtots (360–441)

The Armenian people were Christianized at an early stage of the religion. However, paganism prevailed in some areas and Mesrop, who had already founded a monastery to train priests, found evangelizing difficult without materials that would be accessible to the populace. Since no existing alphabet reproduced the sounds of their language, he and his assistants produced a new one. This painting depicts Mesrop presenting the Armenian alphabet at the court of King Vramshapuh. The presence of an angel presages his elevation to sainthood.

Source: Used with permission, courtesy of Gevork Nazaryan.
http://www.armenianhighland.com/images/nkarner/nkar_4488.jpg.

3. St. Cyril (c.827–69) and St. Methodius (c.815–85)

Cyril and Methodius were dispatched to Moravia to evangelize the inhabitants at the urging of their Christian prince, who wanted his people to have access to the Gospels in their own language. Like others faced with the difficulty of proselytizing among unlettered populations, the brothers were inventive. In this painting, the saints present their Glagolitic alphabet to the royal court. A version of this alphabet, refined by a disciple, Clement of Ohrid, became the Cyrillic used today in Russia and other nations of eastern Europe.

Source: Painting "Saints Cyril and Methodius" by Zahari Zograf (1810–53).
http://en.wikipedia.org/wiki/File:Cyril-methodius-small.jpg.

4. Jacques Amyot (1513–93)

A prelate who became Bishop of Auxerre, Amyot was known as "Prince of Translators" and "Plutarch of France". He was one of the first humanists to translate from the original Greek rather than Latin translations. He became tutor and chaplain to the dukes of Orléans and Angoulême, who became Kings Charles IX and Henri III, respectively. This statue stands in front of the city hall in his hometown of Melun, southwest of Paris.

Source: Publicly available photographs of the statue; Delisle and Lafond (2012).*

5. William Caxton (c.1422–91)

The illustration is a presumed portrait of Caxton, the translator who introduced printing to England. He was for some years an international trader in Europe and he learned the printing trade in Cologne. He moved to Bruges in 1474, taking with him a printing press and sets of English characters. There he printed the first English book: *The Recuyell of the Historyes of Troye,* by Raoul Lefèvre, which Caxton himself had translated from French. He later moved to England, setting up his shop near Westminster Abbey.

Source: *Civilisations, peuples et mondes.* Paris: Éditions Lidis, 1966. Vol. 4, p. 308; courtesy of Jean Delisle.

6. Joost van den Vondel (1587–1679)

A Dutch poet, dramatist and translator, Vondel is known for his biblically-inspired lyrical compositions, satires and religious tragedies. During his translation career of fifty years, his works included versions made from French, Italian, Latin and Greek originals. An imposing monument stands in the Vondelpark named for him in Amsterdam. This portrait is by the Dutch Golden Age artist Govert Flinck (1615–1660); Vondel was close to him and wrote poems to accompany his paintings.

Source: Rijksmuseum Amsterdam. Used with permission.

7. Okot p'Bitek (1931–82)

This Ugandan writer, poet and translator returned to his homeland after completing his studies in law and anthropology in England and took up a teaching position at Makarere University. Subsequently, he taught at the University of Nairobi in Kenya. He won considerable acclaim for his novel, *Lak Tar.* Over his career, he translated numerous African works into European languages and vice-versa, and is considered one of the literary pioneers of his country.

Source: East African Literature Bureau, Nairobi.

8. Matteo Ricci (1552–1610)

The first Jesuit missionary to China in 1582, Ricci initiated the custom of translating works of Western science as well as Christian texts to facilitate relations with the Chinese. The missionaries were often assisted by Chinese collaborators such as Xu Guangqi, a scientist and prime minister during the last years of the Ming dynasty, who assisted Ricci when he translated Euclid's *Elements* in 1607. Ricci worked with Li Zhizao, another scientist and government official, when he translated the *Astrolabium* by German Jesuit and mathematician Christophorus Clavius. This portrait of Ricci in a scholar's robe was painted in 1610 by the Chinese brother Emmanuel Pereira (born Yu Wen-hui) and is now kept in a church in Rome.

Source: Courtesy of the Chiesa del Gesù de Roma. http://www.chiesadelgesu.org/documenti/120212_Clavius_RatioStudiorum_ViaLibrorum_it.pdf.

9.   Yesudas Ramachandra (1821–80)

A mathematician, scientist and journalist, Ramachandra translated Western scientific works into Urdu for use as textbooks at Old Delhi College, his alma mater. His treatise on mathematics was considered an outstanding text in India and also in Europe. Regarded as one of the most brilliant intellectuals at Old Delhi College, he later held various positions in the Ministry of Education in Delhi and the Punjab.

Source: S.R. Kidwai, New Delhi.

10.   Doña Marina (c.1501–50)

Also known as La Malinche, she was among twenty young women presented to the Spaniard Hernán Cortés on his arrival in Mexico. Fluent in at least two major native languages, she is said to have quickly mastered Castilian. As an interpreter, she was indispensable, informing Cortés of threats, tribal rivalries and ways to win over suspicious tribes. This illustration, showing Cortés and Marina meeting the Emperor Moctezuma in Tenochtitlan in 1519, emphasizes her importance to Cortés's mission, showing her to be larger than he is. Until recently, however, she was nearly forgotten in her homeland: only a single extinct volcano bears her name.

Source: *Lienzo de Tlaxcala* (1585). Courtesy of The Bancroft Library, University of California, Berkeley.

11.   Barbara Godard (1941–2010)

Educated in Canada and France, Godard enjoyed a sterling interdisciplinary career of nearly 40 years at York University, Toronto. A prolific and gregarious scholar, she published eight books, 80 book chapters and 115 articles in several fields, including literature in both English and French, social and political thought, and women's studies. She translated major Quebec feminist writers, including Nicole Brossard, Yolande Villemaire and Louky Bersianik, and introduced pioneering perspectives to translation studies.

Source: Photo by James Gillespie. Used with permission.
http://pi.library.yorku.ca/dspace/handle/10315/2911.

12.   Xuan Zang (c.600–64)

In 645, the Chinese monk Xuan Zang returned from a pilgrimage to India with hundreds of Buddhist documents written in Sanskrit. He spent the remaining twenty years of his life in the then-capital, Chang'an (modern Xi'an), translating them into Chinese. These translations contributed greatly to the flowering of Buddhism as one of the major religions of China.

Source: Brochure of the city of Xi'an.

13.   William Tyndale (1494–1536)

This image shows Tyndale with his New Testament, translated from the original Greek. The first Bible printed in English, its small size was meant to suit common folk and to make it easily smuggled into England, where it was forbidden. Any person caught with it was excommunicated and the translator himself was condemned to burn at the stake. Only one copy of his Bible survives, in the British Library. However, Bible translations in English for the next four hundred years relied heavily on Tyndale's striking idiom and writing style.

Source: Courtesy of the Bible Society Library, Cambridge University Library.

14. King Alfonso X (1221–84)

The Spanish King of Castile and Leon from 1252 to 1284, Alfonso was more of a scholar than a statesman, largely responsible for the translation activity that made thirteenth-century Toledo and other parts of Spain so well known. He was deeply religious but also commissioned scholars to translate works of science from Arabic to Castilian and had them compile a code of law and write a history of Spain. A writer, poet and astronomer, known as Alfonso the Wise, he is shown here with translators / scholars at his court. Also considered the founder of the Castilian language, he commissioned a set of texts in the vernacular that came to be known as the *Book of the King*.

Source: Miniature from the thirteenth-century "Cantigas de Santa Maria" (vellum), Biblioteca Monasterio del Escorial, Madrid. Used with the permission of Bridgeman Art Library International.

15. Yan Fu (1854–1921)

Despite coming from a poor family in the port city of Fuzhou, Yan Fu attended naval college and travelled abroad for studies, during which he learned English. When posted to England, he immersed himself in philosophical and scientific texts. Returning to China, he undertook the translation of numerous English works into Chinese. He held a succession of posts in academe and the military, including supervising several translation bureaus and being the first president of what is now Beijing University. He remains an inspiration to Chinese translators of today, who debate the ideas set out in the preface to his translation of Thomas H. Huxley's *Evolution and Ethics*.

Source: Courtesy of Tony Ryan; from his personal website, http://www.tonyinchina.com/china5/tianjin/tianjin.html.

16. Nicolas Oresme (c.1320–82)

This image depicts Oresme presenting his translation of Aristotle's *Ethics* to King Charles V (Charles the Wise) of France. A theologian and scholar, he was acquainted with Greek, a rarity in his time. He had been the private tutor of Charles V, whose patronage assisted Oresme to legitimize vernacular translation. He also translated treatises on physics and astronomy by Aristotle and Ptolemy and is credited with having enriched the French language.

Source: Photo of a painting, courtesy of the *Bibliothèque Nationale de France*.

17. Robert Estienne (1503–59)

Lexicographer, translator and printer, Estienne became known as the "Prince of Typographers". When he wrote and published the *Dictionnaire françois-latin* in 1539, it was the first time the word *"dictionnaire"* (dictionary) was used in the title of a French work of this kind. He also used the Italianism *"traduire"*, introducing it into French. As a translator, he produced vernacular versions of the *Bible* (1551) and the *Psalms* (1552).

Source: *L'Art du livre à l'Imprimerie nationale*. Paris: Imprimerie nationale, 1973; courtesy of Jean Delisle.

18. Hieroglyph depicting interpreting (c.3000 BCE)

This cartouche, read from top to bottom and left to right, shows a seated man with outstretched forearm and a fisherman's boat with net (Gardiner 1969). The cartouche is double because it signifies the interpreter receiving a message (top) in a foreign tongue and then repeating it (bottom) in another language.

Source: Delisle and Lafond (2012); image provided by Henri Van Hoof, Belgium.

19. Nuremberg Trials (1945–46)

The large-scale multilingual simultaneous interpreting used at the War Crimes Trial at the end of World War II was made possible by improvements in technology. The victorious Allies, the United States, Great Britain, France and the U.S.S.R., prosecuted surviving German Nazi leaders. The languages of the tribunal were English, French, Russian and German. The technical system was perfected by Antoine (Tony) Pilon, a Canadian bomber pilot and audio engineer. Interpreters were recruited from the School of Translation and Interpretation at the University of Geneva and from among people who had acquired their proficiency in languages by other means.

Source: Delisle and Lafond (2012).

20. St. Jerome (c.347–420)

One of the best known translators of all time, St. Jerome has come to be regarded as the patron saint of translators. Since 1992, FIT's International Translation Day has coincided with St. Jerome's feast day, September 30. From the fourteenth to the seventeenth centuries, he was one of the Christian saints who most frequently inspired painters and artists. Shown in this painting at work in his study, Jerome is credited with being the first to have translated the Old Testament into Latin directly from the original Hebrew. His version, The Vulgate, served the Western Church as its sacred text for over a thousand years. Though he was born a Christian in Dalmatia and served as a papal secretary and adviser, only later in life did he take up an ascetic life in Bethlehem, becoming a prodigious and prolific scholar and translator.

Source: "St. Jerome in his study", painting by Domenico Ghirlandaio. Courtesy of the Chiesa di Ognissanti, Florence, which holds the painting under the auspices of the Ministry of the Interior (Fondo Edificio di Culto).

21. The Venerable Bede (c.673–735)

It has been speculated that Bede came from a well-to-do family that sent him at age seven to be educated in a monastery. He became a leading ecclesiastic and one of the most prolific writers of his time, famous for his *Historia ecclesiastica gentis Anglorum* (*Ecclesiastical History of the English People*) and other works of Latin scholarship. His disciple Cuthbert has depicted him as a champion of the English vernacular. Cuthbert's description of Bede on his deathbed dictating St. John's Gospel into English is depicted in this 1902 painting by J. D. Penrose.

Source: "The Venerable Bede Translates John", painting by J. D. Penrose. In *An Outline of Christianity: The Story of Our Civilization*. New York: Bethlehem Publishers, 1926. vol. 2, p. 204. Courtesy of The Penrose Collection, Sussex, England.

22. Great Wild Goose Pagoda

This pagoda, whose title is apparently taken from a namesake in India, was built for the Chinese monk Xuan Zang by emperor Tai Zong in Chang'an (present-day Xi'an). Here the monk and his assistants spent decades translating Buddhist texts, which he had brought back from India, from Sanskrit into Chinese. The Indian temple was named Wild Goose Pagoda because it was built on the site where a goose fell from the sky in answer to the prayers of starving monks. In gratitude, the monks buried the goose rather than eat it and built their temple (Kaplan et al. 1986:600).

Source: Photo by Lindsay Crysler, 1995.

23. Constance Garnett (1861–1946)

Thanks to Garnett, Anglo-Saxon readers became familiar with many of the greatest works of Russian literature of her time. She translated the novels of Dostoyevsky and Turgenev, the complete works of Gogol, as well as titles by Tolstoy, Chekhov and other Russian writers. During the first half of the 20th century, her translations gave a wide audience to the dissident voices of novelists, poets and dramatists who opposed the institution of the Soviet Communist regime.

Source: Richard Garnett. *Constance Garnett: A Heroic Life*. London: Sinclair-Stevenson, 1991.

24. A. H. Birse (1889–1981)

A British subject born in St. Petersburg, A. H. (Arthur Herbert) Birse lived in Russia for more than 20 years, becoming fluent in the language. He joined the military at the outbreak of the Second World War and was pressed into service as Churchill's interpreter in 1942. He continued in that role throughout the war and in the immediate post-war period. When he left the military, he returned to his former career of banker in London while also teaching interpreting courses at the University of Cambridge. He is shown here flanked by British leader Winston Churchill and Russia's Joseph Stalin in July 1945.

Source: A. H. Birse, *Memoirs of an Interpreter*. London: Michael Joseph, 1967.

*   I am indebted to Jean Delisle for having initiated the collection of images of translators and interpreters, now forming a vast archive available on his history of translation DVD (Delisle and Lafond 2012), and for having drawn my attention to several of the illustrations in this edition.

Contributors, translators and proofreaders

This book is the result of the efforts of translation historians from twenty countries, who participated as the principal authors and coordinators of the nine chapters, or as contributing authors, translators or proofreaders. The list below includes those who worked on the original edition, along with others who have lent their support to the second edition, and sets out the place of residence and institutional affiliation at the time the contribution was made.

Chapter authors and coordinators

Jean-Claude Boulanger, Université Laval, Québec, Canada (Chapter 8)
Margareta Bowen, Georgetown University, Washington, U.S.A. (Chapter 9)
Jean Delisle, University of Ottawa, Canada (Chapter 1)
Yves Gambier, University of Turku, Finland (Chapter 7)
André Lefevere, University of Texas at Austin, U.S.A. (Chapter 5)
Charles Atangana Nama, University of Buea, Cameroon (Chapter 2)
Myriam Salama-Carr, University of Salford, United Kingdom (Chapter 4)
Sherry Simon, Concordia University, Montreal, Canada (Chapter 6)
Judith Woodsworth, Concordia University, Montreal, Canada (Chapter 3)

Contributing authors

Anneliese Abramowski, Humboldt-Universität, Berlin, Germany (Chapter 2)
Lourdes Arencibia Rodriguez, professor and interpreter, Havana, Cuba (Chapter 5)
Michel Ballard, Université d'Artois, France (Chapter 5)
Michel Bastiaensen, Inst. Cooremans / Univ. libre de Bruxelles, Belgium (Chapter 7)
Ronald H. Bathgate, translator and writer, The Hague, The Netherlands (Chapter 4)
David Bowen, Georgetown University, Washington, U.S.A. (Chapter 9)
Robert Bratcher, United Bible Societies, Chapel Hill, U.S.A. (Chapter 6)
Amila Butorovic, Haverford College, Haverford, U.S.A. (Chapter 6)
Pierre Cloutier, professional translator, Montreal, Canada (Chapter 1)
Michael Cronin, Dublin City University, Ireland (Chapter 3)
Jean Delisle, University of Ottawa, Canada (Chapter 4)
John Denton, University of Florence, Italy (Chapter 7)
Lieven D'hulst, Université d'Anvers, Belgium (Chapters 3 & 7)
Bill Findlay, literary translator, Glasgow, Scotland (Chapter 3)
Clara Foz, University of Ottawa, Canada (Chapters 4 & 5)
Ana Gargatagli, Universitat Autònoma de Barcelona, Spain (Chapter 3)
Jean-Marc Gouanvic, Concordia University, Montreal, Canada (Chapter 7)
Theo Hermans, University College, London, United Kingdom (Chapter 3)
Paul A. Horguelin, Université de Montréal, Canada (Chapter 2)
Francine Kaufmann, Bar-Ilan University, Ramat Gan, Israel (Chapters 6 & 9)

Achmed A.W. Khammas, translator, Berlin, Germany (Chapter 6)
Ingrid Kurz, University of Vienna, Austria (Chapter 9)
Charles Atangana Nama, University of Buea, Cameroon (Chapter 3)
Li Nanqiu, University of Science and Technology, Hefei, China (Chapter 4)
Alexis Nouss, Université de Montréal, Canada (Chapter 7)
Moses Nunyi Nintai, University of Buea, Cameroon (Chapter 2
Domenico Pezzini, University of Verona, Italy (Chapter 6)
Joëlle Prungnaud, Université de Lille, France (Chapter 7)
Anthony Pym, Universitat Rovira i Virgili, Spain (Chapters 5 & 7)
Shantha Ramakrishna, Jawaharlal Nehru University, New Delhi, India (Chapter 4)
Margaret Rumbold, Melbourne, Australia (Chapter 7)
Arvind Sharma, McGill University, Montreal, Canada (Chapter 6)
Sherry Simon, Concordia University, Montreal, Canada (Chapter 5)
D. J. M. Soulas de Russel, Fachhochschule Nürtingen, Germany (Chapter 5)
George Talbot, University of Hull, England (Chapter 5)
Colette Touitou-Benitah, Bar-Ilan University, Ramat Gan, Israel (Chapter 5)
Henri Van Hoof, professor and professional translator, Waterloo, Belgium
     (Chapter 8, 1995 edition)
Rachel Weissbrod, The Open University of Israel, Tel Aviv, Israel (Chapter 2)
Lars Wollin, University of Uppsala, Sweden (Chapters 2 & 4)
Judith Woodsworth, Concordia University, Montreal, Canada (Chapters 2, 6 & 9)
Xu Shi Gu, Commercial Press, Beijing, China (Chapter 7)

Translators

Marie-José Bissonnette, Montreal, Canada (Chapter 9)
Michael Carr, Prestwick, United Kingdom (Chapter 4)
Glenn Clavier, Montreal, Canada (appendix)
Enrico Caouette, Montreal, Canada (Chapter 8)
Patrick Gionet, Montreal, Canada (Chapter 2)
Danny Godin, Montreal, Canada (Chapter 2)
Pamela Ireland, Montreal, Canada (preface)
Richard Jacques, Barcelona, Espagne (Chapter 3)
Christophe Jaeglin, Munster, France (Chapter 5)
Terry Knowles, Montreal, Canada (preface)
Lucette Laramée, Montreal, Canada (Chapter 6)
Matthieu Leblanc, Moncton, Canada (Chapter 2)
Sarah Lott, Ottawa, Canada (Chapter 1)
Sherry McPhail, Ottawa, Canada (Chapter 1)
René Morin, Hull, Canada (Chapter 3)
Meghan O'Connell, Vancouver, Canada (Chapter 8)
Jean-Pierre Patry, Ottawa, Canada (Chapter 2)
Anthony Pym, Calaceite, Spain (Chapter 7)
Elizabeth Rasmussen, Montreal, Canada (Chapter 3)
Andrée Sirois, Hull, Canada (Chapter 3)
Sébastien Stavrinidis, Montreal, Canada (Chapter 8)
Lise Vincent, Ottawa, Canada (Chapter 2)
Zhao Wenli, Hefei, China (Chapter 4)

Proofreaders

Glenn CLAVIER, Montreal, Canada
Monique C. CORMIER, Université de Montréal, Canada
Lindsay CRYSLER, Concordia University, Montreal, Canada
Sheryl CURTIS, Montreal, Canada
Marcel DELISLE, Hull, Canada
Clara FOZ, University of Ottawa, Canada
David HOMEL, Montreal, Canada
Paul A. HORGUELIN, Université de Montréal, Canada
Philip NOSS, American Bible Society, Gainesville, U.S.A.
Douglas PARKER, Ottawa, Canada
Hilary PARKER, Ottawa, Canada
Elizabeth RASMUSSEN, Montreal, Canada
Frances SLINGERLAND, Montreal, Canada

Acknowledgements

We would also like to thank the following people for their assistance with the first edition: Cay Dollerup, Center for Translation Studies & Lexicography, Copenhagen; S. R. Kidwai, Dean of the School of Languages of Jawaharlal Nehru University, New Delhi, and member of the Royal Asiatic Society of London; Ingrid Kurz, University of Vienna; Jacques Mantoux, Grenoble; Aglika Markova, cultural agent at the Bulgarian Embassy in London; Dora Sakayan, McGill University, Montreal; Josef Schmidt, McGill University, Montreal; and Yu Min, doctoral student, Concordia University, Montreal. Thanks, also, to Marie Leconte, Concordia University, Montreal for her help with the second edition.

Figure 21. The Venerable Bede

Figure 22. Great Wild Goose Pagoda

Works cited

Abdul-Raof, Hussein. 2005. "Cultural Aspects in Qur'an Translation". In *Translation and Religion: Holy Untranslatable?*, Lynne Long (ed.). Clevedon, UK: Multilingual Matters. 162–172.

Achebe, Chinua. 1975. *Morning Yet on Creation Day*. New York: Anchor Books.

Aitken, A. J. and Tom McArthur (eds). 1979. *Languages of Scotland*. Edinburgh: Chambers.

Agorni Mirella. 2005. "A Marginal(ized) Perspective on Translation History: Women and Translation in the Eighteenth Century". *Meta: journal des traducteurs / Meta: Translators' Journal* 50 (3): 817–830. http://id.erudit.org/iderudit/011598ar. Accessed January 2012.

Alarcón, Norma. 1981. "Chicana's Feminist Literature: A Re-Vision through Malintzin / or Malintzin: Putting Flesh Back on the Object". In *The Bridge Called My Back: Writings by Radical Women of Color*, Gloria Anzaldúa and Cherríe Moraga (eds). New York: Kitchen Table. 182–190.

Alarcón, Norma. 1989. "Traddutora, Traditora: A Paradigmatic Figure of Chicana Feminism". *Cultural Critique*. 13 ("The Construction of Gender and Modes of Social Division"): 57–87.

Aldhelm, Saint. 1925. *The Riddles of Aldhelm*. Translated by James Hall Pitman. Yale Studies in English, 67. New Haven, CT: Yale University Press.

Alembert, Jean-Baptiste le Rond d'. 1967. "Observations sur l'art de traduire en général [...]". Introduction to *Essai de traduction de quelques morceaux de Tacite* and excerpt from *Mélanges de littérature, d'histoire et de philosophie. 1760*. In *Œuvres de d'Alembert*. Genève: Statkine Reprints. [Excerpted in English in Lefevere 1992]

Alverny, Marie-Thérèse d'. 1994. "Deux traductions latines du Coran au Moyen Âge". In Marie-Thérèse d'Alverny. *La Connaissance de l'Islam dans l'occident médiéval*, Charles Burnett (ed.). Aldershot, UK. 69–131.

Andersson, Thorsten. 1987. "Svensk medeltid i fornsvenskt perspektiv". In *Svensk medeltidsforskning idag. En forskningsöversikt utarbetad på uppdrag av Humanistisk-samhällsvetenskapliga forskningsrådet*, Göran Dahlbäck (ed.). Uppsala: HSFR. 119–153.

Arberry, Arthur J. 1955. *The Koran Interpreted*. London: George Allen & Unwin Ltd.

Arencibia Rodriguez, Lourdes. 2006. "The Imperial College of Santa Cruz de Tlatelolco". In *Charting the Future of Translation History*, Georges L. Bastin and Paul F. Bandia (eds). Ottawa: University of Ottawa Press. 263–275.

Arndt, Erwin (ed.). 1968. *Martin Luther. Sendbrief vom Dolmetschen und Summarien über die Psalmen und Ursachen des Dolmetschens. Mit einem Anhang ausgewählter Selbstzeugnisse und Übersetzungsproben*. Halle/Saale: Max Niemeyer Verlag.

Arndt, Erwin and Gisela Brandt. 1987. *Luther und die deutsche Sprache: wie redet der Deudsche man jnn solchem fall?* Leipzig: Bibliographisches Institut.

Aroga Bessong, Dieudonné Prosper and Michael Kenmogne. 2007. "Bible Translation in Africa: A Post-Missionary Approach". In *A History of Bible Translation*, Philip Noss (ed.). Rome: Edizioni di Storia e Letteratura. 351–385.

Arrivabene, Andrea (ed.). 1547. *L'Alcorano di Macometto, nel qual si contiene la dottrina, la vita, i costumi e le leggi sue.* Venezia: Arrivabene.

Augustine, Saint, Bishop of Hippo. 1951–1956. *Letters.* Translated by Sister Wilfrid Parsons. 5 vols. New York: Fathers of the Church.

Aulotte, Robert. 1959. "Jacques Amyot, traducteur courtois". *Revue des Sciences Humaines* 94: 131–139.

Aulotte, Robert. 1965. *Amyot et Plutarque: La tradition des Moralia au XVIᵉ siècle.* Geneva: Droz.

Aulotte, Robert. 1980. "Jacques Amyot et la formation de la prose littéraire française". *Travaux de linguistique et de littérature* 18 (2): 49–56.

Aulotte, Robert. 1986. "Amyot et l'humanisme français du XVIᵉ siècle". In *Fortunes de Jacques Amyot*, Michel Balard (ed.). Paris: Nizet. 181–190.

Bachet de Méziriac, Claude-Gaspar. 1998. *De la traduction [1635].* Introduction and bibliography by Michel Ballard. Arras: Artois Presses Université / Ottawa: Les Presses de l'Université d'Ottawa.

Badawî, Abdurrahman. 1968. *La Transmission de la philosophie grecque au monde arabe.* Paris: Vrin.

Baigorri Jalón, Jésus. 2004. *De Paris à Nuremberg: naissance de l'interprétation de conférence*, traduit sous la direction de Clara Foz. Ottawa: Les Presses de l'Université d'Ottawa.

Bakker, D. M. and G. R. W. Dibbets (eds). 1977. *Geschiedenis van de Nederlandse Taalkunde.* Den Bosch: Nalmberg.

Balard, Michel (ed.). 1986. *Fortunes de Jacques Amyot.* Paris: Nizet.

Balliu, Christian. 2005. *Les Confidents du Sérail: Les interprètes français du Levant à l'époque classique.* Beyrouth: Université Saint-Joseph.

Bandia, Paul F. 2008. *Translation as Reparation: Writing and Translation in Postcolonial Africa.* Manchester: St. Jerome.

Barber, Charles. 1976. *Early Modern English.* London: Andre Deutsch.

Barnes, Annie. 1938. *Jean Le Clerc (1657–1736) et la République des Lettres.* Paris: Droz.

Barratt, Alexandra. 1984. "Works of Religious Instruction". In *Middle English Prose*, A. S. G. Edwards (ed.). New Brunswick, NJ: Rutgers University Press. 413–432.

Barthel, Manfred. 1982. *Die Jesuiten.* Düsseldorf & Vienna: Econ Verlag.

Bäse, Hans-Jürgen. 1966. "Osteuropäische Sprachen". *Lebende Sprachen* 11 (4–5–6).

Bassnett, Susan and André Lefevere (eds). 1990. *Translation, History and Culture.* London & New York: Pinter.

Bassnett, Susan and Harish Trivedi (eds). 1999. *Post-Colonial Translation: Theory and Practice.* London: Routledge.

Bastin, Georges L. and Paul F. Bandia (eds). 2006. *Charting the Future of Translation History.* Ottawa: University of Ottawa Press.

Baudier, Michel. 1625. *Histoire de la religion des Turcs.* Paris: Cramoisy.

Baugh, Albert C. 1957. *A History of the English Language.* Englewood Cliffs, NJ: Prentice Hall.

Bayle, Pierre. 1702. *Dictionnaire historique et critique.* Rotterdam: Leers. [c1697]

Beal, Samuel. 1895. *Si-Yu-Ki. Buddhist Records of the Western World. Translated from the Chinese of Hiuen Tsiang [Xuan Zang].* 2 vols. London: Kegan Paul. [c1884]

Bede, the Venerable, Saint. 1969. *Historia ecclesiastica gentis Anglorum*, Bertram Colgrave and R. A. B. Mynors (eds). Oxford: Clarendon. [English and Latin edition]

Béjoint, Henri. 2000. *Modern Lexicography: An Introduction.* Oxford, Oxford University Press.

Béjoint, Henri. 2010. *The Lexicography of English.* Oxford: Oxford University Press.

Bennett, Henry Stanley. 1952. *English Books and Readers, 1475–1557, being a study in the history of the book trade from Caxton to the incorporation of the Stationers' Company*. Cambridge: Cambridge University Press.

Bennett, Henry Stanley. 1965. *English Books and Readers, 1558–1603, being a study in the history of the book trade in the reign of Elizabeth I*. Cambridge: Cambridge University Press.

Ben-Shahar, Rina. 1998. "The Language of Plays Translated into Hebrew from English and French – A Cultural-Stylistic Study", *Meta: journal des traducteurs / Meta: Translators' Journal* 43 (1): 54–67.

Bergsträsser, Gotthelf. 1913. *Hunain Ibn Ishaq und seine Schule*. Leiden: E. J. Brill.

Berman, Antoine. 1984. *L'Épreuve de l'étranger*. Paris: Gallimard.

Berman, Antoine. 1989. "La traduction et ses discours". *Meta: journal des traducteurs / Meta: Translators' Journal* 34 (4): 672–679.

Berman, Antoine. 1992. *The Experience of the Foreign*. Translated by S. Heyvaert. New York: State University of New York Press. [Translation of Berman 1984]

Bernard, Roger. 1990. "Cyrille et Méthode – IXᵉ siècle". *Encyclopaedia Universalis*. vol. 6.

Besch, Werner, Anne Betten, Oskar Reichmann, and Stefan Sonderegger (eds). 1984. *Sprachgeschichte. Ein Handbuch zur Geschichte der deutschen Sprache und ihrer Erforschung*. vol. 1. Berlin & New York: Walter de Gruyter.

Bhabha, Homi K. 1994. *The Location of Culture*. London: Routledge.

"Bible Translations by Language". http://en.wikipedia.org/wiki/Bible_translations_by_language. Accessed January 2012.

Bibliander, Theodore. 1550. *Machumetis, Saracenorum principis, eiusque successorum vitae ac doctrina, ipseque Alcoran*. Basel. [c1543]

Binark, Ismet and Halit Eren. 1986. *World Bibliography of Translations of the Meanings of the Holy Qurʾân*. Istanbul: IRCICA.

Binns, J. W. 1990. *Intellectual Culture in Elizabethan and Jacobean England: The Latin Writings of the Age*. Leeds: Cairns.

Birse, A. H. (Arthur Herbert). 1967. *Memoirs of an Interpreter*. New York: Coward McCann.

Bjornson, Richard. 1991. *The African Quest for Freedom and Identity: Cameroonian Writing and the National Experience*. Bloomington & Indianapolis: Indiana University Press.

Blake, Norman Francis. 1969. *Caxton and his World*. London: Andre Deutsch.

Blake, Norman Francis (ed.). 1973. *Selections from William Caxton*. Oxford: Clarendon Press.

Blake, Norman Francis. 1991. *William Caxton and English Literary Culture*. London: Hambledon Press.

Blake, Norman Francis. 1996. *A History of the English Language*. New York: New York University Press.

Bolgar, R. R. (Robert Ralph). 1954. *The Classical Heritage and its Beneficiaries*. Cambridge: Cambridge University Press.

Bolle, Kees W. 1979. *The Bhagavadgita: A New Translation*. Berkeley: University of California Press.

Bondzio, Wilhelm. 1984. "Hermeneutik und Übersetzung bei Martin Luther". In *Luthers Sprachschaffen. Grundlagen – geschichtliche Wirkungen*, Joachim Schildt (ed.). vol. 1. Berlin. 260–272.

Bonno, Gabriel. 1955. *Les relations intellectuelles de Locke avec la France (D'après des documents inédits)*. University of California Publications in Modern Philology, vol. 3, no 2. Berkeley: University of California Press.

Bonsal, Stephen. 1944. *Unfinished Business*. Garden City, NY: Doubleday, Dean & Co.

Bonsal, Stephen. 1946. *Suitors and Suppliants: The Little Nations at Versailles*. New York: Prentice-Hall.

Borges, Jorge Luis. 1924. *Inquisiciones*. Buenos Aires: Proa.

Borges, Jorge Luis. 1932. *Discusión*. Buenos Aires: Emecé.

Borges, Jorge Luis. 1936. *Historia de la eternidad*. Buenos Aires: Viau y Zona.

Borges, Jorge Luis. 1952. *Otras inquisiciones (1937–1952)*. Buenos Aires: Sur.

Boserup, Ivan. 1981. "The Angers Fragment and the Archetype of the Gesta Danorum". In *Saxo Grammaticus: A Medieval Author between Norse and Latin Culture*, Karsten Friis-Jensen (ed.). Copenhagen: Museum Tusculanum Press. 9–26.

Boulanger, Jean-Claude. 2003. *Les inventeurs de dictionnaires: De l'eduba des scribes mésopotamiens au scriptorium des moines médiévaux*. Ottawa: Les Presses de l'Université d'Ottawa.

Bourdieu, Pierre. 1979. *La Distinction: Critique sociale du jugement de goût*. Paris: Minuit.

Bourdieu, Pierre. 1992. *Les Règles de l'art: Genèse et structure du champ littéraire*. Paris: Seuil.

Bowen, David and Margareta Bowen (eds). 1990. *Interpreting – Yesterday, Today and Tomorrow*. ATA Scholarly Monograph Series 4. Binghamton: State University of New York.

Bowman, Martin. 2000. "Scottish Horses and Montreal Trains: The Translation of Vernacular to Vernacular". In *Moving Target: Theatre Translation and Cultural Relocation*, Carole-Anne Upton (ed.). Manchester: St. Jerome. 25–33.

Brandon, William (ed.). 1988. *The American Heritage Book of Indians*. New York: American Heritage/Bonanza Books.

Brendler, Gerhard. 1983. *Martin Luther. Theologie und Revolution*. Berlin: Deutscher Verlag der Wissenschaften.

Brendler, Gerhard. 1991. *Martin Luther: Theology and Revolution*. Translated by Claude R. Foster, Jr. New York: Oxford University Press. [Translation of Brendler 1983]

Brunot, Ferdinand. 1966. *Histoire de la langue française des origines à nos jours*. vol. 5. Paris: Armand Colin.

Brunot, Ferdinand. 1967. *Histoire de la langue française des origines à nos jours*. vol. 9. Paris: Armand Colin.

Bühler, Curt F. 1960. *William Caxton and His Critics: a critical reappraisal of Caxton's contributions to the enrichment of the English language*; with Caxton's Prologue to *Eneydos* in facsimile, and rendered into present-day English by Curt F. Bühler. Syracuse, NY: Syracuse University Press.

Burford Mason, Roger. 1996. *Travels in the Shining Island*. Toronto: Dundurn.

Burke, David G. 2005. "The Translation of the Hebrew Word *'ish* in Genesis: A Brief Historical Comparison". In *Translation and Religion. Holy Untranslatable?*, Lynne Long (ed.). Clevedon, UK: Multilingual Matters. 129–140.

Burke, David G. 2007. "The First Versions: The Septuagint, the Targums, and the Latin". In *A History of Bible Translation*, Philip Noss (ed.). Rome: Edizioni di Storia e Letteratura. 59–89.

Burke, Peter. 1966. "A Survey of the Popularity of Ancient Historians 1450–1700". *History and Theory* 5: 135–152.

Burke, Peter (ed.). 1992. *New Perspectives on Historical Writing*. University Park, PA: The Pennsylvania State University Press.

Burke, Peter and R. Po-chia Hsia (eds). 2007. *Cultural Translation in Early Modern Europe*. Cambridge: Cambridge University Press.

Burnett, Charles. 1990. "Adelard of Bath and the Arabs". In *Rencontres de cultures dans la philosophie médiévale: Traductions et traducteurs de l'antiquité tardive au XIVᵉ siècle*, Jacqueline Hamesse and Marta Fattori (eds). Louvain-la-Neuve: Cassino. 89–107.

Burnham, Philip. 1996. *The Politics of Cultural Difference in Northern Cameroon*. Washington, D.C.: Smithsonian Institution Press.

Burwash, Nathanael. 1911. "The Gift to a Nation of a Written Language". *Proceedings and Transactions of the Royal Society of Canada*. 3rd series, vol. 5. Section II: 3–21.

Butterfield, Bonnie "Spirit Wind-Walker". 2010. "Sacagawea: From Captive to Expedition Interpreter to Great American Legend". http://bonniebutterfield.com/NativeAmericans.html. Accessed October 2011.

Caillé, Pierre-François. 1955. Introduction to the first issue of *Babel*. *Babel* 1 (1). [untitled article]

Callewaert, W. M. and Shailanand Hemraj. 1983. *Bhagavadgitanuvada: A Study in Transcultural Translation*. Ranchi: Satya Bharati Publication.

Calvet, Louis-Jean. 1981. *Les Langues véhiculaires*. Paris: Presses Universitaires de France.

Cary, Edmond. 1956. *La Traduction dans le monde moderne*. Geneva: Georg & Cie.

Cary, Edmond. 1962. "Pour une théorie de la traduction". *Journal des traducteurs* 7 (4): 118–125.

Cary, Edmond. 1963a. *Les Grands traducteurs français*. Geneva: Georg & Cie.

Cary, Edmond. 1963b. "Pour une théorie de la traduction (suite et fin)". *Journal des traducteurs* 8 (1): 3–11.

Caxton, William. 1490. *Caxton's Eneydos, 1490: Englisht from the French "Liure des Eneydes", 1483*, M. T. Culley and F. J. Furnivall (eds.). London: N. Trübner & Co. for the Early English Text Society, 1890.

Chaballe, J.-H. and Pierre Daviault. 1945. *English-French, French-English Military Dictionary*. Ottawa: Bureau of Bilingual Publications of the Canadian Army / General Staff of the Canadian Army.

Chan, Sin-wai and David E. Pollard (eds). 1995. *An Encyclopaedia of Translation: Chinese-English, English-Chinese*. Hong Kong: The Chinese University Press.

Chaucer, Geoffrey. 1977. *The Complete Poetry and Prose of Geoffrey Chaucer*, J. H. Fisher (ed.). New York: Holt, Rinehart and Winston.

Chavy, Paul. 1974. "Les premiers translateurs français". *The French Review* 47 (3): 557–565.

Chavy, Paul. 1988. *Traducteurs d'autrefois. Moyen Âge et Renaissance*. 2 vols. Paris: Champion/ Geneva: Slatkine.

Cheyfitz, Eric. 1991. *The poetics of imperialism: translation and colonization from "The Tempest" to "Tarzan"*. New York: Oxford University Press.

Chia, Emmanuel N., Joseph C. Suh and Alexandre Ndetto Tene (eds). 2009. *Perspectives on Translation and Interpretation in Cameroon*. Bamenda (Cameroon): Langaa RPCIG.

Christensen, Thomas G. 1990. *An African Tree of Life*. Maryknoll: Orbis Books.

Cohen, Israel. 1957. "The Beauty of Shem in the Languages of Yefet". *Moznayim* 5 (2). [In Hebrew]

Cohen, J. M. (John Michael) 1962. *English Translators and Translations*. London: Longmans, Green and Co.

Cohen, Paul A. 1997. *History in Three Keys: the Boxers as Event, Experience, and Myth*. New York: Columbia University Press.

Coindreau, Marcel-Edgar. 1974. *Mémoires d'un traducteur. Entretiens avec Christian Giudicelli*. Paris: Gallimard.

Colebrooke, Henry Thomas. 1972. *Algebra with Arithmetic and Mensuration, translated from the Sanskrit of Brahmegupta and Bhascara*. London: John Murray. [c1817]

Coles, Mike. 2001. *The Cockney Bible: Well, bits of it anyway...* Oxford: Bible Reading Fellowship.

Conley, C. H. (Carey Herbert). 1927. *The First English Translators of the Classics*. New Haven, CT: Yale University Press.

Conot, Robert E. 1983. *Justice at Nuremberg*. New York: Carroll & Graf Publishers.

Considine, John. 2008. *Dictionaries in Early Modern Europe: Lexicography and the Making of Heritage*. Cambridge: Cambridge University Press.

Copeland, Rita. 1991. *Rhetoric, Hermeneutics and Translation in the Middle Ages: Academic Traditions and Vernacular Texts*. Cambridge: Cambridge University Press.

Cronin, Michael. 1993. "The Irish Language: Past and Present". *Van Taal tot Taal* 37 (2): 80–83.

Cronin, Michael. 1996. *Translating Ireland: Translation, Languages, Cultures*. Cork: Cork University Press.

Cronin, Michael. 2002. "The Empire Talks Back: Orality, Heteronomy, and the Cultural Turn in Interpretation Studies". In *Translation and Power*, Maria Tymoczko and Edwin Gentzler (eds). Amherst & Boston: University of Massachusetts Press. 45–62.

Cronin, Michael. 2006. *Translation and Identity*. London: Routledge.

Cypess, Sandra Messinger. 1991. *La Malinche in Mexican Literature: From History to Myth*. Austin: University of Texas Press.

Dagut, Menachem. 1981. "Semantic 'Voids' as a Problem in the Translation Process". *Poetics Today* 2 (4): 61–71.

Dah, Jonas N. 1986. "African Responses to Christian Presence". [Unpublished]

Daniel, Norman. 1960. *Islam and the West: The Making of an Image*. Edinburgh: University Press.

Daniel, Norman. 1975. *The Arabs and Medieval Europe*. London: Longman.

Daniell, David (ed.). 1989. *The New Testament Translated from the Greek by William Tyndale in 1524; in a Modern Spelling Edition and with an Introduction by David Daniell*. New Haven, CT: Yale University Press.

Daniell, David (ed.). 1992. *Tyndale's Old Testament: Being the Pentateuch of 1530, Joshua to 2 Chronicles of 1537, and Jonah*. New Haven, CT: Yale University Press.

Daniell, David. 1994. *William Tyndale: A Biography*. New Haven & London: Yale University Press.

Daniell, David. 2003. *The Bible in English: History and Influence*. New Haven & London: Yale University Press.

Davis, Calvin DeArmond. 1975. *The United States and the Second Hague Peace Conference: American diplomacy and international organization, 1899–1914*. Durham, NC: Duke University Press.

Dawson, Christopher. 1966. *Mission to Asia*. New York: Harper & Row.

De Blaghad, Earnán. 1931. *Earnán De Blaghad Papers*. University College Dublin Archives.

Dédéyan, Gérard (ed.). 1982. *Histoire des Arméniens*. Toulouse: Privat.

de Groot, Alexander H. 2000. " Dragomans' Careers". In *Friends and rivals in the East: Studies in Anglo-Dutch relations in the Levant from the seventeenth to the early nineteenth century*, Alastair Hamilton, Alexander H. de Groot and Maurits H. van den Boogert (eds). Amsterdam: Brill. 223–246.

Degros, Maurice. 1984. "Les jeunes de langues [*sic*] sous la Révolution et l'Empire". *Revue d'Histoire Diplomatique* 99 (2): 77–107.

Delater, James Albert. 2002. *Translation Theory in the Age of Louis XIV: The 1683 "De optimo genere interpretandi" of Pierre-Daniel Huet (1630–1721)*. Manchester: St. Jerome.

Del Castillo, Adelaida R. 1977. "Malintzin Tenépal: A Preliminary Look into a New Perspective". In *Essays on la Mujer*, Rosaura Sánchez and Rosa Martinez Cruz (eds). Los Angeles: University of California. 2–27.

Delabastita, Dirk and Lieven D'hulst (eds). 1993. *European Shakespeares: Translating Shakespeare in the Romantic Age*. Amsterdam/Philadelphia: John Benjamins.

Delavenay, Émile. 1960. *An Introduction to Machine Translation*. Translated by Katharine M. Delavenay and Émile Delavenay. London: Thames and Hudson.

Delisle, Jean. 1977a. "Les pionniers de l'interprétation au Canada". *Meta: journal des traducteurs / Meta: Translators' Journal* 22 (1) : 5–14.

Delisle, Jean. 1977b. "Les interprètes français au Brésil au XVIe siècle". *Le Linguiste* 1–2: 1–4.

Delisle, Jean. 1984. *Bridging the Language Solitudes. Growth and Development of the Translation Bureau of the Government of Canada, 1934–1984*. Ottawa: Secretary of State. [Also published as *Au cœur du trialogue canadien. Historique du Bureau des traductions du gouvernement canadien, 1934–1984*. Ottawa: Secretary of State.]

Delisle, Jean. 1990. *The Language Alchemists. Société des traducteurs du Québec (1940–1990)*. Ottawa: University of Ottawa Press. [Also published as *Les Alchimistes des langues. Société des traducteurs du Québec (1940–1990)*. Ottawa: Les Presses de l'Université d'Ottawa.]

Delisle, Jean. 1996. "Littré, traducteur érudit, provocateur et illusionniste ". *Circuit* 52: 20–21.

Delisle, Jean (ed.). 2002. *Portraits de traductrices*. Ottawa: Les Presses de l'Université d'Ottawa.

Delisle, Jean. 2005. "Les nouvelles règles de traduction du Vatican ". *Meta: journal des traducteurs / Meta: Translators' Journal* 50 (3): 831–850.

Delisle, Jean (ed.). 2011. *International Directory of Historians of Translation / Répertoire mondial des historiens de la traduction*. http://aix1.uottawa.ca/~jdelisle/fit_index.htm.

Delisle, Jean and Gilbert Lafond (eds). 2012. *History of Translation*. Multimedia DVD. 8th edition. [Continuously updated since 1999; distribution: jdelisle@uOttawa.ca.]

Delisle, Jean and Judith Woodsworth (eds). 1995. *Translators through History*. Amsterdam/Philadelphia: John Benjamins.

Denton, John. 1992a. "Metaphors the Elizabethans Translated by. Aspects of Late 16th Century English Translation Metalanguage". In *Early Modern English: Trends, Forms and Texts*, Carmela Nocera Avila, Nicola Pantaleo and Dominco Pezzini (eds). Fasano: Schena. 255–271.

Denton, John. 1992b. "Plutarco come lo leggeva Shakespeare: la traduzione delle Vite parallele di Thomas North (1579)". In *Plutarco: Le vite di Coriolano e Alcibiade*, Barbara Scardigli (ed.). Milan: Rizzoli. 57–78.

Denton, John. 1993. "Plutarch in English from Sir Thomas North to the Penguin Classics". In *Aspects of English and Italian Lexicology and Lexicography*, David Hart (ed.). Rome: Bagatto. 265–278.

Desai, Mahadev. 1970. *The Gospel of Selfless Action or the Gita According to Gandhi*. Ahmedabad: Navajivan Publishing House.

Devic, Marcel. 1883. "Une traduction inédite du Coran". *Journal Asiatique*, 8th series (1): 343–406.

D'hulst, Lieven. 1994. "Enseigner la traductologie: pour qui et à quelles fins?". *Meta: journal des traducteurs / Meta: Translators' Journal* 39 (1): 8–14.

Díaz del Castillo, Bernal. 1983. *Historia Verdadera de la Conquista de la Nueva España*, Genaro García (ed.). Mexico: Editorial Porrua S.A. [c1575. Previously translated by A. P. Maudslay as *The True History of the Conquest of New Spain*. London: Hakluyt Society, 1926; and by D. Jourdanet as *Histoire véridique de la conquête de la Nouvelle-Espagne*. Paris: G. Masson, 1877.]

Diderot, Denis. 1976. *Encyclopédie*. In *Œuvres*, John Lough and Jacques Proust (eds). vol. 4. Paris: Hermann.

Diringer, David. 1952. *The Alphabet: A Key to the History of Mankind*. London: Hutchinson.

Dollmann, Eugen. 1963. *Dolmetscher der Diktatoren*. Bayreuth: Hestia-Verlag.

Dollmann, Eugen. 1965. *J'étais l'interprète de Hitler et de Mussolini*, traduit par René-Marie Jouhan. Paris: Éditions France-Empire. [Translation of Dollmann 1963]

Dollmann, Eugen. 1967. *The Interpreter, Memoirs of Doktor Eugen Dollmann*, translated by J. Maxwell Brownjohn. London: Hutchinson. [Translation of Dollmann 1963]

Du Ryer, André. 1647. *L'Alcoran de Mahomet, translaté de l'arabe en français*. Paris: Somaville. [1647–1649]

Dulles, Allen Welsh. 1947. *Germany's Underground*. New York: Macmillan Co.

Dvornik, Francis. 1970. *Les Slaves, Byzance et Rome au IXe siècle*. Hattiesburg, MS: Academic International. [c1926]

Ebel, Julia. 1967. "A numerical survey of Elizabethan translations". *The Library*. 5th series (22): 104–127.

"Ebla tablets". http://en.wikipedia.org/wiki/Ebla_tablets. Accessed January 2012.

Eco, Umberto. 1985. "Towards a New Middle Ages". In *On Signs*, Marshall Blonsky (ed.). Baltimore: Johns Hopkins University Press. 488–504.

Edwards, A. S. G. (ed.). 1984. *Middle English Prose*. New Brunswick, NJ: Rutgers University Press.

Einstein, Lewis. 1902. *The Italian Renaissance in England*. New York: Franklin.

Ekvall, Robert Brainerd. 1960. *Faithful Echo*. New York: Twayne Publishers.

Ellis, Roger (ed.). 1989. *The Medieval Translator: The Theory and Practice of Translation in the Middle Ages*. Cambridge: D. S. Brewer.

Ellis, Roger (ed.). 1991. *The Medieval Translator II*. London: Centre for Medieval Studies. Queen Mary and Westfield College. University of London.

Embree, Ainslie T. (ed.). 1972. *The Hindu Tradition*. New York: Random House.

Eoyang, Eugene Chen. 1993. *The Transparent Eye: Reflections on Translation, Chinese Literature, and Comparative Poetics*. Honolulu: University of Hawaii Press.

Esnoul, Anne-Marie and Olivier Lacombe. 1972. *La Bhagavad Gîtâ*. Paris: Librairie Arthème Fayard.

Etkind, Efim. 1977. *Dissident malgré lui*. Translated by Monique Slodzian. Paris: Éditions Albin Michel.

Even-Zohar, Itamar. 1976. "What did Gitl Cook and what did Čičikov eat? On the Status of Denotation in Hebrew Literary Language Since the Revival Period". *Ha-sifrut/Literature* 23. [In Hebrew]

Even-Zohar, Itamar. 1978. "The Position of Translated Literature within the Literary Polysystem". In *Literature and Translation: New Perspectives in Literary Studies*, James S Holmes, José Lambert and Raymond van den Broeck (eds). Leuven: Acco. 117–127.

Even-Zohar, Itamar. 1990. *Polysystem Studies*. Special issue of *Poetics Today* 11:1.

Falk, Marcia. 1982. *Love Lyrics from the Bible: A Translation and Literary Study of the Song of Songs*. Sheffield: Almond Press.

Février, James Germain. 1948. *Histoire de l'écriture*. Paris: Payot.

Filliozat, Jean. 1949. *La Doctrine classique de la médecine indienne, ses origines et ses parallèles grecs*. Paris: Imprimerie nationale.

Filliozat, Jean. 1963a. "Ancient Indian Science". In *History of Science*, René Taton (ed.) and A. J. Pomerans (trans.). vol. 1. London: Thames/Hudson.

Filliozat, Jean. 1963b. "Indian Science from the 15th to the 18th century". In *History of Science*, René Taton (ed.) and A. J. Pomerans (trans.). vol. 2. London: Thames/Hudson. 602–604.

Filliozat, Jean. 1963c. "Indian Science in 1800–1960". In *History of Science*, René Taton (ed.) and A. J. Pomerans (trans.). vol. 4. London: Thames/Hudson. 591–593.

Filliozat, Jean. 1964. *The Classical Doctrine of Indian Medicine: Its Origins and its Greek Parallels*. Translated by Dev Rav Chanana. New Delhi: M. Manoharlal. [Translation of Filliozat 1949]

Findlay, Bill (ed.). 2004. *Frae Ither Tongues: Essays on Modern Translations into Scots*. Clevedon, UK: Multilingual Matters.

Findlay, Bill. 2005. "*Gallus* meets *joie-de-vivre*". In *Montreal-Glasgow*, Bill Marshall (ed.). Glasgow: University of Glasgow French and German Publications. 179–195.

Fischbach, Henry. 1992. "Translation, the Great Pollinator of Science". *Babel* 38 (4): 193–202.

Flexner, James Thomas. 1965. *George Washington: The Forge of Experience, 1732–1775*. Boston & Toronto: Little, Brown and Co.

Folkart, Barbara. 1991. *Le Conflit des énonciations*. Montréal: Balzac.

Forcada, Mikel L. 2010. "Machine Translation Today". In *Handbook of Translation Studies*, Yves Gambier and Luc van Doorslaer (eds). vol. 1. Amsterdam/Philadelphia: John Benjamins. 215–223.

Foz, Clara. 1988. "La traduction-appropriation: le cas des traducteurs tolédans des XIIᵉ et XIIIᵉ siècles". *TTR* 1 (2): 58–64.

Foz, Clara. 1998. *Le Traducteur, l'Église et le Roi*. Ottawa : Les Presses de l'Université d'Ottawa.

Frantzen, Allen J. 2010. "The Englishness of Bede, from then to now". In *The Cambridge Companion to Bede*, Scott DeGregorio (ed.). Cambridge: Cambridge University Press. 229–242. *Cambridge Collections Online*. http://cco.cambridge.org/extract?id=ccol9780521514958_CCOL9780521514958A019. Accessed September 2011.

Gale Biography in Context. Contemporary Authors Online. 2001. "A(rthur) H(erbert) Birse". Detroit: Gale. http://ic.galegroup.com/ic/bic1/ReferenceDetailsPage/ReferenceDetailsWindow?displayGroupName=Reference&prodId=BIC1&action=e&windowstate=normal&catId=&documentId=GALE%7CH1000008831&mode=view&userGroupName=loc_main&jsid=56a422f11ba74ae8825620e6080f7a20. Accessed March 2011.

Gallant, Christel. 1990. "L'influence des religions catholique et protestante sur la traduction des textes sacrés à l'intention des Micmacs dans les provinces maritimes: du livre des prières de l'abbé Maillard (1710–1762) à la traduction des Évangiles par Silas Tertius Rand (1810–1889)". *TTR* (3) 2: 97–109.

Gandhi, Mohandas Karamchand. 1950. *Hindu Dharma*. Ahmedabad: Navajivan Publishing House.

Gardiner, Alan Henderson. 1969. *Egyptian Grammar, Being an Introduction to the Study of Hieroglyphs*. 3rd, revised edition. London: Oxford University Press.

Gargatagli, Ana. 1992. "La traducción de América". Barcelona: First International Congress on Translation. [Unpublished paper]

Garnett, Richard. 1991. *Constance Garnett: A Heroic Life*. London: Sinclair-Stevenson.

Garnier, Bruno. 2002. "Anne Dacier, un esprit moderne au pays des Anciens". In *Portraits de traductrices*, Jean Delisle (ed.). Ottawa: Les Presses de l'Université d'Ottawa. 13–54.

Gaulmier, Jean. 1950. Notice biographique sur l'interprète Jean-Michel Venture de Paradis (1739–1799), secrétaire-interprète du Roy pour les langues orientales et interprète de Bonaparte en Égypte. In *La Zubda Kachf al-Mamâlik de Khalîl Az-Zâhirî*. Beirut: Institut français de Damas.

Gelhaus, Hermann. 1989 and 1990. *Der Streit um Luthers Bibelverdeutschung im 16. und 17. Jahrhundert*. 2 vols. Tübingen: Max Niemeyer Verlag.

Gentzler, Edwin and Maria Tymoczko. 2002. "Introduction". In *Translation and Power*, Maria Tymoczko and Edwin Gentzler (eds). Amherst & Boston: University of Massachusetts Press. ix-xxviii.

Gil, José Sangrador. 1974. *Los colaboradores judíos en la Escuela de traductores de Toledo*. Washington, D.C.: The Catholic University of America.

Girardot, Norman. 2002. *The Victorian Translation of China: James Legge's Oriental Pilgrimage*. Berkeley: University of California Press.

Girardot, Norman J. and Terry F. Kleeman. 2005. "Chinese Religion: History of Study". In *Encyclopedia of Religion*, Lindsay Jones (ed.). vol 3. 1629-1640. Gale Virtual Reference library. http://0-go.galegroup.com.mercury.concordia.ca. Accessed January 2012.

Glazemaker, Jan Hendrik. 1658. *Mahomets Alkoran, door de Heer Du Ryer [...] in de Fransche taal gestelt [...] Alles van nieus door J. H. Glazemaker vertaalt*. Amsterdam: Jan Rieuwertsz.

Godard, Barbara. 1990. "Theorizing Feminist Discourse/Translation". In *Translation, History and Culture*, Susan Bassnett and André Lefevere (eds). London: Frances Pinter. 87-96.

Godard, Barbara. 1991. "Translating (With) the Speculum". *TTR* 4 (2): 85-121.

Goodman, Paul (ed.). 1943. *The Jewish National Home: the second November, 1917-1942*. London: Dent.

Goodwins, Christopher. 2001. *The New Testament in Limerick Verse*. Arlesford, UK: John Hunt.

Gouanvic, Jean-Marc. 1994. *La Science-fiction française au 20ᵉ siècle (1900-1968): essai de sociopoétique d'un genre en émergence*. Amsterdam & Atlanta: Rodopi.

Gouanvic, Jean-Marc. 1999. *Sociologie de la traduction: La science-fiction américaine dans l'espace culturel français des années 1950*. Arras: Artois Presses Université.

Gray, Douglas. 1990. "Some pre-Elizabethan examples of an Elizabethan art". In *England and the Continental Renaissance: Essays in Honour of J. B. Trapp*, Edward Chaney and Peter Mack (eds.). Woodbridge: Baydell and Brewer. 23-36.

Greenblatt, Stephen. 1991. *Marvelous Possessions*. Chicago: University of Chicago Press.

Gretsch, Mechthild. 1973. *Die Regula Sancti Benedicti in England und Ihre Altenglische Übersetzung*. Munich: W. Fink Verlag.

Grizzard, Frank E., Jr. 2002. *George Washington: a Biographical Companion*. Santa Barbara, CA: ABC-Clio.

Grousset, René. 1973. *Histoire de l'Arménie des origines à 1071*. Paris: Payot.

Gullberg, Ingvar E. 1981. "Outline bibliography of dictionaries between German and the Scandinavian languages". *Lebende Sprachen* 26 (3): 138-144.

Guha, Ranajit. 1983. *Elementary Aspects of Peasant Insurgency in Colonial India*. Delhi: Oxford.

Gutas, Dimitri. 1998. *Greek Thought, Arabic Culture: the Graeco-Arabic Translation Movement in Baghdad and Early ᶜAbbâsid Society (2nd-4th/8th-10th centuries)*. London: Routledge.

Gyasi, Kwaku Addae. 1999. "Writing as Translation: African Literature and the Challenges of Translation". *Research in African Literatures*. 30 (2): 75-87. http://0-muse.jhu.edu.mercury.concordia.ca/journals/research_in_african_literatures/v030/30.2gyasi.pdf. Accessed June 2011.

Haefeli, Evan. 2007. "On First Contact and Apotheosis: Manitou and Men in North America". *Ethnohistory* 54 (3): 407-443.

Hamer, Richard. 1978. *Three Lives from the Gilte Legende*. Heidelberg: Carl Winter Universität Verlag.

Hannay, Margaret Patterson. 1985. *Silent but for the Word: Tudor Women as Patrons, Translators and Writers of Religious Works*. Kent, Ohio: Kent State University Press.

Hansson, Stina. 1982. *Afsatt på Swensko. 1600 talets tryckta översättningslitteratur*. Göteborg.

Harl, M., G. Dorival and C. Munnich. 1988. *La Bible grecque des Septante: Du judaïsme hellénistique au christianisme ancien*. Paris: Éditions du Cerf et du CNRS.

Harris, Brian. 1992. "A Nineteenth-Century Diplomatic Interpreter in Japan". University of Ottawa. [Unpublished]

Harris, Brian. 2003. "Ernest Satow's Early Career as Diplomatic Interpreter". *Diplomacy & Statecraft* 13 (2): 116–134.

Hartmann, Reinhard (ed.). 1986. *The History of Lexicography*. Amsterdam/Philadelphia: John Benjamins.

Haskins, Charles Homer. 1967. *Studies in the History of Medieval Science*. New York: Frederick Ungar.

Haskins, Charles Homer. 1970. *The Renaissance of the Twelfth Century*. Cleveland & New York: The World Publishing Co.

Helvétius, Claude Adrien. 1973. *De l'Esprit*. Verviers: Marabout. [c1758]

Hemming, John. 1970. *The Conquest of the Incas*. New York: Harcourt Brace Jovanovich.

Hérault de Séchelles, Marie-Jean. 1970. "Éloge d'Athanase Auger". In *Œuvres littéraires et politiques*. Paris: Éditions Rencontre.

Hermans, Theo. 1985a. "Vondel on Translation". *Dutch Crossing: Journal of Low Countries Studies* 26: 38–72.

Hermans, Theo. 1985b. "Images of translation. Metaphor and imagery in the Renaissance discourse on translation". In *The Manipulation of Literature: Studies in Literary Translation*, Theo Hermans (ed.). London: Croom Helm. 103–135.

Hermans, Theo (ed.). 1991. *Studies over Nederlandse vertalingen*. The Hague: Stichting Bibliographia Neerlandica.

Herren, Ricardo. 1992. *Doña Marina, la Malinche*. Barcelona: Planeta.

Hibbert, Christopher. 1975. *Benito Mussolini: The Rise and Fall of Il Duce*. Harmondsworth: Penguin Books.

Highet, Gilbert. 1949. *The Classical Tradition: Greek and Roman Influences on Western Literature*. London: Oxford University Press.

Hoernle, A. F. Rudolf. 1987. *The Bower Manuscript (1893–1912)*. New Delhi: Aditya Prakashan.

Hoffman, Andy. 2011. "Need to Talk to China? Go Through Him". *The Globe and Mail* (Toronto, Canada). August 27, 2011. F6–7.

Holmes, James S, José Lambert and Raymond van den Broeck (eds). 1978. *Literature and Translation: New Perspectives in Literary Studies*. Leuven: Acco.

Holmstrom, John Edwin. 1969. *Bibliography of Interlingual Scientific and Technical Dictionaries*. 5th edition. Paris: UNESCO. [c1951]

Horguelin, Paul A. 1981. *Anthologie de la manière de traduire – Domaine français*. Montreal: Linguatech. [Out of print: 2nd edition on Delisle and Lafond 2012]

Howard, Philip. 1994. "Philip Howard Column: Tyndale's language of the common man is the bedrock of English literature today". *The Times* (London). April 29, 1994.

Hunayn ibn Ishâq. 1925. "Risalat ilâ ᶜAli Ibn Yahya fi dhikr mâ Turjima min Kutub Jâlinûs bi ᶜilmihi wa baᶜd mâ lam Yutarjam". In *Hunain ibn Ishâq über die syrischen und arabischen Galenübersetzungen zum ersten mal herausgegeben und übersetzt*, Gotthelf Bergsträsser (ed.). Leipzig: F. A. Brockhaus. [Arabic text and German translation]

Hutchins, W. John. 2000. *Early Years in Machine Translation. Memoirs and Biographies of Pioneers*. Amsterdam/Philadelphia: John Benjamins.

Hutchins, W. John. 2011. "The history of machine translation in a nutshell". http://ourworld. compuserve.com/homepages/WJHutchins. Accessed June 2011.

Ibn Abî Usaybiᶜa. 1882. ᶜ*Uyûn al-anbâ' fî tabaqât al-attibâ'*. Cairo.

Ibn al-Nadîm, M. 1871–72. *Kitâb al-Fihrist*, mit Anmerkungen herausgegeben von Gustav Flügel. Leipzig: F. C. W. Vogel .

Intersol Inc. 2011. *Global Advisor Newsletter*. http://www.intersolinc.com/newsletters/africa. htm. Accessed June 2011.

Irfan Habib, S. and Dhruv Raina. 1989. "The Introduction of scientific rationality in India: a Study of Master Ramachandra". *Annals of Science* 46 (6): 597–610.

Ivir, V. 1987. "Procedures and Strategies for the Translation of Culture". *Indian Journal of Applied Linguistics* 13 (2): 35–46. [Also published in *Translation Across Cultures*, Gideon Toury (ed.). New Delhi: Bahri Publications, 1987.]

Jackson, Peter (ed. and trans.). 1990. *The Mission of Friar William Rubruck: His Journey to the Court of the Great Khan Möngke 1253–1255*. London: The Hakluyt Society.

Jagic, Vatroslav. 1936. "The Conversion of the Slavs". In *The Cambridge Medieval History*, J. R. Tanner, C. W. Previté-Orton and Z. N. Brooke (eds). [Planned by J. B. Bury]. vol. 4, chapter 7(b). Cambridge: Cambridge University Press. 215–229.

Jean, Georges. 1987. *L'Écriture, mémoire des hommes*. Paris: Gallimard.

Jinbachian, Manuel. 2007. "Introduction: the Septuagint to the Vernaculars". In *A History of Bible Translation*, Philip Noss (ed.). Rome: Edizioni di Storia e Letteratura. 29–57.

Johnson, Micheline D. 1974. "Pierre Maillard". In *Dictionnaire biographique du Canada*. vol 3. Québec: Presses de l'Université Laval. 448–449.

Joinville, Jean de. 1963. *Chronicles of the Crusades: The Life of Saint Louis*. Translated by Margaret R. B. Shaw. Harmondsworth: Penguin Books. [Translation of *Mémoires de Jean Sire de Joinville, ou Histoire et Chronique du très Chrétien Roi Saint Louis*]

Jones, Lindsay (ed.). 2005. *Encyclopedia of Religion*. 15 vols. Detroit: MacMillan Reference USA.

Jones, Richard Foster. 1953. *The Triumph of the English Language*. Stanford: Stanford University Press.

Jordan, Clarence. 1968. *The Cotton Patch Version of Paul's Epistles*. New York: Association Press.

Kaplan, Fredric M., Julian M. Sobin and Arne J. de Keijzer (eds). 1986. *The China Guidebook*. 7th edition. New York: Eurasia Press.

Kaufmann, Francine. 2005. "Contribution à l'histoire de l'interprétation consécutive: le *metourguemane* dans les synagogues de l'Antiquité ". *Meta: journal des traducteurs / Meta: Translators' Journal* 50 (3): 972–986.

Karttunen, Frances E. 1994. *Between Worlds: Interpreters, Guides and Survivors*. New Brunswick, NJ: Rutgers University Press.

Kelen, Emery. 1963. *Peace in their Time: Men who Led us in and out of War (1914–1945)*. New York: Alfred A. Knopf.

Kelly, J. N. D. (John Norman Davidson). 1975. *Jerome: His Life, Writings, and Controversies*. London: Duckworth.

Kelly, Louis G. (trans.). 1976. *To Pammachius: On the Best Method of Translating*. Ottawa: University of Ottawa, "Documents de Traductologie" 1. [St. Jerome's Letter 57, translated with an introduction and notes by L. G. Kelly]

Kelly, Louis G. 1979. *The True Interpreter: A History of Translation Theory and Practice in the West*. Oxford: Blackwell.

Kelly, Nataly. 2011. Interview with Ray Kurzweil on Translation Technology. http://vimeo.com/25021517. Uploaded June 13, 2011; accessed September 2011.

Ketterer, David. 1974. *New Worlds for Old – The Apocalyptic Imagination, Science Fiction, and American Literature*. Garden City, NY: Anchor Books.

Keynes, John Maynard. 1949. *Two Memoirs. (Dr. Melchior: A Defeated Enemy & My Early Beliefs)*. 2nd edition. New York: Augustus M. Kelley/London: Rupert Hart-Davis.

Kiberd, Declan. 1993. *Synge and the Irish Language*. London: Macmillan.

Kissinger, Henry. 1979. *White House Years*. Boston: Little, Brown and Co.

"Klingon Bible Translation Project". http://www.kli.org/wiki/index.php?Klingon%20Bible%20Translation%20Project. Accessed January 2012.

Kna'ani, Ya'akov. 1989. *Dictionary of Shlonsky's Neologisms*. Tel Aviv: Sifri'at Poalim. [In Hebrew]

Kna'ani, Ya'akov. 1998. *The Comprehensive Hebrew Dictionary*. 7 vols. Revised edition. Israel: Milonim Laam.

Koenig, Edna L., Emmanuel Chia and John Povey (eds). 1983. *A Sociolinguistic Profile of Urban Centers in Cameroon*. Los Angeles: Crossroad Press.

Koller, Werner. 1984. "Übersetzungen ins Deutsche und ihre Bedeutung für deutsche Sprachgeschichte". In *Sprachgeschichte. Ein Handbuch zur Geschichte der deutschen Sprache und ihrer Erforschung*, Werner Besch, Anne Betten, Oskar Reichmann, and Stefan Sonderegger (eds). vol. 1. Berlin & New York: Walter de Gruyter.

Krishna, V. V. 1991. "The Emergence of the Indian Scientific Community". *Sociological Bulletin* 40 (1–2): 89–107.

Kritzeck, James. 1964. *Peter the Venerable and Islam*. Princeton, NJ: Princeton University Press.

Krontiris, Tina. 1992. *Oppositional Voices: Women as Writers and Translators in the English Renaissance*. London and New York: Routledge.

Kurz, Ingrid. 1985. "The Rock Tombs of the Princes of Elephantine. Earliest References to Interpretation in Pharaonic Egypt". *Babel* 31 (4): 213–218.

Kurz, Ingrid. 1986. "Dolmetschen im alten Rom". *Babel* 32 (4): 215–220.

Kurz, Ingrid. 1990. "Christopher Columbus and his Interpreters". *The Jerome Quarterly* 5 (3).

Labourt, Jérôme. 1949. *Saint Jérôme, Lettres*. Texte établi et traduit par J. Labourt. 8 vols. Paris: Belles Lettres.

Lambert, José. 1993. "History, Historiography and the Discipline. A Programme". In *Translation and Knowledge: Proceedings from the Scandinavian Symposium on Translation Theory (SSOTT IV)*, Yves Gambier and J. Tommola (eds). Turku: University of Turku Centre for Translation and Interpreting. 3–25.

Lange, Johann. 1688. "Vollständiges Türckisches Gesetzbuch [...] und jetzo zum allererstenmahl in die Hochdeutsche Sprache versetzet durch Joh. Lange". In *Thesaurus exoticorum*, Eberhard Werner Happel (ed.). Hamburg: von Wiering.

Lansing, Robert. 1921a. *The Big Four and Others of the Peace Conference*. Boston & New York: Houghton Mifflin.

Lansing, Robert. 1921b. *The Peace Negotiations: A Personal Narrative*. Boston & New York: Houghton Mifflin.

Lanson, Gustave. 1931. *Manuel bibliographique de la littérature française*. Paris: Hachette.

Lanson, Gustave. 1964. *Histoire de la littérature française*. Paris: Hachette.

Larbaud, Valery. 1946. *Sous l'invocation de saint Jérôme*. Paris: Gallimard.

Larson, Kenneth E. and Hansjoerg R. Schelle (eds.). 1989. *The Reception of Shakespeare in Eighteenth-Century France and Germany*. Special Issue of *Michigan Germanic Studies* 15:2.

Lathrop, Henry Burrowes. 1967. *Translations from the Classics into English from Caxton to Chapman, 1477–1620*. New York: Octagon Books. [c1933]

Lee, Sidney. 1968. *The French Renaissance in England: An Account of the Literary Relations of England and France in the Sixteenth Century*. New York: Octagon Books.

Lefevere, André. 1981. "Translated Literature: Towards an Integrated Theory". *Bulletin of the Midwest Modern Language Association* 14 (1): 86–96.

Lefevere, André (ed.). 1992. *Translation/History/Culture: A Sourcebook*. London: Routledge.

Legge, James. 1970. *The Chinese Classics*. 5 vols. Hong Kong: Hong Kong University Press. [c1960; originally published 1861–72]

Lemay, Richard. 1962. *Abu Maꞌshar and Latin Aristotelianism in the Twelfth Century; The Recovery of Aristotle's Natural Philosophy through Arabic Astrology*. Beirut: American University.

Lemay, Richard. 1963. "Dans l'Espagne du XIIᵉ siècle. Les traductions de l'arabe au latin", *Annales Économies, Sociétés, Civilisations* 18 (4): 639–665.

Lengenfelder, Helga and Henri Van Hoof. 1979. *International Bibliography of Specialized Dictionaries*. 6th edition. Munich: K. G. Saur.

Léry, Jean de. 1972. *Histoire d'un voyage fait en la terre du Brésil*, Michel Contat (ed.). Lausanne: Bibliothèque Romande.

Léry, Jean de. 1975. *Histoire d'un voyage fait en la terre du Brésil*, présentation et notes par Jean-Claude Morisot; index des notions ethnologiques par Louis Necker. Genève: Droz.

Léry, Jean de. 1990. *History of a Voyage to the Land of Brazil, Otherwise Called America*. Translated by Janet Whatley. Berkeley: University of California Press.

Levine, Suzanne Jill. 1991. *The Subversive Scribe: Translating Latin American Fiction*. Saint Paul, MN: Graywolf Press.

Lévy, Maurice. 1974. "English Gothic and the French Imagination: A Calendar of Translations, 1767–1828". In *The Gothic Imagination: Essays in Dark Romanticism*, Gary Richard Thompson (ed.). Pullman: Washington State University Press. 150–176.

Lévy, Maurice. 1978. "Bibliographie du roman gothique anglais en traduction française". *Les Cahiers de l'Herne* 34: 363–375.

Lewis, M. Paul (ed.). 2009. *Ethnologue: Languages of the World*. 16th edition. Dallas: SIL International. http://www.ethnologue.com. Accessed March 2011.

Li, Nanqiu. 1993. *The History of Science Document Translation in China*. Hefei, China: University of Science and Technology of China Press. [In Chinese]

Lilova, Anna. 1979. "In memoriam. Pierre-François Caillé (1907–1979)". *Babel* 25 (4) : 227–230.

Lin, Kenan. 2002. "Translation as a Catalyst for Social Change in China". In *Translation and Power*, Maria Tymoczko and Edwin Gentzler (eds). Amherst & Boston: University of Massachusetts Press. 160–183.

Lindsay, W. M. (Wallace Martin). 1917. "The Philoxenus Glossary". *The Classical Review* 31: 158–163.

Lloyd, David Colles. 1987. *Nationalism and Minor Literature: James Clarence Mangan and the Emergence of Cultural Nationalism*. Berkeley: University of California Press.

Long, Lynne (ed.). 2005. *Translation and Religion: Holy Untranslatable?*. Clevedon, UK: Multilingual Matters.

Lotbinière-Harwood, Susanne de. 1991. *Re-Belle et Infidèle: La traduction comme pratique de réécriture au féminin / The Body Bilingual: Translation as Rewriting in the Feminine*. Montréal: Les Éditions du Remue-Ménage / Toronto: The Women's Press.

Luca, Francis Xavier. 1999. "Re-'Interpreting' the Role of the Cultural Broker in the Conquest of La Florida". Florida International University. http://www.kislakfoundation.org/prize/199901.html. Accessed March 2011.

Luca, Francis Xavier. 2004. *Re-'interpreting' the Conquest: European and Amerindian Translators and Go-Betweens in the Colonization of the Americas, 1492–1675*. Ph.D. dissertation. Florida International University [AAT 3128610].

Lusignan, Serge. 1986. *Parler vulgairement: Les intellectuels et la langue française aux XIIIe et XIVe siècles*. Paris: Vrin / Montréal: Les Presses de l'Université de Montréal.

Ma, Zuyi. 1995. "History of Translation in China". In *An Encyclopaedia of Translation: Chinese-English, English-Chinese*, Chan Sin-wai and David E. Pollard (eds). Hong Kong: The Chinese University Press. 373–387.

Machan, Tim William. 1989. "Chaucer as Translator". In *The Medieval Translator: The Theory and Practice of Translation in the Middle Ages*, Roger Ellis (ed.). Cambridge: D. S. Brewer. 55–67.

MacMillan, Margaret. 2002. *Paris 1919: Six Months that Changed the World*. New York: Random House.

Mac Nioclais, Máirtín. 1991. *Seán Ó Ruadháin: Saol agus Saothar*. Dublin: An Clóhomhar. [In Irish]

MacNutt, Francis Augustus (ed. and trans.). 1977. *Fernando Cortes: his Five Letters of Relation to the Emperor Charles V*. 2 vols. Glorieta, NM: Rio Grande Press. [c1908]

Madariaga, Salvador de. 1942. *Hernan Cortés Conqueror of Mexico*. London: Hodder & Stoughton Ltd.

Madariaga, Salvador de. 1974. *Morning without Noon: Memoirs*. Farnborough, England: Saxon House.

Makdisi, George. 1990. *The Rise of Humanism in Classical Islam and the Christian West: with Special Reference to Scholasticism*. Edinburgh: Edinburgh University Press.

Mallarmé, Stéphane. 1945. "Le tombeau d'Edgar Poe". In *Poésies*. Paris: Gallimard. [c1877]

Mantoux, Paul. 1992. *The Deliberations of the Council of Four (March 24–June 28, 1919): Notes of the Official Interpreter, Paul Mantoux*, Manfred F. Boemeke (ed.) and Arthur S. Link (ed. and trans.). 2 vols. Princeton, NJ: Princeton University Press.

Marienstras, Élise. 1976. *Les Mythes fondateurs de la nation américaine*. Paris: Maspero.

Marlowe, Michael D. 2003. "An Open Letter on Translating by Martin Luther, 1530", revised and annotated by Michael D. Marlowe. http://www.bible-researcher.com/luther01.html. Accessed July 2011.

Marracci, Ludovico. 1691. *Prodromus ad refutationem Alcorani*. Patavii (Padua): Seminarium.

Marracci, Ludovico. 1698. *Alcorani textus universus*. Patavii (Padua): Seminarium.

Martindale, Joanna. 1985. *English Humanism – Wyatt to Cowley*. London: Croom Helm.

Masson, Denise (trans.). 1967. *Le Coran*. Paris: Gallimard.

Matthiessen, Francis Otto. 1931. *Translation: An Elizabethan Art*. Cambridge, MA: Harvard University Press.

McClintock, John and James Strong. 1885. *Cyclopaedia of Biblical, Theological, and Ecclesiastical Literature, Supplement*. vol 2. New York: Harper.

McCrum, Robert, William Cran and Robert MacNeil. 1986. *The Story of English*. New York: Viking.

McLean, John. 1890. *James Evans, Inventor of the Syllabic System of the Cree Language*. Toronto: Methodist Mission Rooms.

Ménage, Gilles. 1715. *Menagiana, ou Les bons mots et remarques critiques, historiques, morales & d'érudition de monsieur Ménage, recueillis par ses amis*. 2 vols. Paris: Chez la veuve Delaulne.

Menut, Albert Douglas (ed.). 1940. *Le livre de ethiques d'Aristote de Nicole Oresme*. New York: G. E. Stechert & Co.

Metzger, Bruce M. and Michael D. Coogan (eds.). 1993. *The Oxford Companion to the Bible*. New York & Oxford: Oxford University Press.

Mirandé, Alfredo and Evangelina Enríquez. 1979. *La Chicana: The Mexican-American Woman*. Chicago: University of Chicago Press.

Mirsky, N. 1978. "The Third Territory: Non-Academic Meditations on the Problems of Literary Translation". *Siman Keri'ah* 8. [In Hebrew]

Monaco, Maria. 1974. *Shakespeare on the French Stage in the Eighteenth Century*. Paris: Didier.

Morgan, H. Wayne (ed.). 1965. *Making Peace with Spain: The Diary of Whitelaw Reid, September-December 1898*. Austin: University of Texas Press.

Mortier, Roland. 1982. *L'Originalité: une nouvelle catégorie esthétique au siècle des lumières*. Geneva: Droz.

Mounin, Georges. 1965. *Teoria e storia della traduzione*. Translated by Stefania Morganti. Turin: Einaudi.

Mounin, Georges. 1994. *Les belles infidèles*. Lille: Presses Universitaires de Lille. [c1955]

Murison, David. 1977. *The Guid Scots Tongue*. Edinburgh: Blackwood.

Nama, Charles Atangana. 1990a. "A History of Translation and Interpretation in Cameroon from Precolonial Times to Present". *Meta: journal des traducteurs / Meta: Translators' Journal* 35 (2): 356–369.

Nama, Charles Atangana. 1990b. "A Critical Analysis of the Translation of African Literature". *Language and Communication* 10 (1): 179–201.

Nama, Charles Atangana. 2009. "A History of Translation and Interpretation in the Littoral Province of Cameroon". In *Perspectives on Translation and Interpretation in Cameroon*, Chia et al. (eds). Bamenda (Cameroon): Langaa RPCIG. 47–56.

Needham, Joseph. 1954. *Science and Civilisation in China*. vol. 1. Cambridge: Cambridge University Press.

Neher-Bernheim, Renée. 1969. *La déclaration Balfour*. Paris: Julliard.

New York Times. 1918. "Quit, says Stowell, to win free speech". March 3, 1918.

Ngugi, wa Thiong'o. 1986. *Decolonising the Mind: The Politics of Language in African Literature*. Nairobi: Heinemann.

Niang, Anna. 1990. "History and Role of Interpreting in Africa". In *Interpreting – Yesterday, Today and Tomorrow*, David Bowen and Margareta Bowen (eds). Binghamton: State University of New York. 34–36.

Nicholson, H. B. (Henry B.). 2002. "Fray Bernardino de Sahagún: A Spanish Missionary in New Spain, 1529–1590". In *Representing Aztec Ritual in the Work of Sahagún*, Eloise Qiñones Kleber (ed.). Boulder, CO: University Press of Colorado. 21–39.

Nida, Eugene A. and Charles Taber. 1969. *The Theory and Practice of Translation*. Leiden: E. J. Brill.

Niranjana, Tejaswini. 1992. *Siting Translation: History, Post-Structuralism, and the Post-Colonial Context*. Berkeley: University of California Press.

Nocera Avila, Carmela. 1992. *Tradurre il Cortegiano: "The Courtyer" di Sir Thomas Hoby*. Bari: Adriatica.

Nørgaard, Holger. 1958. "Translations of the Classics into English before 1600". *Review of English Studies* 9: 164–172.

Noss, Philip. 1981a. *Grammaire Gbaya*. Meiganga: Centre de Traduction Gbaya.

Noss, Philip. 1981b. "The Oral Story and Bible Translation". *The Bible Translator: Technical Papers* 32 (3): 301–318.

Noss, Philip. 1982a. *Dictionnaire Gbaya-Français*. Meiganga: Centre de Traduction Gbaya. [With Père Yves Blanchard, o.m.i.]

Noss, Philip (ed.). 1982b. *Grafting Old Rootstock*. Dallas: International Museum of Cultures.

Noss, Philip. 1985. "The Ideophone in Bible Translation: Child or Stepchild". *The Bible Translator: Practical Papers* 36 (2): 423–430.

Noss, Philip. 1987. "Communicating the Scriptures Across Cultures". In *Developments in Linguistics, Semiotics, Language Teaching and Learning*, Simon Battestini (ed.). Washington, D.C.: Georgetown University Press. 195–213.

Noss, Philip. 1993. "Les héros et l'héroisme dans la tradition et la vie gbaya". In *Peuples et Cultures de l'Adamaoua (Cameroun)*, Hermanegildo Adala and Jean Bostrich (eds). Paris: ORSTOM. 203–217.

Noss, Philip. 2001. "Ideas, Phones, and Gbaya Verbal Art". In *Ideophones*, F. K. Erhard Voeltz and Christa Killian-Hatz (eds). Amsterdam/Philadelphia: John Benjamins. 259–270.

Noss, Philip. 2003. "Translating the Ideophone: Perspectives and Strategies of Translators and Artists". In *The Creative Circle: Artist, Critic, and Translator in African Literature*, Angelina E. Overvold, Richard Priebe and Louis Tremaine (eds). Trenton, NJ: Africa World Press. 40–58.

Noss, Philip (ed.). 2007. *A History of Bible Translation*. Rome: Edizioni di Storia e Letteratura.

Obolensky, Dimitri. 1967. "Cyrille et Méthode et la christianisation des Slaves". In *La Conversione al cristianesimo nell'Europa dell'alto mediœvo*. Spoleto: Presso la Sede del Centro. 587–610.

O'Driscoll, Kieran. 2011. *Retranslation through the Centuries: Jules Verne in English*. Oxford: Peter Lang.

Ó Faracháin, Roibeárd. 1937. "Regarding An Gúm". *Bonaventura*. Summer: 174–175.

Ofek, Uriel. 1985. *The Who's Who of Children's Literature*. Tel Aviv: Zmora Bitan. [In Hebrew]

Olin, John C. 1979. "Erasmus and Saint Jerome". *Thought* 54 (3): 313–321.

Ó Lúing, Seán. 1989. *Saoir Theangan*. Dublin: Coiscéim. [In Irish]

Ó Rinn, Liam. 1933. "Tugtar Cead a gCinn Do Lucht Ceaptha Rudaí Nua". *The United Irishman*, May 13. [In Irish]

Orlinsky, Harry M. 1974. *Essays in Biblical Culture and Bible Translation*. New York: Ktav Publishing House.

Orlinsky, Harry M. and Robert G. Bratcher. 1991. *A History of Bible Translation and the North American Contribution*. Atlanta: Scholars Press.

Pall Mall Review. 1897. "Dr. Legge, The Chinese Professor". December 1, 1897, p. 10. [Signed "By One Who Knew Him"]

Palmer, John McAuley. 1937. *General von Steuben*. New Haven, CT: Yale University Press.

Panikkar, Kavalam Madhava. 1963. *The Foundations of New India*. London: George Allen & Unwin.

Paplauskas-Ramunas, Antanas. 1956. "Le rôle du traducteur dans la société internationale". *Revue de l'Université d'Ottawa* 26 (1).

Paz, Octavio. 1992. "Translation: Literature and Letters". *Theories of Translation*, Rainer Schulte and John Biguenet (eds). Chicago: University of Chicago Press. 152–163.

p'Bitek, Okot. 1974. *Horn of My Love*. London: Heinemann.

Pearsall, Derek. 1977. *Old English and Middle English Poetry*. London: Routledge & Kegan Paul Ltd.

Peel, Bruce B. 1974. *Rossville Mission Press: The Invention of the Cree Syllabic Characters, and the First Printing in Rupert's Land*. Montreal: Osiris.

Peeters, Paul. 1929. "Pour l'histoire de l'alphabet arménien". *Revue des études arméniennes* 9: 203–237.

Pelletier, André (ed.). 1962. *Lettre d'Aristée à Philocrate*. Paris: Éditions du Cerf.

Perry, Menakhem. 1981. "Thematic and Structural Shifts in Autotranslations by Bilingual Hebrew-Yiddish Writers: The Case of Mendele Mokher Sforim". *Poetics Today* 2 (4): 181–192.

Pezzini, Domenico. 1991a. "Brigittine Tracts of Spiritual Guidance in Fifteenth-Century England: a Study in Translation". In *The Medieval Translator II*, Roger Ellis (ed.). London: Centre for Medieval Studies. 175–207.

Pezzini, Domenico. 1991b. "Versions of Latin Hymns in Medieval England: William Herebert and the English Hymnal". *Mediaevistik* 4: 297–315.

Pezzini, Domenico. 1992. "Wordis of Christ to his spowse: una compilazione di testi brigidini nel Ms. Oxford, Bodleian Library, Rawl. C. 41". *Aevum* 66 (2): 345–360.

Pfister, Lauren F. 1995. "James Legge". In *An Encyclopaedia of Translation: Chinese-English, English-Chinese*, Chan Sin-wai and David E. Pollard (eds). Hong Kong: The Chinese University Press. 401–422.

Pfister, Lauren F. 2004. *Striving for 'The Whole Duty of Man': James Legge and the Scottish Protestant Encounter with China*. 2 vols. Frankfurt am Main: Peter Lang.

Pingree, David. 1963. "Astronomy and Astrology in India and Iran". *Isis* 54: 229–246.

Pingree, David. 1978. "History of Mathematical Astronomy in India". In *Dictionary of Scientific Biography*, Charles C. Gillispie (ed.). vol. 15. New York: American Council of Learned Societies, Scribner & Sons. 531–633.

Pocock, J. G. A. 1985. "The Sense of History in Renaissance England". In *William Shakespeare: his World, his Work, his Influence*, John F. Andrews (ed.). vol. 1. New York: Scribner. 143–157.

Priestley, Herbert Ingram (trans.). 1971. *The Luna Papers, Documents Relating to the Expedition of Don Tristán de Luna y Arellano for the Conquest of Florida in 1559–1561*. 2 vols. Freeport, NY: Books for Libraries Press. [c1928]

Prungnaud, Joëlle. 1994. "La traduction du roman gothique anglais en France au tournant du XVIIIᵉ siècle". *TTR* 7 (1): 11–48.

Prungnaud, Joëlle. 1997. *Gothique et Décadence: Recherches sur la continuité d'un mythe et d'un genre au XIXe siècle en Grande-Bretagne et en France*. Paris: Champion.

Pym, Anthony. 1992. *Translation and Text Transfer*. Frankfurt: Peter Lang.

Pym, Anthony. 1998. *Method in Translation History*. Manchester: St. Jerome.

Pym, Anthony. 2000. *Negotiating the Frontier: Translators and Intercultures in Hispanic History*. Manchester: St. Jerome.

Pym, Anthony. 2007. "On the Historical Epistemologies of Bible Translating". In *A History of Bible Translation*, Philip Noss (ed.). Rome: Edizioni di Storia e Letteratura. 195–215.

Qiñones Kleber, Eloise (ed.). 2002. *Representing Aztec Ritual in the Work of Sahagún*. Boulder, CO: University Press of Colorado.

Radó, György. 1964. "La traduction et son histoire". *Babel* 10 (1): 15–16.

Radó, György. 1967. "Approaching the History of Translation". *Babel* 13 (3): 169–173.

Rafael, Vicente. 1993. *Contracting Colonialism: Translation and Christian Conversion in Tagalog Society Under Early Spanish Rule*. Durham: Duke University Press.

Rahman, Abdur et al. (eds). 1982. *Science and Technology in Medieval India – A bibliography of source Material in Sanskrit, Arabic and Persian*. New Delhi: Indian National Science Academy.

Raina, Dhruv and S. Irfan Habib. 1993. "The unfolding of an engagement: 'The Dawn' on science, technical education and industrialization: India, 1896–1912". *Studies in History* 9 (1): 87–117. http://sih.sagepub.com/content/9/1/87

Raina, Dhruv and S. Irfan Habib. 2004. *Domesticating modern science: a social history of science and culture in colonial India*. New Delhi: Tulika Books.

Reboul, Pierre. 1962. *Le Mythe anglais dans la littérature française sous la Restauration*. Lille: Bibliothèque universitaire.

Reddick, Allen Hilliard. 1990. *The Making of Johnson's Dictionary, 1746–1773*. Cambridge & New York: Cambridge University Press.

Reland, Adrian. 1717. *De religione Mohammedica libri duo*. 2nd edition. Traiecti ad Rhenum: Brœdelet.

Reland, Adrian. 1721. *De la religion des mahométans*. Traduit par David Durand. The Hague: Isaac Vaillant. [Translation of Reland 1717]

Rener, Frederick M. 1989. *Interpretatio: Language and Translation from Cicero to Tytler*. Amsterdam & Atlanta: Rodopi.

Richards, Kel. 2006. *The Aussie Bible (Well, bits of it anyway!)*. Sydney: Bible Society, New South Wales.

Richards, Kel. 2008. *More Aussie Bible*. Sydney: Bible Society, New South Wales.

Riddell, George Allardice, 1st Baron Riddell. 1933. *Lord Riddell's Intimate Diary of the Peace Conference and after, 1918–1923*. London: Victor Gollancz Ltd.

Ride, Lindsay. 1970. "Biographical Note". In James Legge. *The Chinese Classics*. vol. 1. Hong Kong: Hong Kong University Press. 1–25.

Robinson, Douglas. 1995. "Theorizing Translation in a Women's Voice: Subversions of the Rhetoric of Patronage, Courtly Love, and Morality by Early Modern Women Translators". *The Translator*. 1 (2): 153–175.

Roditi, Édouard. 1978. "How I Became a Conference Interpreter". Washington, D.C.: Georgetown University. [videotape]

Roditi, Édouard. 1982. "Interpreting: Its History in a Nutshell". Washington, D.C.: Georgetown University. National Resource Center for Translation and Interpretation Outreach Paper.

Roger, Sarah. 2011. "A Metamorphosis? Rewriting in Borges's Translations of Kafka". *Comparative Critical Studies* 8 (1): 81–94.

Roland, Ruth A. 1999. *Interpreters as Diplomats: A Diplomatic History of the Role of Interpreters in World Politics*. Ottawa: University of Ottawa Press.

Rosenberg, Eleanor. 1955. *Leicester, Patron of Letters*. New York: Columbia University Press.

Ross, Alexander. 1649. *The Alcoran of Mahomet translated out of the Arabique into French by the Sieur Du Ryer [...] and newly Englished by A. Ross*. London: Randal Taylor.

Ross, Raymond. 2005. Obituary of Bill Findlay. *The Scotsman*, May 23, 2005. http://news.scotsman.com/obituaries/Bill-Findlay.2628820.jp. Accessed August 2010.

Rossi, Sergio and Dianelli Savoia (eds). 1989. *Italy and the English Renaissance*. Milan: Unicopli.

Roulon-Doko, Paulette. 2008. *Dictionnaire gbaya-français*. Paris : Éditions Karthala.

Rudin, Harry R. 1944. *Armistice 1918*. New York: Yale University Press.

Rumbold, Margaret E. 1991. *Traducteur huguenot: Pierre Coste*. Frankfurt: Peter Lang.

Sadan, Dov. 1965. *The Question of Yiddish in Bialik's Opus*. Jerusalem: Academon. [In Hebrew]

Sahagún, Bernardino. 1978. *The War of Conquest, How It Was Waged Here in Mexico. The Aztecs' Own Story As Given to Fr. Bernardino de Sahagún, Rendered into Modern English* [*The Florentine Codex*, Book XII]. Translated by A. J. O. Anderson and C. E. Dibble. Salt Lake City: University of Utah Press.

Said, Edward W. 1978. *Orientalism*. London: Routledge & Kegan Paul.

Salama-Carr, Myriam. 1990. *La Traduction à l'époque abbasside: L'école de Hunayn Ibn Ishâq et son importance pour la traduction*. Paris: Didier Érudition.

Salomon, Jean-Jacques. 1993. "Paul Mantoux et la Révolution industrielle". *Les Cahiers d'histoire du CNAM* (2–3): 59–86.

Sánchez-Martí, Jordi. 2001. "Chaucer's 'Makyng' of the Romaunt of the Rose". *Journal of English Studies*. 3: 217–236. http://dialnet.unirioja.es/servlet/fichero_articulo?codigo=720785&orden. Accessed September 2011.

Santoyo, Julio-César. 2006. "Blank Spaces in the History of Translation". In *Charting the Future of Translation History*, Georges L. Bastin and Paul F. Bandia (eds). Ottawa: University of Ottawa Press. 11–43.

Sargent, Michael G. 1984. "Minor Devotional Writings". In *Middle English Prose: a Critical Guide to Major Authors and Genres*, A. S. G. Edwards (ed.). New Brunswick, NJ: Rutgers University Press. 147–163.

Sarma, D. S. (Dittakavi Subrahmanya). 1956. *Hinduism Through the Ages*. Bombay: Bharatiya Vidya Bhavan.

Satow, Ernest Mason. 1979. *Guide to Diplomatic Practice*, (Lord) Paul Henry Gore-Booth and Desmond Pakenham (eds). 5th edition. London: Longmans.

Schäler, Reinhard. 2010. "Localization and translation". In *Handbook of Translation Studies*, Yves Gambier and Luc van Doorslaer (eds). vol. 1. Amsterdam/Philadelphia: John Benjamins. 209–214.

Schildt, Joachim. 1983. "Die Sprache Luthers – Ihre Bedeutung für die Entwicklung der deutschen Schriftsprache". In *Martin Luther. Leben – Werk – Wirkung*, Günter Vogler (ed.). Berlin: Akademie-Verlag. 307–324.

Schulte, Rainer and John Biguenet (eds). 1992. *Theories of Translation*: An *Anthology of Essays from Dryden to Derrida*. Chicago: University of Chicago Press.

Schwarz, Werner. 1963. "The History of Principles of Bible Translation in the Western World". *Babel* 9: 5–22.

Schweigger [Swigger], Salomon. 1616. *Alcoranus Mahometicus, das ist: Der Türken Alcoran, Religion und Aberglauben [...] Erstlich auß der Arabischen in die Italienische: jetzt aber in die Deutsche Sprach gebracht. Durch Herrn Salomon Schweiggern*. Nuremberg: Lochner.

Schweigger [Swigger], Salomon. 1641. *De Arabische Alkoran [...] wt de Arabische spraecke/ nu nieuwelijcks in Hoogduytsch ghetranslateerd/ [...] door Salomon Swigger [...] ende wederom uyt het Hoogduytsch in Nederlantsche spraecke ghestelt*. Hamburg: Barent Adriaensz, Berentsma.

Scott, Mary Augusta. 1916. *Elizabethan Translations from the Italian*. Boston: Riverside Press.

Seleskovitch, Danica. 1968. *L'Interprète dans les conférences internationales: problèmes de langage et de communication*. Paris: Minard.

Seleskovitch, Danica. 1978. *Interpreting for International Conferences: problems of language and communication*. Washington, D.C.: Pen & Booth.

Sen, S. N. (Samarendra Nath). 1966. *A Bibliography of Sanskrit Works on Astronomy and Mathematics: Part I, Manuscripts, Texts, Translations and Studies*. Calcutta: Sree Saraswati Press.

Sen, S. N. (Samarendra Nath). 1972. "Scientific Works in Sanskrit, Translated into Foreign Languages and Vice-versa in the 18th and 19th Century A. D." *Indian Journal of History of Sciences* 7 (1): 44–70.

Serpieri, Alessandro (ed.). l988. *Nel laboratorio di Shakespeare*. Coll. "I drammi romani" 4. Parma: Pratiche.

Shackford, Martha Hale. 1929. *Plutarch in Renaissance England, with Special Reference to Shakespeare*. Wellesley, MA: Wellesley College.

Shamir, Ziva. 1986a. *Poet of Poverty: Folkloristic Elements in Bialik's Works*. Tel Aviv: Papyrus. [In Hebrew]

Shamir, Ziva. 1986b. *Not for Adults Only: Children's Literature by Ch. N. Bialik*. Tel Aviv: Papyrus. [In Hebrew]

Shandler, Jeffrey. 2005. *Adventures in Yiddishland: Postvernacular Language and Culture*. Berkeley: University of California Press.

Sharma, Arvind (trans.). 1983. *Abhinavagupta Gitarthasangraha*. Leiden: E. J. Brill.

Sharma, Arvind. 1993. *Our Religions*. San Francisco: Harper.

Sharma, Arvind. 2008. "The Hermeneutics of the Word 'Religion' and Its Implications for the World of Indian Religions". In *Hermeneutics and Hindu Thought: Toward a Fusion of Horizons*, Rita D. Sherma and Arvind Sharma (eds). New York: Springer. 19–31.

Sherma, Rita D. and Arvind Sharma (eds). 2008. *Hermeneutics and Hindu Thought: Toward a Fusion of Horizons*. New York: Springer.

Sherma, Rita D. 2008. "Introduction". In *Hermeneutics and Hindu Thought: Toward a Fusion of Horizons*, Rita D. Sherma and Arvind Sharma (eds). New York: Springer. 1–18.

Shipley, Nan. 1966. *The James Evans Story*. Toronto: The Ryerson Press.

Simon, Sherry. 1996. *Gender in Translation: Cultural Identity and the Politics of Transmission* London & New York: Routledge.

Simon, Sherry. 2002. "Germaine de Staël and Gayarti Spivak: Culture Brokers". In *Translation and Power*, Maria Tymoczko and Edwin Gentzler (eds). Amherst & Boston: University of Massachusetts Press. 122–140.

Simon, Sherry. 2006. *Translating Montreal: Episodes In The Life Of A Divided City*. Montreal: McGill-Queen's University Press.

Simon, Sherry. 2011. *Cities in Translation: Intersections of Language and Memory*. London & New York: Routledge.

Simon, Sherry and Paul St-Pierre. 2000. *Changing the Terms: Translating in the Postcolonial Era*. Ottawa: University of Ottawa Press.

Singh, B. Chhajju. 1971. *Life and Teachings of Swami Dayanand Saraswati*. 2nd edition. New Delhi: Jan Gyan Prakashan.

Sinn, Elizabeth. 1995. "Yan Fu". In *An Encyclopaedia of Translation: Chinese-English, English-Chinese*, Chan Sin-wai and David E. Pollard (eds). Hong Kong: The Chinese University Press. 429–447.

Smalley, William Allen. 1991. *Translation as Mission: Bible Translation in the Modern Missionary Movement*. Macon, GA: Mercer University Press.

Sokolov, Nahum. 1919. *History of Zionism, 1600–1918, with an introduction by the Rt. Hon. A. J. Balfour*. London: Longmans, Green, & Co.

Sonderegger, Stefan. 1984. "Geschichte deutschsprachiger Bibelübersetzungen in Grundzügen". HSK 2 (1): 129–185.

Staël, Germaine de. 1821. "De l'esprit des traductions". In *Œuvres complètes de Mme la baronne de Staël*, publiées par son fils. vol. 17. Paris: Treuttel et Würtz.

Stein, Leonard. 1961. *The Balfour Declaration*. London: Valentine & Mitchell.

Steiner, George. 1975. *After Babel*. New York & London: Oxford University Press.

Stolt, Birgit. 1983. "Luthers Übersetzungstheorie und Übersetzungspraxis". In *Leben und Werk Martin Luthers von 1526–1546*, Helman Junghans (ed.). Berlin: Evangelische Verlagsanstalt. 241–252.

Stolt, Birgit. 1990. "Luther, die Bibel und das menschliche Herz. Stil- und Übersetzungsprobleme der Luther-Bibel damals und heute". In *Textgestaltung – Textverständnis*. Stockholm: Almqvist & Viksell. 110–137.

Stover, Leon E. 1972. *La Science-fiction américaine – Essai d'anthropologie culturelle*. Paris: Aubier Montaigne.

Stradal, Otto. 1982. *Der andere Prinz Eugen: Vom Fluchtling zum Multimillionar*. Vienna: Österreichischer Bundesverlag.

Stratford, Philip. 1978. "Translation as Creation". In *Figures in a Ground: Canadian Essays on Modern Literature Collected in Honor of Sheila Watson*, Diane Bessai and David Jackel (eds). Saskatoon: Western Producer Prairie Books. 9–18.

Sturel, René. 1908. *Amyot, traducteur des Vies parallèles de Plutarque*. Paris: Champion.

Sugirtharajah, Sharada. 2008. "Max Müller and Textual Management: A Postcolonial Perspective". In *Hermeneutics and Hindu Thought: Toward a Fusion of Horizons*, Rita D. Sherma and Arvind Sharma (eds). New York: Springer. 33–43.

Swanton, Michael (ed. and trans.). 1975. *Anglo-Saxon Prose*. London: Dent.

Szasz, Margaret Connell (ed.). 1994. *Between Indian and White Worlds: the Cultural Broker*. Norman: University of Oklahoma Press.

Tachiaos, Anthony-Emil N. 2001. *Cyril and Methodius of Thessalonica: the Acculturation of the Slavs*. Crestwood, NY: St. Vladimir's Seminary Press.

Taylor, Robert. 1965. "Les néologismes chez Nicole Oresme, traducteur du XIVe siècle". In *Actes du Xe Congrès international de linguistique et de philologie romanes*. vol. 2. Paris: Klincksieck. 727–736.

Technik, Wissenschaft und Wirtschaft in fremden Sprachen: Internationale Bibliographie der Fachwörterbücher. 1969. 4th edition. Munich: Verlag Dokumentation.

Terrall, Mary. 1995. "Émilie du Châtelet and the Gendering of Science". *History of Science* 33 (3): 283–310.

Thompson, E. A. 1966. *The Visigoths in the Time of Ulfila*. Oxford: Clarendon Press.

Thorndike, Lynn A. 1923–58. *A History of Magic and Experimental Science during the First Thirteen Centuries of our Era*. 8 vols. London: Macmillan.

Tilak, Bal Gangadhar. 1965. *Srimad Bhagavadgita – Rahasya or Karma-Yoga Sastra*. Translated by Bhalchandra Sitaram Sukthankar. Poona: Tilak Bros.

Time Magazine U.S. 1929. "Camerlynck Obituary". February 25, 1929. http://www.time.com/time/magazine/article/0,9171,880475,00.html. Accessed October 2011.

Titley, Alan. 1991. *An t-úrscéal Gaeilge*. Dublin: An Clóchomhar. [In Irish]

Torgerson, Sten. 1982. *Översättningar till svenska av skönlitterär prosa 1866–1870: 1896–1900*. Göteborg: Litteraturvetenskapliga institutionen vid Göteborgs universitet edition.

Toury, Gideon. 1977. *Translational Norms and Literary Translation into Hebrew, 1930–1945*. Tel Aviv: Porter Institute for Poetics and Semiotics. [In Hebrew]

Toury, Gideon. 1980. *In Search of a Theory of Translation*. Tel Aviv: Porter Institute for Poetics and Semiotics.

Translations of the Meaning of the Noble Qur'an. http://alagr.com. Accessed October 2011.

Tremblay, Michel. 1988. *The Guid Sisters*. Translated by Martin Bowman and Bill Findlay. Toronto: Exile Editions.

Tremblay, Michel. 1991. *The Guid Sisters: 3 Plays*. Translated by Martin Bowman and Bill Findlay. London: Nick Hern Books.

Tymoczko, Maria and Edwin Gentzler (eds). 2002. *Translation and Power*. Amherst & Boston: University of Massachusetts Press.

UCLA Language Materials Project. http://www.lmp.ucla.edu/Profile.aspx?LangID=17&menu=004. Accessed June 2011.

United Bible Societies. http://www.unitedbiblesocieties.org. Accessed October 2011.

Van Hoof, Henri. 1962. *Théorie et pratique de l'interprétation avec application particulière au français et à l'anglais*. Munich: Max Hueber Verlag.

Van Hoof, Henri. 1990. "Traduction biblique et genèse linguistique". *Babel* 36 (1): 38–43.

Van Hoof, Henri. 1991. *Histoire de la traduction en Occident*. Paris & Louvain-la-Neuve: Éditions Duculot.

Van Hoof, Henri. 1994. *Petite histoire des dictionnaires*. Louvain-la-Neuve: Peeters.

Venuti, Lawrence (ed.). 1992. *Rethinking Translation: Discourse, Subjectivity, Ideology*. London: Routledge.

Vermeer, Hans J. 1992. *Skizzen zu einer Geschichte der Translation*. 2 vols. Frankfurt/M.: Verlag für interkulturelle Kommunikation.

Vian, Boris. 1953. "Un robot-poète ne nous fait pas peur". *Arts* 10 (16): 219–226. [Reprinted in *Cantilènes en gelée*. Paris: UGE, 1970]

Vian, Boris and Stéphan Spriel. 1951. "Un nouveau genre littéraire: la Science-Fiction". *Les Temps modernes* 72: 618–627.

Vittorini, Elio (ed.). 1984. *Americana*. Milan: Tascabili Bompiani. [c1941]

Voltaire. 1961. *Traité sur la tolérance*. In *Mélanges*, Jacques Van den Heuvel (ed.). Paris: Gallimard. [c1763]

Voltaire. 1963. *Essai sur les mœurs et l'esprit des* nations, René Pommeau (ed.). Paris: Garnier. [c1756]

Von Flotow, Luise. 1997. *Translation and Gender: Translating in the "Era of Feminism"*. Ottawa: University of Ottawa Press.

Von Flotow, Luise. 2002. "Julia E. Smith, traductrice de la Bible à la recherche de la vérité par le littéralisme ". In *Portraits de traductrices*, Jean Delisle (ed.). Ottawa: Les Presses de l'Université d'Ottawa. 291–319.

Von Flotow, Luise (ed.). 2011. *Translating Women*. Ottawa: University of Ottawa Press.

Walters, Vernon. 1978. *Silent Missions*. Garden City, NY: Doubleday.

Walters, Vernon. 2001. *The Mighty and the Meek: Dispatches from the Front Line of Diplomacy*. London: St. Ermin's.

Wang, Hui. 2008. *Translating Chinese Classics in a Colonial Context: James Legge and his Two Versions of the 'Zhongyong'*. Bern: Peter Lang.

Watson, George (ed.). 1974. *The New Cambridge Bibliography of English Literature*. vol. 1. Cambridge: Cambridge University Press.

Watters, Thomas. 1904–05. *On Yuan Chwang's Travels in India (629–645) with two maps and an itinerary by Vincent A. Smith*, T. W. Rhys Davids and Stephen W. Bushell (eds.). 2 vols. London: Royal Asiatic Society.

Weintraub, Stanley. 1985. *A Stillness Heard Around the World: The End of the Great War: November 1918*. New York: E. P. Dutton.

Weissbrod, Rachel. 1989. *Trends in the Translation of Prose Fiction From English to Hebrew: 1958–1980*. Tel Aviv: Tel Aviv University. [Unpublished PhD Dissertation in Hebrew]

Weizmann, Chaim. 1949. *Trial and Error*. London: Hamilton.

Weizmann, Chaim. 1957. *La naissance de l'État d'Israël*. Paris: Gallimard.

Werrie, P. 1969. "L'École des traducteurs de Tolède". *Babel* 15 (4).

White, Andrew Dickson. 1905. *Autobiography of Andrew Dickson White*. 2 vols. New York: The Century Co.

White, Andrew Dickson. 1939. *Selected Chapters from the Autobiography of Andrew D. White*. Ithaca, NY: Cornell University Press.

Whitfield, Agnès. 2002. "Émilie du Châtelet, traductrice de Newton, ou la 'traduction-confirmation'". In *Portraits de traductrices,* Jean Delisle (ed.). Ottawa: Les Presses de l'Université d'Ottawa. 87–115.

Wolfram, Herwig. 1988. *History of the Goths*. Translated by T. J. Dunlop. Berkeley: University of California Press.

Wollin, Lars. 1991. "The Monastery of Vadstena. Investigating the Great Translation Workshop in Medieval Scandinavia". In *The Medieval Translator II*, Roger Ellis (ed.). London: Centre for Medieval Studies. 65–88.

Wollin, Lars. 2000. "Birgittine Biography at Vadstena: a Bilingual Affair?" In *The Medieval Translator 7. The Translation of the Works of St. Birgitta of Sweden into the Medieval European Vernacular*, V. O'Mara and B. Morris (eds). Turnhout, Belgium: Brepols. 53–74.

Wong, Wang-chi Lawrence. 2004. "Beyond *Xin Da Yu*: Translation Problems in the Late Qing". In *Mapping Meanings: The Field of New Learning in Late Qing China*, Michael Lackner and Natascha Vittinghoff (eds). Leiden & Boston: Brill. 239–264.

Woodsworth, Judith. 1988. "Traducteurs et écrivains: vers une redéfinition de la traduction littéraire". *TTR* 1 (1): 115–125.

Woodsworth, Judith. 2000. "Fragments d'une théorie de la traduction : Paul Valéry traducteur". *Littératures. Mélanges à la mémoire de Jean-Claude Morisot*, Mawy Bouchard, Isabelle Daunais et al. (eds). Montréal: Université McGill. (21–22): 245–263.

Wright, Louis B. 1935. *Middle Class Culture in Elizabethan England*. Chapel Hill: University of North Carolina Press.

Wurzbach, Constant von. 1869. *Biographisches Lexikon des Kaiserthums Österreich*. Vienna: k.k. Hof- & Staatsdruckerei.

Young, Egerton Ryerson. 1899. *The Apostle of the North: Rev. James Evans*. London: Marshall Brothers.

Zuber, Roger. 1968. *Les "Belle Infidèles" et la formation du goût classique*. Paris: Armand Colin.

Figure 23. Constance Garnett

Figure 24. A. H. Birse

Index of names

About the authors

JUDITH WOODSWORTH holds a PhD in French literature from McGill University. She has published widely on French literature, literary translation and translation history. She currently holds the position of Professor of Translation Studies at Concordia University after serving for several years as vice-president and president at three Canadian universities. She is founding president and an honorary member of the Canadian Association for Translation Studies (CATS).

JEAN DELISLE holds a doctorate from the Sorbonne Nouvelle (Paris III). After a distinguished career of teaching at the University of Ottawa from 1974 to 2007, he now holds the title of professor emeritus. He is the author, editor or co-editor of about twenty books and many articles dealing with translation history and teaching translation. His work has been translated into at least seventeen languages. He is an honorary member of the Canadian Association for Translation Studies (CATS).